The Development of
Mobile Logistic Support in
Anglo-American Naval Policy, 1900–1953

New Perspectives on Maritime History and Nautical Archaeology

UNIVERSITY PRESS OF FLORIDA

Florida A & M University, Tallahassee
Florida Atlantic University, Boca Raton
Florida Gulf Coast University, Ft. Myers
Florida International University, Miami
Florida State University, Tallahassee
New College of Florida, Sarasota
University of Central Florida, Orlando
University of Florida, Gainesville
University of North Florida, Jacksonville
University of South Florida, Tampa
University of West Florida, Pensacola

Replenishment in the Yellow Sea, 1951: HMAS *Sydney*, RFA *Wave Premier*, USS *Hanna*, and HMS *Alert*, (Photograph courtesy Fleet Air Arm Museum)

The Development of Mobile Logistic Support in Anglo-American Naval Policy, 1900–1953

Peter V. Nash

Series foreword by
Gene Allen Smith
and James C. Bradford

Foreword by
Vice Admiral Sir Alan Massey

University Press of Florida

Gainesville/Tallahassee/Tampa/Boca Raton
Pensacola/Orlando/Miami/Jacksonville/Ft. Myers/Sarasota

Copyright 2009 by Peter V. Nash
Printed in the United States of America. This book is printed on
Glatfelter Natures Book, a paper certified under the standards of
the Forestry Stewardship Council (FSC). It is a recycled stock that
contains 30 percent post-consumer waste and is acid-free.
14 13 12 11 10 09   6 5 4 3 2 1

Library of Congress Cataloging-in-Publication Data

Nash, Peter V.
   The development of mobile logistic support in Anglo-American
naval policy 1900–1953/Peter V. Nash; series foreword by James C.
Bradford and Gene Allen Smith.
     p. cm.—(New perspectives on maritime history and nautical
archaeology)
   Includes bibliographical references and index.
   ISBN 978-0-8130-3367-9 (alk. paper)
1. United States. Navy—Procurement—History—20th century.
2. Great Britain. Royal Navy—Procurement—History—20th century.
3. United States—Military relations—Great Britain. 4. Great Britain—
Military relations—United States. 5. Logistics—History—20th
century. I. Title.
   VC263.N37 2009
   359.4'110973090419–dc22   2009017141

The University Press of Florida is the scholarly publishing agency
for the State University System of Florida, comprising Florida
A&M University, Florida Atlantic University, Florida Gulf Coast
University, Florida International University, Florida State University,
New College of Florida, University of Central Florida, University of
Florida, University of North Florida, University of South Florida, and
University of West Florida.

University Press of Florida
15 Northwest 15th Street
Gainesville, FL 32611-2079
http://www.upf.com

For Emmy and Stephane

Contents

Illustrations

Conversion Tables

Marine Fuel Oil

1 U.K. long ton (L/T; 2,240 lb)	=	6.7 barrels (bbl) U.S.
1 U.K. L/T (2,240 lb)	=	234 gallons (gal) Admiralty
1 U.K. L/T (2,240 lb)	=	282 gal U.S.
1 metric ton (t; 2,204 lb)	=	277 gal U.S.
1 t (2,204 lb)	=	6.595 bbl U.S.
1 t (2,204 lb)	=	230 gal imperial
1 t (2,204 lb)	=	37 cubic feet (cu ft)
1 gal imperial	=	9.4 lb
1 gal imperial	=	0.02859 bbl U.S.
1 gal imperial	=	1.20094 gal U.S.
1 gal U.S.	=	7.8 lb
1 gal U.S.	=	0.8335 gal imperial
1 bbl U.S.	=	35 gal imperial
1 bbl U.S.	=	42 gal U.S.
1 bbl U.S.	=	5.6146 cu ft
1 bbl U.S.	=	158.984 liters

JP-5 Aviation spirit

1 U.K. L/T (2,240 lb)	=	7.97 bbl U.S.
1 U.K. L/T (2,240 lb)	=	278 gal Admiralty
1 U.K. L/T (2,240 lb)	=	334 gal U.S.
1 t (2,204 lb)	=	329 gal U.S.
1 t (2,204 lb)	=	274.4 gal imperial
1 t (2,204 lb)	=	7.84 U.S. bbl
1 t (2,204 lb.)	=	44 cu ft

Avgas

1 U.K. L/T (2,240 lb)	=	8.85 bbl U.S.
1 U.K. L/T (2,240 lb)	=	310 gal Admiralty
1 U.K. L/T (2,240 lb)	=	372 gal U.S.
1 t	=	8.71 bbl U.S.
1 t	=	304.85 gal imperial
1 t	=	356 gal U.S.

1 gal imperial	=	7.1 lb
1 gal U.S.	=	5.9 lb
1 bbl U.S.	=	35 gal imperial
1 bbl U.S.	=	42 gal U.S.
1 gal imperial	=	1.2 gal. U.S.
1 gal U.S.	=	0.84 gal imperial

Diesel

1 U.K. L/T (2,240 lb)	=	7.60 U.S. bbl
1 U.K. L/T (2,240 lb)	=	266 gal Admiralty
1 UK L/T (2,240 lb)	=	319 gal U.S.
1 t	=	314 gal U.S.
1 t	=	261.8 gal imperial
1 t	=	7.48 bbl U.S.
1 gal U.S.	=	7.8 lb fuel oil
1 gal U.S.	=	0.834 gal imperial
1 gal imperial	=	1.2 gal U.S.

Units of Flow

1 U.S. gal/hr	=	0.0167 U.S. gal/min
	=	0.0038 cu m/hr
1 U.S. gal/min	=	60 U.S. gal/hr
	=	0.2271 cu m/hr
1 cu m/hr (M^3/hr or simply CZ)	=	264.2 U.S. gal/hr
	=	4.43 U.S. gal/min
	=	219.964 U.K. gal/hr
	=	3.67 U.K. gal/min

Shortcuts

L/T/hour FFO	=	U.S. gal/min ÷ 4.69
L/T/hour FFO	=	n cu m × 220 (for Imperial gal p/h) ÷ 234

Sources: NARA2, ATP-16 "Replenishment at Sea" (1955); USNHC "NWIP 11–22 Fuel Consumption and Endurance Data" (1953); Sundry Unclassified Naval Documents, EXTAC 1003 (Rev. A) USN "Replenishment at Sea" year 2000 Manual; AL, Admiralty, BR103 "Conversion Tables"; TNA(Kew),ADM 1/24432, APM307 Admiralty "Logistics Planning Data" (1952).

Series Foreword

Water is unquestionably the most important natural feature on earth. By volume, the world's oceans compose 99 percent of the planet's living space; in fact, the surface of the Pacific Ocean alone is larger than that of the total land bodies. Water is as vital to life as air. Indeed, to test whether the moon or other planets can sustain life, NASA looks for signs of water. The story of human development is inextricably linked to the oceans, seas, lakes, and rivers that dominate the earth's surface. The University Press of Florida's series New Perspectives on Maritime History and Nautical Archaeology is devoted to exploring the significance of the earth's water while providing lively and important books that cover the spectrum of maritime history and nautical archaeology broadly defined. The series includes works that focus on the role of canals, rivers, lakes, and oceans in history; on the economic, military, and political use of those waters; and upon the people, communities, and industries that support maritime endeavors. Limited by neither geography nor time, volumes in the series contribute to the overall understanding of maritime history and can be read with profit by both general readers and specialists.

"Amateurs talk strategy. Professionals talk logistics," says the old adage that reflects the crucial nature of logistics, especially in modern warfare when it is impossible for a military force to "live off the land." Hundreds of works analyze strategy and tactics, campaigns and battles, and leaders, but very few focus on the sinews of war, and until recently those works that did so dealt more with production than with the supply systems that got the men and material to the theater of operations and then supported the forces deployed there. None before this study focused on the logistics involved in keeping warships operational while deployed far from bases.

To a large degree logistics has been a challenge of the twentieth century. During the Age of Sail warships could carry enough supplies to sustain themselves for months while "on distant stations," but when sail gave way to steam much of a vessel's carrying capacity had to be allocated to fuel rather than provisions. During the same transitional era advances in ordnance led to increased rates of gunfire, which necessitated much larger ammunition supplies than warships had carried in the past. The space needed for fuel and munitions multiplied again with the development of carrier aviation in the interwar decades and the dominant role it assumed during World War II.

During that conflict the logistical support for naval forces became exponentially greater than during peacetime or even World War I, when most operations were conducted within easy range of shore bases which could be replenished with relative safety because sea lanes of supply were relatively immune to attack everywhere but waters off the British Isles. Anglo-American naval planners recognized the need to virtually revolutionize naval logistics to make it possible to replenish supplies of fuel, ordnance, and provisions far from fixed bases, which had fulfilled this function in the past. Americans first confronted the need to devise a new system following the Spanish-American War, when studies by the General Board concluded that the limited number of bases available to the U.S. Navy in Hawaii, Guam, and Samoa were inadequate to sustain a fleet in combat-ready condition as it transited from the west coast of North America to the newly acquired Philippine Islands. The need to depend on foreign-owned bases and colliers during the globe-encircling cruise of the Great White Fleet, December 1907 through February 1909, further highlighted problems of sustaining U.S. warships on extended operations. Great Britain possessed a system of coaling stations and bases superior to any other nation, but its leaders, too, recognized the requirements brought by the revolution in naval warfare.

In this, the first study of its kind, Peter V. Nash traces the development of long-ran logistical support systems and techniques of underway replenishment. He describes its testing and the development of doctrine in a series of fleet problems conducted between the world wars and explains how both Great Britain and the United States designed and constructed ammunition, liquid and dry cargo vessels with adequate speed and endurance and formed these into the fleet train upon which the battle fleets of the Pacific War depended. Most fundamental was the decision to abandon fixed shore bases and instead to rely on the fleet train, which, with the ability to transfer all types of supplies directly to warships while underway, became "the most vital link in the logistics chain." In the second half of this book Nash assesses the lessons learned during the war, the plans made to cope with postwar demobilization while maintaining the ability to mobilize reserve forces in time of crisis, the organizations and doctrine developed to execute the mobilization, and the success of the system in meeting the challenges presented by the war in Korea. Throughout, Nash compares and contrasts developments and operations conducted by the U.S. and Royal navies and the bonds forged between the two, particularly in the post-1945 era.

This is a nuanced study with lessons for planners operating in the modern world of joint and combined operations in which interoperability plays a key role in both current and future operations. Civilians and naval officers engaged multinational planning and operations will recognize in today's navies much of the service cultures described by Nash.

Gene Allen Smith, Texas Christian University
James C. Bradford, Texas A&M University

Foreword

ULTIMATELY, LOGISTICS IS about combat power. Today, seaborne logistic support is a well-established and indispensable enabler for achieving sustained reach, freedom of maneuver, and operational flexibility in maritime operations—the hallmarks of any genuine blue water navy. The ability to replenish, maintain, and even repair warships at sea gives the commander the capacity to conduct protracted operations, at varying tempo and intensity, far from any home or friendly base. But there is a risk of taking such logistic support for granted, because the practicalities of supporting ships at sea, along with the associated planning disciplines, are now very much part and parcel of the everyday business of navies with global reach. Advanced technology, too, has significantly enhanced the transfer of liquid and solid stores under way and has extended the capacity of afloat maintenance facilities to the point where such activities can be conducted routinely, swiftly, and safely. Yet maritime technological advances—whether for platforms or ordnance—have also multiplied the logistic challenges for modern navies as they strive to sustain the high tempo of operations that are often required—and by no means only in times of conflict. Sustained aircraft carrier operations are a particular case in point.

So it is salutary, from time to time, to stand back and consider what these challenges may mean for current and future maritime logistics capability. Indeed, for the Royal Navy in particular, this is a most apposite time to reflect, as we plan for a new generation of combatant ships and the vessels and systems that will support them into the coming decades. Unsurprisingly perhaps, one can glean very useful guidance from the lessons of history not only by examining and codifying the steps by which we acquired our current capabilities but also by identifying and focusing honestly on those questions that need to be asked (or reasked) in defining future solutions. There is much recent history to help us better gain that perspective, not least from the Falklands and the Gulf wars, whereby much of the received wisdom can still be gleaned from those who were actually involved. But as one travels further back in time, this becomes increasingly problematic. Not only are there fewer firsthand witnesses to hand but the corporate memory has in many cases also been lost, with little documentation retained for the records. There are valuable insights to be gained from more geographically distant operations, too. The rigorous study of "logistics" or "supply" has rarely attracted the same attention or influence as other disciplines. It was not until the experiences of the Pacific War in 1942–45 that the vital importance of mobile logistic support afloat became self-evident. Without it, the reach, endurance, and flexibility necessary for Allied expeditionary ocean warfare, particularly where carriers were involved, would simply never been have attained.

With many modern navies committed to global maritime operations, this book provides a relevant and timely insight into the many difficulties encountered by both the Royal Navy and United States Navy as each adapted to the geostrategic implications of Japan's entry into the war in 1941. The Allies could succeed only by winning the war at and from the sea. With victory ultimately hard won, both navies then had to adjust to the corresponding rundown in the postwar environment and the Cold War that followed, not only because of contemporary financial constraints but also because of the inevitably reduced tempo and intensity of those maritime operations that still had to be conducted. At least that was the case until the Korean War broke out, when both navies once more had to gear up to high intensity operations, albeit of a very different character to those faced during World War II.

But this book is more than just a study of the administrative and technical developments in supporting large numbers of ships under way, along with the opportunities and constraints that these presented. It also examines the cultural issues that influenced the profile of logistics within both navies during this period, an important topic that has attracted less attention from historians and indeed the services in the past. In taking us back to this period of rapid evolution, this book makes the case that the experience gained in both the war and the peace between 1945 and 1953 changed forever the way serious navies need to address the issues of reach, pace, sustainability, and versatility in a global maritime battle-space. An especially telling factor is the advent of new technology— particularly that associated with jet aircraft—in influencing the design of both warships and the necessary scale of logistic support to an extent that was impossible to foresee during the previous half century. Even then, as this book demonstrates, it was no foregone conclusion that maritime logistics would flourish and demand appropriate priority in the deliberations and structures of senior naval hierarchies throughout this period. Indeed, this book helps to explain why the logistics dimension struggled to find its rightful place in naval doctrine and planning in both the Royal Navy and U.S. Navy after 1945 despite clear evidence that without such afloat support the war would never have been so successfully prosecuted.

Finally, this book describes the pursuit of convergence and standardization in Allied logistics doctrine between 1945 and 1953, a subject of considerable interest to those concerned with coalition interoperability, which remains challenging to this day despite so much postwar progress having been won. In the logistics world, this was truly a period of trial and tribulation, both in developing this core maritime capability in practical terms and in taking forward the underlying principles to guide and nurture its future evolution in peacetime. This was a fundamental issue when, on the one hand, military priorities were difficult to determine at a time of rapid and extensive demobilization; yet, on the other hand, there could be no certainty about what the future might demand. Despite this, as the author notes, everything to do with mobile logistics "which was discovered, experienced, recorded, or codified during this time also touched the future."

There is no doubt that we, as modern naval practitioners, have been very much the beneficiaries of the enormous maritime logistics effort depicted during this period. One need only look, for example, to British Maritime Doctrine (BR 1806) to see how the principles underpinning our own current approach to the logistic dimension reflect those very same ideas first enunciated by Rear Adm. Henry E. Eccles at the U.S. Naval War College more than half a century ago. Discovering how this came to be is a first step toward understanding the evolution of maritime logistics and appreciating why we find ourselves where we are today. This book, the first of its kind on this particular subject embracing both the Royal Navy and U.S. Navy, helps us greatly along that path of discovery.

Vice Adm. Sir Alan Massey, KCB CBE ADC, Royal Navy
Second Sea Lord and Commander in Chief Naval Home Command

Acknowledgments

THERE ARE A number of people who have helped me during the course of writing this book, for whom I would like to record my sincerest gratitude and appreciation.

From Britain's Royal Fleet Auxiliary, my thanks to Commodore William Walworth, OBE RFA, who provided invaluable practical insights on my early drafts on the science of replenishment at sea. To Capt. Dale Worthington, OBE RFA, and his team on RFA *Wave Ruler*, my thanks for all the help and advice willingly given in response to my attempts to understand and film the many replenishment operations while on board during June 2005. In a similar vein, I am grateful to Capt. Bill Baldwin of Military Sealift Command, who provided valuable technical feedback on my early drafts regarding American aspects of mobile logistics, as well as Capt. Craig Upton and the officers and crew of USNS *Patuxent* for their advice and help during my time on board to witness how replenishment evolutions were conducted with the U.S. Navy.

To Andrew Lambert I would like to extend my particular appreciation for his guidance and support including his perspicacious gems and subtle turn of phrase that on many an occasion helped to unclog my otherwise cluttered mind. Also, my thanks to Greg Kennedy for his helpful advice about the interwar period in naval history.

I have had to rely very heavily on archive material, which would not have been either as enjoyable or even possible to find without the help and wealth of experience generously afforded by so many in various archives around the world. In the United Kingdom, I must particularly thank Chris Page, Jock Gardner, Malcolm Llewellyn-Jones, Kate Tildesley, and Jenny Wraight for giving their time, experience, and the space to work at the Ministry of Defence's Naval Historical Branch, particularly when they were still at their crowded premises in Whitehall. I am especially indebted to Dr. Llewellyn-Jones for his invaluable guidance and willingness to critique so constructively my efforts throughout.

Abroad, I am most grateful to Peter Dennerly at the RNZN Museum in Auckland, New Zealand, for helping me find hitherto unpublished photographs of the British Pacific Fleet in 1945. As for the United States, where I spent a very enjoyable time as the Edward S. Miller Research Fellow in Naval History at the Naval

War College, I am very glad for the opportunity to record my warm thanks for the guidance and tremendous help willingly given by Dr. Evelyn Cherpak, Head of the Naval Historical Collection as well as Prof. John Hattendorf, for his practical support and insights on the breadth and depth of logistics research material located there.

My thanks also go to Kathy Lloyd at the U.S. Naval Historical Center, Washington, D.C., as well as Michael Coles in New York, for all his advice and support over the years. Finally I must thank those referees commissioned by the University Press of Florida who provided such constructive and helpful comments to my earlier drafts. I would like to convey my special appreciation to Meredith Morris-Babb, director, Jacqueline Kinghorn Brown, project editor, and Patricia Bower, copy editor, for all their diligent attention and valuable advice throughout.

One of the endearing joys that this whole project engendered was that of discovering the help and support available from others who have been through similar experiences. I am grateful to a number of the "ol' fogeys" in London for generously sharing their ideas and experience, including Dr. Tony Hampshire; Maj. John Ross; Col. John Abbatiello, USAF; Dr. Warwick Brown; and Dr. Nicholas Black.

Last but not least, I would like to warmly thank my wife, Emmy, for all her patience and support during this long project, and my son, Stephane, without whose practical assistance my computer (and all that goes with it) would never have functioned properly, if at all.

Introduction

The Challenge of Logistics Support

When peace returned to the Pacific in August 1945, both Britain and the United States were deploying the most potent fleets ever created.[1] It was not just the sheer numbers either. The necessary flexibility to win a war stretching across vast oceans had required a unique capacity for sustaining huge combat fleets at sea for lengthy periods many thousands of miles from their shore bases. This ability to keep carrier task forces regularly on station, in action at high tempo for months at a time had required frequent restocking of fuel, gasoline, aircraft, provisions, spares, and ammunition from specialist ships while they remained under way at sea. The magnitude of this logistics challenge was therefore quite daunting. Its application was decisive. For without fleet trains to provide essential logistic support, Allied task forces had neither the mobility nor endurance to seek out and destroy the Japanese air, sea, and garrison forces before them.

A measure of the challenge can be deduced by looking at the amount of fuel oil, diesel oil, and aviation gasoline issued while under way by a fleet train of sixty-seven fleet oilers and merchant tankers to support just one American task force off Okinawa between March 17 and May 27, 1945.[2] This requirement alone represented more petroleum than Japan produced or imported for the whole of 1944.[3] In hindsight this must surely rank as one of the most significant indicators of the war's eventual outcome.

Yet neither navy had been prepared for the scale and intensity of the Pacific campaign, and both had been compelled to develop their replenishment capability the hard way—by trial and tribulation. It was presumed however that the difficulties they had encountered would at least provide lessons that, if heeded, would avoid a repeat in the future of their early fraught experience. Logistics, after all, was undoubtedly expected to stay in some form or other. By the end of the war both navies employed a vast, complex—if rather prosaic—logistics infrastructure that not only took on a life of its own but, at least for the Americans, was to become the hallmark in planning for the rest of the century.

Within months, however, both became constrained by budget cutbacks, decimated by rapid demobilization, and disoriented by the immediate contraction in operational imperatives. Uncertainty of purpose soon permeated through each as the vacuum left by the defeated enemy remained unfilled. This was further compounded by the debilitating effects of interservice rivalry, a confusing role transition in peacetime, and perceptions of base vulnerability in the new atomic age, all of which posed new problems for naval planners and leaders alike. Yet much that was learned about supplying and sustaining large combat-ready forces at sea was seemingly relegated or forgotten. As Thomas Wildenberg noted, "The financial and personnel cutbacks were so severe in the post-war period that the [U.S.] navy found itself temporarily forced to abandon mobile logistic support as a practice."[4] The Korean War therefore became a timely reminder as the struggle to reassemble as well as relearn the art of logistic sustainability provided testament to the problems that can arise if core capabilities and skills, perhaps not sufficiently recognized for their relevance at the time, are allowed to wither.

Purpose of This Book

This book will explore how the Royal Navy (RN) and U.S. Navy (USN) initially went about developing and refining the art and science of mobile logistic support from the early years of the twentieth century, leading up to their transformational baptism of fire in 1945. It will then examine how progress was subsequently defined by the constraints and opportunities that governed the early postwar period of peace until five years later, when the sudden outbreak of the Korean War forced both navies to reconsider their priorities. After analyzing why the contribution of mobile logistics was so critical by 1945, the book will then seek to establish the extent to which this capability became a core competency to be preserved in peacetime to meet new challenges, many of which have remained as relevant as ever to this day.

Much has been written about how navies have prepared themselves for war and even more on how they have operated in one. Relatively little illumination, however, has been shed on how navies manage contraction with its consequential effect on decisions, priorities, and plans. Yet history has shown the Royal Navy, for example, to be quite adept at protecting its core capabilities during previous postwar cutbacks, so would this occasion prove any different? Inevitably, certain political, financial, and economic forces (including, for example, appropriations or the unification of the armed forces) have affected naval logistics planning and outcomes throughout the period covered by this book, but this book does not intend to study the specific causes of these external forces. Nevertheless, such constraints do raise important dimensions. For example, were the postwar financial appropriations for the U.S. Navy, or estimates for the Royal Navy, always so predominant and always negative? And would naval logistics be recognized for its potential as a force multiplier to compensate for the reduction in forces debilitated by financial and economic restraint? Was contemporary naval thinking for logistics rigid and precedent-dependent rather than flexible and forward looking? Often challenges posed by trying to do more with less demand imagination and experience. Ethos nourishes the former. Rapid demobilization denies them the latter. How did each navy fare?

The essence of logistics, however, is all about the supply of men, ships, facilities, bases, and combat support afloat. But such an observation demands some focus since there are three different processes at work: needs identification/ planning, procurement and production, and distribution. Procurement and production were generally civilian managed whereas planning and distribution remained essentially a military prerogative. While it was the function of logistics to bridge the gap between production and consumption, the focus here will predominantly be upon planning and distribution.[5] Such related aspects covering the rail, air, and shipping administrations, including naval transportation, will also remain outside the scope of this book, given their limited direct impact on theater mobility. Nevertheless, it will still require looking at what balance, if any, was achieved in allocating limited resources between "teeth" and "tail" for peacetime requirements as well as those required for potential war. How, for example, could reserves be reactivated expeditiously to avoid a prolonged ramp-up? Did the concept of having reserve fleets fulfill expectations? This book will therefore be looking at the relationship between postwar strategic and logistic planning functions, with particular emphasis on how logistics mobilization plans factored in how reserve fleets were to be managed.

Although mobility and endurance were established as important contributors to the successful outcome in the Pacific, their postwar strategic relevance was something that still needed to be validated as both navies tried to determine how much afloat support remained necessary or even affordable in peacetime. Hence the need to look at the ramifications of operational fleet speeds and endurance upon auxiliary ship design and why these were important considerations in, for example, the Admiralty's assessment of what might be the most appropriate policy for its overseas bases in the postwar period.

Finally, there were the tactical outcomes. A key enabler for optimizing tactical or even strategic choice was the ability to replenish combat forces at sea, whether en route or while operating off potential enemy territory. A thorough appreciation of the limitations as well as the potential benefits of this capability is therefore an essential building block for understanding how naval logistics became an indispensable component in theater strategy during this period. For this reason, the book will examine in some detail that most vital link in the logistics chain: the operational art and science of replenishing ships at sea.

The Relevance of Logistics to National and Alliance Planning and Strategy

In his book *The Leverage of Sea Power*, Colin Gray argues that sea power, if effectively harnessed, can provide the holder with the ability to control the geostrategic terms of war. As he put it,

> . . . Depending on who controls the sea, water is a highway or a barrier. The continuity of the world's seas and oceans translates into a global mobility and agility for maritime forces and for merchant shipping which can have no continental parallel. That mobility and agility has been used time and time again, in all historical periods, to achieve surprise and the full strategic advantage of surprise effect.[6]

The value of this leverage persuaded Britain and the United States to make an enormous strategic investment to ensure their continuing dominance at sea. Sea power, of course, can only act as the enabler in wars, particularly if a continental land power is the enemy, because such wars must ultimately be won on land. The challenge for maritime dependent nations, therefore, was to ensure they did not lose sea control to continental land powers. And if mobility was to be the enabler for securing such maritime supremacy globally, then a responsive logistics support capability was sine qua non. With self-sustainability being the key to mobility and independence from the land, this would help to solve what Corbett called "the main problem which lies at the root of all naval history, the problem of reconciling sea endurance with free movement."[7]

This sophisticated and complex capability is, however, an expensive proposition in times of peace, and while navies have always represented major national investments, the scramble for scarce resources made them no less vulnerable to being marginalized by planners and commanders alike. Indeed, to some degree World War II contemporary logistics theory was hijacked by such logic. The capacity of a nation to wage war was the sum of many factors, but its various resources could not in themselves represent military force until they were organized. Organization and mobilization could transform a market economy into a war economy—the fusion, as it were, of what was economically feasible with what was militarily desirable. Logistics was therefore perceived as essentially a function of war with urgency, shortages, and haste reflecting the military hazards of such war.[8] However, these imperatives tended to evaporate when the danger was past, at which point a new and potentially dangerous mindset could develop. Military officers, seduced to the notion that the economic aspects of war were no longer their concern, would quickly forget the lessons. For the politicians, on the other hand, domestic reconstruction would be the first priority, and military budgets therefore represented an attractive source for reallocation toward economic and social development.

But how a nation positions its logistic capability can speak volumes about its intent, both strategically and tactically. In World War II, 25 percent of the total industrial output of the United States was channeled into the building and support of its wartime navy.[9] Such allocation in peacetime was clearly neither sustainable nor warranted, but one test for ascertaining a nation's true global maritime aspiration is to look beyond the political rhetoric. Instead, one should evaluate what scarce resources were allocated to the more prosaic but critical fleet auxiliary support rather than the more overt but sometimes inert symbols of power and prestige.[10] It will therefore be important to establish whether each navy was successful in creating a cultural as well as intellectual climate that would enable logistics to find its appropriate level within strategic and operational planning.

Brief Survey of Existing Literature

Despite the decisive contribution of naval logistics to the successful outcome in the Pacific, and compared to the amount of literature produced on British or American naval operations or policy from World War II onward, the subject of mobile logistics has been lamentably served. Only a handful of books have been published, most within the first ten years after World War II and all by American authors.[11] Given such a paucity of material, a brief survey might help to provide some context, for although most books on the subject are now somewhat dated, they are no less masterly or relevant for that.

Duncan Ballantine's classic work *U.S. Naval Logistics in the Second World War* was based on his PhD with the benefit of access and authority from the historical section of the Office of the Chief of Naval Operations (CNO). The result is a comprehensive, radical understanding of the role of logistics as the communications bridge between what is strategically required militarily and the limits of what can be economically produced. It goes beyond providing a statistically driven operational analysis in distribution (which it does well) by looking at logistic issues from different perspectives at political, economic, and general command levels. Admiral Dyer's book *Naval Logistics* is written more for the naval officer, particularly the logistician, covering both the theory and application of logistics, much of it derived from his distinguished career including flag officer spells as Chief of Logistic Plans, Naval Operations in 1945 and commander of the United Nations (UN) Blockade and Escort Force in Korea in 1951–52. The seminal work on the wartime operational history of naval logistics, bar none, is Worrall Read Carter's *Beans, Bullets and Black Oil*, together with its companion *Ships, Salvage and Sinews of War*.[12] Written by the officer responsible for most of the logistics operation in the Pacific, both became, in effect, the official histories of logistic distribution for the U.S. Navy in the Pacific and Atlantic, respectively. A more recent but absolutely indispensable book, both from an historic as well as technical viewpoint, is Thomas Wildenberg's *Gray Steel and Black Oil*. This book complements

Carter's book on wartime activity but also looks at how, in practice, combat logistics support emerged as an integral component of operational postwar planning and execution.

Despite the important role that reserve fleets played in postwar contingency planning, there has been precious little published on this subject, even in the United States, and then almost exclusively through contemporary journal articles that tended to be either technical treatises on the art of mothballing, or wake-up calls on the problems of reserve fleet manning. The only book published exclusively on the subject was very interesting with excellent photographs but unfortunately inchoate for key statistics.[13]

As for British books devoted to contemporary naval logistics, none was produced during this postwar period nor, indeed, have any really surfaced since. Only two journal articles were published on British postwar underway replenishment, both excellent and surprisingly informative, given that much of the information was only later released by the Ministry of Defence (MoD) to the public archives.[14] The only publications on the Royal Fleet Auxiliary (RFA) are Sigwart's *Royal Fleet Auxiliary*—a rather dated brief history of the service and fueling at sea, together with the histories and descriptions of all its ships; this was recently surpassed by a most authoritative publication celebrating the RFA's centenary that provides an essential source of facts and information.[15]

Approach

The central premise underpinning this book is that the logistic challenges confronting both navies in 1945 required such innovative solutions that their successful outcome was not simply the most radical turning point in the history of mobile logistic support; the logistics solutions also formed the yardstick by which foreseeable future mobile logistic support (particularly for carrier based warfare) was to be judged.

Chapter 1 provides historical context by reviewing the more important milestones in the period from the early 1900s until World War II, when each navy sought to modify its rather static supply infrastructure to become more responsive to the increasing global expeditionary nature of fleet deployment. Both navies developed their plans based on what they perceived to be the geopolitical threats prevailing at the time, taking into account the availability of permanent bases to provide the necessary logistic support for any global response. If fixed bases were unavailable, then an alternative way for supporting fleets had to be found. This led to the development of fleet trains, which only really came in to their own in 1945. Chapter 2 looks at how and why this extremely vital and effective capability was developed for both navies during World War II. It also introduces some of the consequences that would influence future logistic planning.

The most crucial component in this newly devised fleet-train model was the science of replenishment at sea, where logistics effectively met the front line. Chapter 3 describes in more detail how this worked and provides a more informed understanding of both the potential and the limitations of the fleet-train model and hence why it was so important to get the whole evolution right. At the tactical level, speed became an increasingly critical consideration for minimizing fleet vulnerability to attack from enemy submarines or aircraft. A more efficient replenishment process meant less time was being diverted from the main course and mission. At the strategic level, more experience gained in the replenishment process increased the chances for improved efficiency and understanding; this ensured more forces could be supplied with a wider variety of stores and liquids under increasingly demanding circumstances. Such improvements led in turn to enhanced task force endurance, range, and capability, thereby maximizing the commander's strategic options. The chapter will demonstrate why a well-developed doctrine, if regularly practiced, was vital to achieve operational consistency and harmony, both prerequisites for convergence and ultimately interoperability between different allied navies.

Chapter 4 looks at how postwar cultural and organizational change was conditioned by recent wartime logistic experience. Many of the logistic challenges during World War II had been faced for the first time and were only resolved by improvisation and sheer grind. A fresh sense of order and pattern were needed so the role of logistics would be better recognized, anticipated, and applied in future wars. Such progression will be explored on two levels. First, we will look through the prism of naval education, rather than just training, by examining how the principles of logistics—which underlie the conduct and relevance of logistics—were inculcated among the future leaders of both navies, particularly those British and American officers attending the logistics courses introduced after the war at the Naval War College (NWC). Second, we will investigate whether either navy modified its organizational administration to reflect and build upon the logistical lessons learned from the past as each navy went about positioning itself to meet the fresh challenges of the future.

Many of these postwar logistic challenges were, however, difficult to address because there was limited precedent and scarce resources available to resolve them. The Royal Navy in particular faced a pressing need to determine postwar whether the way forward was to have more afloat support or simply revert to prewar strategies using permanent bases. Chapter 5 looks at the ramifications for choosing either afloat support or permanent bases, how each choice affected the establishment of appropriate endurance levels for warships, and the subsequent impact this had on auxiliary ship design. The second major challenge for planners, highlighted by the collective experience at the beginning of World War II, was the need for better preparation and efficiency at marshalling logistic resources in the event of another war. Exacerbating the problem after 1945 was the debilitating effects from very rapid demobilization of both ships and manpower. Chapter 6 will investigate how this was managed and whether the mobilization plans—including the role of reserve fleets and their methods of preservation—worked, based on the evidence about naval mobilization efforts for the Korean War.

Chapter 7 focuses on the tactical aspects of logistic support as both navies realigned their command structures and operating fleets to meet existing obligations and anticipated worldwide threats. It will then explore why and how tactical doctrine for logistic support was refined to cope with the increasingly complex challenges caused by technological advances in carrier development, jet aircraft, and weaponry, all against the constant backdrop of heightened risk from potential enemy fast submarine or air attack. This line of inquiry will include postwar fleet exercises, war-gaming, and trials programs, all of which provided the only peaceful means to improve skills, understanding, and the actual equipment associated with replenishment at sea. It will conclude by examining how the Korean War logistic experience affected doctrine and why it acted as a catalyst for introducing new technology and ships that would improve both navies' future capability in the art and science of replenishing ships at sea.

Finally, chapter 8 draws some conclusions that place the key period between 1945 and 1953 into context, particularly in terms of its enduring legacy upon future developments for mobile logistic support.

Abbreviations

(U.K./RN terminology unless marked otherwise)

AE	Fleet Replenishment Ammunition Stores ship (USN)
AF	Supply ship for fresh/frozen/dry provisions (USN)
AFO	Admiralty Fleet Order
AH	Hospital ship (USN)
AK	General Stores/Cargo ship (USN)
AKA	Attack Cargo vessel (USN)
AKS	Fleet Replenishment Stores ship (USN)
AO	Oiler for all petroleum products (USN)
AOE	Fast Combat Support ship (1964 USN)
APD	Administrative Plans Division
ARL	Repair Ship Landing craft (USN)
A/S	Antisubmarine
ASIS	Armament Stores Issuing ship
ASW	Antisubmarine Warfare
BAD	British Admiralty Delegation, Washington, D.C.
BJSM	British Joint Staff Mission, Washington, D.C.
BPF	British Pacific Fleet (1945–46)
BuSandA	Bureau of Supplies and Accounts (USN)
CAP	Combat Air Patrol
C-in-C	Commander in Chief
CinCLant	Commander in Chief, Atlantic (USN)
CinCNELM	Commander in Chief, U.S. Naval Forces, Eastern Atlantic and Mediterranean
CinCPac	Commander in Chief, Pacific (USN)
CNO	Chief of Naval Operations (USN)
CNS	Chief of Naval Staff, Admiralty
CominCH	Commander in Chief United States Fleet (USN)
ComNavEu	United States Commander Naval Forces Europe (USN)
ComServLant	Commander Service Force Atlantic (USN)
ComServPac	Commander Service Force Pacific (USN)
DNI	Director of Naval Intelligence, Admiralty
DNO	Director of Naval Ordnance, Admiralty
DNOR	Director of Naval Operational Studies or Director of Naval Operational Research, Admiralty

DTSD	Director of Training and Staff Duties Division, Admiralty or Director of Tactical and Staff Duties Division, Admiralty
dwt	dead weight tons
IEP	Information Exchange Programs
JCS	Joint Chiefs of Staff (USA)
LSD	Landing Ship, dock
LSG	Logistic Support Group (RN BPF)
LSF	Logistic Support Force (USN)
MFA	Merchant (or Mercantile) Fleet Auxiliary
MOF	Ministry of Food
MOT	Ministry of Transport
MOWT	Ministry of War Transport
NATO	North Atlantic Treaty Organization
NDRF	National Defense Reserve Fleet (USN)
NSIS	Naval Stores Issuing Ship
NWC	Naval War College, Newport, Rhode Island (USN)
NWP	Naval Warfare Publication (USN)
NWIP	Naval Warfare Information Publication (USN)
PD	Plans Division, Admiralty
PD (Q)	Plans Division (Q), Admiralty
RAFT	Rear Admiral Commanding, Fleet Train (BPF)
RAN	Royal Australian Navy
RAOC	Review of Admiralty Organization Committee
RAS	Replenishment at Sea
RCN	Royal Canadian Navy
Rear Adm.	Rear Admiral
RFA	Royal Fleet Auxiliary
RN	Royal Navy
RNZN	Royal New Zealand Navy
SACLANT	Supreme Allied Commander Atlantic
TSD	Tactical Staff Duties Division, Admiralty
TSDD	Training and Staff Duties Division, Admiralty
UNREP	Underway Replenishment at Sea (USN)
URG	Underway Replenishment Group (USN)
USA	United States Army
USN	United States Navy
VCNO	Vice Chief of Naval Operations (USN)
VERTREP	Vertical Replenishment using helicopters
Vice Adm.	Vice Admiral
VSIS	Victualling Stores Issuing Ship

1 | Naval Logistics, 1900–1940
Historical Perspective, Political Context

ANY NATION'S STRATEGIC foreign policy reflects a myriad of often conflicting perceptions and interests even within their own elites—particularly financial, economic, diplomatic, or military—as well as other domestic or external pressures. For brevity's sake, the following strategic overview is confined to the naval perspective as it related to the Pacific during the interwar period. The intention is to provide some broader context to the logistic challenges confronting each navy as both sought to address what they perceived to be the main but invariably changing maritime threats, most notably those emanating from Japan's growing navy.

General Interwar Strategic Overview

From a mobile logistics perspective, the Admiralty's experience in naval operations during World War I reaffirmed its belief that future battle fleets would continue to be dependent on permanent base support that would remain relatively close to operations/theaters. Even for those actions beyond the North Sea and Mediterranean, namely the battles of Coronel and the Falkland Islands, warships were still able to access coal bases on the coast of Chile and in the Falkland Islands themselves. So there was little incentive after the war to redesign and build new warships simply to extend their endurance or achieve a higher degree of self-sufficiency. Yet over the subsequent decades a number of milestones would shape the Royal Fleet Auxiliary (RFA) from being a static supply organization that happened to use ships for transportation into a mobile logistics force that, albeit with some struggle forty years later, would nevertheless transform the way British warships could remain in theater for extended periods without having to return to their traditional network of bases.

For the U.S. Navy, conversely, its World War I experience in terms of endurance had proved the opposite. Once their warships, whether large or small, were obliged to operate far from their traditional naval bases for long periods, sufficient afloat logistic support proved essential to enable them to operate either on their own or with minimum host-nation support. The likelihood of needing such a capability in the future could not be ruled out, so at least this valuable experience would help define some of the logistics challenges that might need to be faced should it once again prove necessary to fight far from home. Thus the genesis for establishing a fleet train was established. Throughout this period each navy inherently assumed a different attitude to mobility and endurance that was reflected not only by how each viewed the geopolitical threats of the time but also how each chose to prepare for them.

By 1919 the U.S. Navy's doctrine and the value of battleships "remained intact and unused," although for what purpose and against whom was unclear, other than the conviction among naval officers that parity must be achieved with the Royal Navy, the world's largest navy.[1] While no one envisaged actual war between the two navies (at least among the political elites) or that they were even a threat to each other, there nevertheless existed virtually throughout the interwar period an extraordinarily competitive distrustful edge between the two, which would only really mellow by the late 1930s.

For much of this period Congress did not believe that the U.S. Navy had an acceptable strategic plan, or indeed even needed one, so funding was denied for new bases or ships until well into the 1930s and any resumption of naval competition was actively discouraged. The Admiralty, conversely, had become increasingly anxious even before the end of World War I about its ability to maintain command of the sea as other naval powers began to grow quickly and significantly.[2] The British were also concerned about America's determination to become a major player in world shipping after the war.[3] Although it was never anticipated that Britain's naval strength in 1919 could be maintained in peacetime, the subsequent retrenchment was not only extremely severe but also brought for the first time the prospect of Britain having to accept naval parity with another power. Moreover, her fleet, much of it aged and worn out from war, was to be limited by international treaty. In the background too was whether Britain's underlying economic power could remain buoyant enough—as it had, for example, during the last major demobilization period, post-1815—to enable it to unleash rapid naval expansion should such a course suddenly prove necessary.[4] The period 1919–29 was therefore the last decade of British maritime supremacy that not only dominated maritime trade but also enabled powerful new fleets to be supported by an unrivalled network of worldwide bases ranging from dockyards and naval harbors to coaling and fueling stations. The Mediterranean Fleet, for example, enjoyed Gibraltar and Malta with additional private docks available in wartime at Port Said and Alexandria. The East Indies Fleet could rely on Aden, Colombo, and Mauritius while the China station deployed from Hong Kong and Singapore with supplementary coaling stations at Penang and Wei-Hai-Wei, China. In North America and the West Indies, a naval dock at Bermuda was supplemented by docks in Bridgetown, Barbados; Trinidad; and St John's. Finally, the Cape Station had a naval dockyard at Simon's Bay with smaller stations for coaling in Port Stanley, Falkland Islands; St Helena; Cape Coast Castle; and Sierra Leone. Considerable assistance could additionally be sought through the naval base facilities of the Dominion navies, principally those of Canada, New Zealand, and Australia.[5] In fact, as John Ferris would argue, Britain was "the only sea power with the strength and bases to be a world power."[6] While a vibrant shipbuilding industry had made this all possible, the enabler undoubtedly had to be this network of bases. For the Admiralty to provide a main fleet to protect Britain herself, defend British trade, and attack foreign commerce yet still be capable of sustaining imperial defense presented a huge challenge that demanded "an elaborate infrastructure of logistics and bases to deploy, concentrate and maintain its forces in all seas essential to the Empire."[7]

However, a number of important events occurred in 1921 and 1922 that would affect how the U.S. Navy and, to a degree, the Royal Navy perceived their future roles and purposes. First, President Warren G. Harding convened the Washington Conference to avoid an arms race developing between the United States, Britain, and Japan. It was largely successful, despite strong U.S. Navy misgivings, because both Japan and Britain were prepared to cooperate. The Four Power Treaty signed in December 1921 was followed by the Naval Arms Limitation Treaty signed in 1922, which imposed capital ships ratios on the five main naval powers including a ten-year holiday in ship construction. In trying to establish a stable framework in the Far East, it had also been agreed earlier that in return for Japanese assurances to respect American concerns about further expansion, the United States in turn would not build any permanent advanced bases or even strengthen existing naval facilities in Guam and particularly in the Philippines (a legacy of the Spanish-American War).[8] Only Hawaii was immune. Unlike the comparatively close links between the Admiralty and the British Foreign Office, the U.S. Navy seemingly received few political guidelines from the American administration and remained forever in doubt as to what the civilian intentions were regarding the circumstances under which the United States might go to war, or even what type of war would be fought if it did. The political implications of such agreements therefore seemed to take no account of the military consequences. Indeed, for one eminent naval historian, U.S. foreign policy and naval policy were seemingly often "divorced from each other."[9] What brought this home was the aforementioned serious American concession that directly challenged the U.S. Navy's ability to protect the United States' Pacific interests because the consequent lack of secure naval bases in the region removed in one stroke the foundations of its strategy of offensive sea control in the western Pacific. In fact, the only positive outcome of the Four Power Treaty from the U.S. Navy's point of view was the concomitant abrogation at long last of the 1902 Anglo-Japanese Alliance, which had become an increasing source of irritation for them. Up to this point Britain's dilemma in trying to protect her interests in the Far East (initially from the Russians but later the Japanese) had essentially pivoted on whether to continue relying on a diplomatic bilateral solution—hence the perpetuation of the Anglo-Japanese Alliance—or whether to rely on her own naval strength instead. As a result, the Alliance, together with Britain's relationship with Japan generally, had become "closely tied to Anglo-American relations, naval building policy and Imperial Defence."[10] The combination of the Four Power Treaty and the Limitations Treaties, however, provided the necessary framework for Britain to disengage from the Anglo-Japanese Alliance without harming her relations with Japan while strengthening her relations with the United States and simultaneously avoiding an unwinnable arms race with Washington.[11] It also provided the opportunity for Britain to replan her military strategy for the Far East in the light of these new circumstances, particularly if Japan continued to consolidate its military, economic, and political influence in the region. For the Admiralty, Singapore was the only base in the Far East to be relied on in the event of any war with Japan, assuming it was properly defended. So any plans for Singapore need to be seen in the context of how the Admiralty planned to mobilize a fleet from Europe, given there was no prospect in peacetime of Britain being able to deploy substantial forces in the region. While Britain therefore retained under the new Four Power Treaty the flexibility to send—should the need arise—a fleet within sixty days to Singapore, there was little expectation that this would ever happen. It was proving much more difficult for Britain to defend her interests alone against an increasingly powerful potential threat that was located in a region so far from her traditional Eurocentric sphere of influence. As Paul Kennedy put it, Britain was effectively neutered and simply "gambling upon the hope that Japan would not be aggressive."[12]

Both the Royal Navy and U.S. Navy had believed it was necessary to maintain a two-power standard as each faced what they saw were two separate potential threats with Japan being the common denominator. But the combination of very tight funding and the constraints imposed by the Washington treaties caused both navies to adopt what was in effect a "fleet in being" strategy with diminished auxiliary support. This vacuum would eventually encourage Japan to pursue her own regional conquests with impunity—not that this led to complete inaction by the Anglo-Americans, just that their options were limited. In 1921, for example, the U.S. Navy had decided to forgo the principle originally established after World War I of keeping the U.S. Fleet divided between the Atlantic and Pacific. This change was because Japan, which had taken over Germany's possessions in the central Pacific and also occupied part of China, was now perceived by the United States (or at least particularly by the U.S. Navy) to be the most likely future enemy.

Although this shift in naval priority was fundamental, the transfer itself still took some years to consummate; it was not until the mid 1930s that the bulk of

U.S. naval power was reallocated to the modern Pacific battle fleet. For the rest of the 1920s the impact of the various treaties upon naval strategy essentially meant that the U.S. Navy was no longer in control of its strategic destiny. Instead it had become very reliant on public support, which preferred to see their navy as "a treaty Navy."[13] Nor was its strategic perspective necessarily in keeping with national policy, which regarded the U.S. Navy's role as simply either defending or deterring any direct attack upon mainland United States, nothing more, nothing less. This constraint, however, never seemed to deter the U.S. Navy from attempting to identify maritime threats globally, if only to assess how these might be initially tackled should potential campaigns became reality.

A number of these campaign or war plans were formulated by the U.S. Joint Army–Navy Board to address a variety of different global threats to the United States. Of all these color-coded plans, War Plan Orange focused on Japan as the potential enemy. Produced in various iterations throughout the interwar period, War Plan Orange was essentially a staff forecast that became the operational centerpiece of the U.S. Navy's doctrine for offensive sea control. As such, it provided the only likely focus of where fleet action might take place, but it remained essentially a doctrine that could never provide justification for authorizing expenditures since it "politically had no meaning and was ignored by civil authorities."[14] The essence of the plan was that the war would be waged in three phases: first the U.S. fleet would be concentrated and move to the main base at Hawaii; phase 2 would see the fleet moved to its advanced operational base; and phase 3 would be the offensive launched against Japan.[15] The problem for the U.S. Navy, however, was in having the right bases ready in the right place at the right time. Hawaii, the core base, required huge development expenditures, which were not forthcoming. Moreover, with any campaign against Japan likely to be a long one, the choices for advanced naval bases was limited for as long as the various treaties, which did not expire until 1936, forbade any modifications to existing facilities.

Unlike the Admiralty, the U.S. Navy had none of the benefits that could accrue from having numerous well-established bases and refueling anchorages dotted around the world, supported by a relatively huge merchant fleet. Perhaps what Plan Orange did achieve was to generate a growing realization that the logistic ramifications for implementing any form of offensive counterattack were quite daunting, requiring, among other things, large troop convoys across the Pacific or amphibious support through a series of island-hopping maneuvers. As a result, much of the effort post-1936, when the treaties expired, was devoted to identifying many of the logistic issues to be faced if the right resources were to be properly established in a timely manner to protect the main base at Hawaii or the Philippines.

If Plan Orange was not part of national strategy, neither was it particularly well received, let alone coordinated, with the Army despite the defense of the Philippines being the Army's responsibility. Nor did Plan Orange take into account British naval interests in the Far East because it was considered politically unwise to suggest any form of collaboration given the significant antagonism still felt in some circles toward the Royal Navy. The Admiralty's policy toward the Americans, conversely, was more inclusive. In the 1920s through the early 1930s, the Admiralty had been concerned whether the U.S. Navy would act as the catalyst for a naval arms race or seek a more mutually accommodating form of cooperation against Japan. But as Greg Kennedy noted, "Tellingly, in all legitimate British naval planning for the Pacific, the United States was factored in, either as a benevolent neutral or an ally of some degree."[16]

Yet by 1933, following President Roosevelt's reinvigoration of the U.S. Navy with new ships and bases, the Admiralty's assessment of potential American combat capability in the Far East became increasingly respectful and intense. In 1930 the London Naval Conference—the last successful arms limitation conference—had established quantitative and tonnage equality across major ship classes between the U.S. Navy and Royal Navy including, to the Admiralty's dismay, the increasingly important category of cruisers of which the Royal Navy retained a significant numerical advantage for trade protection. Although the treaty expired in 1936, this margin was more or less maintained throughout the rest of the 1930s, which lead many observers to believe that when all was said and done, the Royal Navy had in fact given up little by way of real power—a perception that was to remain a source of resentment within certain circles in the U.S. Navy for some years to come. That said, by the late 1930s Anglo-American relations had become much closer, reflected by the increasing amount of information exchange conducted between the two on a range of matters dealing with policy as well as technical issues relating to the Pacific.[17]

Yet not all was entirely well in terms of the Royal Navy's effective order of battle. As was pungently noted, "In 1900, only when every other sea power joined forces was Britain at risk. By 1936 any sea power could endanger Britain," and the government realized that a crisis was now imminent.[18] By 1935 Britain's navy would be hard pressed to win a war against any two powers; while this relative decline had developed in fits and starts, it was not hard to see why it had occurred. Before World War I the Royal Navy had been allocated £50 million, some 25 percent of total government expenditure; by 1932 it received more or less the same amount, but with rising and broader costs this now only represented some 6 percent of government expenditure.[19] Although Imperial Defence chiefs were becoming increasingly concerned about the potential for overstretch by having to face simultaneous commitments in the Far East and Europe, there was still no clear threat, even if it was becoming hard to ignore the growing pace of German rearmament and mounting aggressiveness from Japan and

Italy. But British public sentiment and treasury fiscal prudence led increasingly to resources being diverted away from military programs (including some shipbuilding) toward domestic social programs. Without some form of rearmament program, the risk grew that the empire would become increasingly difficult to defend, arguably made worse if the widespread dissipation over the previous decade of economic resources and skills, caused by the cutback in naval and maritime construction, was allowed to continue.[20]

The reasons for this relative decline were various and far-reaching, but invariably most could eventually be traced back in some form to a combination of a weak economy still drained from the war and a lack of political will to rearm in the absence of any compelling threat. Meanwhile the British government no longer felt bound to rely exclusively on traditional sea power despite the continuing need for a sizable fleet to defend the British Empire. Instead it chose to divert scarce resources to build up the newly created Royal Air Force with, for example, bombers to preempt the fear of aerial bombing attacks—initially from the very powerful French air force but later from the German air force.[21]

The Admiralty's intense battle with the air lobby led to many distortions and confusion over time, but one of the far-reaching consequences was the Admiralty being almost forced to promote its battleship/battle fleet doctrine as being supreme because it was indestructible from the air. As a result, given the economic constraints of the time, the aircraft carrier even with its own air arm and despite ingenious early development, was considered comparatively less attractive and limited in purpose—a view not shared by Japan or the United States. For them, the concept of using carriers as part of a balanced battle task force capable of deploying modern naval aircraft in large numbers as an offensive weapon was to become an integral part of their carrier doctrine. Indeed, the first seeds can be found in the U.S. Navy even as early as 1929. Conversely, British aircraft carrier policy generally emphasized the role of carriers as being primarily defensive in nature for reconnaissance or trade protection. That is not to say there was no offensive or task force planning at all—there was, as the later successful attack on Taranto would demonstrate—but it was never intended to deploy carriers for offensive air operations on a major scale. This prerogative remained largely the preserve of the Royal Air Force. As a result, fleet air arm aircraft were never specifically tailor-made for offensive carrier operations and therefore suffered inadequate power, payload, range, or speed. The outcome for adopting such different approaches on the role of carriers and their air component, particularly given their consequent logistic ramifications, would come home to roost for all three navies a few years later during the Pacific War, as we shall see later.

All throughout the 1930s it was becoming increasingly evident to allied planners that Japan posed a growing and real maritime risk. The early treaties from 1921 onward had initially enabled Japan to adopt a modest posture thereby helping to assuage Western fears that it was out of control. By the mid 1930s however, the dissention between the moderate forces in the Japanese government and the militarist elements had grown alarmingly; the "peacemakers" wanted to avoid an arms race by having the Imperial Japanese Navy act as a defensive force designed to deter American countermeasures in the Asian region, which Japan had secured through these treaties. The Japanese Naval Staff, conversely, took the Mahanian approach by adopting an offensive naval strategy that required a strong battle fleet ready for the inevitable decisive battle in the Pacific against the United States and her allies, who had in their eyes denied Japan her rightful status as an equal naval power. This came to a head by 1935 at the Second London Naval Conference when the Japanese broke ranks and walked out. With the treaty structure thereafter in a state of collapse, an arms race soon got under way.

To redress significant weaknesses in naval strength to meet potential European theater threats, particularly from Germany but also the Mediterranean, and to preserve the ability (at least theoretically, if not intentionally) to counter Japanese aggression in the Far East, Britain thereafter initiated a new warship program. Although the Imperial Conference of 1937 had suggested that the security of both the United Kingdom and Singapore were the cornerstones for the survival of the British Commonwealth, within two years the plan for the Far East was virtually abandoned. As war in Europe approached, all efforts to continue building large capital ships was postponed as the massive need for smaller escort ships prevailed to counter the growing submarine threat against Britain's lifelines. At the outset of war in 1939, Britain, together with France, had a comfortable superiority over Germany and Italy in terms of capital ships, but in the Far East they remained very exposed. Indeed, according to Paul Kennedy, Japan's energetic shipbuilding program had produced a frontline fleet of ten battleships and ten carriers with sizable cruiser and destroyer fleets such that despite the recent resurgence of British naval shipbuilding it remained the case that "the entire Royal Navy would have had an enormously difficult task in taking on the Japanese alone."[22]

By 1940 the need for Britain to divert large naval forces to the Mediterranean effectively killed off any further thoughts of developing a Far Eastern fleet. Consequently, the United States was left to assume responsibility for the Pacific while complex negotiations began between the two navies about how and under what circumstances the U.S. Navy would commit substantial resources to meet the growing threats developing in the Atlantic. The U.S. Navy's revival in the 1930s had initially been the result of massive ship building contracts that, along with other military contracts, were designed to help the United States recover from the Depression. All these new ships, however, were only replacements for those being scrapped. As events unfolded in Europe, it was becoming increasingly evident to the United States that its Navy might need to be significantly involved in two different oceans, so in 1938 Congress expanded the U.S. Navy to include incremental tonnage for the first time since World War I. A year later this initiative was followed by the equally significant decision to reintroduce a two-ocean navy and immediately concentrate a fleet in the Atlantic/Caribbean while adopting a more defensive posture pro-tem in the Pacific.

This dramatic switch in strategic objectives was reflected in the new so-called Rainbow war plans, which dealt with multiple enemies/alliances in different theaters but did not address the need to harmonize strategies with resources. As the prospect of war in Europe accelerated, four bills were presented to Congress in quick order through July 1940 to fund an essential rapid naval expansion to protect American interests should a global war erupt in either ocean. Although by now potential European allies were already fighting for their survival, the United States remained officially neutral but increasingly engaged; for example, the U.S. Navy provided key support to the Royal Navy under difficult domestic political circumstances. Meanwhile, the attack on Pearl Harbor, as Professor Baer noted, was "a genuine strategic surprise. Yet it is not a mystery why war came to the Pacific. War came because the Japanese government had committed itself to a policy of aggressive expansion and the domination of Asia, which the United States opposed."[23]

Naval Logistics: British Progress, 1900–1940

One of the most challenging problems that the Royal Navy had always had to contend with from earliest times was keeping large numbers of warships operational and fully replenished throughout the world's oceans. Store ships became necessary as warfare moved away from the coasts of Britain and maritime exploration between the sixteenth and eighteenth centuries gave rise to trading routes that would eventually become part of a global trading empire. These store ships were largely obsolete warships or merchantman acquired as the need arose; given that there were only relatively minor differences in hull shape during this period their cargo was generally confined to victuals, powder and shot, canvas, and timber. As sail gave way to steam, ship support became a more complex matter, requiring for the first time not just well-equipped bases but also coaling stations to support and maintain what by then had become the most powerful and ubiquitous navy in the world. It was not until the twentieth century, however, that the Admiralty formally separated the roles of war fighting and support when, in 1905, the Lords Commissioners instructed that "the title 'HMS' shall in future be strictly confined to commissioned ships flying the white ensign. . . . Auxiliaries which belong to the Admiralty shall in future be styled 'Royal Fleet Auxiliaries' [RFA] while those on charter were to be styled 'Merchant Fleet Auxiliaries' [MFA]."[24]

Nevertheless, since such auxiliaries were to be registered under the Merchant Shipping Acts and classified at Lloyds Register of Shipping, they would all be subject to the rules and regulations of the Department of Trade and Lloyds Surveyors. Because they were still owned by the Crown however, an Order in Council also had to be passed on March 22, 1911, to formally establish the Royal Fleet Auxiliary Service exempting it from certain rules, despite being manned by officers and men of the Merchant Navy. This qualification did not apply to any purpose-built depot, tender, or repair ships commissioned under the White Ensign of the Royal Navy, despite the auxiliary nature of their function. Indeed, such vessels retained their naval status even when they were eventually pooled together with the RFA vessels in 1945 to form fleet trains designed to harness the necessary mix and type of mobile logistic support required for the fleet.[25]

The first fleet auxiliary of modern times, however, was not a supply ship or tanker but a 2,860-ton vessel originally loaned by the Atlantic Trading Company to the American Ladies of Maine Committee (headed by Lady Randolph Churchill) that was fitted out during the Boer War as a hospital ship called HMHS *Maine*, a name for hospital ships perpetuated until after World War II.[26] Moreover, it was not until 1913 that the term "Royal Fleet Auxiliary" first appeared in the Admiralty's *Navy List* despite being regularly featured in all the Admiralty Transport Department records.[27] This relationship with the Admiralty was, and indeed remained for many decades, unique; no other naval force in the world was serviced by ships manned by merchant officers and men under a civilian administration.

Coal to Oil

The Royal Navy's adoption of fuel oil rather than coal for its warships was gradual and rather cautious. Coal, after all, was less flammable than oil and posed less of a risk of fire if the ship was under attack. Emanating first from trials in 1902, oil was therefore initially regarded as only an auxiliary power to be used in conjunction with coal. The growth in its use was modest such that, after three years in use, the annual consumption of fuel only amounted to a few thousand tons, compared to over 1 million tons of coal for the same period.[28] In hindsight, the Royal Navy's approach seemed remarkably perfunctory, although it must be remembered that the Royal Navy had access to the best Welsh steam coal in the world—and plenty of it—while the existence of vast oil deposits around the world was not yet as well known, and whatever was available was foreign owned. Such apprehension was therefore understandable, yet oil had many factors in its favor, not least its greater thermal efficiency, easier storage, and more efficient handling characteristics. Not only did oil fuel help to increase warship speed and endurance but it was also a significantly cleaner burning fuel, without the debilitating effects of dust, smoke, and ashes.

The first small tanker to be owned and managed by the Admiralty, RFA *Kharki*, was acquired as a collier in 1903 and converted in 1906.[29] Trials that year using HMS *Hannibal* and HMS *Mars* eventually led to six *Dominion*-class battleships being fitted for oil burning in conjunction with coal.

To meet this growing demand for fuel oil, the first large (7,000 dwt) oil tank vessel, the *Petroleum*, was purchased and fitted for fueling ships in port. Ironically, she was still a coal burner, "as if to express lack of confidence in oil as a fuel," a Fourth Sea Lord at the Admiralty was later to note rather dryly.[30] However, it was the naval maneuvers in 1906 that marked the real beginning of the switch from coal to furnace oil as the benefits of increased speed and efficiency became more apparent. From 1907 onward, when the *Petroleum* was not required for maneuvers or in port, she was deployed to freight oil from Port Arthur, Texas, and New York.[31] This idea of tankers undertaking a dual role to optimize operating returns eventually became standard practice for the Admiralty, but to some extent, as will be seen later, this became a somewhat double-edged sword.

The first introduction to oiling ships at sea came in 1906 by suspending a 5-inch hose astern on a stirrup to the warship in station seven hundred to eight hundred feet behind. These early experiments were not particularly auspicious due to the many problems encountered with the equipment, but at least the potential benefits for pursuing this type of operation were well evident, and the incentive for overcoming these handicaps was therefore compelling. Following Sir John Forsey's call for more transportation to meet the growing use of oil, the Admiralty designed and introduced their first RFA oiler construction program in 1911, starting with *Burma*.[32] Two years later, however, the Admiralty privately admitted to the U.S. Navy that, despite considerable practice typically at about 6 knots, no satisfactory method for oiling at sea had been found to replace what was otherwise virtually the same method originally used for coaling at sea.[33] However, a report in *Shipping Illustrated* recorded that "great skill has been attained in bunkering British warships with liquid fuel at sea while travelling at full speed," with the battleship towing the fuel vessel *Petroleum* at "about 19 knots," something that is "regularly carried out by way of training."[34] To the outside world, with war just two years away, such progress was clearly being portrayed very differently.

World War I

Despite the Admiralty's concealed frustration, progress converting to oil nevertheless continued. Although the large majority of capital ships during World War I were coal burning, practically all the destroyers were oil fired, the first having entered service some years earlier. The combination of improved efficiency and habitability encouraged the Admiralty to convert as many of the rest of the fleet as soon as possible, so that by the time the war was concluded oil had become the primarily fuel. The monthly oil requirement, for example, in January 1915 of 80,500 tons rose to more than 190,000 tons by January 1917.[35] This was also reflected in the rapid expansion of the RFA tanker fleet. At war's outbreak there were only three RFA tankers in commission: *Petroleum, Kharki,* and *Burma.*[36] Three other small oilers were completing with four still being built while the rest of the RFA comprised only a hospital ship and a store carrier. After 1916, as more and more fuel oil depots replaced many of the coaling stations, the biggest requirement was for small tankers to attend the fleet in port, so a major expansion program was undertaken over the next few years for twenty-two small 1,000-ton harbor oilers to fulfill this function. The five recently completed *Burma* class, while advanced for their day, proved rather unstable, so an additional ten improved 2,000-ton and six larger 5,000-ton *Leaf*-class tankers were built, all fitted out for fueling at sea, notably as convoy escort tankers. In addition, eighteen merchant cargo ships of between 5,000–7,000 tons, mostly *War*-class freighters, were converted to tankers for the Admiralty during the War and run as merchant fleet auxiliaries. After 1918, most were then either sold or placed in reserve while others, such as the wartime built *War* class, were eventually used to freight oil from the oil ports to the naval dockyards, or they were put out to charter.[37]

Despite its inauguration in 1911, in reality the RFA still hardly existed at the end of World War I because the harbor ships were run by the coaling offices, leaving the Naval Store Department with only a vague role to play, while most ships were laid up anyway. Meanwhile the nucleus of the RFA officers worked for various commercial companies such as Lane and MacAndrews, which had successfully managed a number of the Admiralty's ships in the past.

1920–1930: Suspended Development

By 1921 the auxiliary fleet comprised twenty-two freighting tankers, twenty small tankers, and a few miscellaneous vessels including a small store carrier, drolly named RFA *Bacchus,* originally acquired and converted for service in Gallipoli as a distilling ship.[38] Six 10,000-ton *Olna*-class commercial type tankers were also built after the war, owned by the Admiralty but permanently chartered out until transferred back in 1934. Throughout the interwar period the remainder of the freighting fleet acted as station ships around the world, without any additions or replacements—reflecting the stringent economies of the 1920s and 1930s. Indeed it seemed deliberate policy to ignore the inevitability of their having to be scrapped by the end of the 1930s.

Although the Royal Navy continued to experiment in fueling at sea, it was never regarded as essential given the ubiquity of base facilities and modest warship deployment aspirations of the time, much of this the lingering legacy from its experience in World War I. Mobility, as the Deputy Director of Intelligence observed, was "a factor of minor importance."[39] The Director of Naval Construction also noted in 1946 that while between the wars "the problem of fuelling at sea was not lost sight of, the records show that though some thought was expended, little money was."[40] Replenishment arrangements therefore remained cautious and the gear cumbersome with low transfer rates, often due to burst hoses. But at least the process worked sufficiently well to meet the modest expectations. Following a series of trials over a number of years, none of which could be characterized as groundbreaking, a new policy was introduced whereby larger ships would not require oil while under way but would instead rely on exposed anchorages, while destroyers would generally be oiled from battleships. Further trials to analyze the relative efficacy of various methods for oiling at sea were undertaken in 1929 by ships on the China and Mediterranean stations, from which it was concluded that "the oiling of the fleet on passage in war is an emergency proposition entailing the use of a large number of commercial oilers. These cannot be fitted with special equipment prior to the emergency arising, and in consequence the older method of employing stirrups, although not so efficient as the hose/hawser, may be more suitable as it does not require such extensive equipment."[41]

In effect, economic expediency overruled the chance to improve efficiency, reflecting the lack of any priority in trying to enable ships to become more independent and mobile. The consequent inability to maintain destroyers at sea for long periods, or even show determination to practice replenishment regularly, increasingly contrasted with how the Americans viewed future operations. This disinterest seemed to be fairly entrenched, despite the caveat in 1926 by the then Deputy Director of Naval Intelligence, that

> Ten of the larger American oilers carry sufficient fuel to move 26 battleships of the *Revenge* class from Plymouth to Singapore via the Suez Canal, and one of them sufficient for 10 destroyers. We are providing shore depots on that particular route, but when the next war comes, some nation other than Japan may be the opponent and the tanks and oil may be required elsewhere, or even if Japan is the enemy, the fleet might have to proceed to the East by some other route.[42]

He then presciently observed that

> A plan that centres around fortresses and fixed bases like Metz and Port Arthur usually contains within itself the germs of strategical failure. On the other hand, a fleet with its oil supplies secured in Australia could have, with the assistance of a supply train organized on the American pattern, the choice of nu-

merous anchorages in Malayan and Chinese waters. The resultant flexibility of movement would enable it to take the initiative and adjust its strategy to the changing circumstances of the war.[43]

To try to emulate the Americans was not only perceived to be exaggerating the problem but very costly to boot. There was admittedly money to save if only by closing some Royal dockyards and shore establishments whose expenditure had increased from just more than 10 percent of total estimates in 1913 to nearly 15 percent in 1925, despite the lack of postwar construction.[44] There was also the potential to overhaul the way cruiser squadrons operated from various world-wide locations, for example, by dispensing with the need to maintain local facilities for maintenance and overhaul that could more economically be handled at home. But these arguments for emulating the American approach to mobility did not win many advocates. The Royal Navy was becoming less confident and imaginative rather than bold and visionary. The Americans, conversely, were starting to gain a march on their British rivals and they knew it.[45]

1930–1940: Admiralty Plans and Development

As the clouds of war loomed ominously on the horizon, the Admiralty's fears of Imperial overstretch, first raised in 1922, became reality.[46] By 1936 the increased likelihood of bombing attacks on fixed bases caused a concerned Admiralty "to consider the number and types of auxiliary vessels" required to supply the fleet "taking into consideration the possibility of certain bases not being available and others having to be improvised."[47] For reasons not disclosed (but probably because they were RFAs), oilers, colliers, and hospital ships were to be specifically excluded from consideration. It seems reasonable to infer from this that there was little desire to look for an integrated or at least all-encompassing response for providing logistic support that would compensate for the loss of any bases. Two years later, after much deliberation, the report was more or less adopted by the Admiralty, with the major exception of the committee's hypothetical proposition that Singapore might be lost in the event of a two-ocean war.

The Admiralty's continued reliance on Singapore was not shared by everyone. The Naval Historical Section of the Admiralty's Training and Staff Duties Division, for example, was convinced that conducting a guerre de course with cruisers and submarines refueled at sea was a far more efficient way to destroy Japanese shipping than having to deploy five times the resources by operating out of Singapore. Tankers, so their logic went, should therefore be naval manned and properly equipped for replenishment under way, while "fuelling at sea must be practiced as in the American and German navies."[48] No evidence was found to suggest this was heeded. Indeed, to the contrary. While Britain's defense spending was increasing significantly by 1937–38, increases were confined to warships only. No real attention had been given to the RFA, which in

1935 comprised fifty-six aging ships that provided some 267,000 of cargo capacity, of which nearly half were chartered out to managers, in reserve or temporarily manned.[49] In fact, it was not until 1937 that the Admiralty's Naval Store Department felt adequately prepared to take control of the various RFA-manned freighting tankers then managed by commercial companies.[50]

Meanwhile, unlike the Americans, the Admiralty had remained unconvinced about the need for ultrafast tankers, but they eventually relented under pressure from Sir William Gick, Director of Naval Stores Department (D of S), who had the foresight in 1937 to recognize the growing need to replace a severely worn out freighting tanker fleet. Six 12–knot 12,259-dwt tankers ordered by the British Tanker Company were therefore taken over by the Admiralty to become the new *Dale* "A" and "B" class, without any apparent "navalization" planned, followed later by two more "C" *Dale* class acquired from the Anglo-Saxon Petroleum Company.[51] With so many naval oilers of a venerable age and the high costs for new construction inhibiting any chance for new specialized shipbuilding, British logistics policy even by 1938 continued to rely upon the peculiar cooperation between the Admiralty and oil companies in sharing the same hull. While expedient, this would never allow for ultrafast speeds (that is, 15 knots or more) because, to the commercial companies, this was neither economic nor necessary.[52]

Naval Logistics: U.S. Navy Progress, 1898–1941

In many ways the story of how the U.S. Navy developed its logistic infrastructure during the same period provides an interesting contrast to the Royal Navy's approach, even if the starting point for both was not too dissimilar.

Coal to Oil

The Spanish-American War (1898) provided the first opportunity for America's steam-powered navy to fight outside continental shores. This was achieved by procuring merchant colliers to supply the fleet from coaling stations located in the United States. These colliers were slow and unable to transfer coal at sea except in sheltered waters, which not only inhibited squadron maneuvers but also relied upon convoys to work. What made coaling at sea a priority was the need to replenish their warships blockading the Spanish fleet at Santiago de Cuba without damaging the colliers docked in Guantanamo Bay specifically captured for the purpose. This was the moment of recognition that enormous benefits would accrue if replenishment could be accomplished under way. While subsequent engineering research developed coaling-at-sea from collier to battleship in 1904, the transfer rates were slow and the machinery cumbersome.[53] But the rate was still adequate enough to justify outfitting ten Russian battleships with half a million tons of coal by sixty chartered merchant colliers during their famous long voyage to the Far East.[54]

The one event that really highlighted the need for a battle force to be accompanied by fuel ships was the famous cruise of the Great White Fleet in 1908. The vast amount of coal required over the fourteen–month voyage by sixteen pre-dreadnoughts required forty-nine mostly British-owned colliers to deliver their cargoes around the world in a timely manner.[55] However, the frequent rendezvous failures convinced the U.S. Navy that in future only a dedicated force of naval colliers would suffice, and so for the first (and only) time, more than 50 percent of the U.S. Navy's appropriation in 1908 was spent on auxiliaries rather than warships.[56] With the switch from coal to fuel oil completed just prior to World War I, new oilers were also built to replace the colliers.[57] Although the nature of the fuel changed, the principles underlying any transfer between two ships remained unchanged. The oilers were still expected to follow the fleet and moor alongside to refuel warships in sheltered waters.

World War I

Underway replenishment itself was not recognized as a serious possibility until 1916 and first tested in 1917. By this time, troopships from the United States were escorted to Europe by cruisers with sufficient range to cross nonstop. However, destroyers required for antisubmarine patrol off Ireland could not transit without a refueling stop. The U.S. Navy's second oiler, USS *Maumee* (AO2), was therefore dispatched in May 1917 to operate three hundred miles south of Greenland as the refueling post. Displacing 14,000 dwt and designed to fuel destroyers while moored alongside in port, she was the first diesel-powered surface ship in the navy, so up to this point no actual oiling-at-sea had ever been conducted. Nevertheless, this did not seem to deter her young executive/engineering officer, Lt. Chester Nimitz, who promptly set up a jury rig that enabled destroyers to cruise alongside at 5 knots with some 40 feet of clear water between them, a method known as "riding-abeam," later called "broadside."[58] Thirty-four destroyers were refueled this way over three months, and while the system was crude and limited to daytime in reasonable weather, the breakthrough was extraordinary and precedent setting.[59]

It is interesting to note that even though the U.S. shipbuilding program produced fifteen oilers, two ammunition ships, and three stores ships by this time, none were actually configured for replenishment at sea.[60] This would suggest that, despite the Atlantic success, replenishment at sea was still perceived as one-off and that supporting the fleet using American ports and dockyards would remain unchanged. But the key to the future was right here. As Nimitz wrote after some decades of further reflection, the *Maumee* fueling-at-sea operations "gave our Navy the experience that was to prove invaluable in supplying mobile logistic support to our great fleets that crossed the Pacific in World War II and ut-terly destroyed the Japanese Navy."[61]

While self-sufficiency in World War I remained an American ideal rather than a realistic objective, the early signs of what later became known as fleet trains were already evident. The initial deployment to the United Kingdom of just six destroyers had increased by the end of the war to nearly four hundred vessels ranging from battleships and cruisers to auxiliaries and coast guard cut-ters. To augment the initial force of tenders, tankers, and repair ships to support them, the U.S. Navy built with the assistance of European host countries some fif-teen naval bases and twenty-seven aviation bases and various operating depots or stations to support this sizable fleet.[62] Half of their fleet operated in British or colonial waters, and it was impossible to service them without imposing upon dockyard resources and tankers that were often in competition with the Royal Navy. In fact the Royal Navy's support was crucial and much appreciated.[63] But it was the small floating repair base operating independently in Brest that would prove to be the prototype for what followed in the next war.[64]

1920–1930: War Plan Orange and the Focus toward Japan

After World War I, refueling under way was regarded by the U.S. Navy as likely to occur only in wartime and therefore relegated to occasional practice by carri-ers or battleships topping up their escorts during annual exercises.[65] Although some fifteen oilers had entered the fleet between 1915 and 1922, the importance of keeping warships or other auxiliaries ready for future service was often over-looked, with many scrapped due to the tonnage limitation treaties set by the Washington Arms Limitations Conference of 1921–22. It was soon recognized, however, that for any plan to work would require, among other things, a supply "train" of logistic forces to support any expeditionary force across the Pacific so temporary supply bases for the battle fleets could then be established in the for-ward areas.[66] This was the catalyst that raised the whole rationale for underway replenishment to a much higher level of appreciation because any such force would have to comprise hundreds of troop transports and cargo ships as well as a battle fleet. The lack of available fixed bases to some extent would explain why "the special training and organization of the marine corps with transports and amphibious technology [was specifically designed] . . . as a small but complete expeditionary force for the capture and defence of temporary bases and anchor-ages," thereby freeing the American fleet from such dependence.[67] The precursor for this was, of course, their experience at Guantanamo Bay.

Most significant, however, was that nearly half of the Fleet Train would be oilers. Given the large steaming distances involved and the lack of refueling bases, the ramifications were far reaching. En route fueling schedules would be essential, and two-thirds of the twenty-one tankers dedicated solely for refueling the battle fleet itself would have to be merchant tankers requisitioned after war had been declared.[68] This reliance upon mobilization became, not for the last time, an important bone of contention with Congress, which remained unconvinced that new auxiliaries deserved funding in peacetime. Nothing new there, of course, but the tempo for change was at least advancing. By 1926 a substantial fleet train, known since its formation after World War I as the Base Force, had been developed to support the U.S. Navy's operating fleet of 296 warships including 15 battleships, 18 cruisers, a carrier, and 106 destroyers.[69] Described by the Royal Navy's Deputy Director of Naval Intelligence as the U.S. Navy's Naval Train Squadron, he reported the Base Force to be "an integral part of the naval organisation" comprising a fleet of auxiliaries, which can be found listed in appendix A.[70] This was, in fact, the precursor to the Service Force, adopted in 1942, about which the official historian of the U.S. Fleet Train would consider some thirty years later as having been "sound" in concept and principle and well organized in practice. Indeed, it was rendering such "valuable and efficient services to the fleet" even by the early 1920s that "some ideas of greater future accomplishments took root."[71] Whether these ever blossomed is not immediately evident; like so much else during the Depression years, they were probably victim to appropriation cuts, but at least the function of logistics had firmly found its métier.

Although War Plan Orange was modified several times over the years, the essential challenge remained unchanged: namely, whether to establish advanced bases to mount successive offensives or to provide logistic support by en route refueling on a massive scale. In truth, these plans were not very realistic as long as the auxiliaries remained nonexistent and the fleet continued to rely on continental home bases for their support. While the U.S. Navy had not entirely stopped developing underway replenishment capability after 1918, it remained categorized as a wartime priority only and was therefore relegated to occasional practice, adopting methods first acquired in World War I.[72] Although attempts were made to improve technology, there was no sense of urgency within the U.S. Navy, and it was not really until 1929 that the first steps were taken to recognize the potential importance of underway replenishment when it was mandated as "a routine peacetime exercise, to be carried out at least once, annually, by each navy tanker."[73] This was an important step however because it placed the practice of refueling squarely on everyone's training agenda for the first time. Indeed, within three years such closer attention started to bear significant fruits, not least in productivity.

1930–1940: U.S. Navy Plans and Development

As the war clouds appeared on the horizon, concerns surfaced in late 1938 about the limited endurance of aircraft carriers, which was first highlighted in 1929 but given little subsequent attention, as well as concerns about the lack of refueling capability between capital ships and smaller escorts.[74] Further successful tests by capital ships using the broadside fueling technique—up to then considered safe only for destroyers—proved how much could be gained from multiple refueling between different sizes of warships or oilers. It also highlighted the disconcerting lack of available fast merchant ships or modern oilers; this forced the recently created U.S. Maritime Commission to initiate building high-speed commercial tankers that could be transferred to the U.S. Navy in emergency for immediate conversion to fleet oilers.[75] The first three of twelve high-speed 16,300-dwt tankers ordered by Standard Oil were therefore promptly acquired by the U.S. Navy and enhanced with certain so-called national defense features so they could be mobilized in emergency as replenishment oilers.[76] The first of these, the *Cimarron*, shown in plate 1.1, was the fastest tanker in the United States and one of the largest in the world. It was delivered to the U.S. Navy on February 6, 1939, fewer than ten months after her keel was laid down. However, it would take another year to "navalize" the tankers by installing such features as oiling-at-sea gear and substantial armament.

By mid 1940 a reassessment of whether the fleet was properly balanced between fighting and support concluded that insufficient funds had been allocated toward strengthening the auxiliary force. The operating force of 344 warships was supported by 120 auxiliaries, but during the fifteen years between 1925 and 1940, although warship numbers had doubled, auxiliaries had languished.[77] In 1928 there was only one navy contract for a combatant ship, and an all-time low in construction was reached in 1935 with only nine ships completed, six for the U.S. Navy. Following the passing of the Two-Ocean Navy bill in 1940, authority was given to expand the fleet's combat tonnage by 70 percent, the largest shipbuilding expansion program in history.[78] Included were 100,000 tons of additional auxiliaries. By early 1941 emergency programs for tankers and liberty ships were rampant as the economic might of the U.S. shipyards kicked in. Within three years the number of shipyards had nearly tripled and the flow of new auxiliary and merchant ships was almost overwhelming.[79] By 1943 more than 17 million tons of new merchant shipping had been built; by the end of the war five thousand merchant ships had been produced at a cost of some $12 billion.[80]

Conclusion

Throughout the interwar period British logistic plans had assumed that, from a geographical standpoint, naval operations would remain relatively parochial, predicated to some extent from their experience during World War I. The Pacific was therefore never in the forefront of strategic deliberations; any future deployments beyond Europe, particularly to the Far East, would have to be adequately supported by a chain of bases and repair facilities spread throughout the empire. Operations over long distances for extended periods were therefore not considered probable; consequently replenishment at sea was effectively ignored.[81] In contrast to this expedient and somewhat arrested perspective, the U.S. Navy's approach had become more inclusive and forward looking for the important reason that it had no choice. For them a two-ocean strategy became increasingly essential as war loomed, although the consequent shift in naval power from Europe to the United States and, more importantly, beyond presented U.S. naval planners with difficult logistical challenges given the distances involved and the lack of available bases other than at Hawaii and the Philippines. As Geoffrey Till noted, the vast distances involved in any Pacific campaign "mandated the allocation of high priority to the development of naval aviation" that, with the absence of available land bases, meant relying on aircraft carriers until enemy territory had been acquired.[82] Thus, each navy developed its logistic capability based on its confidence and ability to meet the new, increasingly ominous geostrategic threats of the late 1930s posed by Japan in the Far East and Germany and Italy in Europe. A key difference in philosophy between the two navies was on the future role of aircraft carriers, which was partly due to how and (more importantly) where such resources were likely to be deployed. What both the British and American experience had shown was how difficult it was, during any prolonged period of decline or national readjustment, to calibrate ship construction and force size to match real or prospective maritime threats.

2 | World War II
The Fleet Train Comes of Age

This chapter charts the progress of both the U.S. and British navies in developing mobile logistic support during World War II. This war would require a new type of expeditionary warfare using carrier task forces that would have to operate for long periods away from any base. Much of the history specifically relating to American logistic experience during World War II has been widely published already and is likely to be familiar to many readers. The Royal Navy's logistic experience, however, is far less well documented, let alone extensively published, so in keeping with trying to shed a fresh focus on aspects of wartime logistic experience, this chapter is disproportionately given over to studying the British effort. This does not imply that their respective contributions to the outcome of the Pacific campaign should be regarded as being similarly balanced, either in importance or in value. The intention is simply to undertake a broad survey of the British contribution but provide some focus on less familiar but still important aspects of how the Royal Navy's logistic effort was transformed during this period.

It was not until 1945, when American insistence that the Royal Navy be self-reliant for operating under their command in the Pacific, that both navies operated together with their respective fleet trains; it was from this moment that the first seeds of logistic convergence were sown. And it was from this critical period onward that virtually all the foundations of modern naval logistic theory and doctrine were laid. How this happened and the difficulties encountered along the way are explored here.

British Logistics Experience, 1940–1944

Britain's response to German rearmament, while initially tardy, had nevertheless accelerated by 51 percent in 1937–38. By 1939, British defense spending had reached a level two and a half times that of the United States, despite the latter's much larger gross national product (GNP), even though the country had yet to be placed on to a war footing.[1] Whether there would be sufficient British warships to protect both U.K. and Dominion interests around the world in the event of war was something that worried the Admiralty a great deal. The prospect of having to extend warship deployment to cover the gaps would inevitably require them to be fully sustained and replenished at bases around the empire. This meant that any such bases would quickly become Britain's first line of defense. However, the available tools to achieve such sustainability were limited—as indeed was the technology and thinking behind them. The 1936 committee's recommendations for naval supply ships in the event of war in the Far East, which was adopted in 1938, had included a number of different ship types, as shown in appendix B.[2] What is striking is the disproportionate number of issuing ships being proposed, mostly for armaments (ASIS), to the exclusion of not just tankers (which, given the terms of reference, was to be expected) but also any repair ships. Second, of the eighteen stores carriers proposed, all but five were for armaments while fourteen more ships were allocated to carry mines, although how these were to be laid remained unclear. Moreover, because no auxiliaries of reasonable size could be fitted out with the whole range of stores for large warships, it was recommended to combine victualling and naval stores into the same issue ship, despite the potential (and, in fact, subsequently realized) impracticability of implementing this, given the technology that was then available. Half would need to be taken up prior to the outbreak of war with the balance delivered as soon as possible thereafter—a reasonable proposition at the time. However, by 1941, the overall shipping situation was so tight that only a small fraction of these recommendations was adopted, and of these only a small proportion of auxiliaries ever reached the Pacific by 1945. Perhaps not surprisingly, the author of the "History of the Fleet Train" felt it was "noteworthy that the findings of this committee were never quoted later in the war; this is understandable in the case of victualling and naval stores ships whose numbers were grossly underestimated, but they might have been used to support bids for ammunition ships."[3]

The other serious deficiency in the committee's recommendations—the lack of any base support ships—was reflected in the order of battle at the outbreak of war. By 1939, the Royal Navy had only one 14,650-ton submarine tender, HMS *Medway*, built in 1928, and a smaller 8,750-ton destroyer depot ship, HMS *Woolwich*, built in 1934. In addition, there were five smaller depot ships for submarines and destroyers, none built after 1915.[4] More critical, however, was the single fleet repair ship, HMS *Resource*, displacing 12,300 tons, built in 1928 to service ships in the large floating dock in Singapore, should the graving dock not be completed. This was to be the only ship throughout the war designed to supplement an existing operational base. This is significant because only after 1941 was any contemplation given to deploying fleets in oceans other than from established operational bases. But for this to become feasible required a number of base repair and depot ships, which would all now have to be conversions from existing armed merchant cruisers, suitably modified to operate in places where shore facilities hardly existed, such as Kilindini and Trincomalee. Even in these early days, the sudden void of available adequate repair vessels was so palpable that recommendations were made there and then to retain in the postwar fleet all such converted repair ships to avoid repetition of the error.

Although the RFA fleet had been expanded in recent months to sixty-six vessels (twenty-eight freighting and thirty-three fleet attendant tankers, four store carriers, and a hospital ship), the vast majority were at the tail end of their serviceable careers.[5] Meanwhile, by 1942 British losses in both warships and merchantmen had become so heavy that no further merchantmen could be taken up. Consequently, neither a properly balanced fleet nor adequate mobile support could be considered for the Far East, let alone produced. It was not so much a lack of intent as simply the lack of ships to establish such a fleet train, although considerable doubts were raised as to whether it was really understood how critical a fleet train—any fleet train—would be for future operations in distant oceans. As Captain Roskill noted in the official history of the Royal Navy in World War II, unless this challenge was addressed, the Royal Navy would have to operate in Far East waters where "base facilities, both fixed and floating, would be totally inadequate."[6]

Nor was there much progress in developing either the intention or the practice for keeping capital ships and cruisers continuously refueled at sea near the operational area. Instead, it was a case of "business as usual" with the emphasis on refueling convoy escorts from tankers, typically from astern.[7] Indeed six naval-designed *Ranger*-class fleet attendant tankers had been launched in 1940, the first since 1914, but these were deployed on mostly North Russian and Malta convoys. While some progress had been achieved in the art of refueling within these convoys, the broader issue of providing fleet mobility to capital ships and cruisers still remained unaddressed. The hunt to locate and destroy the German battleship *Bismarck* in 1941 proved a timely wake-up call. In all, five battleships, two carriers, three battle cruisers, nine cruisers, and twenty-three destroyers needed to be harnessed due to the turnover caused by the continuous need for warships to return to base for refueling.[8] Despite the scale of the operation, however, the Admiralty remained undeterred. Because the vast majority of their work was conducted in what was perceived to be the rather narrow waters of the North Sea and Mediterranean against a heavy U-boat menace, it accepted "the limit of endurance of our ships as the limit of their mobility."[9]

After three years of war, with the Admiralty's continued reliance on fixed bases for support and leaving replenishment at sea confined mostly to destroyers, it had become increasingly evident that the Royal Navy was ill prepared for extending its fleet beyond India toward the East Indies in 1944, and eventually to the Pacific. In March 1943, the first recognition of a need for more mobility came with the proposal for two Mobile Fleet Base Organizations, as they were to be called, in the Indian and Pacific Oceans "for the rapid provision of the facilities necessary for the sustained operation of the fleet in an area far removed from established bases."[10] Within six months, however, plans for sending large forces to the Far East receded with any residual logistic support expected to come from either American or Dominion partners.[11]

This was wishful thinking. The subject of a fleet train was, after all, first tabled at the Quebec conference in August 1943. As their talks with both the Americans and Ministry of War Transport progressed down their tortuous path, the Admiralty quickly came to grips with just what was involved. As it tried to determine precisely what Britain's future role in Southeast Asia and the Pacific should be, it was becoming manifestly clear that the fundamental issue at stake was all about logistics. How could a logistics plan be formulated that would support, on the one hand, British aspirations for maintaining large naval forces as part of the Allied offensive against Japan while meeting American demands, on the other hand, that any such contribution be largely self-sustaining and mobile? Behind this precondition was the U.S. Navy's concern about whether the Admiralty's organization for logistic planning both in the U.K. and in theater was adequate.

In trying to explain to the Deputy First Sea Lord what was behind these concerns, Admiral Dorling, the British supply representative at the British Admiralty Delegation in Washington (BAD), emphasized that the Americans would only be willing to supply equipment "where there is clear operational need," provided there existed a well-thought-out logistic plan prepared in advance of the operation that clearly justified the various needs. Perhaps the most important requirement was that there existed "a suitable organization for the receipt, custody and distribution of the equipment supplied."[12] What the Americans were looking for was a mirror of their own structure, which featured a flag officer close to the theater C-in-C responsible for all its logistic service needs while also reporting directly to a dedicated "logistics" admiral in Washington, close to the CNO, Planning, and Co-minCH.[13] By comparison, the Admiralty's logistic organization was, according to the Deputy Director of Plans (Q), "almost nonexistent."[14] It might be helpful to explore why this was still so.

Admiralty Plans Division: Logistic Planning, 1940–1944

The Admiralty's Plans Division (PD) was originally set up during World War I to fulfill two functions previously handled by the Operations Division or the Mobilization Division.[15] The PD was first to conceive and produce plans for operations, both current and future, and second, to prepare the necessary procurement program. After the war, operational planning was returned to Operations Division, and Plans Division was developed into the section to advise the Admiralty on naval policy in general. This function, however, became subordinated to the various interwar political negotiations and security arrangements such that, by 1931, the incoming Deputy Chief of Naval Staff (CNS) claimed, for example, that he found the task of preparing war plans being completely neglected due to other more pressing demands.

The early period of World War II witnessed a further realignment of the Naval Staff Divisions in which Plans Division assumed more responsibility for joint operational planning—a task that involved considerable administrative planning, in particular providing other Admiralty departments with guidance on implications for manpower, material, and supply matters. It also provided the naval contribution to the Joint Planning Staff. Eventually it became necessary to merge different sections of both Plans Division and Training and Staff Duties Division (TSDD) into a new section titled Plans Division (Q). Among its duties was that of planning and coordinating the necessary administrative, technical, and supply arrangements for carrying out future operations. Although responsible to the Director of Plans, the head of PD(Q) had considerable autonomy because he not only had direct responsibilities for certain matters to both the First and Second Sea Lords but he was also naval assistant to the Fourth Sea Lord as well as the link between the Admiralty and the chief of Combined Operations.[16]

Throughout 1942 and 1943, as offensive initiatives involving the Home and Mediterranean fleets were intensified, and as thoughts progressed for building an Eastern Fleet, strategic planning within the Admiralty became, not surprisingly, considerably more complex and demanding. With the deputy CNS preoccupied by current operations, the Director of Plans had to assume responsibility for working with both the Joint Planning Committee and the combined British and United States chiefs of staff, which meant attending their meetings, including the conferences between Prime Minister Churchill and President Roosevelt. Such logistic planning that was undertaken outside of the various departments themselves was otherwise handled by PD—in particular, the Administrative Planning section of PD(Q) under a deputy director (Q). It was never designed to cover all aspects of logistics; in fact neither Plans Division (Q) nor Plans Division as a whole dealt with all naval activities, the independent Fleet Air Arm being a case in point.

By December 1943, as the logistics functions (still termed administrative planning) became increasingly applied across all the services, PD(Q) blossomed into a separate division tasked with estimating operational requirements for particular operations and keeping the Admiralty Board informed on the progress of preparations for executing such plans.[17] Only four months later, as the prospect for switching the main fleet to the Pacific advanced, PD(Q) was obliged to emphasize that unless there were adequate and timely supplies of equipment, then neither the naval bases nor the fleet auxiliaries would be found to provide the necessary regional logistic support. In other words, a fleet train had to be devised and immediately organized. However, the First Sea Lord (1SL) strongly objected to any requests for Naval Staff complement increases to help plan for such a transition, so the Division continued to operate along the lines shown in appendix C, with the functional aspects of logistics, including freighting and material, handled by the deputy director while the geographic planning was governed by the head of PD(Q). It was not until September 1944, only a brief period before the BPF was actually formed, that the Director of PD(Q) was finally able to form the important bases section in the division, responsible for establishing staff requirements for such bases and coordinating and progressing their further development.

One of the problems in developing an integrated comprehensive logistic plan was that, unlike the American logistics command structure, there was no one Admiralty Board member responsible for logistics as a whole; different aspects were covered by different members. For example, the Fourth Sea Lord was responsible for supplies and transport, among other things, while the Controller was responsible for warship production. There was not a centralized logistic command structure in the fleets or in the theater commands, so supply coordination was managed at a relatively low level, mainly for day-to-day issues. The Eastern Fleet, admittedly, had a rear admiral (administrative) at Kilindini, but although this was an improvement, his effectiveness was hampered by his being detached geographically from the commander in chief.

For a number of reasons, some of them unappealing to certain members within the Admiralty, the recommendation was eventually made to "follow the American [logistics] model, which despite fault has the merit of being a logical arrangement for modern conditions."[18] What this implied was setting up a dedicated logistics planning division, nominating one board member for all logistics matters, having a logistics admiral or captain on the staff of the commander in chief, and having logistics planning officers on all main staffs. Although the Fourth Sea Lord "resented the implied criticism of our Allies," he recognized that "the Admiralty [logistic] organization is by no means ideal," nor did it "look particularly sound on paper."[19] But, he argued, it had functioned for a very long time, and although not always successful, it "on the whole compares favourably with anything achieved on the other side of the Atlantic." While he agreed it made sense to move supply departments dealing with postproduction from controllers to his domain, any wholesale reorganization on such a scale was, he conceded, not possible in wartime. Needless to say, the controller concurred.[20] It was therefore proposed that the best interim solution was to enhance the seniority of administration within the fleets and prepare a draft Admiralty Fleet Order (AFO) to explain the naval organization for planning and implementing supplies to theater. Although it was intended to keep a draft for Admiral Badger USN, Head of Logistics in Washington who was about to visit London, the whole initiative was subsequently shelved when it became apparent that any such document would demonstrate "very clearly that we have no logistics organisation."[21] With that, the whole matter was set aside for later consideration by the newly created Administrative Planning Department, which a year later indeed pointed this out to the new Fourth Sea Lord: "The original subject of this paper, namely steps to convince the Americans that we had a logistic planning system as they understand it, whereas in fact we have not, have now I think lapsed. However, [given the views expressed earlier about the difficulty of realigning departments under different Board members] . . . I am wondering whether it should be tabled as a 'post-war problem'?"[22]

With the Sea Lord's predictable concurrence, the reorganization was finally shelved. However, at least one of the key building blocks for any logistic organization to work—that is, the need for more senior logistics officers to be in theater—was identified through this exercise; to that extent, some progress was achieved. Whether it would be adequate to cope with organizing a fleet train remained to be seen because many of the logistic challenges that were starting to descend upon the Royal Navy would become the most complex in its history, requiring not just dynamic planning but also new methods and new designs for a broader range of vessels capable of sustaining warships at sea over longer periods than had ever been dreamt possible.

Before considering this challenge further, it is perhaps appropriate to examine the extent to which the U.S. Navy traveled the same or different paths in developing its own mobile logistic capability during the early years of World War II.

U.S. Navy, 1941–1944: Building the Logistic Network

Supporting U.S. naval forces in the Atlantic during the early years of World War II was simplified logistically by the availability of naval bases on both sides of the ocean, so the critical demand was invariably for more combatants rather than auxiliaries.[23] The early years of the war in the Central and South Pacific, however, could be characterized as a battle for advanced bases using amphibious forces to establish supply ports, ship repair facilities, and landing strips that could then act as a backstop for the continuing offensive. Some of these bases were general, others were for special purposes, and many were temporary due to the fluidity of changing battle lines. Once built, however, every base had to be maintained. The problem of supplying this growing web was both complex and colossal, requiring a continuous flow of munitions, manpower, and supplies from sources throughout the United States and elsewhere. In 1941 the base force of the Pacific Fleet had been reorganized into four squadrons of fewer than one hundred ships. The name was changed in April 1942 to Service Force, which rapidly expanded its range of support capability to become an auxiliary fleet composed of a number of squadrons with each being allocated a different function. Before the end of the war the Service Force would collectively comprise more than sixteen hundred vessels.[24]

In very broad terms, the war in Europe was dominated by armies; for the Pacific, it was predominantly a naval war. This meant, among other things, that no fleet could operate effectively without employing aircraft for power projection or protection. By early 1944 the U.S. Navy's strategy for waging war had become increasingly mobile, flexible, and innovative. American fast carrier task forces, suitably replenished at sea, were able to roam at will into distant waters for months at a time to inflict severe damage to Japanese shipping and island installations. The raids on Truk and the Marianas also introduced another new concept—escort carriers that accompanied the oiler group to furnish replacement aircraft.[25] As the nature of battle changed from undertaking raids or seeking pure fleet engagements to one of advancement and attrition, the role of carrier task forces was adapted accordingly. Their great attribute now was that they could be alternately concentrated or moved to provide air cover and sea control wherever American amphibious assaults against Japanese-held islands were required, without the need to rely on advance bases on land. By positioning large carrier task forces within striking distance of the enemy defensive positions, particularly airfields, they could neutralize resistance while furnishing close air cover for the amphibious landings. Although substantially more shipping would be required to move and maintain an army in the Pacific compared to Europe, a unique element of this particular campaign was the ability to move troops from island to island, and to put them ashore against opposition.[26] This demanded a full command of the sea, an ability to "leapfrog" when it was expedient, and—most vitally—a regular, extensive, but flexible supply chain. In fact, during the final campaigns, such as the Marianas, the Philippines, Iwo Jima, and Okinawa, where Japanese resistance was very prolonged, it also became essential to have both fleet and light/escort carrier forces linger out of view, in a wholly unprecedented manner, so naval ground support aircraft could reach inland far beyond the maximum range of battleship guns to provide continuing support beyond the beachhead. This ability to linger was critical until land air bases could be established to provide the necessary air cover.

From a logistics perspective, supporting task force naval units was comparatively easier than supporting the expeditionary or amphibious operations. Even then, although it proved relatively straightforward to predict demand flow for maintenance and support to a typical task force deployment, the real difficulty was being able to anticipate well in advance where the "customers" would be when the support was likely to be required. For expeditionary or amphibious forces, the unpredictable exigencies of a land campaign imposed such wide variables when trying to establish requirements that it proved exceptionally difficult to plan with any degree of accuracy. Capturing the Marianas Islands in the summer of 1944 had required a force of more than six hundred vessels ranging from carriers to high-speed transports and tankers, more than two thousand aircraft, and three hundred thousand naval, marine, and army personnel.[27] Yet it was the sheer scale and frequency of these types of operations that enabled logistic skills to be quickly honed, and mistakes to be made but lessons learned, as the inexorable American advance continued across the islands with typical vigor and tenacity.

By 1944, according to Fleet Admiral King in his reports to the Secretary of the Navy, the U.S. Navy had gained considerable experience in addressing two distinct but related problems in trying to supply combatant forces that were constantly growing and always in a hurry. The first problem was the procurement, mobilization, and transportation of personnel, materiel, and supplies from the United States to the advance bases in areas that lacked suitable port facilities. This entailed not only delivering "at the sharp end" huge quantities of ammunition and supplies following the initial amphibious assault but also securing and building airfields for local control of the air and positioning repair facilities for ships and depots for supplying all the necessary stores for base activities, fleet units, and vessels of the fleet train. Docks and harbors had to be improvised, adequate stocks of spare parts handled, and living quarters built.

Three service squadrons provided these needs for the Fifth and Third fleets (alternating) with occasional support also given to the Seventh Fleet. Service Squadron Two administered the fleet repair ships, salvage, mobile hospitals, and mail. Service Squadron Ten, created in March 1944, took over most of the functions of Service Squadron Four by acting as the mobile advanced bases providing floating dock facilities, for example, for battle damage, emergency repairs, and ship upkeep as well as all the other necessary services and storage facilities applicable for fleet anchorages. Service Squadron Eight bridged the gap between the United States West Coast and the forward areas by deploying a large force of oilers, stores, and ammunition issuing ships as well as chartered tankers and provision ships for the supply, transportation, and distribution of all fuel products, ammunition stores, and provisions.[28] In 1940 the only properly equipped advance base was Pearl Harbor, Hawaii. By 1945, more than four hundred advance bases had been established in the forward areas, ranging in complexity from relatively modest staging bases for refueling fleets and armadas of transports to those equipped with dry docks to repair and refit the largest capital ships.[29] All this was on a scale of both size and complexity that any objective analysis would be outside this chapter's scope. Nevertheless, its relevance becomes an important consideration in the postwar reassessment of mobile logistics policy, discussed further in chapter 4.

The second major logistics problem identified by King was keeping ships supplied at sea, partly due to the speed of the American advance and partly due to the huge increase in the number of vessels in theater. After three years of contending with both these problems, King acknowledged that resolving the first had proven initially to be less successful than the second, because "in peacetime we had less opportunity to obtain such actual experience," whereas the latter had at least been practiced in fleet exercises before the war.[30] Even then the occasions for replenishing at sea in peacetime had been limited to providing naval units with a predictable and relatively modest quantity of fuel or supplies at predetermined, if variable, meeting points. With the introduction of fast carrier task forces, such deployments were by nature far reaching and constantly changing, and they comprised a huge number of ships and men in a vast ocean initially dominated by the enemy. The ability to keep all these warships sustained at sea with the necessary fuel, aircraft, provisions, and ammunition was a much more complex affair than peacetime training or planning could have envisaged. It says a great deal about the fortitude and ingenuity of all those whose task it was to design and deliver the relevant logistic support, because without it no task force could ever have operated effectively, if at all.

U.S. Navy Underway Replenishment Matures

The progression from conducting peacetime replenishment exercises, usually in calm seas, to Pacific operations, particularly in bad weather, proved disconcerting.[31] Due to the small number of available warships and lack of suitable auxiliaries, oiling at sea in the early part of the war was used solely to increase the steaming radius of the task forces engaged in hit-and-run strikes. Refueling carriers by fleet oilers after all had only become an operational requirement in 1939.[32] Moreover, it was not until July 31, 1940, that the first battleship was fueled under way at sea.[33] As the U.S. Navy prepared to campaign across the Central Pacific, augmented by substantial increases to the fleet, so came the first major change in doctrine for fueling carriers. Until then, the practice had always been for the replenishment oilers to approach the carrier, but during the Gilbert Islands operation in late 1943, combatants including carriers lined up on the oiler, without running into the wind, with the traditional rigging of abreast and spring lines discarded.[34] In November 1944, the first comprehensive set of instructions exclusively dealing with fueling at sea for all ships was issued.[35] The abeam or broadside method was thus confirmed as the standard method, and refueling from astern was relegated to emergencies only. This has virtually remained so ever since, exemplified in the emergency refueling of two U.S. Navy mine countermeasures ships in November 2007 off Hong Kong in heavy weather, which had to be conducted astern due to their size and speed.[36]

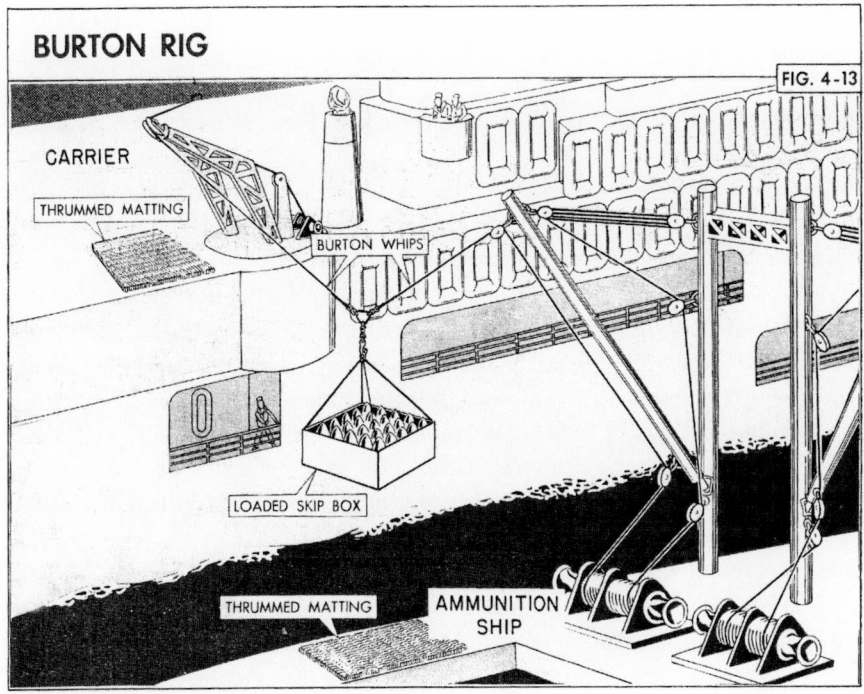

Diagram 2.1. USN burton rig (NARA2, RG38, ATP-16, 1955)

Although by 1944 refueling at sea had become a relatively routine business, very little attention had been given to devising a similar safe method for ammunition or stores. True, oilers had started to carry limited quantities of ammunition, lubricants, different fuels and gases, general stores, and provisions; nevertheless, it was still necessary for the fleet to return to Ulithi in the Western Pacific—some ten to twelve days turnaround—for proper replenishment. As Admiral Spruance, Commander Fifth Fleet, was to warn Fleet Admiral King in December 1944, any plans for the invasion of Iwo Jima in February and Okinawa in April would depend on finding a way to avoid these lengthy turnarounds.[37] The scope of the ammunition supply problem can be gauged by the fact that a single reload of the whole U.S. Pacific Fleet in 1945 required 180,000 tons of ammunition, and an average ammunition ship could hold only about 6,500 tons.[38]

Within weeks however, a method called the burton method was devised for transferring heavy loads (see diagram 2.1). This method used standard winches and booms on the ammunition cargo ships to supply carriers with the necessary aircraft ordnance. This rig became the first and perhaps most famous of the solids transfer rigs deployed during World War II. Now that ships could theoretically be fully rearmed under way, the next critical phase in the campaign, the assault on Okinawa, would provide the opportunity and logistic framework to prove it.

Okinawa 1945 (Operation ICEBERG): The U.S. Fleet Train Comes of Age

The final phase of the war witnessed the assault on Iwo Jima and Okinawa, both outer defenses of Japan itself, with the latter a particularly difficult undertaking given the size of force required and distances involved.

As can be seen from map 2.1 and distance chart in appendix D, supply lines from Australia and the U.S. mainland were stretched and variable due to the constantly changing battle lines. This operation became the milestone of the whole Pacific campaign because it witnessed the full-scale application of a new concept that revolutionized how task forces could be kept at sea for extended periods. Based on lessons learned from past campaigns, this operation saw the first historical application of a new group, known in operations orders initially as the "Logistic Support Group," established on December 5, 1944, and designated Service Squadron Six.[39]

It is important to reflect on how this came to fruition. With the mobile base system having reached full development by 1945, Service Squadron Ten remained responsible for the logistic support, including repairs of the fleet at forward area bases, and the routing and sailing of service ships required by those forces operating in the combat area. Commanding more than six hundred vessels in five anchorages, the squadron supported Operation ICEBERG, for example, with forty-six major auxiliaries, including ammunition ships, fleet tugs, merchant tankers, destroyer tenders, and a hospital ship all anchored at Ulithi.[40] To give the task force commanders more operational flexibility and greater sustainability, Service Squadron Six was created as a designated task group within the combat area to replenish fleet units under the task organization of the fleet commander in the forward area. The logistics commander was not just responsible for coordinating the fueling schedules with the carrier task groups; most importantly, he exercised direct command of all replenishment activities while under way at sea.

Thus the Logistic Support Group—operating some forty oilers "borrowed" from Service Squadron Eight, five ammunition ships, two provisions and stores ships, four transport carriers, two escort carriers, four fleet tugs, and thirty escorts/destroyers and a light cruiser (flagship)—remained at sea for up to three months at a time while the fleet commander enjoyed the freedom to pursue his objectives, whether searching, fighting, or loitering, without having to return to base.[41] The first opportunity to test this had been the three-week Iwo Jima campaign, which "proved a successful experiment," providing "valuable and needed experience." The Okinawa ICEBERG operation that followed almost immediately, however, was described as providing "the real test of replenishment

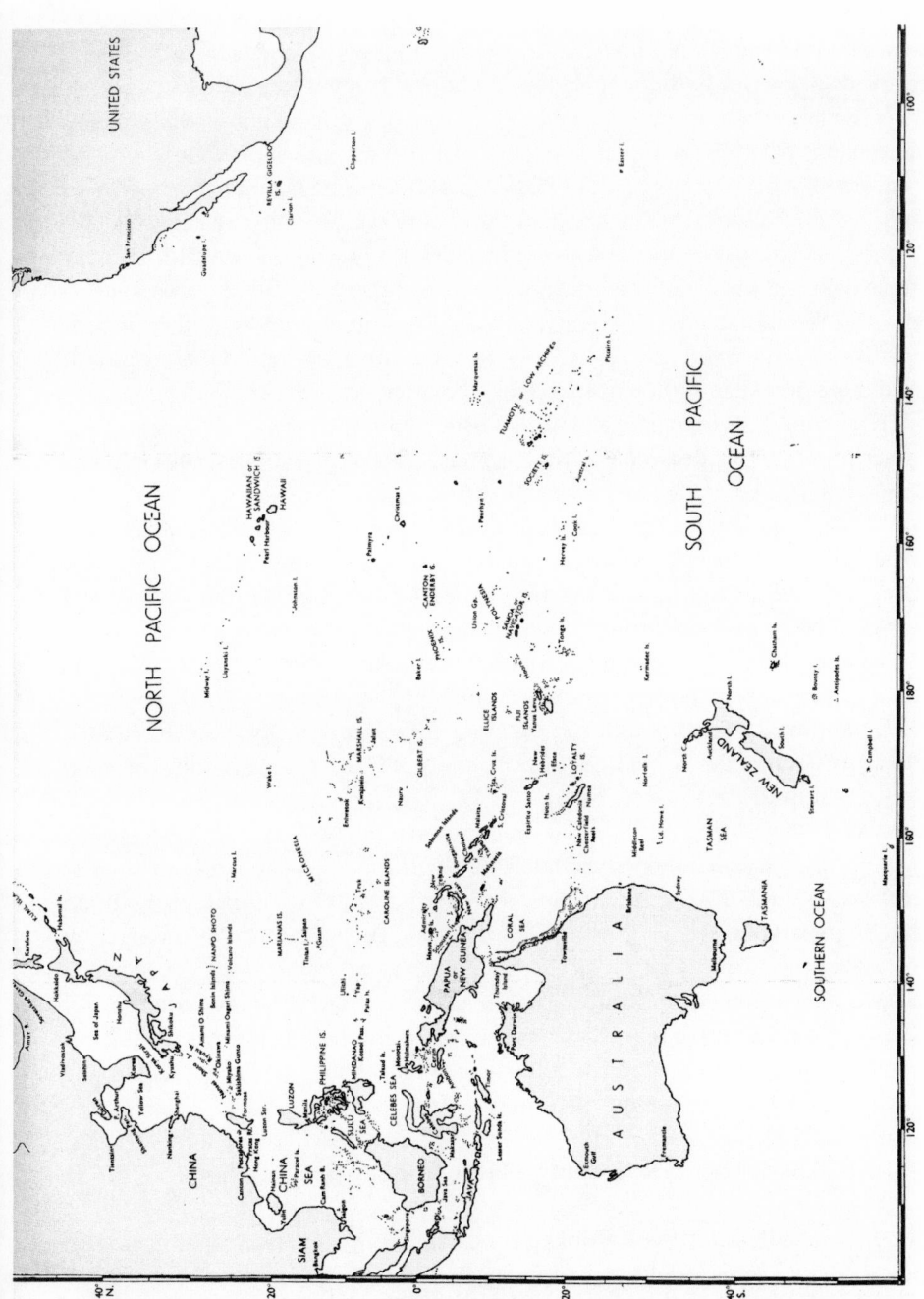

Map 2.1. Pacific region, 1945. (MoD(N), *War with Japan*, Vol. VI: Maps) Courtesy Naval Historical Branch

at sea."[42] Indeed, not only was it the first time that such support had been rendered for such an extended period on so large a scale, it also became the benchmark for all future operations and the source from which much of the future logistic doctrines for both the U.S. Navy and Royal Navy were crafted.

The largest group in the Service Force were the oilers, each carrying about 15,000 tons of cargo, of which 80 percent was fuel oil with the balance comprising diesel, lubricating oils, and aviation gasoline.[43] The fast fleet carriers were organized into four divisions, usually with three or four oilers assigned to replenish each division. Initially, five fully laden oilers would leave Ulithi for the replenishment rendezvous every four days, modified later to every two to three days. Ammunition and stores ships took their positions in the second replenishing line, about two thousand yards astern. All combatants would then approach and thereafter keep station abreast while being replenished—usually one large ship at a time, but two destroyers were possible simultaneously.[44] A more detailed description of how this replenishment process worked, with disposition plans and a description of the risks involved, is provided in chapter 3.

Of particular note regarding replenishment during ICEBERG was that it was much more than just petroleum products. According to the official historian for Service Squadron Six, also transferred to the fleet during this time were 16,373 tons of bombs and ammunition; 998 replacement aircraft; 220 replacement aircrews; 2,219 tons of refrigerated provisions; 4,000 tons of dry provisions; 15,398 mail bags; 1,240 passengers; and 1,032 replacement personnel.[45] In all, some 318 U.S. Navy major warships and 1,139 auxiliaries took part in Operation ICEBERG, together with elements from the Royal Navy's BPF and a huge number of troop landing ships.[46]

As the fleets gathered for their final pre-invasion carrier operations against Japan, which again included elements of the BPF, plans were ready to harness more than three thousand warships and auxiliaries (excluding all of the troop landing boats) for the final assault on Kyūshū. The possibility of invasion on such a massive scale clearly indicates the extraordinary progress achieved by the Service Force in matters of supply and support. For the U.S. Navy, after nearly four very hard years of relentless effort to cope with the constantly growing but rapidly changing demand from ships throughout the whole Pacific region, the Okinawa operation witnessed its fleet train truly "come of age."

British Experience in Developing a Fleet Train, 1945

As mentioned earlier, the Royal Navy was also obliged to develop a fleet train to enable its carrier task force to operate alongside the Americans in 1945 (designated according to the American task force system as TF57 or TF37, depending on whether it was assigned to the U.S. Fifth or Third fleets). But the contrast in how the British fleet train came to existence and eventually operate could not be more striking.

The Challenge

One of the American preconditions for the BPF was it must be logistically self-reliant over long periods because American logistic support would be limited primarily to fuel. The consequent urgent need to create a fleet train was therefore a daunting challenge for the Admiralty given its previous lack of experience or need for this sort of logistic mobility. Even as recently as 1944, replenishment operations at sea were essentially confined to refueling smaller warships on the grounds that in relatively narrow but submarine-infested seas, it was more expedient for the larger ships to rely on the existing network of bases, given the modest distances and types of risks involved. Now five completely new challenges faced the Admiralty's naval planners and logisticians, for which there was little if any experience to call upon. First, the proposed scale of the task force was huge, requiring several carriers in formation and battleships with attendant cruisers and an escort screen. Second, these forces would be operating thousands of miles from bases, constantly moving from theater to theater as the Allied naval advance progressed. Third, any fleet replenishment would require more than just furnace fuel; it would also need ammunition, planes, and aviation fuel as well as (to a lesser degree) provisions of refrigerated and dry goods. Moreover, all this would be required regularly over a protracted period from ships that were not only ill equipped to transfer such cargoes at sea but also incapable of steaming at sufficiently high speeds to keep up with fleet requirements. Finally, any fleet train must provide floating support with repair ships, hospital ships, stores issuing ships, and other specialist craft at temporary anchorages to support both warships and those auxiliaries that occasionally needed to be withdrawn from the combat operation. This was no small order.

Planning and Build-up

Much of the delay in getting both the BPF and its fleet train up and running was caused by the long-running political and military dilemma over whether Britain's role alongside the Americans should be in the Pacific or Southeast Asia, or both. In May 1943, the Admiralty's Director of Plans acknowledged that any future Pacific campaign would require mobile and rapid afloat support. The Admiralty also recognized that British shipbuilding repair and conversion capacity could not absorb the demand; therefore, "it was obvious that assistance from the U.S.A. would be required. Everything possible was to be waterborne so as to avoid shore commitments."[47] By March 1944, planners began to realize that there might be insufficient amphibious forces available for Operation CULVERIN, the proposed amphibious landings in northern Sumatra and Malaya, let alone the shipping required for both its fleet train and that for the BPF.[48] The strategic dilemma, however, could not be separated from the means; yet with such little experience to hand, "Fleet Train estimates [were] based on compromise and guesswork."[49] Planning had become a nightmare. Allocation of shipping commenced in 1944, but any planning was handicapped by uncertainties surrounding the employment of the fleet and its operating area, exacerbated by the unavailability or underestimation of the right type of auxiliary required for the various tasks.[50] American skepticism of whether Britain really understood the kind of warfare being fought in the Pacific remained high during this time, and not without reason.[51] According to Vice Adm. Lynde McCormick, assistant CNO for Logistic Plans (Op-12) in 1944–45, who was charged by Fleet Admiral King to evaluate the British logistic proposals (which he later confessed was "a difficult and delicate job"), much of the British proposal looked "rather 'iffy.'"[52] However, as the reliance upon U.S. auxiliary and base support had seemingly been "squeezed to a minimum," he recommended after much deliberation "a green (or at least an orange) light."[53] Eventually politics prevailed and the decision was made at the Second Quebec conference in September 1944 to commit a British fleet to the Pacific.

The Director of PD(Q), responsible for drafting operational plans for a fleet train to support the BPF, found the task painful and protracted, not least because the Americans' rapid advance across the Pacific required continuous recalculation of the length of supply lines. The demands for more fleet train shipping became increasingly unacceptable to the Ministry of War Transport (MOWT), which insisted that policy priorities should be settled once and for all before these fleet train and various amphibious issues were tackled.[54] Eventually the British War Cabinet decided in January 1945 that in view of the acute shortage of shipping even for the annual 24 million tons of U.K. imports, which had first priority, and in recognition of the fact that the fleet train was proving a heavy drain on manpower, the proposed fleet size would have to be reduced accordingly.[55] As Churchill later wrote rather pithily to Alexander, the First Lord, "The Fleet . . . must be limited by the Fleet Train. It is not a question of making the Fleet Train up to your ideas of the Fleet."[56]

While the actual role and operating area of the BPF remained uncertain, planning—including conversion work for appropriate supply ships—remained seriously hampered.[57] As the staff "History of the Fleet Train" recorded, it said much for Admiralty optimism in November 1944 that it was tacitly assumed that all available warships would be sent to the Pacific and that "logistic support would be scraped up somehow."[58] There were even proposals to expand the RFA by transferring Admiralty-owned and Lend-Lease White Ensign vessels for noncombatant duties, although for a number of administrative reasons this was resisted by the Admiralty's Director of Stores.[59] The reality, however, soon set in.

First, large numbers of supply ships were essential to cover the huge distances. Australia was already 12,500 miles from the fleet's home bases and was not extensively equipped with naval base facilities either.[60] Adm. Sir Bernard Rawlings later described his task as the equivalent of sailing from Plymouth to strike at Rio de Janeiro, replenishing once from harbor tankers in the Cape Verde islands with the second replenishment at sea—coincidentally not so different from the Falklands campaign some thirty-seven years later.[61] In similar vein, Admiral Fraser used the analogy of having the fleet based in Alexandria with advanced anchorages in Gibraltar and the Azores attacking the North American coast between Labrador and Nova Scotia.[62]

By the time the BPF was at full strength, supply lines from Australia to the front line would increase from 2,000 to 3,500 miles, requiring even more supply ships.[63] Yet less than a third of the freighting and replenishment tonnage needed for a fleet train was available at the end of November 1944 and delays in getting the Australian naval base facilities developed and tankers suitably fitted out were becoming particularly vexing.[64] But the alternative, setting up huge base installations on obscure Pacific islands, was extravagant in cost and time because the rapid advances meant that new bases were needed before the previous ones were completed. For the Americans, they could afford to have vast temporary bases that could be dismantled and moved to the next site, as the war advanced. It did not take long for Britain to recognize this was not a realistic option for it, so any reliance beyond Australia would rest upon having more modest mobile bases and the ability to replenish at sea.[65]

The Admiralty's struggle throughout 1944 to get ships allocated to the fleet train was, according to at least one naval historian, because the Ministry of War Transport "failed to comprehend the magnitude of the task."[66] But with 54 percent of Britain's prewar tonnage lost, together with the worn out state of several of the fleet auxiliaries and merchantmen after five years of war, it was impossible to reach the standard either in numbers or appropriate types of ships or crews.[67] Given past agreement with the United States, British yards had concentrated on warship building leaving the United States to provide normal merchant shipping; therefore, no provision had been made for such auxiliaries to come from British naval sources.[68] Furthermore, the shipping demands of Operation OVERLORD, the Allied invasion of Europe in 1944, were overwhelming; it became belatedly recognized that this would get worse at the end of the European war due to repatriation of all the Commonwealth forces as well as of prisoners of war.[69]

As for the quality of the shipping that was eventually forthcoming, this proved problematic too. By far the biggest complaint was the lack of any homogeneity with all vessels in need of constant repair. Vice Admiral (Q) in Brisbane signaled the Admiralty never again to "allow any ship to join the BPF in such a shocking state of inefficiency." "Such complaints," the Staff History records, "were many and various."[70] Ammunition supply vessels were bereft of gyro-compasses, making station-keeping difficult while the tankers "were old slow and designed for the leisurely transportation of fuels from port to port." [71] The need for speed in excess of 15 knots was critical if tankers were to keep station with the fleet during fueling at sea, but the *Dale* class's maximum speed was only 11–12 knots. The Admiralty was therefore obliged to take over nine of the new faster *Empire*-class tankers being built for the Ministry of War Transport; while the RFA eventually took twenty of the twenty-one built (called the *Wave* class, which eventually formed the backbone of the postwar tanker fleet), only three actually arrived in theater by August 1945. The essential difficulty was that none of the auxiliaries had been designed from the beginning for the exacting fleet standards demanded by continuous underway replenishment. All were ad-hoc conversions, and many were worn out and required inordinate levels of ingenuity and improvisation to keep operational. Moreover, the fundamental problem was that the Royal Navy was essentially short-haul. Of 560 auxiliaries on the books in March 1944, 114 were colliers (inappropriate for the Pacific), 165 were decommissioned, and the vast bulk were small or coastal craft providing temporary facilities or supplementing existing shore bases.[72] Of the 2,250,000 tons of merchant shipping under direct Admiralty control, 44 percent was under charter for single voyages only, and 22 percent was committed to operational support that could not be curtailed. Despite a fleet train need for 256 ships, only 111 ships were oceanic, most of which required lengthy refitting before they would be suitable for Pacific duty.[73]

Despite no settled agreement on what role Britain's fleet would be undertaking in the war against Japan, Rear Admiral Fleet Train (RAFT) was nevertheless appointed in October 1944, with temporary offices in Sydney, to assume responsibility for preparing the fleet train and providing logistic support at sea for the fleet.[74] Timing for the fleet to arrive at Sydney was predicated on how long it would take to establish stocks in Australia, but as it happened, the BPF was constituted on November 22, 1944, three or four months earlier than anticipated.[75] With Australia unready to receive it, the BPF undertook its first operation en route against Sumatran oilfields combining with elements of the British East Indies Fleet. The fleet train meanwhile remained in embryo until its formal inauguration on January 1, 1945. Organizational inadequacy in Sydney, however, was widespread—reflected in a report in January 1945 that the Admiralty's provisions for water appeared to have been "governed either by child-like faith or ostrich-like escapism."[76] Accommodation for Vice Admiral (Q)'s staff, for example, initially consisted of some tents on a racecourse where offices were nonexistent. The fleet train engineering staff comprised five officers who were luckier in having a room in a barracks, but they were only equipped with one desk and chair. The U.S. liaison officer, meanwhile, was surprised that no one section of staff dealt with estimating and accounting for oil for the fleet.[77] It would be several more months for the organization to reach the necessary staffing levels to cope with the myriad of operational needs. A measure of the lateness in decisions was that 90 percent of requested aircraft stores had not arrived in Australia by the time the BPF set sail from Manus for Operation ICEBERG.[78]

Operations ICEBERG I and II

Having eventually arrived at Sydney on February 10, 1945, the BPF departed again eighteen days later under the American task designation TF57. The task force—including three fleet carriers (HMS *Illustrious* having been temporarily detained at Sydney for urgent repairs), two battleships, five cruisers, sixteen destroyers, and eight escorts—headed for Manus two thousand miles away in the Admiralty Islands north of New Guinea, shown in map 2.2.

After a very confusing and difficult birth for the BPF, the build-up phase was at last finally over. The supporting fleet train had two distinct duties. First was the transportation from Australia and distribution of all facilities and supplies at the designated advanced bases, and second was the replenishment of TF57 at sea when necessary. This latter task was charged to a Logistics Support Group (LSG) not dissimilar in concept to the American Logistic Support Force and with the object "to furnish direct logistic support at sea to the Fleet in and near the combat zone, in order to maintain the mobility and striking power of the Fleet."[79] Furnace fuel oil was to be transported from U.S. bulk supplies at Manus, Leyte, and later Eniwetok. The choice of Manus as principal base with Leyte as the advanced base achieved the objective of setting up the smallest establishment onshore in the forward areas while also satisfying the American requirement that the British possess an independent but temporary support system.[80] Inevitably, the doubling in distance complicated operations and directly affected the number and deployment of ships; the huge anchorage for the initial twenty-seven fleet train ships, for example, required numerous harbor craft, and there were many problems to contend with given the remoteness and environmentally harsh nature of the site.[81]

At last, on March 14, 1945, TF57 sailed under the umbrella of Admiral Spruance's U.S. Fifth Fleet, tasked with attacking airfields in Sakishima Gunto. The first deployment was for thirty days at sea and the second for thirty-two days interspersed with a replenishment period of a week in Leyte.[82] TF57 averaged two battleships, four fleet carriers, four to five cruisers, and between eleven and fourteen destroyers. Actual replenishment was undertaken at sea every four or five days, usually taking two days to complete (compared to one for the U.S. Navy, which by now had become well practiced) in a designated fueling area about seven hundred miles from Leyte and two hundred miles behind the striking area, as shown in map 2.3.

Map 2.2. Map: Manus to Japan. (MoD(N), *War with Japan*, Vol. VI: Maps) Courtesy Naval Historical Branch

Altogether sixty-seven vessels, including escorts, were employed on fleet train duties from Leyte, and an additional thirteen arrived at Manus toward the end of May 1945.[83] The procedures for replenishing TF57 were adapted from recent American experience, with typically three or four "task units" comprising three oilers, a replenishment carrier, and two or three escorts each plying back and forth from Leyte to the designated replenishment area.[84] Once there they would temporarily join with other ships permanently stationed in the fueling area to form the LSG under the tactical command of the Commander Logistic Support Group. Screened by some fifteen escorts, the LSG comprised nine oilers each with an average capacity of about 9,000 tons, five escort carriers, an ammunition supply issuing ship (ASIS), a victualling supply issuing ship (VSIS), a hospital ship, and a rescue tug.[85]

For both deployments during ICEBERG, 180,000 tons of fuel and 2,056 tons of avgas were transferred under way on thirteen occasions, as well as 140 aircraft. Fortunately, the weather was generally favorable and the fleet train and most of the fleet (except the carriers) escaped the attention of Japanese planes and sub-

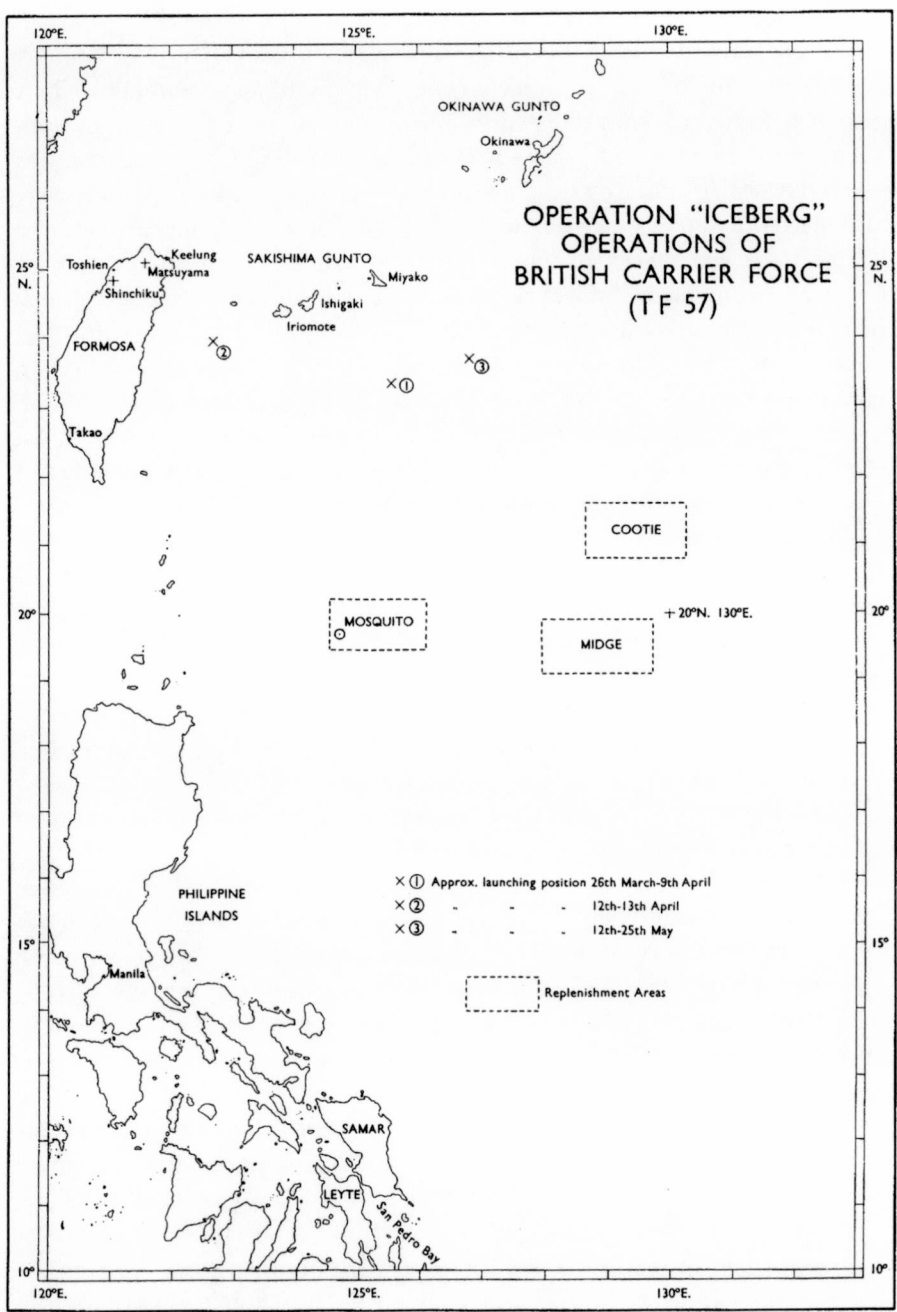

Map 2.3. TF57 fueling areas and operational strike points, March–May 1945. (MoD(N) *War with Japan*, Vol. VI: Maps) Courtesy Naval Historical Branch

marines, which was just as well because the Admiralty's Director of Plans would note later, "there was certainly no margin for casualties in the Fleet Train."[86] Nevertheless, the time taken to fuel during each evolution or serial proved far greater than had been anticipated from peacetime fueling at sea, and—until the new tankers appeared—the typical method of trailing fuel lines astern was much slower than the American abeam method. These early operations were also marred by burst hoses due to swells, insufficient pumping capacity, and the inevitable general lack of both training and spares.[87] Nor had much victualling been accomplished under way at sea by this time because the issuing ships remained either at Manus or Leyte. Notwithstanding these handicaps, the fleet train continued to expand, including two repair ships and a destroyer depot ship that conducted most repairs not requiring docking.[88] Despite official American reticence to provide support other than fuel, whenever more serious attention was required, this was willingly handled by the U.S. Navy at the local level until Britain's floating docks, still on passage, arrived.

Air replacements, however, remained a headache throughout, and here American support was less relevant because the planes were either British or American ones significantly modified to British requirements. British carriers lost 81 percent of their air establishment during ICEBERG alone, mostly through operational hazards rather than enemy action.[89] To rationalize the four different organizations attending to the specialist nature and problems associated with aircraft support for the carriers, it had eventually become necessary for the BPF to create a separate Air Train, which still reported to RAFT.[90]

After the first phase of ICEBERG, most of the BPF was obliged to withdraw to Sydney for much-needed major replenishment. The U.S. Navy, meanwhile, covered the one-month gap from within its own resources until the BPF returned to Manus on June 29 for their next assignment. Now designated TF37, the BPF averaged eleven major combatants and eighteen destroyers and was deployed on July 6 for the Japanese mainland. Manus rather than Leyte was the advance base so that refueling was near Japan—albeit still a distance of 2,500 miles; American bulk fuel arrangements at Eniwetok reduced this gap by 1,000 miles.

A new problem, however, was that due to weather and target changes, the fueling area was moved by the American commander at frequent and irregular intervals, often more than 500 miles, which particularly affected the slow tanker groups. In all, twelve tankers supplied 160,000 tons of fuel over six refueling periods. Burst hoses and low pumping rates continued to debilitate service capability while half the oilers in the second sortie had no experience of formation fueling large ships at all. Speeds were therefore reduced, forcing five cruisers to be fueled by the Americans during the two operations.[91]

On the positive side, as can be seen in appendix E, LSG complement had by now grown to twelve tankers, two ASIS, a hospital ship, a tug, two VSIS, five replenishment carriers, a CAP carrier, a radio maintenance ship, and twenty-three escorts. Most significantly, inherent good seamanship combined with growing confidence and improved or hastily adapted equipment brought important improvements to service. Ammunition replenishment occurred twice, for example, which was a major breakthrough. Also for the first time, reprovisioning in the fueling area was undertaken when the VSIS *Glenartny* (see plate 2.1) successfully transferred fresh provisions and other stores on seventy-seven occasions, sometimes at twice the normal embarkation rate at Sydney![92] While transfer techniques and ship-handling at greater speeds measurably improved throughout this period, all ships were in a poor state of repair. Of the twenty-three tankers deployed (including the three *San*-class MFAs), only the three new *Wave*-class tankers and the first fast naval tanker HMS *Olna* were capable of achieving 15 knots and able to adopt the American practice of abeam refueling. The major lesson for the British had been the discovery that the American system of oiling at sea could transfer a greater quantity of fuel in a given time than the British system because British warships had insufficient intake capacity, their tankers had insufficient pumping capacity at sea, and there were an insufficient number of fuel and avgas hoses or suitable derricks on the tankers.[93]

OLYMPIC

The BPF's final major deployment from July 13 to August 20 was as TF37 under Admiral Halsey's U.S. Third Fleet against the Japanese mainland. At this point the BPF, together with its Fleet Train designated TF112.1, had reached its zenith—the most powerful aggregation of naval power Britain had ever assembled in one place during World War II. Appendix B details the extraordinary growth of the BPF and fleet train, from the planning stages in 1941 to May 1946. Appendix F breaks down the growth of each auxiliary ship category from December 1944, when ships were being assembled, to those vessels on station by August 1945. By V-J Day, TF112 was manned by 26,200 officers and men, and consisted of 20 naval and 60 civilian auxiliaries and 45 escorts, with a further 23 vessels en route to join. What is particularly striking, however, is the plan to increase this to 315 ships by January 1946, which would more than double the required fleet train manpower levels to 53,600 officers and men. Of the 238,000 Empire personnel employed by the BPF overall, including 11 admirals, 5 commodores, and 81 captains, nearly 100,000 were now permanently at sea, mostly in the forward areas.[94] This extraordinary growth had been achieved despite the complete lack of previous experience in this type of logistics procedure. Although it was believed this would hold the Royal Navy in good stead for the future, the unfortunate fact was, however, that assembling everything in such haste resulted in no standardization in equipment or homogeneity in composition, along with all the attendant risks and problems this caused and would continue to pose for many years.[95]

As a postscript, Operation OLYMPIC, the invasion of Kyūshū planned for October, would have required two British task forces, thus placing a potentially enormous strain on the BPF Fleet Train—at least thirty tankers would have been required. The evidence would suggest that this would have proved impossible to accomplish, even more so the earlier it was required. In the end, the sudden cessation of hostilities diverted the fleet train to all manner of transport, repair, and repatriation tasks throughout the region before being reduced, on November 11, to just nineteen repair and hospital ships together with a mix of accommodation ships and tugs. Soon thereafter the fleet train was reintegrated into the BPF (which in turn reverted from U.S. to Admiralty command) and it was finally wound up on February 28, 1946.[96] Again, appendix F shows the extraordinary reduction in the BPF's Fleet Train from 131 in August 1945 to just 10 by January 1946, in sharp contrast to plans that five months earlier had called for a total of 315 auxiliaries to be on station by then.

Conclusion

The first four years of World War II witnessed improved techniques that incrementally enhanced mobile logistic support for both navies but were hardly revolutionary because any major changes to doctrine during this time were not deemed necessary. In truth, neither navy had foreseen during the interwar period, or even in the early years of the war, the full strategic and logistic ramifications of operating carrier task forces, which explains why mobile logistic support for this type of warfare was not prioritized until it was almost too late. British oiling-at-sea policy remained essentially confined to convoy escorts in the Atlantic. Even the U.S. Navy, although much more familiar with some of the complexities of replenishing capital ships at sea (albeit on a comparatively modest scale, compared to later years), was forced to learn very quickly how to sustain both amphibious support operations and large-scale carrier task forces across a vast and constantly changing battle space. This challenge soon spawned an effective, if not necessarily efficient, mobile logistic support system very much reflecting the prewar convictions outlined in War Plan Orange. While American plans had remained more or less intact throughout the war, Britain's prewar plans for the Far East were turned upside down by the fall of Singapore, with its large graving dock, and Hong Kong, thereby effectively eliminating any fixed base logistic support in the region. The Pacific naval campaigns of 1945 thus required unprecedented immense fleet trains to provide all the necessary logistic support.

At least for the U.S. Navy, the war-winning "secret weapon" of using such fleet trains had been the culmination of several years of hard experience in which to learn, build, and eventually organize them properly. For the Admiralty, prior to World War II there had been little cohesive or integrated planning to establish the outer limitations of wartime endurance based on the potential for logistic support that would only be available from the RFA. Hence there existed a less-than-dynamic tanker policy, too much reliance on traditional fueling astern, and the belief that capital ships would not require refueling at sea given the proximity of bases for any support.[97] As a result, 1945 felt more like a sudden rude shock, which required learning fast the hard way, often through extemporization, with borrowed ideas or resources from the U.S. Navy.

The last few months of the Pacific War in 1945 attested for both navies how the character of logistic support had changed profoundly. Despite coming as they did from such different experiences, culture, and doctrine, both navies nevertheless reached their peak of power projection capability by 1945, made possible by having in place the necessary mobile logistic support to sustain their operations on a grand scale. As Commodore Barraclough, the new commander of the Fleet Train that had so valiantly supported the BPF, was to note soon after the war, "the idea of a fleet remaining at sea for offensive operations for prolonged periods without returning to harbour is now adopted as a principle. This is only possible if such a fleet can be replenished at sea. The assumption is made, therefore, that the fleet train has 'come to stay.'"[98]

Although the routes both navies undertook to reach this point had been significantly different, the combination of the challenges they both faced and the chance to work alongside each other by 1945 in many ways encouraged a closer alliance despite their different styles and understanding of each other's procedures. Both were forced to learn from trial and error, and both relied heavily on improvisation to get the job done. Despite their very different size and makeup, in other words, both found the challenges equally demanding within their respective context while demonstrating at the same time the advantages to be obtained for all if interoperability received priority attention in future operations. For the British, such sentiment was as politically motivated as it was practical. For the Americans, the advantages were more confined to the operational level, and any motivation remained culturally rather than politically or even militarily inspired. For the U.S. Navy, the combination of economic might that could make things happen together with a clearer vision of what was needed to overcome the logistic challenges led to their being better planned, prepared, and able to respond with the tools that mattered for successfully prosecuting this new type of carrier-based air warfare.

In a sense, though, it would be very surprising to discover if this had not been the case, given the size, motivation, and power of the U.S. Navy, underpinned as it was by the strongest economy in the world. Perhaps what is more surprising, therefore, is that the Royal Navy, despite having started from so far behind in 1940, was able to accomplish as much as it did in the Pacific with the limited resources then available to it. Indeed, the same comparison could be applied after the war too. Despite Britain's comparatively much weaker economic and military status, the Royal Navy was still able to continue closing the logistic capability gap between the two navies, at least in technological terms if not in fleet size and numbers.

With both navies having survived their critical baptism of fire, albeit on different scales, the question for each was whether this fundamental paradigm shift should remain the model for future naval logistic planning in peacetime. There was no easy answer, given, on the one hand, that the prospect of another global war at some future point meant the need for having armed forces properly prepared while, on the other, new fiscal cutbacks were rapidly eroding on a major scale many of the preliminary ideas for postwar fleet strengths and capabilities. Given that peacetime requirements would not demand the same high-tempo operations and need for long endurance, the pressure to develop and maintain afloat support would clearly be reduced. The challenge was to find the right balance.

3 | Underway Replenishment at Sea (UNREP/RAS)

Cʜᴀᴘᴛᴇʀ 2 ᴅᴇsᴄʀɪʙᴇᴅ the key to achieving mobility and endurance by using fleet trains replete with mobile bases for floating medical, repair, and salvage facilities that could also act as staging posts to transport fuels, aircraft, and all forms of supplies to the carrier task forces in the battle zone. The final link in this long supply chain, replenishing the ships at sea, was the most critical component because it was extremely complex to plan and organize, and whenever it was conducted, it always put the fleet into a position of great tactical disadvantage. As a result, all replenishment evolutions had to be undertaken expeditiously to minimize interference with the operation in progress or risk exposure to enemy action while under this handicap. The level of efficiency in its entire operation therefore had significant strategic and tactical implications.

Although replenishment at sea, in some form or other, has been around during most of the twentieth century, for the most part it remained in arrested development until toward the end of World War II. The challenges of the Pacific War in 1945, with carriers at the forefront, had required both the U.S. and British navies to find and then apply new skills, equipment, and technology to enable auxiliaries to transfer under way whatever was needed as consistently, safely, and efficiently as possible, whenever it was required. This new type of ocean warfare had forced everyone to realize that if this was to be the standard for the future, then above all else, it must be recognized for what it was—an everyday but complex practical application of power that depended upon a well-honed logistic support system to work. As one of the Royal Navy's experts put it, "Mobile or floating logistic support is the means by which this end can be attained; therefore fuelling at sea must be regarded as an everyday operation."[1]

Some useful progress in developing replenishment doctrine had already been achieved during the first years of the war, but the Pacific campaign would stretch this by comparative leaps and bounds. While the necessity for change naturally diminished when peace returned, there still prevailed a significant awareness in some quarters—in contrast to the interwar period—that further change must be embraced for advantage. While this did not extend to finding new ships, at least it encouraged new handling techniques to be tested and advanced, new designs to be contemplated, and even the doctrine itself to be continually enhanced and better codified. A more detailed description of how replenishment at sea actually worked in practice during this period will therefore help to gain a more informed understanding of both its potential and its limitations and consequently why it was so important to get the whole evolution right.

Definition

It is perhaps useful first to review how both navies were defining replenishment at sea during this postwar decade. For the Royal Navy, it was "the act of transferring a solid weight from one ship to another or supporting a hose carrying a liquid between ships. These transfers are made either by ships abeam of one another or, in the latter case, abeam or astern."[2] Its purpose was, "to increase a ship's endurance in a strictly limited range of supplies, up to the endurance of the ship in the majority of commodities. It will be necessary in operational areas far from bases and exposed to enemy attack. It must be treated as an evolution to be carried out with the utmost dispatch in order to minimize interference with the operation in progress and the risk of damage due to enemy action or the weather."[3]

For the U.S. Navy, with a comparatively better-developed logistics doctrine, the concept was elevated to a more institutional level and described as "a branch of naval science . . . embodying the minute and exacting operations that take place when ships are engaged in the underway transfer of fuel, munitions, supplies and men."[4] The overall principle established as an operational guide was that "Every effort consistent with safety must be made to reduce to a minimum the time required to accomplish replenishment."[5]

The following acronyms have been applied according to each navy's convention. "Replenishment at sea" becomes RAS in a strictly Royal Navy or general context, and it becomes UNREP when applied in its U.S. Navy context. The U.S. Navy typically applied the term "oilers" (for example AO for Auxiliary, oiler) both for naval transportation and for those ships that replenished others at sea; otherwise bulk or commercial tankers were called "tankers." For the Royal Navy, the nomenclature for either function was normally "fleet tanker" or simply "tanker." Finally, a brief history of applicable doctrine on replenishment at sea published during this time is covered in chapter 7, which, given its tactical dimension, emphasizes the technical challenges that both navies faced in supporting carrier-based warfare.

History of Replenishment at Sea

The process of oiling ships at sea was first introduced to the Royal Navy in 1906, but these early replenishment arrangements were cautious and the gear cumbersome. It involved having a wire passed between two ships in line intended to steady but not actually tow the receiving ship while the hose from the tanker was suspended from a long rail by hanging straps, or "stirrups," fitted every few feet with rollers for running along the rail.[6] The first really significant, if not particularly auspicious, oil transfer took place between the RFA *Petroleum* and HMS *Dominion* in June 1906, but despite a 37–57 tons per hour (tph) flow rate, the transfer proved bulky, prone to breakages, and took hours to set up.[7] In 1924, the Hose Hawser method was introduced, in which the towing hawser was actually inside the fuel hose, thereby enabling a straighter course to be taken, which improved flow rates to about 100 tph. However, any defects in the hose invariably caused lengthy suspension of operations; after a series of trials, this method was eventually abandoned in 1932 in favor of the stirrup method again. This remained more or less unchanged as "the standard and primary procedure for oiling ships at sea and exposed anchorages" until 1937 when the first experiments were undertaken that were a complete departure from the traditional astern method of transfer.[8]

The pace of American progress in oiling at sea more or less followed the same course through to the mid-1930s. The U.S. Navy's first attempt at replenishment had occurred a little later than the attempt by the British, in 1916, when the crew of the conventional tanker USS *Maumee* devised a scheme to fuel destroyers alongside. The first opportunity to test this in other than calm water arose in 1917, when a squadron of American destroyers en route to the United Kingdom required refueling mid-Atlantic, which was undertaken by sailing abeam. After World War I the U.S. Navy continued experimenting with refueling techniques and equipment, including the first "over the stern" method in 1921, but this and subsequent trials proved disappointing. In 1923, an automatic tensioning engine was even introduced to improve the necessary tautness in the towline, but the results were equally disappointing and further work on astern refueling was eventually cancelled in 1931.[9] The "riding abeam" tests, on the other hand, continued to flourish, particularly with the number of multiple refueling sessions that were undertaken. Most encouraging was the first occasion involving a ship larger than a destroyer, the cruiser USS *Omaha* on January 11, 1924, for this proved that fueling large capital ships was eminently feasible.[10] From then on for the rest of the decade, however, all technological development in replenishment stalled, partly due to lack of funds and partly because more and more warships were still learning or adapting themselves to the equipment they already had.

The combination of increased fleet practice and a growing awareness of the need to extend endurance reawakened the need for further improvements in refueling capability in the early 1930s. For example, by 1932 oilers could now refuel two destroyers alongside simultaneously, with as many as seven 4-inch fuel hoses.[11] By contrast, it would be another six years before British tankers regularly refueled a destroyer abeam rather than astern.[12] While this may simply be the result of each navy responding to differing degrees of strategic anxiety, it would also suggest that there was little, if any, sharing of information or cooperation to resolve issues raised by underway replenishment. Although during the interwar period both navies had shared ideas and concerns about the broader objectives and the strategic risks of war in the Pacific, there was very little if any dialogue—let alone cooperation or information sharing—at any substantive tactical level. Within the Admiralty, for example, while the policy divisions such as Plans or Naval Intelligence welcomed a closer exchange rapport with the U.S. Navy, the technical divisions were very much opposed to the idea. As war became ever-more likely in the late 1930s, there eventually developed a form of exchange between the two navies purely on a quid pro quo basis, but this was never very enthusiastically adopted by either party.[13] Indeed, even as late as 1941, the Admiralty's Director of Naval Intelligence (DNI) had to admit that they had no files at all on oiling at sea undertaken by American capital ships.[14]

Meanwhile, in 1938 the Royal Navy took a comparatively significant step forward as the clouds of war started to form on the horizon. Long delayed tests of the new "trough" system were undertaken by the China, Mediterranean, and Home fleets; this system required warships to sail abeam of each other at about 50 feet distance, tied together by 8-inch manila spring and breast lines. These not only proved suitable for oiling destroyers from larger ships in fair weather using two 3½-inch flexible metallic hoses to achieve about 80 tph but also it allowed more than one vessel to be refueled at a time.[15] After it was confirmed that this was intrinsically superior to the old stirrup method, it was formally adopted on December 30, 1938, as "the standard procedure for oiling at sea." Although the Admiralty still assumed it was "unlikely that ships larger than destroyers will require to oil under way," this was still a significant step forward because it encouraged plans for putting the new rig on the RFA tankers as well.[16]

Yet even after World War II was well under way, there was still no contemplation within the Admiralty that capital ships and cruisers might require continuous refueling near the operational area. Nor was much attention given to improving rates of supply (then about 90 tph) or tanker speeds (8 knots was "comfortable").[17] The point was that the challenge of oiling ships at sea had originally been limited to refueling large ships in open anchorages or destroyers at sea, with the experiments conducted accordingly. The fueling of escort vessels in the mid Atlantic or elsewhere in all weathers had not been anticipated either. Although by 1941 the Admiralty considered using an American transfer rig as standby, the necessary modifications to the warships and RFA tankers were soon deemed too costly and difficult to implement, so the idea was dropped. Following a series of tests in various fleets, both the stirrup and trough rigs were eventually fitted on some 120 commercial and Admiralty tankers to refuel escorts in all weathers, and this at least provided some flexibility for coping with different conditions at sea.[18] The exercise was fairly low-key, using no special derricks or bollards but leaving it to those tankers to use their normal equipment for deploying a 3½-inch hose (later 5-inch) about fifty feet between each ship designed to transfer at about 90 tph. A book of instructions was also issued to assist their masters, which was useful because only twenty-one tankers had gyrocompasses.[19] Meanwhile, the search for a more buoyant hose, which would allow the complicated paraphernalia required for the stirrup method to be discarded altogether, took a rather dramatic turn in 1941 when recently captured German replenishment equipment (including a rubber hose) was tested in trials already being conducted by the Royal Navy using a British-manufactured rubber hose produced by Goodyear.[20] Because of the urgency by 1942 for longer "sea legs" during the Battle of the Atlantic, chartered tankers and RFAs on convoy oiling duties were gradually fitted out with a buoyant rubber hose, which increased transfer rates to 120 tph; this was first successfully deployed by the RFA *Aldersdale* to destroyers escorting convoy PQ17 to Russia in July 1942.[21] However, because rubber was still a scarce commodity, the old stirrup gear had to be retained for up to another year or more, until these could be replaced by rollers at the first available refit. Over the next two years, further evidence of improvements could be seen with carriers gradually becoming equipped to refuel escorts from the flight deck using a buoyant hose over the stern, and RFA tankers were being equipped during refit with long 70-ft derricks each capable of supporting two bigger 5-inch hoses.[22]

Of some 177 British escort tankers equipped in one form or other with oiling-at-sea equipment by the end of 1944, in all about 80 percent operated the buoyant hose over the stern with the rest able to refuel abeam or on the quarter, using mostly American canvas hose; this left just two having to deploy metallic hoses.[23] As a result, by 1943 transfer rates increased from 120 tph to 250 tph using two 5-inch hoses, which was a gratifying improvement. Nevertheless, replenishment speeds still remained below 10 knots—well short of desired fleet speed, let alone contemporary American standards.[24]

The most important catalyst—indeed, milestone—took place the following year. One of the American preconditions for the BPF being allowed to operate as part of the American-led offensive was that the BPF be self-reliant over long periods at sea. This new and most daunting challenge severely tested the navy's replenishment doctrine, such as it was, because apart from a modest effort in the South Atlantic in 1939–40, the British had never supplied large quantities of fuel—let alone ammunition—to a fleet at sea before. Moreover, the proposed scale of the task was huge, both in terms of distance from supplies and in terms of the sheer size of the proposed combat force. Several carriers, battleships with attendant cruisers, and an escort screen would require substantial replenishment of fuel oil and aviation spirit as well as naval stores, planes, and ammunition. With the increasing prospect of substantial forces and their escort screens being moved to the Far East, so the need for improvement in refueling capability had become readily apparent. The provision, for example, of a dual method for enabling destroyers to be refueled astern with the buoyant hose or abeam (when seas were calm or when two escorts needed fueling simultaneously) was therefore to be "given high priority."[25] Once the fleet train was up and running during 1945, operational necessity forced transfer techniques to improve and ship-handling speeds increase, but the essential problem remained that because none of the auxiliaries had been designed specifically for the task, their performance remained well below that of their relatively well-equipped and more experienced American partners.[26]

When the Pacific War ended, plans for introducing a new fast tanker were put on hold while many important unresolved operational questions remained outstanding. How, for example, could a stronger buoyant hose be produced with a self-sealing coupling to avoid repeating the huge, potentially unsustainable fuel losses that had occurred in wartime due to oil bursts, weather, or defective hose. Further investigation was required on pumping capacities of the new *Wave*-class tankers; more trials were needed on ship interaction while alongside, particularly with the improved American "Elwood" abeam rig. Manning RFAs in war and peace also needed overhauling, but at least an important hurdle had been met.[27] Fueling at sea had at last become universally regarded as a normal fleet operation. The buoyant hose and trough methods continued to be enhanced and then standardized into what eventually became known postwar as the astern and abeam methods, respectively; these methods are examined in more detail later in this chapter.

Also examined later will be the problems involved in transferring stores and ammunition while under way, the development of which was less protracted partly because the challenges were difficult to address, British experience was limited, and the results were relatively modest. When the Central Pacific campaign surged in 1945, requiring heavy shore bombardments and continuous bombing, the ability to replenish ammunition while under way became vital. This proved a most dangerous exercise due to the variety in size and weights. Also, the general nature of ammunition replenishment was very difficult to deliver efficiently because, unlike fuel, it could not be consolidated in the operating area.[28] Of equal importance to carrier groups, given the high attrition rate, was the need to replenish aircraft and flight crews. This process became so complex and demanding that the British had to create a separate air train organization with temporary mobile airfields.[29] Suffice it to say here that while this was considered part of the overall fleet train concept for the BPF, it nevertheless attracted such a unique set of problems and accomplishments that only a proper understanding of its complex history can be achieved if this major subject is studied in its own right. A good place to start would be David Hobbs's 2007 book, *Moving Bases: Royal Navy Maintenance Carriers and Monabs.*

Fleet Train Disposition for Replenishment

Understanding how a fleet train serviced the fleet units at sea is important because this set the benchmark for both future doctrine and operational comparison. The following describes how the U.S. Navy's Logistic Support Force (LSF) acted as the last link in the supply chain to the warships in the combat zone. The Royal Navy's fleet train fulfilled a similar function, albeit on a more modest scale, adopting the title Logistic Support Group (LSG) in support of the BPF throughout 1945.[30]

The LSF normally comprised oilers (AO), ammunition ships (AE), provisions store ships (AF), hospital ships (AH), tugs and salvage ships, cargo ships (AK) and general stores issue ships (AKS), and aircraft transport carriers (CVET), all suitably rigged to transfer supplies or services to fleet units while under way. The transfer usually took place every two or three days by rendezvous at different locations in a designated replenishment area, protected by antisubmarine and antiaircraft escort screens with a dedicated carrier for air cover.[31] In 1945 it was not unusual to have the whole armada of more than one hundred ships lining up along a forty-mile front spread over nearly two thousand square miles.

The fast fleet carriers of the task force were organized into four divisions of three or four, usually with three or four oilers assigned to replenish each division. Fueling was conducted in daylight hours only because it was too hazardous at night given blackout requirements. To minimize transfer time, a fueling schedule was drawn up the night before, with speed and course determined in the light of prevailing conditions. Usually at dawn three of the four oilers, sailing about 1,500 to 2,000 yards apart, would form into a single line to establish the fueling course, typically into the wind at about 10 knots. Appendix G shows a typical American replenishment disposition based on doctrine established in 1945. Behind the oilers, ammunition and stores ships would then take up their positions in the second replenishment line, about 2,000 yards astern. All combatants would then approach the ammunition ship and keep abreast on station until the particular evolution was finished. Normal transfer was over the port side of supply ship, typically with one large ship rearmed at a time, but two destroyers could be rearmed simultaneously in need.[32]

Fuel consolidation would then be undertaken among the oilers so those whose tank levels had been reduced to 35,000 bbl could then return to mobile reloading bases, preferably no more than three days' sailing away. Occasionally, as shown in plate 3.1, other auxiliaries in the LSF might benefit from the consolidation to extend their time on station. No consolidation, however, was possible for ammunition ships because these tended to become destabilized after 50 percent had been unloaded.[33] The really useful breakthrough was the introduction of temporary shuttle units that were assigned to rendezvous with the LSF and consolidate cargoes, thereby achieving a more even flow of supplies, freight, mail, and personnel to the fleet.[34]

Various factors affected the force composition and dispersion of the LSF including the number and type of combatants, likelihood of attack, amount of available daylight hours to transfer product, distance to resupply the base, duration of operation being supported, and, of course, weather. Despite the large forces involved, the American logistic support forces were only attacked twice—both by air, of which only one caused any casualties with three oilers hit.[35] No British replenishment operation was attacked either by submarine or air, but both navies were forced to assume that logistic forces would be more vulnerable in the future to homing torpedoes and the Russian type XXI fast submarine that was believed to have speeds similar to that of the mobile force. Protection could not be taken for granted, so closed escort screens became regarded as essential—unlike the open screens of World War II.[36]

Although evolutions were unlikely to exceed 15 knots, cruising dispositions for the fleet train were constantly being modified to accommodate threats from either submarine or aircraft.[37] Appendix H shows a British cruising disposition for replenishment, applicable to 1947 but based on the Pacific model, which highlights how important it was for the replenishment carrier and the protecting carrier providing combat air (CAP) and antisubmarine (A/S) patrols to be given as much room for maneuverability as possible within the closed screen, to allow for flying operations.[38]

Despite such detailed preparation for large-scale tactical maneuvers involving a fleet train, this particular Pacific model never actually had to be adopted after 1945 on the scale envisaged. That said, the doctrine was in place; it is very important to remember that virtually throughout this uncertain postwar period, both navies had to assume that another global war was not out of the question. The Pacific fleet train model, which was after all the only one they knew and understood, was therefore considered the only way to retain the necessary mobility and flexibility to survive the initial attack and secure the necessary resilience to fight back anywhere in the world. Equally important, under the umbrella of this general fleet train doctrine existed some core underlying principles for achieving a successful evolution, which were codified and remained virtually unchanged even through the Korean War. What differed by 1950 was just the scale. The usual complement of U.S. Navy replenishment vessels to support TF77, for example, was two oilers, a provisions ship, and an ammunition ship, while the British managed their underway fueling with usually only one tanker at a time.[39]

Factors Affecting Replenishment Evolution

How the LSF operated was to some extent also governed by limitations and risks inherent with each evolution. Over time, techniques and guidelines were established that reflected experience and improved technology, but many of these enduring principles for achieving a successful evolution also reflected the value and importance attached to "seamanlike judgment."[40] Transfers at sea maneuvers, for example, typically involve at least these six important factors: course, speed, approach, station keeping/water interaction, night transfers, and the breakaway.

Course

Weather, wind, and sea state could seriously affect the viability of undertaking any replenishment; it was often necessary to test the sea by actual turn movements of the task force before a dawn operation to disclose the best replenishment course. If, for example, the commander accepted a 10–20 degree roll, this penalized the oilers because their rigs were too sensitive and the winches and winch men typically "too slow" to respond to the changing distances between ships.[41] If the commander tried to reduce roll by heading into the sea, the resultant pitch could penalize weight allowances for stores transfers. In choosing the optimum course and speed, preference was therefore typically for heading into the wind, although this became less rigid as rig capabilities and techniques improved.[42] In adverse conditions, the best course for abeam replenishment was with the sea and wind 10 to 20 degrees on the bow, to give a lee to the smaller ship or the ship deploying the rigs. Once the replenishment was under way, the group could only alter course in steps, each of 20 degrees, with individual supply ships controlling the alteration procedure in five-degree movements.[43] This practice still applies today. The standard tactical diameter for replenishment ships was normally 1,500 yards.[44] Zigzagging was permitted during World War II but discouraged during peacetime.[45] For refueling astern, the course was immaterial unless the weather precluded safe working on the forecastle of the receiving ship, in which case a course before the wind was advisable.

Speed

Apart from sea state and weather, an important limitation on speed was set by the tanker. The additional need for steam to power the pumps and heat the oil incurred a significant diversion of power that could cost the tanker 2 or more knots. Replenishment speed therefore ranged between 8 and 15 knots with the BPF

Fleet Train tending toward the lower figure. Anything slower caused insufficient maneuverability or control in close steaming.[46] Replenishment speed was therefore controlled by the delivering ship, altered in 1 knot increments (or 3 knots, if only destroyers were involved).[47] By 1953, ship speeds were improving; the U.S. Navy regarded 16 knots as achievable, although 12–14 knots was more flexible. British postwar experience was consistent, but up to 20 knots abeam was claimed as possible.[48] Today both navies typically still transfer at 14 knots.[49]

Approach

The safest method of approach for cruisers or larger vessels was to take station abeam at about one cable and then close to position not less than seventy-five feet from the supplier ship, to avoid the disturbance to ship-handling caused by the interaction effect of the two ships. Plate 3.2 shows the British battleship HMS *Duke of York* on her approach to the tanker, which has the rig prepared for transferring fuel. In good weather, the approach could be made from the quarter but would be too dangerous at night or in poor visibility. In fog, tankers left fluorescent dye trails. Flags, in particular the Romeo signal, were the primary method for communicating each ship's intention and readiness to begin an evolution or serial. The initial connection between ships was by means of a line-throwing rifle (also known as a "gun line" in the Royal Navy), which was normally fired from the supply ship to avoid entanglement in rigging derricks. For a carrier, the reverse applied to avoid possible damage to parked aircraft. The gun line had a messenger attached that carried the distance line, telephone cables, and lines for the rig to be used. A separate gun line could be used to pass another messenger for other jackstay rigs being used.[50]

Station Keeping/Water Interaction

During most of World War II, the oiler would normally be the base unit upon which other ships converged and kept station, except fleet carriers or battleships that would otherwise "tow" the oiler alongside.[51] Towing in this context was not a deadweight task but an exercise in station keeping aided by a towline to check on sudden surges and with booms and lines set to avoid the hose touching the water. By 1945, however, it was common practice for all receiving ships to keep station upon the supply ship. A distance line, usually the first to be passed by the supply ship and the last to be recovered, was marked with different colored numerals showing distances in feet.[52] The transfer positions were marked along the length of the ships using hand flags: red for fuel oil, green for stores and ammunition positions, yellow for aviation fuel, blue for diesel/lubricating oils, and white for water. When jet fuel was introduced, a yellow-blue triangle flag was adopted.[53] The maximum number of ships that could be grouped around a tanker, assuming it had the necessary pumping capacity, was four: one arranged on each beam with two astern.[54] Carriers could only refuel abeam on the tanker's port side to provide a clear view from their bridge; cruisers preferred to fuel also from the port side while destroyers generally fueled from the tanker's starboard side. For British frigates, this varied by class.

When two ships run in close company, the steering of each is affected by the presence of the other due to the modification of the flow pattern. The effects arise from the increased pressure around the bow and stern and the zone of reduced pressure along most of the length. The inevitable yawing is compensated by appropriate rudder correction, with the best position being exactly abeam or, if the receiving ship was much smaller, in the intermediate area between the bow and stern pressure zones and at least eighty feet apart.[55] Except in shallow water (i.e., less than ten fathoms), the interaction effects at normal speeds on ship handling are not severe unless ships are very close, as demonstrated in plate 3.3. Even by 1952, however, not all British replenishment ships had gyrocompasses or automatic steering, so maintenance of accurate speed and course was down to good seamanship, with no tow or breast lines.[56] Heavy swells, particularly on the quarter, would badly affect steering and maneuvering. Automatic pilots received a mixed reception from RFA Masters, some refusing to use them because, with only one source of power supply, the ship would not be under immediate control in an emergency. Normal steering was therefore often manually by telemotor. Others regarded automatic steering as essential in bad weather, given constant crew changes with unknown helming experience.[57]

The key point to remember is that only by conning ships further abeam would transfers become safer and easier to manage during bad weather or at higher speeds—both of which were increasingly becoming determining factors, hence the continual need to improve rigging technology and handling methods to accommodate faster and heavier loads.

Night Transfers

The pressure for introducing night transfers as a regular practice did not really materialize until the Korean War. This was entirely due to the sheer volume of ordnance and aviation fuel being consumed by the American carriers every day. A number of precautions were taken to avoid collision, including red lifejacket light markers on the distance line. Trials carried out under "moonlight," "moonless," and "moonless and starless" conditions, and with ships darkened and undarkened, suggested that replenishment was easier under rigid blackout conditions, rather than with deck lighting in use. Although blue torch lighting was acceptable, the main concern was that any light source tended to blot out the outline of the ship, which made judgment of distances and angles difficult.[58] A fluorescent distance line was not successful and experiments for the gun line were inconclusive during this period. To avoid fuel loss, the supply ship must communicate immediately should there be a sudden loss of backpressure, suggesting a burst hose.[59]

Breakaway

After passing the gear back in reverse sequence, breakaway was achieved by a slight divergence before hauling off. Axes and wire-cutters were available at the transfer stations for emergency disengagement. Regular opportunities were taken to practice emergency breakaways because the circumstances that could call for such action were numerous and varied. Apart from having to react swiftly to air or submarine attack, other reasons to separate could be fire or safety related on one of the ships, particularly as the number of transfer points on both auxiliaries and warships were increased to achieve higher flow rates. Other hazards to cause an emergency breakaway were the effect of interaction between the ships, forcing one to veer toward the other; an emergency recovery of an aircraft; man overboard; or wire ropes having parted or malfunctioned.

Abeam versus Astern Method

Two transfer positions existed: astern and abeam. Astern refueling was the dominant transfer method in the very early years and would remain more popular with the Royal Navy than the U.S. Navy until improved abeam rigs were introduced late in the War.[60] Plate 3.4 illustrates both methods used in 1945.

The astern method was often adopted in lieu of, or in addition to, the abeam method depending on either weather conditions or the number of ships that needed refueling. The normal procedure was for the tanker to stream from her stern up to three or four hoses attached to a float grappled by the receiving ship over the bow, see in plate 3.5.

When refueling abeam, the hose was secured in troughs slung outboard, either from the supplying ship's derrick or crane or from travelers running on a jackstay rigged between the two ships. If there occurred any rolling or yawing, enough slack must exist in the rig to ride through the motion, providing the ships kept station. During World War II, this was the most vulnerable part of the operation because the hose-handling bight lines were hand-tended on both ships and required constant immediate adjustment to avoid either dunking the hoses or stretching them to the breaking point. By the end of 1945, the British and American methods were quite similar; the most noticeable difference was the absence of any connecting lines with the British method.[61]

Only cruisers or larger vessels would receive more than one hose astern. Once grappled, the hose was secured and the ship kept on station with the assistance of a marker buoy streamed at 320 or 500 feet from the tanker floating abreast the receiving ship's bridge. This method became difficult at speeds of 8–10 knots

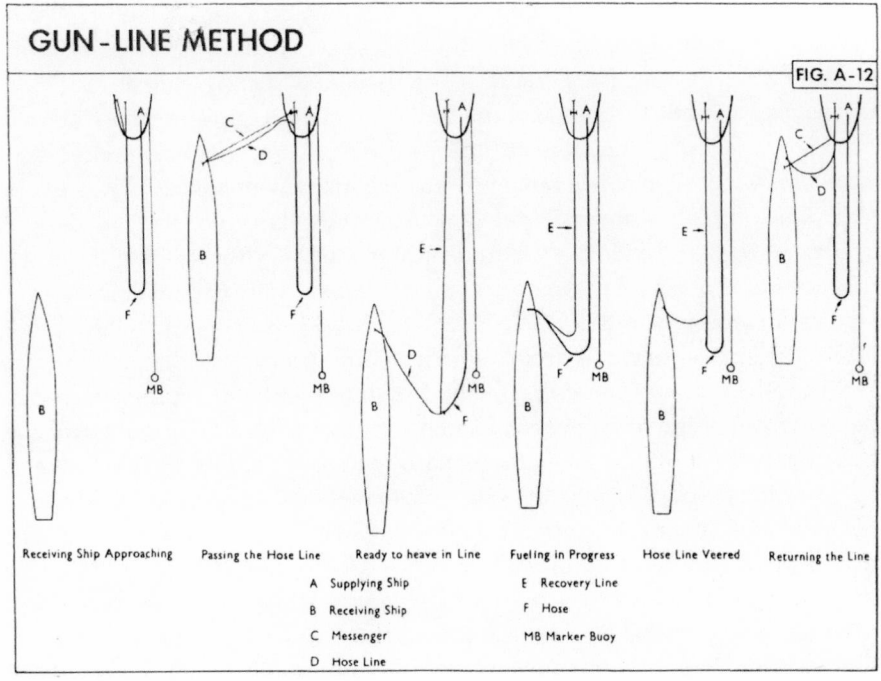

GUN-LINE METHOD

FIG. A-12

Receiving Ship Approaching   Passing the Hose Line   Ready to heave in Line   Fueling in Progress   Hose Line Veered   Returning the Line

A Supplying Ship   E Recovery Line
B Receiving Ship   F Hose
C Messenger   MB Marker Buoy
D Hose Line

Diagram 3.1. RN gun-line procedure for astern fueling (NARA2, RG38, ATP-16, 1955)

in rough weather, so an alternative procedure provided for the hose to be initially transferred using a gun line fired from the tanker across the bows of the receiver ship with the messenger passed as the receiving ship closed on the quarter of the supply ship. Diagram 3.1 illustrates how the gun-line method was expected to work, but it had its detractors among RFA masters because "it requires too many hands and hoses [are] more liable to damage than Float method."[62] Working distance was typically about four hundred feet in fair weather, otherwise six hundred feet.[63] Astern fueling from a large warship was also feasible.[64] Self-sealing fueling couplings were not used because the hose had to be filled with air between each fueling operation so it would float.[65] Instantaneous couplings were not regarded as essential either because ships had more sea room and a less likely degree of urgency compared to the abeam method.[66] American doctrine from World War II throughout this period regarded astern fueling as a secondary method used either by commercial tankers without the right booms or in emergencies for smaller ships.[67] Their procedure was therefore modeled on the British method, although on the occasions when it was necessary to adopt astern refueling, such as in poor Arctic conditions, only the RFAs were prepared to refuel NATO ships in joint exercises.[68]

Broadly speaking, the advantages of abeam refueling were the shorter hoses that made for easier handling by the receiving ship and higher ship speeds, particularly when passing gear because, in astern fueling, speed would be restricted to whatever was safe for men working on the forecastle. Light stores such as mail or bread could also be transferred simultaneously, and telephone communication was possible.[69] The major advantage of the abeam concept, however, was that it was inherently better suited for potential improvements in speed and rig design. The intent was to provide more latitude in ship motion while keeping ships further abeam, which made "things easier and safer . . . and hence enables replenishment to be carried out in heavier weather and at higher speeds, which latter is always desirable from the anti-submarine point of view."[70]

The advantages of the astern method, on the other hand, were greater freedom for using ships' armaments under attack, greater freedom of maneuver, the gear was simpler to fit, and less risk of parting in heavy swells or bad weather.[71] Plate 3.6 illustrates such hazards well. Korean replenishment experience in 1951 demonstrated continuing support within the Royal Navy for using the astern method, particularly to light vessels in bad weather conditions.[72]

If merchant tankers were used for fleet replenishment, they were expected to be able to use at least one of the abeam methods as well as the astern method. However, it is important to remember that one of the key reasons for the Royal Navy's need for perpetuating astern refueling capability was that in any future emergency, large numbers of commercial tankers would be required at short notice to refuel convoy escorts. The astern method, therefore, with its simple requirements for just hose, wire, and a few rollers, might well prove to be the only practical solution from a production standpoint.[73]

Liquids Transfer

Various methods were used to transfer fuel under way, none of them thoroughly satisfactory and all suffered from improvisation until the introduction of specialist replenishment ships after the Korean War. Whatever method was used, the underlying principle was that the elasticity of the hose rig had to cope with both ships' movements under varying sea and weather conditions. Another underlying principle was the burden of rigging and handling assumed by the supplier ship, thereby enabling warships to respond to any attack with the minimum of delay.[74]

Each tanker was loaded predominantly with ship fuel oil. Other products in both type and volume were also incorporated as the demand, particularly for different aviation fuels, increased. Consequently, considerable progress was made in developing simultaneous transfers utilizing improvements in hose size, rig design, and pumping capacity. During 1952 the old wartime British 5-inch and 3½-inch hoses were mostly replaced by 6-inch hose while diesel fuel, petrol, lubricating oil, and water were passed through a special 4-inch hose.[75] The U.S. Navy used 4-inch and 6-inch hoses during the World War II, and this remained unchanged even though the Royal Navy had found in trials during 1948 that a new 7-inch hose combined "both robustness and astonishing lightness."[76] Today the 7-inch hose is NATO standard.

Oil would be pumped at temperatures best suited to promote its flow, never higher than 100°F, with the object of trying to top up as near to 95 percent capacity as possible.[77] Although not normal practice except between tankers, all fuel rigs could be used in the reverse for receiving fuels.[78] Cruisers and larger ships received at least two fuel hoses, and carriers an additional avgas hose. American destroyers could also take two hoses, but their British and Canadian equivalents were initially only fitted for one. Lubricating oils were transferred in drums by the light jackstay or highline method. It became necessary during the Korean War to outfit the American carriers with equipment to receive three transfer rigs instead of the one used in World War II because of the huge increase in demand for aviation fuel caused by jet aircraft that burned gasoline four times faster than propeller-driven aircraft.[79]

During and immediately after the World War II, most of the rigs for fueling abeam proved adequate given the low ship speeds and relatively low transfer rates possible. However, as fleet demand for improvement intensified, each rig had to be redesigned (or increasingly modified) to contend with more severe sea states or weather conditions while coping with heavier loads at faster rates without compromising safety. The challenge was to try to keep the length of hose in the rig to a minimum to reduce pumping effort and increase delivery rate while each ship reacted independently to wave and swell effect, thereby constantly changing the transfer distance.[80] Appendixes I and J summarize the various functions and limitations of the liquids and solids transfer rigs, respectively, as used by both navies between the interwar years through to mid 1950s. The following paragraphs describe some of these rig structures in more detail.

For the Royal Navy, transfer of fuel had traditionally been either by the crane rig on larger warships to replenish, for example, the escorts (see plate 3.7) or small derrick (see diagram 3.2). The third type of rig, called the small ship jackstay rig, was normally only employed between small ships when the aforementioned more orthodox methods proved unavailable.

The most common abeam rig used by BPF tankers in 1945 was the 40-ft trough rig designed before the war (see plate 3.8) that was eventually surpassed by the more successful 70-ft large derrick method, seen in diagram 3.3 and plate 3.9, adapted from the N.D.("net defence") boom rig. This was fitted to four Sam-

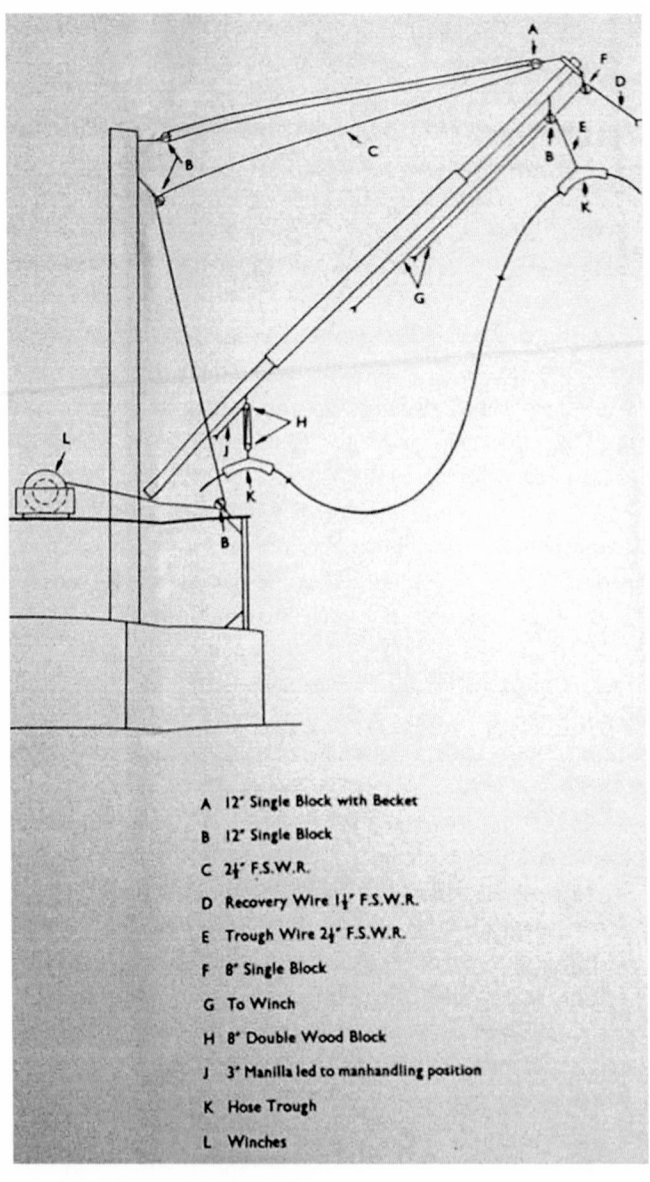

A   12" Single Block with Becket

B   12" Single Block

C   2¼" F.S.W.R.

D   Recovery Wire 1¼" F.S.W.R.

E   Trough Wire 2¼" F.S.W.R.

F   8" Single Block

G   To Winch

H   8" Double Wood Block

J   3" Manilla led to manhandling position

K   Hose Trough

L   Winches

Diagram 3.2. Small derrick rig (NARA2, RG38, ATP-16, 1955)

LARGE DERRICK RIG

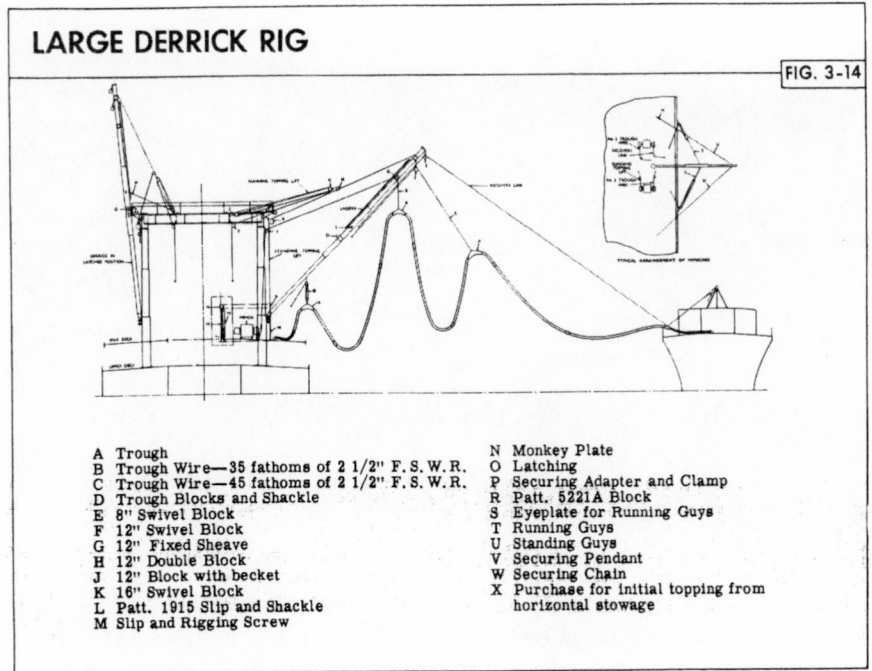

FIG. 3-14

A	Trough
B	Trough Wire—35 fathoms of 2 1/2" F.S.W.R.
C	Trough Wire—45 fathoms of 2 1/2" F.S.W.R.
D	Trough Blocks and Shackle
E	8" Swivel Block
F	12" Swivel Block
G	12" Fixed Sheave
H	12" Double Block
J	12" Block with becket
K	16" Swivel Block
L	Patt. 1915 Slip and Shackle
M	Slip and Rigging Screw
N	Monkey Plate
O	Latching
P	Securing Adapter and Clamp
R	Patt. 5221A Block
S	Eyeplate for Running Guys
T	Running Guys
U	Standing Guys
V	Securing Pendant
W	Securing Chain
X	Purchase for initial topping from horizontal stowage

Diagram 3.3. Large 70-ft derrick fuel rig—the standard RFA fueling rig from 1945 until replaced by the jackstay method (NARA2, RG38, ATP-16, 1955)

son posts, two port and two starboard, which enabled up to four 5-inch hoses to be passed on either beam that became the standard rig for most seas and weather.[81]

Warships or tankers would stow the derrick in the vertical position and then extend by topping out over the side. The hose would rest in saddles or hose troughs, each positioned by deck winches, seen in plate 3.10, thereby reducing the number of attendant personnel.[82] Plate 3.12 shows how this type of rig enabled the gap between ships to become much wider at higher sailing speeds, compared to 1945.

The most significant new rig for the Royal Navy during this period, designed to accommodate even greater distances between the ships, was the jackstay fueling rig (see diagram 3.4). Here the hose was lashed in four troughs, of which one was triced to the kingpost with the remainder slung on travelers that ran along a jackstay.[83] By 1952 this was still confined to the trials tanker HMS *Bulawayo*, shown in plate 3.11 fueling a cruiser, because no decision could be reached on how this could be fitted more widely. The problem was that it required either more powerful steam winches than were available on tankers or

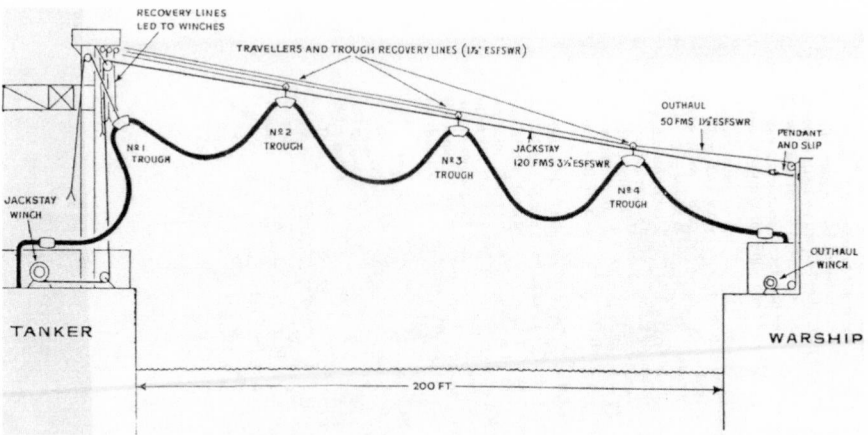

Diagram 3.4. RN jackstay fueling rig (1951) (AL, Admiralty, BR67 (2/51))(Courtesy Admiralty Library Ministry of Defence)

an efficient means of automatic compensation such as the tensioning winch that was still under development and not yet generally fitted to either American or British tankers.[84]

For the U.S. Navy, two rigs were used during and just after World War II called the close-in rig (diagram 3.5) and the Elwood or span-wire rig (diagram 3.6). For both rigs, the hose was supported by boom whips and bight lines that lead from saddles on the hose to booms or other high projections on one or both ships. The complexity involved in such rigging lines caused some Royal Navy officers to be overwhelmed by "far too much string."[85] The difference between the British and American rig was in the method employed to extend the hose between the ships. Instead of just saddles fixed to the bight lines, the Elwood required a span-wire (similar to a British jackstay) to be stretched between the two ships, with the hose hanging from trolley blocks that would then ride along the wire. This enabled wider separation for the ships and eliminated the need for tow and spring lines. As a result, the fueling course could be closer to the desired direction of advance, thereby substantially reducing interference in the primary mission of the task force.

The real perceived benefit of the Elwood method, however, was that it enabled "the operation to become a simple station keeping problem."[86] The manila saddle and retrieving lines could be substituted by wire lines if enough winches existed at the rigging stations, which is why the rig method was called "all wire span-wire."[87] Its main postwar variant, called the Elokomin rig, was specifically modified by the U.S. Atlantic and Mediterranean fleets to be more compatible with NATO ships.

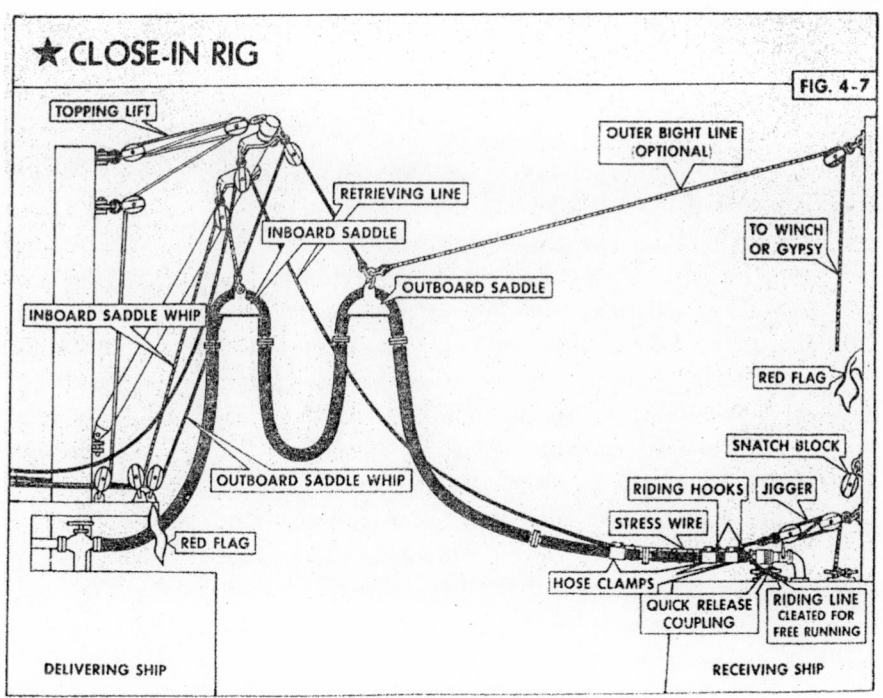

Diagram 3.5. USN close-in fueling rig (USNHC, NWP-38, 1953)

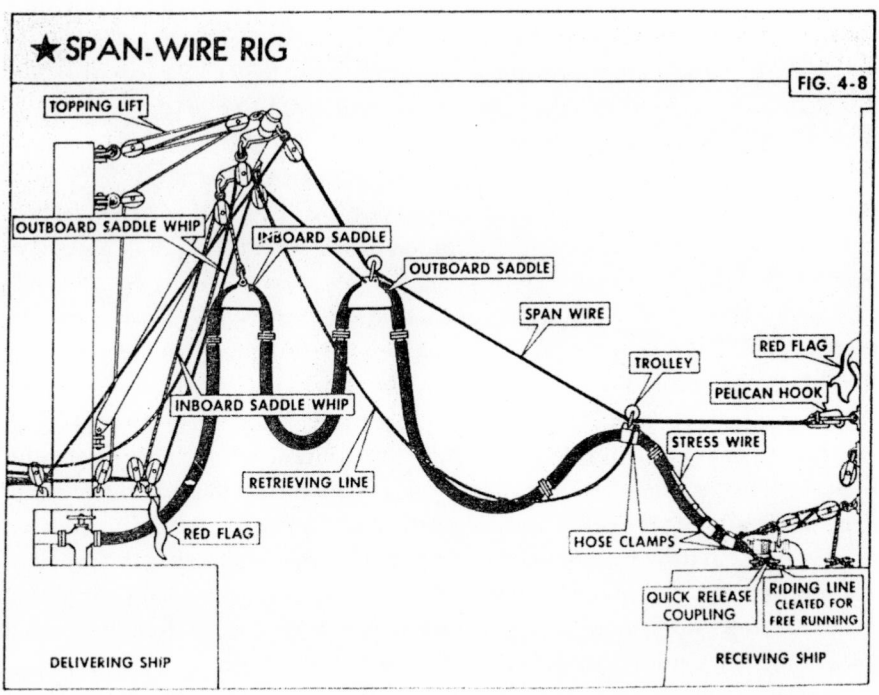

Diagram 3.6. USN span-wire or Elwood fueling rig (1945) (USNHC, NWP-38, 1953)

Stores Transfers

Although the transfer of solids at sea only became a regular feature during the last few months of the Pacific War, further significant progress was stunted until new purpose-built replenishment ships could be built to accommodate the necessary new rig designs, none of which could be retrofitted on wartime-built converted merchant hulls. Even after three years of design development, the Admiralty's Director of Victualling could only bear out the Royal Navy's limitations, by acknowledging "It is quite clear that we have a long way to go before we can undertake as a regular arrangement a full replenishment of victualling stores at sea. As things stand at present the most we can do is to top up HM Ships with items most needed, such as fresh provisions."[88]

The problems for fleet issue of stores are numerous and peculiar to every operation, and the transfer process remained throughout this period "unduly slow and laborious" primarily due to the nature and quantity of stores required to meet the needs of such a wide variety of different warships.[89] One constant problem was that to access every item, a lot of cargo space must be sacrificed to provide passageways. In other words, fleet-issue-loaded ships "are not loaded to capacity but are loaded for mobility."[90] Apart from the issue of safety, ammunition posed particular problems for planners and handlers. In fact, the hazards of organizing and transferring ammunition at sea, first experienced in World War II, had not diminished at all during the Korean War. For the supplier ship, it was critically important to estimate proper loading levels given the variety of different ordnance expended at different rates by so many different types of ships or planes. A typical ammunition ship had five holds, two between decks and at least two derricks to each hold, fitted to enable transfer by the heavy jackstay from two points on either side (see plate 3.14). There were also a variety of safety-related precautions unique to handling ammunition that required strict rules for which "there is [to be] no exception . . . irrespective of what is done in harbor."[91] However, as the volume of demand increased, so did the risks. With each carrier in the Korean War typically deploying up to ninety aircraft, this meant that some 75 tons of ordnance could be expended every day. It was therefore not unusual for the three carriers of Task Force 77 to require restocking up to 750 tons of bombs and rockets every fourth day. As a result, ammunition would often have to be broken out twenty-four hours in advance and temporarily stored on the weather deck of the ammunition ship because there was neither the time nor available crew to perform this task simultaneously with the actual transfer.[92] The problem did not stop there; once the ammunition had been transferred across, it would then take crews up to eight hours to move such a large volume from the hanger deck to the magazines, an exercise that was both time-consuming and perilous. Aside from carriers, it was also not uncommon in the Korean shore bombardment operations for an American ammunition ship to be alongside the warship to starboard while the latter was simultaneously firing her guns to port; indeed on one occasion the cruiser USS *Manchester* was actually firing the very ammunition being delivered simultaneously by the auxiliary.[93]

The limiting factor for provisions was usually volume, not weight, and transfer rates were also slow, often dictated by how fast the receiver ship could actually receive and redistribute the loads. It was therefore noteworthy that on at least one occasion, carriers found it quicker to embark victualling stores at sea via the flight deck rather than alongside in harbor owing to the better internal routes from the flight deck.[94] Water became an important requirement for destroyers during the Korean operation, and although tankers were accordingly modified to accommodate five hundred transfer tons, in general water was considered "a secondary object to be carried out within the time allotted to fuelling."[95] Refrigerated cargoes were essential if the deployments were prolonged, despite the constant breakdown of the refrigeration units on British ships, and with storage costs being about 250 percent higher than base storage, available space tended to be restricted.[96]

Air replenishment presented many unique problems for the British, particularly in World War II when planning the correct number of aircraft and crew replacements in operational trim proved very difficult. Pilots were ferried by air and sea to the replenishment carrier to fly back replacement aircraft, which could only land on the carriers when they themselves were not being replenished. Often the replenishment carrier was ill equipped or designed to handle all types of aircraft.[97]

In terms of overall progress in the immediate postwar period, some limited improvement was achieved in terms of both volume and transfer rate, most particularly for ammunition from American auxiliaries.[98] For the Royal Navy, progress in both ammunition and general provisions was less impressive, mainly due to their limited experience and lack of suitable supply ships. In the second final major deployment of the BPF in July–August 1945, some 532 tons of provisions were transferred in seventy-seven evolutions, averaging 7½ tph per evolution or 9½ tph on a first-to-last net basis.[99] Not surprisingly, given longer experience with better ships and equipment, the U.S. Navy transfer rates for provisions were considerably better, averaging 10 tph for destroyers but still only 17 tph for carriers, albeit a figure that was improving quickly toward the end of the Pacific campaign.[100] After 1945, however, perhaps not surprisingly these rates plummeted. Provisions replenishments undertaken during the U.S. Atlantic Fleet exercises in 1947, for example, averaged a transfer rate for all ships of only 2½ tph, the worst rate belonging to the largest carrier at only 0.86 tph.[101]

Korea changed all this. Dry stores transfer rates from U.S. Navy auxiliaries shot up to average over 35 tph while transfer rates in ammunition improved dramatically from a typical figure of between 32 and 45 tph by the end of World War II to as high as 186 tph by 1952.[102] One report suggested it was not unusual to transfer about 125 tph to U.S. Navy fleet carriers using two burtoning points.[103] Plate 3.13 shows the ammunition ship USS *Rainier* off Korea in 1952 issuing bombs and rockets to the carrier USS *Antietam* and shells to the battleship USS *Wisconsin*. A reflection of how Korea nevertheless was beginning to stretch the ability of the Service Force to sustain the carriers with enough ordnance, particularly bearing in mind the respective size of U.S. Navy forces between 1945 and Korea, can be gauged from looking at the skyrocketing expenditure rates. In the first ten months of the Korean War, U.S. naval and marine aircraft expended one fourth as much aircraft ammunition as all the marine and naval ship or shore-based aircraft put together, covering all theaters in World War II.[104]

As for the British, Royal Navy replenishment experience in Korea was limited to refueling with "nothing in the way of a major replenishment attempted."[105] No British supply ships deployed in Korea were fitted with the heavy jackstays for handling underway loads up to one ton although both warships and tankers were fitted with a light jackstay for transferring up to five hundred pounds, usually provisions that could be controlled by a winch. Despite requests to London for deploying an RFA armament supply issue ship to Korea with underway capability, none was deemed available.[106] On some occasions, therefore, Commonwealth warships resorted to receiving British ammunition from American auxiliaries to avoid returning to base.

To summarize the progress in solids transfers by both navies since 1945, it would seem that while the doctrine, methodology, and designed weight limitations for solids transfers were broadly similar between both navies, the U.S. Navy not only undertook much more frequent transfers but they also operated a wider variety of rigs to suit different needs or ships, particularly for ordnance.

British auxiliaries relied on just two types of jackstay rigs to transfer light and heavy loads. Both were controlled by the supply ship unless refueling was also under way, in which case the receiving ship handled the light jackstay due to the limited complement on board RFA tankers.[107]

The heavy jackstay (see diagram 3.7) was the workhorse, used for safely transferring stores, including ammunition, up to a maximum of one or two tons, provided weather conditions were good and the distance was kept as narrow as possible to reduce the strain. The jackstay line, on the end of which were the jackstay and outhaul, was clipped to the messenger and passed over the water. When secured, the jackstay and inhaul were tended by winches on the supply ship. The loads were slung from a block called "the traveler," which was then hauled along the jackstay. Warships were equipped with a light jackstay and could receive but not supply stores to others using the heavy jackstay.

Plate 3.15 shows a typical transfer of stores, in this case eggs, by light jack-

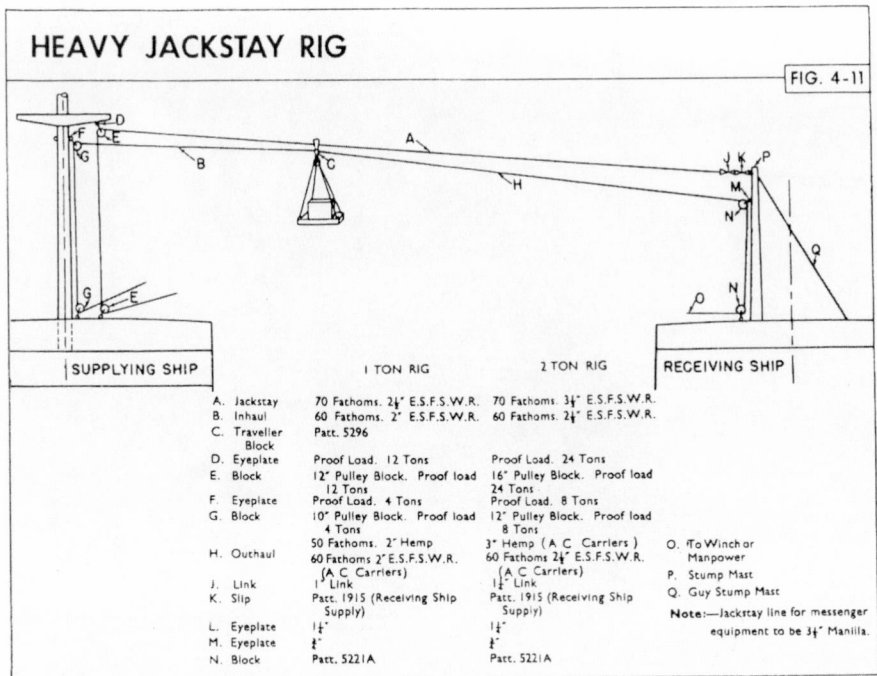

Diagram 3.7. RN heavy jackstay stores rig (NARA2, RG38, ATP-16, 1955)

stay between a cruiser and destroyer in 1945. Even torpedoes could eventually be transferred by this method, as shown in plate 3.16. Men, however, were transferred by stirrup or chair, shown in plate 3.17, or by medical stretcher if necessary, shown in plate 3.18.

Up to 1945, the U.S. Navy standard method for transferring light loads to destroyers was the wire highline method shown in diagram 3.8. Such a line between two ships would support a trolley with a cargo hook attached. The load was then secured to the cargo hook and moved between ships by means of an inhaul and outhaul line. Tension was maintained on the highline by the supplier ship. If the receiver ship had the necessary special fittings, then the wire highline would be similar to the heavy jackstay capable of transferring medium to heavy loads up to two tons. Light loads up to 200 lb, conversely, were transferred by the "manila highline" shown in diagram 3.9. Equivalent to the light jackstay, the manila highline was identical to the wire highline except a manila line was substituted for a wire and tended by hand or gypsy head. All were interoperable with Canadian and British warships.

The rig was modified after 1945 into a number of variations under the "housefall" banner and became particularly appropriate for NATO interopera-

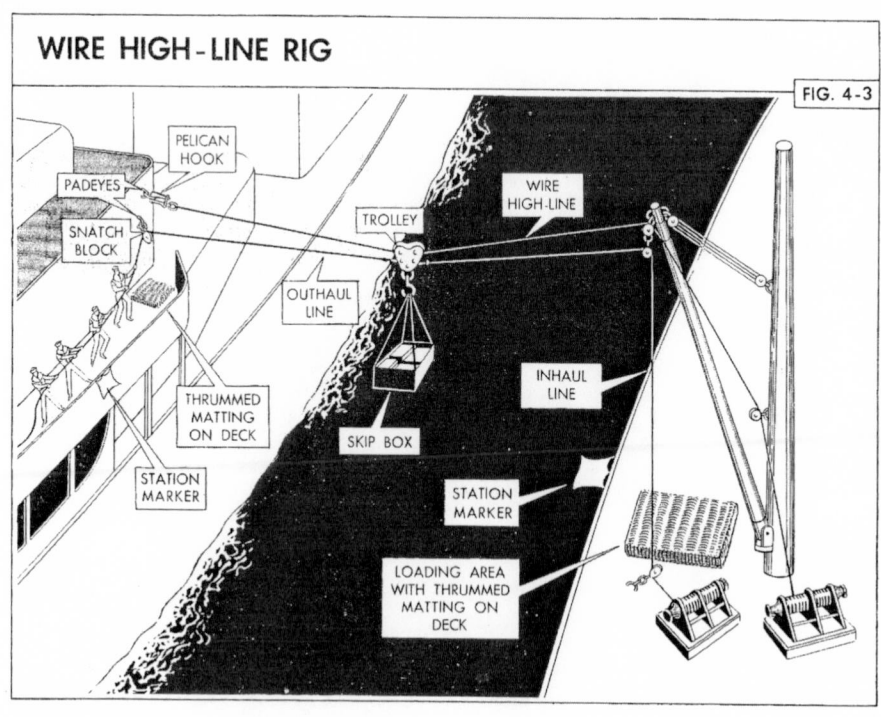

Diagram 3.8. USN wire highline rig (NARA2, RG38, ATP-16, 1955)

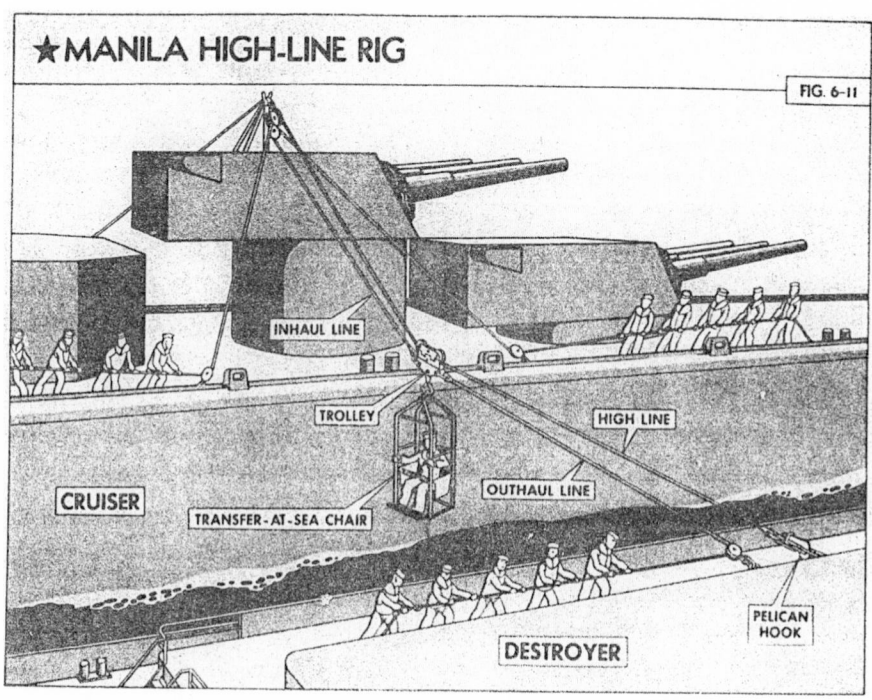

Diagram 3.9. USN manila highline rig (USNHC, NWP-38, 1953)

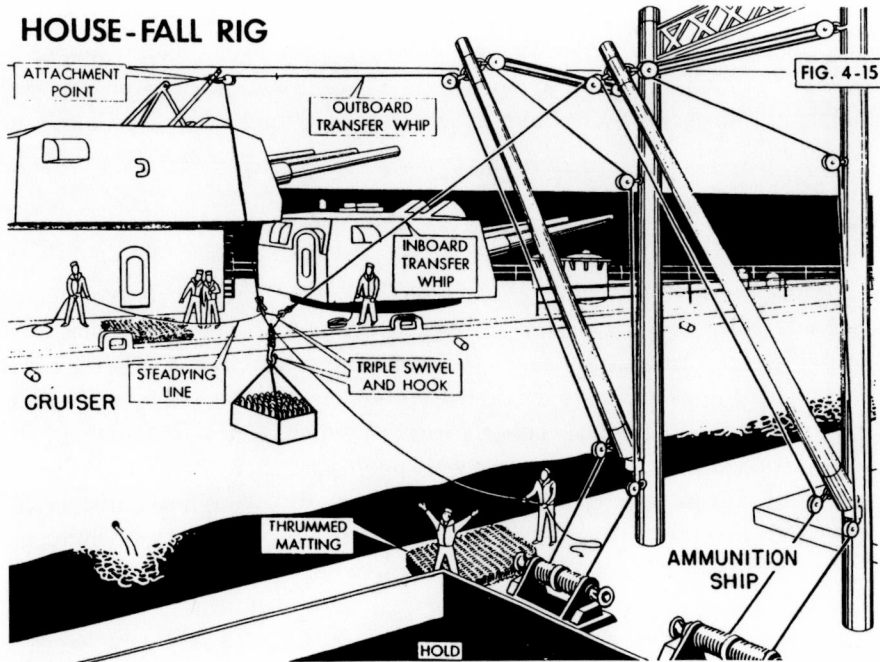

HOUSE-FALL RIG

ATTACHMENT POINT

FIG. 4-15

OUTBOARD TRANSFER WHIP

INBOARD TRANSFER WHIP

STEADYING LINE

CRUISER

TRIPLE SWIVEL AND HOOK

THRUMMED MATTING

AMMUNITION SHIP

HOLD

Diagram 3.10. USN housefall rig (NARA2, RG38, ATP-16, 1955)

bility. This was because the housefall enabled the delivering ship to operate and tend all transfer winches and whips, thus taking entire control of the load procedure during transit. The double housefall consisted of two adjacent housefall rigs employing two housefall blocks shackled together and suspended from a single suspension point on the receiving ship. One housefall rig would deliver a loaded net while the other returned an empty one. The so-called modified housefall combined the housefall and highline methods, in that a trolley block was added to the standard housefall rig, which would then ride on the transfer whip, doubling as a highline and outhaul line, thereby keeping the load higher above the water during transfer.

Perhaps the most significant and long-lasting improvement for transferring heavier loads to carriers was the introduction of the burtoning method, particularly given the requirement for increasingly large amounts of ordnance and replacement parts. Here the receiving and delivering ships each operated a winch and wire. The receiving ship's suspension point ("burton" point), together with the wire and winch, acted as an extended movable yard of the yard-and-stay rig. The delivering ship's boom, wire, and winch, on the other side, took the part of the stay. By using two booms for transfer and hoisting, this method enabled loads of up to 3,500 lb to be moved under favorable conditions; by 1953 this had been modified to handle up to 6,000 lb and became the standard rig for transferring ammunition to carriers during the Korean War. Even so, with ammunition consumption increasing so much, it soon became necessary to increase the number of transfer receiver points on each carrier to three. (See diagram 2.1 in chapter 2.)

Transfer Rates

While theoretically ships could remain at sea for the entire period between major overhauls or dry-docking, the sea-keeping capability for the fleet as a whole was invariably dependent upon the replenishment of two key components: the least self-sufficient ships, typically the destroyers, which at least could be topped up by capital ships, and more crucially, the carriers, which needed to be replenished with aviation gasoline. Every time replenishments occurred, the fleet was put at a tactical disadvantage, so it was important to find ways to improve transfer efficiency. Certain general principles were established as operational guidelines, of which the most important was that "every effort consistent with safety must be made to reduce the time required to accomplish replenishment."[108]

Because fueling was the primary requirement for most ships, this tended to determine the initial time allocated to replenishment. Success for the Royal Navy, for example, was therefore measured by "the rate of replenishment and the progress made in the direction required by the operation in progress."[109] In fact, the experience during the Korean War had confirmed that for the Royal Navy "the largest factor in over-all time of refueling is the rate of pumping." [110] The object had been to maximize the transfer rate, which could only be achieved "by rigidly adhering to the equipment and methods outlined in ["Replenishment at Sea," BR1742] and disseminating this widely to ensure that "a high state of training is attained."[111] In other words, technology and practice would be the limiting factors. Therefore, analyzing and comparing transfer rates should in theory be a potentially useful way to compare progress even though they could not be expected to reflect the whole picture. However, in following this line of inquiry further it became evident that there were some important obstacles when trying to establish any meaningful comparison. Apart from the more obvious variable caveats such as weather or sea states, there were the important variables of experience, confidence, and training among the officers and deckhands of both oilers and particularly the different warships. Other factors would include the time taken to approach, rig, and then break away, all of which could be subject to a variety of variables—not least successful communication between parties or, indeed, within each ship. The most constraining factor of all was the extent to which warships could receive oil at the higher rates without throttling, a fault generally less prevalent in American warships because they were specifically designed to take higher flow rates from larger hoses by having wider trunks leading into larger tanks.[112] The most critical bottleneck in carrier replenishment during Korea, for example, was the delivery rate of aviation gasoline for jet aircraft, which was not easy to resolve. Not only did it require significant design changes to the carrier avgas tank capacity but better flow rates would only be achieved by improved pump capacity, increasing the number of filling connections, and improving tank pressure limitations.[113] By way of comparison, the problem for the British was even worse because ship design in the past had never needed to compensate for long endurance sorties. Warship fuel tank receiver rates were therefore constrained by comparatively smaller tank size/capacity and by the receiver's fuel filling system, which was not conducive to high flow rates. These handicaps would remain a problem for so long as wartime-built ships constituted the vast bulk of the Royal Navy fleet with little prospect of funds being allocated to new construction.[114] Even today tankers can theoretically pump fuel at much higher rates than warships can receive, despite the limitation caused by back pressure and despite fuel filtration systems required for delivery to "customers" powered by certain types of modern engines. Other technical factors including the pressure maintained by the tanker; oil temperature; and the number, bore, and length of hose also influenced flow rates during the postwar period.

Given all these underlying diverse factors involving equipment, technique, and skill, every evolution really becomes unique—even among ships of the same class. As a result, any comparison on transfer rates in isolation can be misleading unless they can be strictly interpreted in a consistent manner within their proper context. Based on the evidence available from records covering the wartime and postwar period, it has not been possible to achieve a consistent interpretation of comparable replenishment evolution performance data within one navy, let alone when trying to compare the two.

Differences between Royal Navy and U.S. Navy Operations

Commenting upon the need for better interchangeability of logistic support, whether shore-based or floating, the Admiralty's Director of Plans (Q) took the view that "reliance by each navy on its own logistic support organisation may be unavoidable today, but it is felt that further examination of the problem could lead to an elimination of at least some of the existing differences of procedure. In war the need for inter-changeability may well become very great."[115]

In the flurry of interest after World War II to find ways for gaining fuller interoperability with the U.S. Navy, the Royal Navy considered adopting the American Elwood rig for their RFAs, but after further trials in 1948, this was abandoned in favor of keeping their existing rig, which had the advantage of being easier to install on merchant ships in emergency. Nevertheless, British ships were fitted at the receiving end with special adapters, and crews were trained to use the Elwood so that they could fuel from U.S. Navy vessels in need.[116] No further attempt appears to have been made to standardize rigs, and this would seem sensible given the same result could be achieved simply by using adapters and adopting the same doctrine.[117]

One-Stop Shopping: The Next Generation

The Korean War exposed a number of fault lines in the composition and capability of both navies, whose ability to provide mobile logistic support for their naval operations had proved to be different from all the plans developed in earlier years. These will be discussed in more detail in later chapters, but to look at how underway replenishment had evolved, a number of observations can now be made.

A key determinant for success, reducing replenishment time, was considerably improved by a number of important enhancements, none of which, however, was revolutionary. Foremost was the improvement in transfer rig design that enabled ships to take a more flexible course and speed, in a broader range of sea and wind conditions, and yet still be able to transfer increasingly heavier loads safely. Second were the increase in transfer rig stations and improved hose design that would increase flow rates during simultaneous refueling for up to four ships. Nevertheless, technological progress was always going to be hampered so long as the only available option for any improvement was to modify or jury-rig existing wartime-built ships and systems. The primary problem was that, due to wartime necessity, all these rigs were adapted from in-port cargo handling systems that, despite improvements, still remained very hazardous and cumbersome to operate at sea. Until each navy acquired replenishment auxiliaries purpose-built from the keel up, nothing was really going to change.

In the end, the difficulties in satisfying the enormous increases in carrier task force consumption during the Korean War of both ordnance and jet fuel led to the 1952 Conference on Mobile Logistic Support in San Francisco, the first but not the last specifically charged by the U.S. Navy CNO to resolve a number of urgent concerns that had arisen about replenishment at sea. The refueling rigs needed to be standardized by choosing either the Elwood (U.S. Pacific Fleet) or Elokomin (U.S. Atlantic Fleet); new, improved rigs using constant tensioning must be introduced (which indeed they were on new ships in 1956); new special-purpose ammunition ships urgently needed to be built, with the first two *Suribachi* class authorized in 1954; and new purpose-built replenishment oilers needed to be built, with the first (AO143 *Neosho*) coming off the blocks only a year later. But it would be another decade before the two most radical enhancements for revolutionizing the transfer process appeared operationally—vertical replenishment (VERTREP) and "one-stop shopping." The former, involving netted, under-slung stores and ammunition carried by helicopter, was first developed in the late 1950s by the U.S. Navy Atlantic Fleet and became an integral design feature of U.S. Navy auxiliaries after 1964, with the same happening to the RFA in the late 1960s.

The concept of one-stop shopping became the most revolutionary development in postwar afloat support. It deserves further mention because so much of the groundwork was established during this postwar period, particularly during the early 1950s. Its most vocal advocate was Capt. E. E. Pare, who had been the first officer in the U.S. Navy to command an oiling group at sea and had served as chief of staff and aide to the commander of Service Squadron Six in the Pacific between December 1944 and January 1945, the period when underway replenishment really flourished. After the war, Pare became commander of the Service Force to the U.S. Atlantic Fleet, during which time he also helped the Naval War College refine their replenishment-at-sea war games to make them more realistic. He retired as a rear admiral in 1950, three years before his concept of one-stop replenishment was tested in trials and sixteen years before it became wartime operational reality in Vietnam.

The original idea was to eliminate the need for warships to go alongside several types of supplier ships to obtain fuel and other liquid or solid commodities that required a variety of different rigs and stations, which wasted precious available time. Earlier mention was made of a fast tanker design that would stay with the fleet all the time, supported by a shuttle of tankers available to top it up when stocks were low. This new concept took the idea to the next level by including provisions, ammunition and spares, all of which would be transferable simultaneously. If larger quantities were needed, then a special product ship would be called up that would otherwise shuttle back and forth from the supply base where they would be faster to reload than a one-stop replenishment ship. The whole exercise would be more efficient as a result. It used a jackstay system similar in principle to the jackstay and heavy jackstay rig described in this chapter, but with better controls and winches to separate the rig into two single-capacity rigs for solids and liquids.[118] The prototype, known as the dual capacity high-performance transfer rig, took enormous time to develop, partly because of the limited choice of appropriate ships to carry out the trials, so its appearance was delayed until 1956.

What would eventually set this project apart from other existing or planned auxiliaries during the Korean War was the scale of the proposed vessels. The first of these, the 26-knot AOE-1 USS *Sacramento*, was commissioned on March 14, 1964. Displacing 53,600 tons, she was capable of providing at very high rates simultaneous replenishment of ship and aviation fuel as well as stores, provisions, and ammunition via six fueling stations, five cargo handling stations, and four fast automatic ammunition transfer stations.[119] With more fuel capacity than the largest oiler, more cargo capacity than an AE, and two helicopters for VERTREP, this extraordinary ship would still be capable of running with the fastest carriers afloat.[120]

Conclusion

The fleet train concept developed in the Pacific in 1945 remained the model for early postwar mobile logistic support doctrine, predicated on the assumption that should a further global war be precipitated, both navies would have the necessary endurance and mobility to pursue their strategic objectives globally. In practice, this meant little change to recent wartime doctrine and procedures because the auxiliaries involved remained unchanged.

At the tactical level, speed became a critical consideration for minimizing the vulnerability to attack from either submarine or aircraft as well as minimizing the deviation from the task force mission. At the strategic level, the more experience gained by all concerned made for a more efficacious evolution, which ensured more forces could be placed into combat properly equipped with an increasing variety of necessary stores, ordnance, and petroleum. This in turn improved task force endurance and range, thereby maximizing the commander's strategic options. What this all proved was that a well-developed doctrine, regularly practiced, was vital if operational consistency and harmony were to be achieved, both prerequisites for convergence and interoperability between navies—the hallmark for future naval operations, as discussed in chapter 7. Yet progress after 1945 was erratic at best, although to some extent inevitable in peacetime, given it was never anything other than evolutionary in nature and peripheral in consequence. Improvements in rig design were driven primarily by the need to transfer fuel and stores safely but at higher speeds under increasingly difficult sea and weather conditions. As replenishment became routine and only susceptible to incremental change, any major advances in replenishment at-sea capability would have to be caused either by some particular major event or by a significant change in warship design or purpose.

The revolution in rig design, like the revolution in auxiliary ship design, took years, and while the result only surfaced after the Korean War, the trigger had been the problems of adapting yesterday's technology in Korea to cope with the logistic demands required by the more modern and versatile carriers and their increasingly powerful air component. To this end, therefore, Korea not only forced changes to the doctrine but also accelerated the pace for designing and building the next generation of fast combat replenishment ships to provide the essential logistic support that even larger and more powerful carriers, many under construction by the mid-1950s, would demand.

4 | Postwar Logistics
Turning Practice into Procedure

Logistically speaking, the primary impetus for strategic change in how global wars could be waged at sea during the first half of the twentieth century was the switch in ship propulsion from coal to oil. The implications for endurance, efficiency, ship displacement, and, ultimately, war-fighting capability were significant and far-reaching. In the second half of the twentieth century, the pace of change was further accelerated by the introduction of jet aircraft, missile technology, increasingly complex maintenance systems, and eventually nuclear power. But it would take a major global war in the middle of the century to bring about the real revolution in logistic capability that enabled Allied navies to uphold and for the first time sustain control of the sea during dynamic intensive and prolonged operations. The transformation from a relatively simple logistic doctrine that relied upon a network of bases during the interwar period into the sophisticated and complex mosaic that was extraordinary for both its pace and versatility was nevertheless achieved in a remarkably unstructured fashion. An entirely new logistics philosophy was born out of World War II, some of it developed from first principles, much of it through bitter experience and expediency. Yet perhaps the problem after 1945, particularly for the U.S. Navy, was that wartime logistics had proved itself to be effective rather than efficient. Peacetime constraints, however, would demand both.

Yet, the fundamental driving force behind a policy that demanded logistic superiority was once described by Admiral King: "Naval accomplishments in this mechanized age are dependent upon production. The best officers and men can do little without an adequate supply of the highly specialized machinery of warfare. Our guiding policy is to achieve not mere adequacy, but overwhelming superiority of material, thereby ensuring not only victory, but early victory with the least possible loss of American lives."[1]

How naval forces were subsequently prioritized, harnessed, and ultimately deployed during World War II were subject to many variables including opportunity, cost, flexibility, distance, sustainability, threat level, and political imperative. All, however, created some form of logistic challenge, and although events often determined both their pace and nature, improvisation or sheer grind usually resolved them. The logistic tasks, whether related to personnel, materials, or services, had certain common elements that could conveniently be categorized as identification and planning, production and procurement, and distribution to the theater of operations. Production and procurement typically comprised staff functions governed by civilian control, whereas planning and distribution remained essentially military prerogatives. But, as Duncan Ballantine wrote in his seminal work on U.S. naval logistics, often quoted by authors on the same subject, "As the link between the war front and the home front, the logistic process is at once the military element in the nation's economy and the economic element in its military operations."[2]

In the early stages of the Pacific War, successful distribution was hampered by the rapidly changing operational/strategic conditions that forced logistic support to be constantly modified. This was exacerbated by inadequate planning or even the data to establish the right framework for a flexible distribution system to the fleet at sea. As Admiral King noted, by the third year of war, "War production had shifted the emphasis from procurement to distribution; that is, while production was still of high importance, a still greater problem was that of getting well balanced materiel support to designated positions at certain fixed times."[3] To what extent did each navy absorb in peacetime the lessons raised by their wartime logistics experience to help them be better prepared and organized for conducting the next war? This will be addressed on two levels, first at the policy level by analyzing whether a more disciplined approach was achievable in the planning process to provide a fresh sense of order and pattern to the role of logistics. In other words, could future challenges be better recognized, prepared for, and resolved by having a more integrated approach within the operational and strategic echelons of both navies? Second, this chapter will gauge the prospects for a more permanent change in culture by looking through the prism of naval education at whether the relevance of logistics became more inculcated among each navy's future leaders—particularly those British and American officers attending the logistics courses introduced after the War at the Naval War College (NWC) in Rhode Island. Finally, a look is taken at how each navy adapted its organizational administration to accommodate the logistic lessons from the past to be better prepared for the challenges of the future.

Perception and Image

> I don't know what the hell this "logistics" is that Marshall is always talking about, but I want some of it.
> —Fleet Admiral Ernest J. King USN[4]

This alleged quotation of Fleet Admiral King has often been cited whenever the subject of logistics arises. In a way, it is rather disheartening to discover the most senior operational commander of the U.S. Navy admit he knew nothing about logistics. In truth, of course, he did. When he was reluctantly commanding the decrepit supply ship *Bridge* in 1921, he regarded logistics, as did most officers of the time, to be "too dull and tedious." Indeed, according to his biographer, King wanted to leave *Bridge* and "anything else relating to logistics as soon as possible."[5] The implication was that logistics was of minor importance to the war-fighting commander and should only be delivered somehow by a staff subordinate whenever it was needed. Many other great American admirals of the wartime era, including Nimitz, Spruance, and Conolly, had also, as Rear Admiral Furer put it "flirted with logistics enough in their early careers to benefit greatly from their experience later on." These officers, he noted, were nevertheless careful "not to get identified too glaringly with materiel."[6] But for many years, line naval officers in the U.S. Navy referred to logistics duty as the "kiss of death" despite, as Admiral Carney reflected, "the extra stars [that] have gone to logistical jobs" with extra promotion spots awarded to logistics experts over the years. To him, and many others, logistics was "still not accorded the respect that it should receive."[7]

But logistics in many ways had a poor reputation throughout the postwar decade because by its very nature it had to embrace a mass of technical administrative detail that could obscure the fundamental principles. It was still too often seen one dimensionally as a supply function rather than an integral element of dynamic strategic planning. This aversion and the reasons for it were not confined to the U.S. Navy. One reason why logistics officers were a scarce commodity in the Royal Navy, according to one admiral who had been heavily involved in logistics planning during World War II, was because the British term for logistics planners was "administrative planner" with all the bureaucratic connotations that this implied.[8]

Twenty-three years after Admiral King had first flirted with logistics, the exigencies of war would replace earlier peacetime expediency, but King was now so preoccupied by grand strategy that he very much left logistical planning to others.[9] Still, after three hard years of fighting, he was compelled to observe, "The War has been variously termed a war of production and a war of machines. Whatever else it is, so far as the United States is concerned, it is a war of logistics."[10]

A common American perspective after the war was indeed that "logistics assured victory in [both world wars] but the logistics way of war has always been the American way."[11] This postwar perception of logistics, sometimes referred to as "the logistics of plenty" very much reflected the American way of war, just as mass production had become the American way of life.

Logistics: A Definition

It is difficult to agree on a precise definition of logistics because it appears to be more of an art rather than a science, with some suggestions attempting to reflect the minutiae while others remain too vague to move the debate forward. One of the most succinct definitions, which also became the standard at the Naval War College, was Thorpe's: "Strategy provides the scheme of utilizing our forces, and Logistics provides the means therefor."[12] Rear Admiral Eccles' postwar definition, however, added a key dynamic when he defined it as "the provision of the physical means by which power is exercised by organized forces. In military terms, it is the creation and sustained support of combat forces and weapons. Its objective is maximum sustained combat effectiveness.[13] This is particularly significant for its last sentence. Logistics was not a one-event exercise in the art of supply. It was a much more complex problem that required an ability to provide and deliver over a protracted period at the choosing of the force commander the full armory of supplies required by naval forces to—and this is the key—to *sustain* the conduct of war in a dynamic environment. Achieving maximum sustainability, however, risked being compromised if the combat force was not properly balanced to the logistical force supporting it. Put another way, because economic capacity limits the creation of combat forces and logistic capabilities limit how these can actually be deployed, both therefore determine the limitations of any strategy.[14] For the purposes of this chapter, strategy is defined as "the comprehensive direction of power to control situations and areas in order to attain broad objectives or aims."[15] It is, in other words, primarily concerned with objectives. Tactics represent the immediate direction of power toward achieving said objectives, entailing the employment of specific forces weapons and techniques, including those related to specific mobile logistic operations. However, the strategic and tactical plans of all naval commanders are limited by only two factors that concern us here. First, by the logistic support made available to them, and second, by their skill in utilizing it. The degree of control over the amount and quality of the available logistic support could vary for a variety of reasons, including the nature and level of organization and their command. But the skill with which they utilize such support, subject, of course, to its own inherent limitation, would determine the practical limits of their strategic and tactical plans.

While most of the lessons ultimately bear on how logistic support can be improved upon, the need for inculcating among the officer class of both navies a more sophisticated understanding for how such support should actually be utilized was vital. It was therefore suggested that progress could best be achieved by promoting its relevance more effectively through the academic curriculum for those young officers attending the various military colleges. This required, among other things, a better understanding of the context for the role of logistics by establishing some underlying principles that could best be found by looking at the lessons discovered from recent experience.

Logistic Lessons from World War II

A significant contributor to the U.S. Navy's logistic success in the Pacific was that the Japanese never realized the importance, or the relative vulnerability, of the U.S. logistic forces and supply lines. The United States, therefore, had three major advantages. First, there was time to build up and prepare forces and equipment. Second, the sheer scale of the Pacific meant that the homeland was not really vulnerable to attack, let alone invasion. Third, bases in the forward area were relatively immune from attack and, once consolidated, the U.S. Navy was able to concentrate vast forces and support facilities with virtual impunity. As a result, the United States achieved both control of the sea and air superiority. However, there are two points to stress. First, a future war may not have any "grace period" in which to prepare and build up support forces. Second, with the advent of more modern weapons and technology, particularly fast submarines and eventually jet aircraft, all these advantages in both time and immunity, whether in the forward areas or at home, could no longer be taken for granted. No assumptions could be made that history would repeat itself.

While it was also recognized after the war that some of the earlier logistic deficiencies were caused by the failure to apply properly what was already known, this should have come as no surprise. There were whole areas where both navies were limited by their imperfect knowledge of the art and science of logistics or even of where its proper place was in their respective military organizations and plans. The crux of the problem for both was that as the war progressed, so the character of logistic support changed profoundly. With everything still relatively new and with little organizational precedent, there was no consensus on what to expect. In peacetime, with the exigencies of war no longer dictating the pace or direction of change, the opportunity for a better understanding of how logistics should apply within the broader scheme of things was there to be grasped. Yet many factors influenced how each navy went about identifying, collating, and acting on such lessons, and not all of them were due to the difference in their capabilities.

Some of the differences in perspective were fairly obvious, such as the relative scale in fleet size, wealth, power, complexity, geographic spread, and time. Others were cultural, such as the different style of command and reporting from theater operations to London or Washington, combined with the way these were then disseminated to experts or officials for comment. Generally, British recommendations from theater chiefs, primarily utilized through their "Reports of Proceedings" or "Reports of Experience," tended to be relatively succinct and yet strategically and tactically all-encompassing. Subsequent analysis within a centralized Admiralty, typically through the circulation of docketed files, became relatively immediate, inclusive, and above all transparent. American operational reporting, by contrast, had to cope with an organization of much greater scale and geographic spread. This handicap, together with American preference for compartmentalized and often autonomous command structures, tended to demand the adoption of a more formalized approach to disseminating information. Both navies could consequently arrive at different solutions at different times for solving the shared predicament.

One particularly outstanding, if perhaps self-evident, lesson of wartime logistics was that logistic mistakes often do not become evident until sometime
after they are made, which usually meant they could not be corrected quickly. It
was therefore inevitable that for both the Royal Navy and U.S. Navy the words
"improvisation" or "extemporization," became synonymous with any logistic
exercise, and this applied no less at the highest levels of command.

Postwar evaluation within the Admiralty of the BPF's experience in 1945
suggested at many levels the need to learn lessons, many articulated in Admiral
Fraser's lengthy report in March 1946 that provided an historical account of its
activities together with an analysis of the operational, logistic, and technical lessons identified. From this evidence were derived a comprehensive series of recommendations "for a Fleet conducting Ocean Warfare" so planners faced with a
similar undertaking in the future might benefit.[16] Incorporated for the first time
also were staff requirements for various types of necessary auxiliary ships and
recommendations for ensuring that appropriate facilities and personnel were
allocated to the various functional headquarters. As the Admiralty's Director of
Plans was to note, the History of the Fleet Train was "a chronicle of learning by
bitter experience and overcoming difficulties and deficiencies.... The Fleet Train
has undoubtedly come to stay as an integral part of the post-war navy. It would
be folly not to hand to posterity the lessons learned in the hard school of which
this report contains so much evidence."[17] Unfortunately, as will become evident
later, the combination of massive economic stricture, widespread demobilization, and changes of perspective in force vulnerability all contributed to a state
of flux that ultimately affected the outcome of many of Fraser's Fleet Train recommendations. Indeed, within months the Director of Plans was obliged to re-
iterate that "it is imperative that the lessons learned in the recent war in regard to
mobility be embodied in all aspects in the post-war fleet. There are already some
signs that more importance is being attached in word than in deed to the future
of the Fleet Train."[18] Yet in general terms it must be remembered that much of
what was accomplished logistically in World War II happened out of necessity,
whereas in peacetime financial constraints invariably impose a choice. While
history might arguably not repeat itself, this doesn't detract from trying to de-
rive from experience some appropriate principles about logistics that, if properly applied, could provide a more enlightened context for resolving the myriad
of logistic challenges that could arise either in peacetime or, more particularly,
in war. What follows is a survey of some key lessons drawn by either or both navies that became fused into practical doctrine development or at least helped to
define some of these principles.

Command

One of the most significant lessons for both navies was that the Task Force leader
must have control of his logistic support to ensure proper harmonization and re-

sponsiveness.[19] U.S. practice ensured that logistics command was colocated with the task force commander, so control in these circumstances was more certain. For the British, this had not been the case either at sea or even within Australia. Its detrimental effect upon efficiency had later caused the Admiralty's Director of Plans (Q) to stress "the importance of co-ordination of operations and logistics, together with the great advantage of having operational and administrative staff at a common HQ."[20]

The transition to a peacetime economy, however, presented a number of logistic challenges for military leaders, some arising for the first time. For example, one of the consequences resulting from such a short history of logistics experience was the growing pattern of uncertainty within both British and American commands as to what was the nature and degree of control that military commanders should now exercise in peacetime over their logistic support; for them, "where did centralization of authority enhance combat efficiency or where did it detract from effectiveness?"[21] The logistics concepts derived from a defensive strategic approach, moreover, are usually inadequate for supporting large-scale offensive operations that tend to produce an entirely different set of problems for which different solutions needed to be found. At the Alliance level too, a different challenge could arise, whether at the practical or political level, because what might work for American forces might not be appropriate for European forces, or vice versa. Either way, logistics cannot be looked at in isolation; it has to be integral to the circumstances.

Planning

The need for integration was equally applicable to the logistical planning process. As Rear Admiral Eccles put it, "Logistics plans are so vital—so ambient—so all-pervasive, that they can be considered to be the common denominator of all plans."[22] Trying to achieve the right balance between the extremes of overplanning or under-planning was nevertheless haphazard at best. This was particularly so for the U.S. Navy in the very early days of the war, with the uncertainties and hand-to-mouth strategy covering immense areas of operation, all of which combined to make it impossible to establish a fixed pattern of activity for logistics.[23] To cope, planners needed to be given firm guidance and accurate information, but as Ballantine pointed out, "Logistic requirements must be determined in the light of strategic aims, and for that purpose logistic planners must have firm guidance and accurate information as to strategic plans. Yet for almost half the war [U.S.] logistic planners lacked the information essential to their task."[24] As a result, American strategic and logistic planning was often confused, with much of the high-level planning defaulted to the bureaus, that is, the procurers. Nor did the CNO's official historian disagree. To him "the Navy did a splendid job of producer logistics during the war although there was more waste than necessary because the basic planning in CNO was crude and amateurish."[25]

The stark reality was, however, that by early 1943 only the Americans were giving much thought to the logistical ramifications in defeating Japan, yet even they had "entered the Pacific campaign with no clear understanding of the function of logistic planning and with even less organization to perform it."[26] Later in 1943, as the Admiralty began to consider plans for moving forces to the Far East, it too faced a daunting task exacerbated by the lack of experience or understanding, let alone doctrine, on what mobile logistic support entailed given their previous reliance on naval bases in the region. Task force operations at sea, for prolonged periods in large force beyond a thousand miles from fixed bases, had been rare.[27] Consequently, logistics was less integrated into the planning process with the result that, as described previously, for the BPF there was undue reliance placed upon improvisation, perseverance, or a quiet helping hand from the Americans in theater. As Rear Admiral Fisher, commander of the BPF Fleet Train, was to confide privately to Admiral Fraser, "If I were to make any remarks about the part played by the Plans Division (Q) in their planning of requirements for logistic support of the BPF, I would have to write on asbestos. I feel that the entire BPF has needlessly suffered a lot."[28]

Not surprisingly, therefore, the Admiralty's postwar recommendations on planning focused more on the time needed to build up infrastructures to avert a breakdown in logistics.[29] Three important themes about planning come through in these various reports. First, that planning "is no good without unity of purpose and rapid executive decision making."[30] Second, an establishment of personnel, material, and shipping for fleet bases should be drawn up and included in the war plan for each contingency.[31] Third, and in some senses the most important yet most difficult to fulfill, a margin must be kept over minimum requirements in both personnel and material to ensure continuous efficient operation. Any augmentation of the fleet train, in other words, should at least be directly proportional to the planned augmentation of the battle fleet. All three themes had much to commend them. Yet for too long and for various reasons all three were seemingly ignored.

In peacetime there existed an additional complication for planners. When forecasting future needs, the dilemma of what to do with surplus resources was twofold. Would it be better to stockpile equipment or place ships in reserve where they would likely deteriorate unless properly preserved, or should everything be kept up to date at considerable expense (both economically and politically) for immediate use in the event of war suddenly breaking out? Yet this dilemma, as it transpired, was in fact only half the problem; unlike in wartime, the availability of funds became so tight that the real question for planners became whether it was more practical or economic to scrap or sell parts of the reserve fleet instead. Chapter 6 explores this issue in depth because it has a direct bearing on the qualification and availability of auxiliaries identified for future mobilization.

There is, however, a direct analogy between the accumulation of ships or materiel and preparing logistic plans. Both, even if they are obsolete, risk giving planners a false sense of security if only because they happen to exist. It is also important to remember that during wartime security considerations could make the "untrammeled interchange of ideas" between the strategists and the logistic planners impossible, given the natural tendency for bureaucracies, particularly American, to work in watertight departments.[32] The evidence, in fact, suggested that strategists, often in their attempt to retain flexibility, were asking too little rather than too much from logisticians. In peacetime, though, planning imposed fewer limitations, less pressure, and more time so efficiency was actually rarely tested. Even the need for closer relationships between the strategists and logisticians could, if not watched, fall back once again to the prewar tendency on both sides of the Atlantic, which was to marginalize all logistic implications at the altar of the more exciting strategic or tactical imperatives. As a result, when World War II broke out, both navies had had few logisticians who could envisage anything beyond purely operational or procurement/supply logistics.[33] This lacuna was, and remained, as much a cultural issue as a practical one; we shall later be looking at what steps were subsequently taken by both navies to avoid such a vacuum of misunderstanding occurring again.

Logistics Infrastructure

Developing an effective logistics administration in war for any navy was invariably difficult because its inherent function attracts all the urgency and unpredictability that war implies. This is quite distinct from the logistics of peace, which tends to be more foreseeable, quantitatively certain, and therefore relatively efficient to manage. For example, fleet exercises were governed by the amount of fuel authorized by government, storage was not a problem, repairs could be conducted in port, and most sea transportation was provided by commercial means. Eventually the U.S. Navy Department recognized in 1942 that the United States was fighting a logistics war that transcended all branches and bureaus of the Navy. Yet it had become too decentralized with no central authority to be effective. This realization led to one of the most important reorganizations of the war, the creation in 1943 of the Logistics Planning Division (OP-12) under the CNO, outlined in appendix K. Appendix L shows where it was placed under an assistant CNO within the CNO hierarchy.[34] Regarded by Eccles as "a wise measure of great importance," this realignment resulted in a greater coordination of strategic and logistic planning in Washington because of its links to the Joint Chiefs of Staff (JCS) organization and Joint Logistics Committee, all conveniently located in Washington.[35]

The problem had been that the bureau system adopted by the U.S. Navy in 1842 to implement the logistic process of the Navy Department had proved deeply entrenched but ill equipped to handle the heavy fleet consumer demands within the CNO infrastructure. So the Navy Department's ability to plan and de- termine logistic requirements was undermined by its lack of authority or organi- zation. This came to a head only when the growing logistical problems created during 1943, particularly those pertaining to maintenance and replenishment, required urgent resolution. From this crisis evolved the post of deputy CNO for Logistics which entailed close collaboration with all the bureaus but also, most importantly, improved collaboration with the strategic planners (shown in ap- pendix M).[36]

The Admiralty, too, was to discover within two years from the start of World War II that it was equally ill equipped to manage properly the logistic require- ments of its wartime fleets beyond home waters. According to Rear Admiral Hughes-Hallett, the "old" days were over when logistics was exclusively handled by the directors of Stores and Victualling between them. The most significant change to come out of this was the creation of the Directorate of Administrative Planning with a dual responsibility, officially to the Vice CNS, on the one hand, but unofficially to every other member of the Admiralty Board, on the other. The Directorate was "the channel for ensuring that logistic requirements arising from operational plans were made known to the supply and design departments in plenty of time."[37] In fact, the Directorate was two-way because not only did it interpret the logistic needs of operational plans but, with the help of the design and supply departments, it would also assess the implication of future plans pro- duced by the operations. This balance was not an easy one, with some depart- ments determined to apply their own high-level planning criteria to operations rather than the other way around. But then, as has been said before, in war logis- tics largely consists of the allocation of shortages.[38] If production capacity and shipping were short—which was typically the case—it was for the logistic plan- ners and staff officers to assess the relative priorities. Therefore, they needed to be involved from the beginning—although half of the problem, consistent with American experience, was simply finding enough experienced officers to under- take the task.

Home Bases versus Afloat Support

The logistic characteristics of naval forces themselves have an important bear- ing on how plans are developed for their deployment. Large naval forces have in- herent logistic endurance when they put to sea after replenishing from any base, typically with enough food for 60–90 days and enough fuel to cruise at moder- ate speeds for 5,000–15,000 miles, with the smaller ships topped up when nec- essary by the larger ones. Naval logistic support, conversely, generally came in three categories—underway replenishment, afloat support, and advanced bases. As with combat forces, there was considerable interchangeability, but whereas replenishment forces were normally limited in type to oilers, stores ships, ammunition ships, carriers, seagoing tugs, and salvage vessels, the concept of afloat support was wider, to include a huge assortment of tenders, repair ships, transports, dry docks, tugs, barges, distilling ships, and so on. Advanced bases, conversely, were by their nature more static and required time and transportation to set up; once running, they could handle elastic demand relatively effectively. Perhaps the most classic conundrum that World War II produced for postwar naval logistic research, the relative advantages between mobility and fixed advanced bases, remained unaddressed for a long time thereafter and was proof, if such was needed, of the complete lack of systematic research conducted in peacetime on this and most other related logistic challenges.

Any attempts to compare the relative merits between these two choices must take into consideration not just their operational efficacy and relative cost but also the degree of politico-economic comfort to be derived from the stability or security attached to either method. Neither Britain nor the United States necessarily faced the same logistical problems simultaneously, whether geographically, economically, politically, or militarily, so what might have worked for one may not have necessarily worked for the other. Yet inherent in either choice was the fundamental logistic principle, that each "should be in harmony with both the economic system of the country concerned and with the combat and operational concepts of its military forces."[39] Trying to reconcile the financial and practical consequences for retaining such mobility was nevertheless difficult. For many officers, logistics had represented a relatively static concept concerned only with bases and supply departments but the Pacific War challenged both navies to become more flexible and mobile. The question for them now was to what degree they could afford or need to be so mobile in the future. Advanced bases for undertaking war damage and repairs were surely no longer so relevant for peacetime ship maintenance. This debate would come to influence attitudes and priorities for the years ahead, no less when it came time to determine what type of naval logistic support was appropriate before, during, and after the Korean War. For this reason, chapter 5 explores why this had such significant ramifications, not only on choosing the appropriate policy underpinning how logistic support should be applied but also its effect upon auxiliary ship design as a consequence.

Achieving a Balanced Fleet

Most of the past failures to achieve a balance between combat and support forces reflected, at the command level, either a lack of good logistic planning or an unwillingness to devote adequate resources or talent to address the underlying problem. But experience had also shown that unless checked, logistic activities tended to grow out of all proportion to the tactical forces they were originally designed to support. Often what happened was that, having underplanned for a particular event or campaign, the immediate unsatisfied demand forced planners to overreact such that the risk of "snowballing"—whereby excesses occur at the mature end of build-ups as the relationship of movement between supply and the front gets out of kilter—becomes a problem that can get out of control.[40]

This tendency has a direct bearing on the relative balance and disposition of the "teeth" and "tail" in any operation, so how logistic forces are made available, as well as whether they were of the right size or mix, are important considerations for achieving maximum sustained support. Chapter 2 explained that British planners were obliged by Churchill to calibrate the size of the BPF combat force around the type and shape of supporting fleet train that could be mustered, given the competing demands upon the few available merchant hulls. Certainly, both navies struggled to establish the correct proportion between "teeth" and "tail," and for Rear Admiral Eccles, determining the proper ratio was "one of the most perplexing problems which high command must decide."[41] Rear Admiral Furer, writing the history of the U.S. Navy Department in World War II, criticized the failure to include in interwar naval shipbuilding programs sufficient types and numbers of auxiliary ships "to provide the necessary logistic support for the operating forces in any war."[42] With such an inadequate understanding of the magnitude of the logistic task ahead, when war eventually intruded, the U.S. Navy "grossly underestimated the proportion of forces that needed to be devoted to logistics."[43]

Although the Americans had not suffered to the same extent as the British in having their operational fleet constrained by the available logistic system, most of the failure to achieve an appropriate balance was considered by many to be owed to the lack of appreciation for the effects of increasingly complex weapons and platform technology that produced ever-increasing demands upon logistic support. One is reminded that toward the end of 1944 some 80 percent of logistic supplies to U.S. naval forces overseas were maintenance items.[44]

Tactical Dimension

Earlier chapters have shown World War II to have been the undoubted catalyst for progressing mobile logistics doctrine in general, and underway replenishment in particular, to new levels of complexity and proficiency. Yet logistic support suffered from poor organization partly because initially "cast off officers were ordered into it" until late 1944 when, according to Eccles, the need for "first class officers for logistic work . . . really began to sink in."[45] In terms of overall performance, though, the Service Force delivered. The most revolutionary development, enabling fleets to remain engaged by being replenished under way from Service Squadron Six, was the tipping point, recognized by its official historian who averred that "complete logistic support at sea has become a fact; it was no longer theory. The endurance of the fleet at sea was limited only by battle damage, human and mechanical endurance."[46] Apart from the huge but perhaps unsurprising demand for oilers, the other more unexpected discovery was the insatiable demand for salvage and rescue tugs.[47] With these valuable resources, however, most damaged warships including battleships could be repaired using floating dry docks rather than having the costly diversion of trekking back to the U.S. mainland or even being abandoned. The fast-changing circumstances in the Pacific, particularly during the final period of the War from late 1944, forced many new techniques and equipment to be introduced for the first time to cope with the ever-increasing levels of complexity for replenishing ships at sea. While chapter 3 described how this was accomplished in practice, chapter 7 explores how postwar tactical doctrine was further refined as a result of postwar trials and additional wartime experience in Korea.

Design

Undoubtedly, the advent of fleet trains introduced a rich source of new ship types and designs for the auxiliary fleets of both navies. Many were built for a specific purpose, such as salvage and repair, floating dock, or aircraft transports. Others, such as cargo and stores ships, were usually modified from civilian general cargo hulls. For the U.S. Navy, these at least reflected naval specification, were naval manned, and were often armed. Most of the hulls, too, were relatively young, although the increasing demands placed on the fleet train as the war progressed required many to be further modified to cope with the volumes and transfer frequency required.

For the British fleet train, very few ships were either naval or single-purpose designed, which meant, for example, that the tankers and fleet issue ships had to be modified beforehand, in some cases significantly, to perform their mission. Even then, from the moment they arrived they proved—more often than not—to be inefficient, too slow and constantly in need of repair.[48] In Admiral Fraser's report of the BPF Fleet Train experience, recommendations addressed various operational and design deficiencies that, if heeded, would at least avoid any repetition.[49] Included were extremely ambitious postwar operating parameters for "The Ideal Fleet Issue" ships as well as "The Ideal Tanker" equipped to replenish under way at 15 knots, with a whole range of petroleum products as well as limited quantities of ammunition and provisions.[50] Here, though, was the genesis of the most important challenge confronting Allied auxiliary design in the postwar era: the requirement for more speed. Although good cruising speeds had been an important consideration for planning replenishment rendezvous during the Pacific War (thereby reducing task force "downtime"), the other reason for seeking higher speeds—to avoid submarine attack—was never actually put to the test. However, it could not be assumed that this would remain the case in future; chapter 5 explores how this risk influenced future auxiliary ship design.

Education: Naval War College and Rear Adm. Henry Eccles, USN

It was proposed earlier that looking through the prism of how each navy educated its officers in the theory and science of logistics might provide insight into the prevailing culture and appetite for adopting a more disciplined approach toward absorbing the logistics lessons coming out of World War II. Given that the initiative for closer integration of logistics with strategic and operational planning was predominantly cultivated within the U.S. Navy, it seems most appropriate to focus on the one person more than any other who helped to promote its relevance to officers in the early postwar period: Rear Adm. Henry Eccles, USN.

Known as the "grand old man of naval logistics," Henry Eccles spent the last forty years of his life studying, teaching, consulting, and writing in this "vital but unglamorous field."[51] He died in 1986 leaving a legacy that has enriched both navies by helping them to recognize that the science of naval logistics played a vital role in any successful military strategy. Having spent much of World War II involved in logistics both at sea and ashore, Eccles served in 1946 on the Joint Operations Review Board tasked with analyzing World War II military operations. Logistics remained very much his expertise throughout his postwar career, particularly after he was assigned in 1947 to the Naval War College, Newport, Rhode Island, charged with organizing and heading up the newly constituted Logistics Department. During the next three and half years, he lectured on logistics, organized the curriculum and logistics library, and wrote his first book, a pioneering work described by the president of the NWC as "devoted to the thesis that while we must expect to make new mistakes in the logistics of a future war, we should not repeat the old ones."[52] The object was to challenge readers to find cheaper and more efficient ways to support military operations.

In 1951 Henry Eccles left the NWC for a dual assignment as Admiral Carney's assistant chief of staff Logistics for CinCNELM and NATO command in Naples (CinCSOUTH) before retiring as rear admiral in June 1952. His four years at the NWC had witnessed a period of rapid turnover, with three college presidents and four chiefs of staff during which time he had been able to build the foundations of a logistics school in spite of the shortage of both funds and key personnel throughout this period.[53] He returned to Newport, and, although not formally employed by the NWC, he continued to lecture and serve as adviser to the college presidents. Among his many professional friends was Dr. Duncan Ballantine, who by then taught at the Massachusetts Institute of Technology and wrote his seminal book on World War II naval logistics while still working at the historical section of the CNO.

In 1956, Eccles returned with his wife to Europe and spent some time in the United Kingdom discussing logistics issues with various British friends, including the Liddell Harts, with whom he and his wife stayed as guests, as well as Royal Navy alumni who had attended his courses at the NWC. His reputation as an authority on the subject of logistics was unchallenged, but one gets the sense from his personal correspondence (particularly when he was seeking a post in academia postretirement) that he could be quite opinionated and single-minded.[54] Eccles meanwhile remained a consultant to the George Washington University Logistics Research project and over the next twenty years produced three landmark works on logistics and military thought: *Logistics in the National Defense* (1959), *Military Concepts and Philosophy* (1965), and *Military Power in a Free Society* (1979).

Theory to Date

The use of the single term "logistics" to denote the broad field of planning and implementation to enable naval warfare strategy or tactics to work seems to have been formally recognized for the first time in a lecture by Cdr. C. T. Vogelsang at the NWC during its 1911 Summer conference.[55] His writing has remained essential reading for all logistics students ever since.[56] However, it was another former graduate and staff member who provided the first valuable insight into the relevance of logistic principles to war in general. In 1917 Lt. Col. Cyrus Thorpe of the U.S. Marine Corps wrote an excellent little book titled *Pure Logistics: The Science of War Preparation*. This initial attempt to develop theory and principle apparently attracted little or no attention until five copies were discovered in the library of the NWC in 1945. Since then many students have pondered how much time and money could have been saved if only some of Thorpe's ideas had been grasped before 1941.[57] The question in its broader sense was also one being asked by the Navy Department as the war drew to a close. Thus were sown the seeds for investigating further how those officers being prepared for higher command could be introduced to both logistic theory and practice, as well as their collective relationship to strategy and tactics. What was needed was a way of taking officers beyond the prosaic aspects of supply and distribution that had so often characterized the function of logistics across both navies.

Naval War College Logistic Courses

As demobilization from World War II ended and reorganization of the armed forces started, it soon became apparent that their educational systems also needed overhauling. New joint colleges were established alongside single-service establishments with the recognition that the study of logistics needed more emphasis. In the U.S. Navy, any integrated study had been virtually ignored until 1946 when the U.S. Navy School (General Line) and the Navy Supply Corps School first introduced logistic courses, followed a year later by courses at the NWC.

Logistics in some form had been taught at the NWC since 1914, but only in very general terms, as part of a broader reading program embracing policy strategy and tactics. By the mid 1920s, a Logistics Division was established that combined naval and national logistics into one program, but given the breadth and complexity of the subject, it was subsumed under the Department of Intelligence in 1928 to reflect the growing awareness of the importance of the Western Pacific in naval policy. For a number of years thereafter, in line with the U.S. Navy's intensifying interest in battle fleet tactical maneuvers, the emphasis in logistics changed from the strategic to tactical employment of naval forces, with tactical proficiency becoming "a prime requisite for promotion." Consequently, planning and supply were relegated to "academic" interest only, a state of affairs that prevailed until shaken at the roots by the scale of effort required to meet the global threat of World War II.[58] A great deal was learned during World War II because at the beginning "the Navy knew little about National logistics, little about planning long overseas campaigns and little about organizing to obtain the most efficient coordination with the other services."[59] As Eccles was to record later, "While the naval officer may intuitively have known much about sound logistic practice, he knew nothing at all of its theory and he was deficient in his understanding of the interdependence of logistic matters and in his knowledge of overall logistic planning and organization."[60]

At the close of World War II, an urgent Navy Board committee headed by Rear Adm. R. E. Jennings was convened by CNO King to study the question of logistics training for naval officers and to make recommendations for establishing a school, including the location, course duration, and curriculum.[61] It was generally recognized that despite the contribution logistics played during the last war, "the science of naval logistics had been neglected and that an appreciation of its importance was lacking." Furthermore, the committee felt that "the increased importance of scientific and industrial developments and the necessity of waging modern warfare at a long range over vast areas has enhanced the importance of logistics to the point where it can no longer be taken for granted but, rather, must be considered a science to which continuous study must be devoted."[62] A number of important recommendations were made that had far-reaching implications. Although the precept from the CNO sought recommendations for establishing a new institution devoted exclusively to logistics, the committee concluded this "was not desirable." After all, "the responsibility of command carries with it the responsibility for logistics, and a commander cannot divest himself of that responsibility."[63] Preparation and execution of logistic plans were therefore not exclusively either a Line or Staff function. They were both, and this interdependence needed to be recognized. Formal logistics training was therefore to be blended progressively into officers' training courses from an early stage, using existing schools at the Naval Academy and NWC. At the end of the report was a separate (and uncalled for) supplementary recommendation to the effect that a Naval Logistics Institute "under the cognizance of the CNO and Chief of Naval Personnel" be set up separately to provide academically trained and experienced logisticians capable of conducting all aspects from the very highest level to the smallest fleet unit.[64] The report, known as the Jennings Board Report was eventually approved by the Secretary of the Navy on June 26, 1946, but the CNO subsequently appointed an ad hoc committee to follow up the supplementary recommendation regarding a number of recommendations for the establishment of the Logistic Research Institute.[65] However, according to Captain Eccles, both admirals Spruance and Carney agreed that establishing an independent school was "a very serious mistake and would tend to increase the cleavage between combat thinking and logistic thinking, with consequent failure of our senior officers to understand the *whole* art and nature of war."[66] After further consultation, it was decided to augment and expand the logistics section of the NWC, to be headed by a flag officer and, most importantly, ensure it received equal recognition by placing it alongside the School of Strategy and Tactics under the president of the College. On January 6, 1947 Admiral Nimitz, CNO, authorized the establishment and proposed outline and scope for the course to be staffed by a rear admiral supported by nine captains and commanders.[67] Three months later, Captain Eccles, who was commanding USS *Washington* at the time, was appointed to head the Logistics Department at the NWC, and within months the staff and materials were mobilized and preparations were in hand for getting the course under way.

Despite now being headed by a captain rather than a rear admiral, the course status was confirmed to be on a par with the other courses. This was important if it was to attract the caliber of officer required for both instructors as well as students. Its mission was "To provide a selected group of student officers from all branches of the armed services with a comprehensive course of instruction and study in the fundamentals of logistics, and their practical application in the prosecution of military campaigns, in order to further their understanding of the fundamentals of future Naval warfare."[68] Despite the acknowledged contribution that naval logistics had achieved in the successful prosecution throughout the Pacific, this recognition soon started to wane. Captain Pare, now commander of Service Squadron Two for the U.S. Atlantic Fleet, wrote to Eccles to commiserate upon the latter's recent involvement "in the unglamorous, thankless job of teaching logistics." He went on to say, "The *necessity* for the teaching is very great because my contacts with naval officers lead me to believe that not over 1% have anything but the vaguest idea where their fuel, food, ammunition etc come from. The rewards to you will be nil. . . . Why not become an aviator instead?"[69] But Eccles was undeterred. Although he too recognized that if this initiative failed, there was the risk the Navy might quickly lose its corporate memory, he nevertheless remained convinced that lessons must be learned and principles identified. To him, this could only be achieved through a more disciplined approach to understanding the theory as well as the practice. His conviction and the circumstances of his time remind one of the struggles which Julian Corbett endured, albeit using a much broader and influential canvas, in trying to inculcate into British naval officers the importance of "uncovering the principles that lay beneath the conduct of maritime operations."[70]

The scope chosen by Eccles was deliberately wide-ranging from broad principles illustrated from World War II, with their significance on modern warfare seen from different perspectives at department, area, theater, and operating force levels. To ensure this interdependent relationship was well understood, the ten-month logistics courses were from the beginning integrated as much as possible with the other senior and junior courses at the NWC for subjects like ship/weapons capabilities, task force dispositions, intelligence, and the like. As if to underpin this, Eccles wrote, "The principle of integration of Logistics and Strategy has been accepted as a fundamental that cannot be sacrificed."[71] He then extended this by having all logistics officers participate in major strategic problems such as mounting amphibious forces or supporting airborne invasions that were being addressed by the other classes so that they could become familiar with higher level logistical planning issues, interservice practice, and procedures as well as the broader aspects of military and industrial mobilization.[72] Although clearly the many lessons to be learned from the last war provided a substantial portion of the content of these courses, the focus was not exclusively directed at history. For example, the two required theses from each student (titled "A Comparison of the War Potential of the U.S.A. and the U.S.S.R." and "The Effects of New Weapons on Naval Logistics") were designed to focus their attention "upon our potential enemy and upon the problems with which logisticians will be faced in the next war."[73]

The first group of 46 students, including representatives from the U.S. Army, Marine Corps, Air Force, and Britain's Royal Navy reported for duty on July 1, 1947, a year ahead of the original plan, to avoid the anticipated cutback of available funds later. The 1948–49 intake expanded to 40 officers from the U.S. Navy, 2 Marine Corps, 8 Army and Air Force, 1 Coast Guard, and 2 British. As the president of the NWC was to note in his report, the continuation thereafter for having "officers from the British Navy as Logistics students is strongly recommended."[74] Over the next three years, 204 logisticians graduated including 6 from the Royal Navy.[75]

The relationship of the NWC to other military educational institutions was complementary rather than duplicated. The Industrial College was primarily considering problems of war mobilization while the National War College covered similar territory but also international affairs, military policy and major operational aspects. The Armed Forces Staff College emphasized the conduct and problems of joint operations in shorter five-month courses. The logistics courses at the NWC devoted less proportionate time to industrial mobilization but more than was undertaken at the Armed Forces College. Uniquely, the NWC would take naval problems, whether tactical or strategic, and try to simulate these using so-called maneuver boards, better known as war-gaming.[76]

In 1950 the course title was changed to Strategy and Logistics Course, with the core subject of strategy remaining unchanged but with the remaining emphasis settled on logistics rather than tactics.[77] In another sign that logistics was becoming an increasingly important aspect of modern warfare, a new correspondence course devoted to logistics was also introduced at this time, specifically designed to enable serving officers to become more proficient in answering comprehensive logistics questions that now formed part of their promotion examinations.[78]

Meanwhile, an enormous body of some three thousand documents covering wartime logistical experience and knowledge recorded in reports, handbooks, manuals, plans, and orders was transferred in June 1947 from the Logistics Research Library at the Navy Supply Corps School in Bayonne (out of some eighty thousand accessions). Together with other logistic material collected within the NWC, this transfer formed the nucleus of the new Logistics Library. Because most of this material was unpublished or in manuscript form, usually very technical and invariably unlogged or unprocessed, everything had to be urgently sorted, compiled, and registered. This was a formidable task exacerbated by the "deplorable shortage" of personnel to screen and evaluate accessions, or even operate the library reference service. Indeed, according to a report in 1950 undertaken at the request of the chiefs of staff, the project "seems to be going backward at an alarming rate" and its mission to provide a reference service "seems almost grotesque."[79] After such a promising start, this state of atrophy represented a sad reflection of changing priorities and lack of funds. But, as the NWC history book would record, "the heart of the college is the library; the college can thrive only as its library thrives; and to neglect the library is to invite the stultification of the whole educational effort for which the college exists."[80]

One of the fundamental requirements of the logistic program—the need for a basic reference textbook of logistic theory and principles—remained unfulfilled for nearly two years due to the pressure of work on the teaching staff. This was only resolved when Captain Eccles took this on as his summer project in 1949. It was published by the NWC as *Operational Naval Logistics*, so named because it "treated chiefly with the problems and considerations of logistic support of naval operating forces."[81] The first edition was available for the autumn intake the same year, and it was distributed widely throughout the U.S. Navy for comment. A modified and substantive limited edition with additional appendices was published in 1950, followed by a run of 13,500 copies the following year.

The idea of creating a formal logistics training course on a par with the more "popular" strategy and tactics disciplines, without specific appropriation was, in hindsight, both visionary and bold. As its founder ruefully noted, however, the logistics department was "started on a financial shoestring and a personnel shoestring. I was the only member of the Department with previous logistic planning experience, and therefore the Department had to feel its way, making many mistakes. It was frequently the case of the blind leading the blind."[82] If the lack of money and available qualified lecturers inhibited any improvement, there also prevailed a broader and in some senses deeper malaise across the general arena of naval education. Because no other military college was primarily concerned with sea power, the NWC was, in fact, the only location where problems of sea power and naval command could be studied objectively. Although it was important that the NWC impart ideas developed elsewhere, the NWC also had to retain for itself research facilities and staff to develop, coordinate, and exchange new ideas. A bold initiative was therefore adopted from the CNO directive of January 6, 1947 to set up a research and analysis division in the Department of Logistics alongside the Library. The problem was that, because the term "logistics" more or less touched on every possible aspect of naval activity, it was important to separate the technical or specialized logistic problems from those that cut across many lines. Understanding the nature and structure of logistics against this broad and very complex canvas was therefore a challenge. Defining with more precision the scope of the basic or pure research compared to applied logistic research could, it was thought, help at least address much of the confusion surrounding their respective relevance in the broader scheme of things.[83] But the lack of available qualified staff or financial support—that is, something beyond mere affirmation—resulted in little progress, even after two years.[84] With the fleets preoccupied in day-to-day problems and the Navy Department focused on budgets, war planning, and interservice politics, nobody would sponsor or undertake research. Seemingly, the original initiative had either run its natural course or run out of steam.

But in March 1950, the chief of Naval Research eventually approached the NWC to establish, de facto if not de jure, a joint venture for managing the Naval Research Logistics Program at George Washington University. This led to a number of exploratory logistics conferences at the Pentagon starting in December 1950 attended by representatives of those offices most associated with logistics, such as the Office of Naval Research, the Naval War College, the Chief of Naval Operations, the Bureau of Supplies and Accounts (BuSandA), and the Navy Supply School in Bayonne.[85] Their proceedings were subsequently published and to this day represent the core of early pure research in Naval Logistics, although the material is unfortunately quite difficult to locate.[86]

Beyond those particular documents about logistics that were produced or distributed by the U.S. Navy, the volume of historiography for this period is very modest. Not surprisingly, it was predominately American oriented, although Eccles was scathing about the growing number of civilian scholars influencing military strategy and organization, who "are completely ignorant of logistics" and either ignoring or, worse, incorrectly appraising key logistical factors. So far as he was concerned, "few logistic writers or commentators relate their work to concepts of war and strategy, therefore they lose the meaning of logistics."[87] Although there was indeed a considerable amount of literature dealing with the technical aspects of logistics at all levels, none provided any comprehensive analysis of the fundamental nature, influence, and principles of logistics, and only a few historical narratives incorporated logistics from the point of view of combat command.[88] Of these, Dr. Duncan Ballantine and Vice Adm. George Dyer have been quoted extensively and need no further comment here.

In trying to determine whether the NWC eventually succeeded in raising the profile of logistics among the officer corps, the fact that by 1954 the logistics faculty felt sufficiently confident to consolidate the logistics strategy and tactics course into one would suggest that the answer was yes. It was also acknowledged, at least internally, that when the logistics course was first established in 1947, logistics was "neither widely understood nor appreciated." Although still relatively new seven years later, its importance had nevertheless gained "service-wide acceptance and the necessity for including the appropriate logistic aspects in all phase of the NWC curriculum had become well established."[89]

War Games

The logistics course program for the first year, outlined in appendix N, enabled logistics students to be involved in four of the five major strategic problems then being addressed by the senior and junior classes, with particular attention given to the various logistics-related issues raised. About 20 percent of the curriculum was devoted to common basic studies, 17 percent to general background, 23 percent to special logistics, and 40 percent to "operations problems" that were logistical in nature. By applying a set of complex maneuver "rules" usually focused on mobility, a series of war games were devised in which the students were expected to address various institutional concerns, including for example a worry that "very little progress has been made" in improving the technique of resupply at sea since 1945.[90] Although the resultant replenishment-at-sea exercises were particularly comprehensive, they were nevertheless predicated—perhaps not surprisingly—on the doctrine prevailing back in 1945.[91] However, additional logistics subjects were introduced the following year, including Army and Air Force logistics, as well as logistic planning factors, international relations, and enemy logistic capabilities.[92] Thus, logistics-related issues expanded to a very respectable 63 percent of the whole curriculum.[93]

What was therefore quite encouraging for the reformers was that not only had the war games concept become a popular aspect of the NWC curriculum generally but the subject of logistics was taking on an increasingly dominant role in all the exercises.

Royal Navy Education, Training, Career, and Specialization

In 1947, during Admiral Spruance's presidency, the first British officers attended courses at the NWC, the first and only non-American officers since two Swedes and a Dane attended in 1894–95.[94] Thereafter, usually two or three British naval officers attended each year until 1951 when invitations were suddenly withdrawn "due to the introduction of atomic warfare studies into the curriculum."[95]

Overall, seven Royal Navy commanders or captains (including two supply officers) and one lieutenant commander(S) attended the logistics course, and a further seven commanders or captains attended the senior course.[96] One of the participants, Cdr. Horace Barnard, found the experience "fascinating, and we were treated with great courtesy." However, he did not believe the British contributed significantly to the understanding of logistics as "we were completely out of our depth as regards the scope and scale of the U.S. war effort." Nevertheless the NWC enjoyed "having the odd U.K. student but the relationship was— quite understandably—more in the nature of big brother to youngster."[97]

In contrast to the American experience, there exists little, if any, evidence to suggest that logistics was regarded within the Royal Navy as an educational issue for officers over and above the normal levels of practical training already available. The Royal Navy's Engineering College started an administrative course in 1947 under a commander (E) who adopted the unfamiliar title of commander (Q), designed to "provide mature officers with an insight into the problems of logistics and the administration of the provisioning of new equipment for the Service."[98] This would suggest that the focus was on administrative matters of supply and distribution at the unit level, rather than providing an introduction of how the science of logistics might fit into strategic and tactical thinking. In any event, the training courses, initially to warrant officers in 1944 and then newly promoted commissioned officers including engineers from 1949, ceased in 1954.[99] A further (Q) course was subsequently started by Vice Adm. D. B. H. Wildish in 1955 for all officers including those in supply, but again, this class was not inclined toward theory.[100] Tactical syndicate courses were also run for some time at the Royal Naval Tactical School in Woolwich, including a course on replenishment at sea that is discussed in more detail in chapter 7. The Royal Naval College at Greenwich organized a number of officer courses (similar to the strategy and tactics courses at the NWC) but only a very small element was allocated to logistic-related issues.[101]

Anglo-American Collaboration in Logistics

Given the relatively cool relationship that prevailed between the two navies prior to World War II, the logistic interrelationship of the U.S. Navy and Royal Navy in 1945 worked well on the whole, but it was always clear who was in charge. As the rear admiral commanding the BPF's fleet train lamented privately to Admiral Fraser in 1945 "I get awfully tired of being the poor relation."[102] Postwar, the overall relationship between both navies strengthened further and perhaps more evenly, partly due to wartime collaboration and partly to mutual interest—at least through the Korean War. This was particularly true in the realm of logistics where a number of examples will be cited later, ranging from replenishment ship design to having observers attend each other's replenishment exercises at sea.

The source for many of the close officer relationships that developed between the two navies after (rather than merely during) World War II can be directly traced to the increasing number of British officers attending courses at the NWC from 1947 onward. As the chairman of the RN/USN collaboration committee was to record, for example, valuable notes had been received from a Captain Briggs regarding American technical developments following his recent completion of the senior course at the NWC—the first British officer to do so.[103] Yet the Admiralty's concerns about whether their officers "were 'pulling their weight'" at the NWC courses surfaced occasionally, which prompted the president of the latter to respond that they were "happy to have them—and we appreciate the valuable suggestions they frequently have to offer."[104] Their attendance, however, did not influence British naval logistics policy when they returned to the United Kingdom, although this was not for the want of trying. Commander Acworth, RN, after graduating from the NWC logistics course in 1949, was appointed to Plans Division (Q) from where he wrote to Captain Eccles

> I have gone to Plans Division (Logistics) in the Admiralty. In that job I find my year at Newport is helping tremendously. It so widened my outlook. On the other hand, it makes me realize more and more how woefully lacking we are compared with the U.S. Navy in logistic thought as a *sine qua non* of strategic planning. Mowll [Lt Cdr Mowll (S) RN graduated from NWC logistics course 1948] and I, among others, are trying hard to persuade people to go into the sub-

ject far more than we do now; but it is a very slow process. I need your advice badly in this respect. Our Naval Staff College (your Senior & Junior course) devotes 8½ working days to logistics! I have been asked how best to use this fantastically short time to teach logistics.[105]

Although Eccles promised to send copies of the logistic planning factors and the "Naval Logistic Manual," he offered no suggestions other than offering himself as a consultant and recommending his book as the core of any course reading material![106] No record was found of whether the courses were ever initiated.

In addition to the regular exchange in operating manuals, naval dispatches, and lectures between the NWC and the Royal Navy's Staff College, Greenwich, the Admiralty remained keen to strengthen ties through more regular officer exchanges, not just as students but also as lecturers, which to date had been too one-sided. The U.S. Army and U.S. Air Force, for example, each had four officers assigned as instructors or students at the Staff Colleges at Camberley and Bracknell, respectively, but the occasional U.S. Navy students, assigned from CinCNELM, only attended short courses of less than one month because the five- month staff course at Greenwich was perceived by American staff officers as impracticable. A British proposition, transmitted to the CNO via CinCNELM in December 1949, suggested that each navy should exchange instructor officers between Greenwich and Newport, and the U.S. Navy should attach two officer students to Greenwich. While this was sympathetically supported by the NWC, provided both the British and American exchange instructors were graduates from the NWC course, nothing came of it.[107] It was not until 1969 that a formal link was established between the two colleges including an annual exchange of visits between the admiral president at Greenwich and the president of the NWC. Formal exchange of instructors came even later, with the initiation in 1974 of Vice Adm. Stanfield Turner, president of the NWC.[108]

Meanwhile, U.S. naval students selected for enrollment to the Imperial Defence College tended to be graduates from Washington's National War College, which had similar missions and courses. While the NWC believed that their own graduates—hitherto ignored—would be better prepared and more likely to gain a rounder experience if they were chosen instead, this does not appear to have been grasped.[109] At the end of 1948, the Admiralty reported that "It is of interest to note that during the period 1st July–31st December 1948 there were 166 U.S. Navy sponsored visitors to the U.K. as against 45 Royal Navy sponsored visitors to the U.S.A."[110] By 1950, however, the flow of British officers to U.S. military colleges had peaked with one captain at the National War College (equivalent to Staff College IDC), one captain at the Industrial College of the Armed Forces, and one captain, two commanders, and one Commander(S) at the NWC. In 1950, no more British officers were allowed by the U.S. government for what would appear to be two reasons. First, U.S. policy prohibited the release of restricted data on atomic energy to non-U.S. persons, and second, allowing British officers to attend courses risked opening the floodgates to all other NATO officers, which was deemed unacceptable. Despite assurances to the Americans from the First Sea Lord that officers could be withdrawn from sensitive lectures, neither he nor even the prime minister, could convince them to change their minds. Such exclusions like this really grated. The First Lord, for example, wrote to the Foreign Secretary, "We welcome them to everything we have to offer here; they treat us as acquaintances rather than close friends."[111] On being appraised of such strong resentment, Sir Oliver Franks, Britain's ambassador in the United States, drew a different conclusion. For him, the problem was simply that "Until we have cured our economic weakness they will not feel they have to listen and we shall get nowhere. The inequity which Mr Thomas has in mind is real and irritating but it reflects a general feature of our relationship with the United States which can only be removed in one way.[112]

Meanwhile, the exclusion of British officers at the National War College and NWC caused their respective directors to admit that their own students "are definitely the losers because they do not get the British point of view at first hand from fellow students as they used to."[113] This point is certainly corroborated by contemporary internal memoranda within the NWC itself, which was also concerned about reciprocity with the Imperial Defence College and the Royal Navy's Staff College at Greenwich, apart from the additional benefit of increased international flavor and prestige for the NWC. The drawbacks for having foreign attendees were partly administrative security matters but otherwise essentially political in nature.[114] The subsequent removal of the formalized Atomic Warfare Study from the curriculum in 1954, combined with the establishment of the Naval Command Course for Senior Free World officers two years later, presented the Royal Navy—along with some twenty-three other navies—the opportunity to send an officer once again to the NWC, but for reasons unrecorded, Britain chose to delay further participation until 1958.

This relative decline in the perceived value placed on closer Anglo-American links may not have hindered but certainly did not help to address the otherwise disappointing lack of any change within the Admiralty on how the role of logistics should be handled within the higher echelons of strategic and operational planning.

Postwar Organizational Structure for the Royal Navy and U.S. Navy

Despite their common logistic experience in 1945, the disparity thereafter between the U.S. Navy and Royal Navy became progressively more marked when it came to the emphasis that should be placed on the strategic role that logistics should command in any preparations for a future war.

Royal Navy: Admiralty Naval Staff

The slow evolutionary change in the role of the Admiralty Naval Staff since the early twentieth century was transformed by the size and scale of operations undertaken during World War II. Subsequent peacetime changes were more gradual, evolutionary, and less remarkable as a result, but its makeup and role were nevertheless subject to other broader domestic political agendas, not least the consideration to unify all three military services under one structure. The period of retrenchment post-1945 was as severe as it was inevitable, but through all this disruption the fundamental purpose of the Naval Staff remained unchanged, namely to support the First Sea Lord and Chief of Naval Staff (CNS) as the operational head of the Royal Navy. Hundreds of warships still remained deployed among the fleets worldwide, commanded by station flag officers or commanders-in-chief whose relevant staffs served afloat and were, from a communications perspective, dispersed and relatively autonomous. This demanded a central organization within the Admiralty that was not only capable of providing coordinated intelligence and direction but also flexible enough to manage the complex realignment of resources induced by demobilization. Thus, the wartime function of the deputy CNS, created to cope with the sheer volume of operational matters, was terminated in 1945 and the various directorates appropriately realigned to reflect the changed priorities. In many ways the structure actually settled back to its prewar configuration with a few additional new disciplines but with a much expanded air element.[115] The autumn of 1945 also saw a return to peacetime methods for the way naval estimates were prepared for the next fiscal year, with expenditure proposals channeled through the proposer's supervising lord and the secretary. The finance committee would then examine these and prepare an annual department estimate whose total would be the subject of discussion between the First Lord and the chancellor of the Exchequer before submission to Parliament.

Further internal reshuffling of departments was undertaken in 1946, which had a modest impact on how logistics was handled; when this was completed, the Naval Staff comprised divisions for Naval Intelligence, Plans, Plans (Q), Operations, Trade, Training and Staff Duties, Gunnery, Torpedo/Antisubmarine/Mine Warfare, Minesweeping, Signals, Navigation and Direction, Air Warfare, Air Organisation and Training, and Combined Operations. In April 1946, the post of deputy First Sea Lord lapsed, but the post of deputy CNS was reintroduced with responsibility for supervising questions of tactics, technical policy, and fighting efficiency, including staff requirements. Further realignments included bringing air warfare under the Fifth Sea Lord with the sole assistant CNS remaining a board member, covering a number of disciplines that affected logistics, staff requirements and operational research, and navigation and direction. Meanwhile, Plans Division and Plans Division (Q) remained completely preoccupied with the effects of demobilization on the Royal Navy's ability to re-deploy the fleet for its postwar responsibilities.

By 1947, fundamental changes in the way the three services were adminis-tered, presaged not so much by the revived Committee of Imperial Defence being retitled the Cabinet Defence Committee as by the fact that the secretariat was the Ministry of Defence headed by a full minister who, in one stroke, replaced the First Lord of the Admiralty and the other single-service ministers. Following the principle that formulation of policy should be combined with implementation it was decided that the single-service staffs would not be immediately supplanted by a central staff, so for the meantime the Naval Staff had to undertake a dual function by having to support the CNS, both as a member of the Defence Com-mittee and as operational head of the Royal Navy. Despite all the changes how-ever, the Naval Staff's practical day-to-day responsibility for formulating and conducting naval operational policy remained much the same as before, partly because the chiefs of staff continued to be members of the successor committees and partly because the new Minister of Defence was provided with neither the authority nor staff to be very effective.[116] Nevertheless the Naval Staff had to face a number of new challenges as the United Kingdom's defense role became more integrated into supporting the NATO Alliance.[117] To a far greater extent than ever before in peacetime, Alliance requirements became the overriding concern for the Naval Staff, which demanded intense liaison between NATO staffs to estab-lish force levels and devise plans and procedures, a common command structure as well as a multitude of other matters affecting the conduct of operations and exercises. Apart from having to devise a fleet capable of opposing an imminent and growing Soviet threat in Europe and the North Atlantic, the Naval Staff was additionally tasked, within less than a year after NATO was formed, to provide and support a very significant contribution to United Nations forces, including aircraft carriers, in response to the outbreak of war in Korea.

Fortunately, strong liaison between the Royal Navy and U.S. Navy had been upheld through the British Admiralty Delegation in Washington D.C., which continued to operate after 1945 under a full admiral representing the First Sea Lord in the Combined Chiefs of Staff Committee, as well as the Royal Navy's member of the Joint Services Mission with overall responsibility to the board for all Admiralty interests in the United States. His staff included a rear admiral as chief of staff, a variety of staff officers, civilian advisers, and the Royal Navy Scientific Service research and development group. At the start of 1948 the Brit-ish Joint Staff Mission (BJSM), as it had become known, was retitled as the BJSM (Navy Staff).

By 1949, as can be seen in appendix O, three admirals in the Naval Staff were subordinated to the CNS, each responsible for a group of related directorates.

The Fifth Sea Lord and deputy CNS (Air) were responsible for air warfare (operational, training and organization); the vice CNS covered operations through the directorates of Intelligence, Plans, Plans (Q), Operations, and Trade and Signals. The third pillar, the assistant CNS, was responsible for the warfare directorates such as Gunnery, Torpedo and ASW, and Navigation. Acting in a coordinating function was the directorate of Tactical and Staff duties, also under the assistant CNS, with support from outside the Naval Staff provided by the directorate of Operational Research. At the start of the Korean War in the summer of 1950, the upper echelon of the Naval Staff was manned at the same strength as in early 1939, with vice CNS (the prewar deputy CNS equivalent) supervising plans and operations while the assistant CNS supervised weapons matters, tactics, and training.[118] The combination of accelerated ship mobilization and stretched resources generally meant that significant realignment and strengthening of central divisions was inevitable. Plans Division (Q)'s tasks, for example, had always been regarded as the logistic planning element of the Naval Staff in support of the Fourth Sea Lord. Not surprisingly, therefore, recommendations were made by the Review of Admiralty Organization Committee (RAOC) in 1950, for these tasks to be merged with other material, supply, and works staffs to form the newly titled Naval Administrative Plans Division (APD) under the Fourth Sea Lord. The CNS, however, wished to retain Plans Division (Q) on the grounds that the drawing up of plans needed to be undertaken within the Naval Staff. Appendix P shows the Naval Staff structure in January 1952 reflecting the new Administrative Plans Division alongside Plans Division under the vice CNS. Despite Plans Division (Q) being replaced the following month by the new Administrative Planning Division, some five years later it was to be acknowledged, without explanation, that Plans Division (Q)'s move to the Fourth Sea Lord had been unsuccessful, so the Administrative Planning Division was once more returned to the Naval Staff as a division under vice CNS.[119]

What this relatively modest shuffle suggests is that logistics planning remained an important but nevertheless still relatively low-profile administrative support function within the Naval Staff. The opportunity for the Admiralty to reconsider afresh the more radical American model, given its closer ties with the U.S. Navy, combined with the accumulated logistic experience gained from its recent Pacific experience, seemed to have been left on hold—presumably because of the growing importance attached to building up the NATO/ North Atlantic link, which did not demand logistic planning convergence.

Royal Navy Postwar: Logistic Support Organization to Change?

In chapter three, reference was made to the difficulties faced by the Admiralty during 1944–45 in trying to meet American expectations that, among other things, the BPF's logistic infrastructure should mirror theirs. This implied not only having proper logistic plans in place and resources suitably prioritized but also an autonomous logistics organization established within the actual area of operation for managing logistic distribution and fleet maintenance, directly accountable to a specific member of the Admiralty's Board responsible for all naval logistic matters.[120] For both practical and political reasons, the recommendations to adopt this American logistic design were discarded, despite the acknowledged advantages, because the problems of trying to reorganize the planning functions into one group were deemed to be best left until after the war. When this was eventually resurrected in 1946, having "recently come to light" in the Fourth Sea Lord's office, further action was still deemed inappropriate.[121] To some extent this was because events had overtaken matters, and that all logistic needs could now be satisfied by a relatively more robust attitude for handling logistics issues following its recent experience in the Pacific. But the earlier underlying weakness of the current system—its lack of empowering the functions of logistic support to the forefront of operational planning—had still not been addressed, let alone resolved. Even by 1949, when logistic planning had become more complex across much of the Admiralty, key advocates of logistics planning such as Admiral Hughes-Hallett were still hoping for the day when "there will be logistic staff officers working alongside the Staff Officer Operations in all big naval staffs."[122]

Yet, apart from the Korean War, which was limited and relatively containable in logistic terms, most of the logistic activity within the Admiralty related either to existing or near-term deployment of fleet units or to longer term contingency planning in the event of global war. But, as will be discussed in chapter 5 on auxiliary ship design and in chapter 6 on mobilization planning, the Royal Navy's methodology and approach to planning was quite different from the U.S. Navy, partly by culture, but also by necessity and circumstance. As mentioned earlier, during World War II the Americans had found it essential to place logistics planning into a central autonomous authority that reported direct to the CNO. It will be important to see therefore whether this was retained during peacetime and whether the unification of the armed forces had as minimal effect on the logistics planning function within the U.S. Navy, as it had within the Royal Navy.

U.S. Navy Postwar: CNO/Fleet Organization

The concept of having formalized joint logistical planning and logistical operations at the field level between the U.S. Army and U.S. Navy only came to fruition in March 1943 when Fleet Admiral King and the Chief of Staff of the Army, Gen. George Marshall, issued a directive titled "Basic Logistical Plan for Command Areas involving Joint Army and Navy Operations." It would be another seven months before a Joint Logistic Plans Committee was formed as part of the JCS organization, but from that moment it was thereafter continually expanded to reflect the growing importance that logistics played in its deliberations.

The Office of the CNO, which during World War II was also CominCH, was for a brief period after August 1945 the senior operational and administrative commander. But in 1946 these powers declined as the military services agreed to establish peacetime unified commands as part of a unified defense organization, which eventually led to the creation of what became, in essence, a federation of the three services.[123] Through the National Security Act of 1947, the U.S. Army, the U.S. Navy, and the U.S. Air Force became the members of the National Military Establishment under Admiral Forrestal, the secretary of defense responsible for the common defense and security of the United States. Certain coordinating agencies were also established within the National Military Establishment, including the War Council, the JCS, the Munitions Board, and the Research and Development Board.[124] A number of duties were directed to the JCS, which carried some very specific responsibilities for integrating and coordinating the strategic planning and direction of the military forces. Second only to these was the preparation of supporting logistic plans, issued primarily for planning guidance and direction, which were issued to each service with responsibility assigned for implementation. Chapter 6 takes this further by looking at how this high-level plan then cascaded down the logistic planning hierarchy within the U.S. Navy itself.

Other types of joint plans included the Joint Long-Range Strategic Estimate, which looked over the next ten years at predicted enemy strength and capabilities, weapons development, predictions of national resources, and so on. Then there was the Joint Strategic Objectives Plan, which covered a four-year build-up based on mobilization that was meant to be disseminated in advance to enable services budget preparation and establishment of peacetime readiness levels. Another plan, the Joint Strategic Capabilities Plan, was essentially the emergency war plan based on current military strength and expected build-up over four years from initiation.

Following representations from James Forrestal, the first U.S. secretary of defense to the president, that his position lacked the authority, powers, and staff to establish the necessary policies and programs, Congress made extensive revisions in 1949 to the National Security Act. In similar fashion to the British model, the traditional rank of the service secretaries was abolished and the Department of Defense became an executive department of the government absorbing the military and nonmilitary components of the National Military Establishment.[125] The National Security Resources Board was established as an advisory body under the president and was essentially responsible for the coordination of the military industrial and civilian mobilization, alongside the National Security Council, which was responsible for the politico-military and diplomatic issues.

The U.S. Naval establishment thus now comprised three principle parts as follows:

- The Navy Department, which was the executive arm located in Washington, comprising the bureaus, boards and offices of the Navy Department as well as the Marine and Coast Guards HQs. From these stemmed the overall policy, administrative command, and logistic direction for the operating forces and the shore establishment.
- The operating forces, comprising the fleets and other seagoing forces, frontier forces, and district forces.
- The shore establishment, which provided the worldwide facilities for servicing, maintaining, equipping, and repairing the operating forces.

U.S. Navy: Logistic Support Organization to Change?

As can be seen in appendix Q, despite these various changes, the logistics arm of the U.S. Navy still remained a separate autonomous group that by 1949 was commanded by Deputy CNO Vice Admiral Carney reporting to the CNO. In effect, what had happened was that since the end of the war, the office of the CNO had been extensively revamped to assume the character more akin to a General Staff.[126] This was particularly true for the Logistic Plans Division (OP-40). Under the U.S. National Security Act of 1947, a new organizational infrastructure was introduced that for the first time enabled logistic planning to be undertaken in a more orderly and systematic manner by addressing both long-range planning issues through the Navy Basic Mobilization Plan as well as plans for coping with the separate challenges for resources required for the present. The vital connection between them was the maintenance of war reserves; this, together with its impact upon auxiliary resources, is addressed in much more detail in chapter 6.

Conclusion

This chapter examined postwar cultural and organizational change conditioned by logistic experience acquired during World War II. The transition from war to peace provided both navies opportunities for reform, but it also caused them to confront difficult challenges as they attempted to define the extent and nature of mobile logistic support required in peacetime. Events had often determined the pace and nature of the various logistic challenges during wartime, and these had too often only been resolved through improvisation. Nevertheless, a substantial and effective core competency had now been developed that needed to be preserved. What was required was a fresh sense of order and pattern so the role of logistics would be better recognized, anticipated, and applied in future wars. Several lessons from wartime logistics helped to identify or define some broad logistics principles that became the foundation for establishing the conduct of logistics and its relationship with strategic and tactical planning. How this translated into improved awareness among officers of the relevance of logistics in the broader context was then analyzed through the prism of postwar naval education, rather than just training. In focusing on the new logistics courses that were introduced in 1947 at the NWC, it was found that on balance the logistic programs achieved what they set out to do but that difficulties continued to persist in creating the necessary cultural change among the officer corps to recognize that logistics merited the same attention as other disciplines, such as naval aviation or gunnery.

Each navy adopted a different organizational approach to managing its postwar logistics needs. The U.S. Navy retained its belief that logistics must remain, even in peacetime, an autonomous organization operating alongside operational forces but controlled from the center directly reporting to the CNO. The Admiralty, however, chose not to adopt a similar approach, first mooted within the Naval Staff in 1944–45 but instead continued to manage its logistics requirements in more or less the same manner as before the war.

5 | Fleet Sustainability and Its Effect on Auxiliary Ship Design

WHEN LOOKING AT the general attributes of either the Royal Navy or the U.S. Navy by the end of World War II, arguably their most outstanding capabilities could be characterized as mobility, flexibility, and sustained high-intensity striking power. These were the legacy of their struggle to achieve strategic flexibility and sustainable air-offensive capability, which were the embodiment of a new form of oceanic warfare discovered in the Pacific. Protecting or trying to extend this core competency during peacetime in anticipation that any future conflict might be equally complex and sophisticated presented a number of different challenges. Not the least of these was the design and procurement or appropriate ships with the right equipment that would allow naval strategies to be pursued with confidence and vigor whether in peacetime or at war.

Lord Fisher once wrote, "Strategy should govern the types of ships to be designed. Ship designs as dictated by strategy should govern tactics. Tactics should govern details of armaments."[1] The trouble is that development rarely follows such a neat prescription, for the challenges imposed on design are always complex, often at different levels, and usually interreactive. This chapter will explore some of the ramifications in peacetime upon worldwide fleet sustainability, particularly as each navy tried to determine how much future logistic support should be concentrated on traditional fixed bases or dispersed by deploying mobile fleet trains. Each choice posed different criteria for establishing minimum acceptable endurance requirements for warships and auxiliaries alike, as well as replenishment speeds to counter certain operational threats. Such challenges affected warship and auxiliary design including whether to convert or build new purpose-built auxiliary ships to meet the demanding Fleet requirements for more speed and flexibility in replenishment capability.

General Appreciation of the Shipping Situation

No study of logistic considerations can ignore the enormous impact that shipping availability and production would have on virtually all aspects of naval planning during this period. The essence of the problem was that, in peacetime, shipyards usually specialized in one type of ship with successors varied only slightly, according to the preferences of future owners. Changing from one type to another reduced the production rate, which had unattractive economic and strategic consequences. At the beginning of World War II, U.K. merchant ship production had been falling for some time, and serviceable available tonnage was therefore small, given expected losses. As a result, the same types of merchant ships continued to be built in wartime as had been built in peacetime, thereby minimizing disruption to production schedules and preserving material. Having studied the merchant ship programs over two world wars, the Admiralty concluded in 1947 that any merchant ship program must be continuous in peace and in war.[2] The problem for the Admiralty, therefore, was how to incorporate wartime requirements into peacetime ship design without compromising commercial economy and efficiency.

Exercise "Trident," a conference held at the Royal Naval College, Greenwich, in April 1949, took this a stage further. Designed to apply the lessons of World War II to a possible war in 1956–57, the conference incorporated a study by the Ministry of Transport (MOT) of the various political, geographic, and economic differences that could affect the shipping position between 1941 and what might be applicable by 1957. The study's main conclusion was that there was every reason to assume that general shortages would be no less critical in later years than during World War II, when every major military operation was affected either in time or scope by shipping considerations. It must be remembered that such operations were rarely sequential but concurrent, and this exacerbated the gap between demand and supply. If the Allies were to maintain their war-making capacity at maximum level and still possess strategic mobility, "which is their greatest asset against the enemy," then ensuring the most economical use of such shipping for all purposes was considered by the study to be "essential."[3] Supporting evidence showed that in September 1939, 2,870 dry cargo ships (10.814 million gross tons) were registered under the British flag (including Dominion). By 1948, this had become 2,733 (12.092 million gross tons), reflecting the postwar priority for export recovery by concentrating shipyard resources on merchant shipbuilding, repairs, and conversions.[4] The projection out to 1952, however, showed only a very modest increase in gross tonnage terms, to just over 12.5 million gross tons.[5]

For British tankers, 510 (3.236 million gross tons) were registered in 1939, increasing to 591 by 1948 (3.788 million gross tons, including 350,000 tons owned by the Admiralty). The projected gross tonnage figure for 1952, however, elevated significantly to 4.750 million gross tons.[6] Given the well-documented difficulties in finding sufficient new hulls for modern fleet train auxiliaries required back in 1944–45, when shipbuilding was then at its peak, this apparent lack of spare future capacity did not bode well.[7] But at least it would explain to some extent why hybrid or dual-purpose designs were still considered essential despite, as we shall see later, their inability to satisfy the conflicting military and commercial requirements that would have to be incorporated into any specification. The figures for the other major flag carrier, the United States, showed the extraordinary acceleration, particularly in cargo and liners, during the war years, after which levels stabilized and were predicted to remain more or less the same well into the 1950s. American tanker tonnage doubled from 2.890 million gross tons in 1939 to 5.796 million gross tons by 1948 whereas the balance of all U.S. merchant shipping more than quadrupled from 5.286 million to 24.862 million gross tons by 1948.[8] The active auxiliary fleet on November 1, 1948, alone comprised 710 tankers, of which 647 were privately owned and 57 were U.S. Navy–owned, with 6 owned by the Army. The U.S. Navy, in fact, owned none of the 1,248 dry cargo ships, and it only owned 6 of the 132 passenger/transports, with the rest spread among private owners or the Maritime Commission. Nor did the U.S. Navy own the inactive U.S. merchant auxiliary fleet totaling some 1,891 vessels, including 38 tankers, 97 passenger/transports, and the balance dry cargo.[9] But here lay the rub, because the feasibility of meeting the anticipated shipping requirements, should war break out, depended "to a large degree" on the condition of this laid up fleet. As will be further discussed in chapter 6 the picture for this was in fact far from encouraging. It was becoming increasingly evident to the U.S. Navy that its reliance upon such an aging and increasingly obsolete auxiliary force was a risk, particularly if the level and type of future logistic support proved to be similar to the past. The questions, now that a war footing was no longer feasible, were how much had the rules changed for retaining logistic self-sufficiency, and how vulnerable was the U.S. Navy to compromising its own strategic mobility and reach.

Strategic Implications upon Fleet Sustainability

As the need for both increased speed and endurance became progressively more important considerations for achieving the right level of fleet sustainability, these variables had an increasingly strong bearing on establishing the parameters of strategic reach both at sea and from appropriately located bases.

Home Bases versus Afloat Support

As discussed in chapter 2, early in World War II the shortage of suitable ships for conversion into effective auxiliaries determined their outer limits logistically as the Allies sought the necessary reach and momentum to prosecute the Pacific campaign. The solution of creating advanced bases and, in some cases, large shore installations was also compromised, given that many were completed after their critical need had already passed. Only later, when the fleet train had been properly augmented, were combat operations properly supported at places such as Eniwetok and Ulithi, which were nearer to the battle zones. Ironically, when plans were drawn up for the eventual invasion of Kyūshū, large naval shore activities were allocated further to the rear to reduce dependence upon afloat facilities because they were becoming increasingly vulnerable to kamikaze attacks.

For the Royal Navy, the lack of adequate dry docks and repair facilities at various strategic locations around the world severely restricted its mobility during World War II. The most notable overseas example would be the loss of Singapore early in the war, which denied the Royal Navy access to one of the largest graving docks in the British Empire. Meanwhile those dry docks and repair facilities that existed elsewhere—particularly in the United Kingdom—were simply deficient (apart from a few private docks for transatlantic liners).[10] The Royal Navy's inherent inadequacy had never come to light because operations had largely been confined to the North Atlantic and North Sea. This persistent neglect of the logistic dimension to some extent reflected the parochial dominance within the Royal Navy toward strategy and tactics that for many invoked the familiar time–distance logistics of the immediate European theater rather than the potential of the Pacific. The lack of previous experience with this intensive type of logistical challenge had deprived the planners of any forewarning with the result that the proportion of logistics forces devoted to the Pacific was grossly underestimated. The Royal Navy's subsequent experience in creating a fleet train, with only a fraction of the vessels actually designed for their purpose, combined with their reliance upon American advanced bases for support and fuel (because it was not economical to build their own) caused the Admiralty some serious reflection after the war. As their Director of Operations Division ruminated, "In spite of the great efforts and masterly improvisation by those concerned, the logistic support of the BPF was achieved only by an uncomfortably narrow margin. . . . Our manifest unpreparedness for long range logistic support raises the question whether, in spite of our worldwide commitments, we had not become too parochial in our conception of the use of sea power."[11]

In a sense, such perspicacity had to surface eventually. Up to 1944, the naval war had been successfully prosecuted on several fronts for years, but it was entirely dependent on fixed bases for maintenance and replenishment, so the ramifications of what had to be taken on were not yet fully comprehended. Neither exercises in peacetime nor the familiarity of a supply system at an established naval base could emulate the urgency, unpredictability, stringency, or, in one word, the "friction" that comes with trying to gain logistic self-sufficiency in a dynamic battle space. So it would be surprising if warnings had not been sounded postwar that the consequences for having insufficient mobility in the future should be ignored at their peril. But if postwar strategic and operational thinking within the U.S. Navy was dominated by their recent experience in the Pacific, this was not necessarily true within the Admiralty. Despite the many advocates for retaining a fleet train, within two months from when the BPF Fleet Train was disbanded in January 1946, the Admiralty reported to the Cabinet Defence Committee that

> . . .the term "Fleet Train" is now obsolete, as the Fleet no longer requires the support in advanced operational areas, which was the original purpose of the Fleet Train. However our operational requirements make it necessary for us to retain a larger fleet east of Suez than we should have in normal times of peace. In addition we are compelled to maintain considerable shore-based staffs in Ceylon, in Singapore, in Hong Kong and in Australia to deal with the administrative work which demobilisation, reduction of naval establishments and rehabilitation of recaptured areas have put upon us, and these staffs have to be fed.[12]

But the political and economic chances of resurrecting naval bases to prewar levels were slim; it was not long before calls were being made that resonated once again the characteristics for the Pacific task force model, with Britain needing to retain a fleet capable of striking "the enemy . . . where it hurts most . . . for as long as possible . . . for weeks if not months from bases which may be 2,000 miles or more away."[13] Whether this was feasible was another matter. On the one hand, postwar contraction in ships and personnel forced many capital ships to be scrapped or placed in reserve, resulting in an increasing proportion of the fleet represented by small, less self-reliant ships that required base support for repair, supply, and accommodation.[14] On the other hand, the perceived threat of air or even atomic bomb attack made such bases more vulnerable, however well dispersed around the United Kingdom, which might result in the fleet and support facilities being moved overseas.[15] Apart from the economic drain such an exodus would cause, recent wartime history has already suggested that new mobile bases for stores (which today would be called forward logistic sites) in any dynamic war would risk immobilizing logistic support that could well become uneconomic. The alternative, keeping stores afloat in temporary anchorages, would at least provide some flexibility, but as we have seen, this again risked tying up scarce shipping and requiring substantial conversion capability to meet the demand for specialized auxiliaries. Perhaps this was the price one had to pay. After all, the atomic bomb had clearly signaled for many the end of static fueling bases as they knew it, so the policy had to be changed anyway. As the Naval Staff History so bluntly put it, the British had to learn replenishment at sea "or content itself with no more than sporadic raids."[16] And so it became the underlying expectation by both navies that, during any future war, warships would have to remain at sea for much longer periods than even in World War II, thereby becoming increasingly reliant upon being replenished at sea.[17] The Admiralty's recommendation for retaining a skeleton fleet train after the war still assumed that the future enemy would be a blue water navy against which Pacific-type battle strategies would apply. For example, the objects for the proposed fleet train stated it was

. . .responsible for the support of a fleet engaged in an ocean war, similar to that which has recently been brought to a successful conclusion in the Pacific, [and] required to discharge two functions:

a) The initial establishment and provision of the necessary facilities at remote anchorages or harbours, of bases on which the support of the fleet can pivot.

b) The supply of fuel ammunition stores and maintenance services for the fleet at sea, thus enabling the fleet to keep at sea for long periods and to maintain continuous operations against the enemy.[18]

The report then acknowledged the need for a Logistics Support Group using a series of bases, with the rear base cited as being in Australia "to establish the ship assembly and main reserves." The intermediate base was defined as "nearer the area of hostilities than the rear base where an operation can be mounted, supplies collected, stored and where repairs and major replenishments can be carried out between operations." The advanced anchorage would be where the fleet would be supplied logistically during an operation, about one thousand miles from the striking force and five hundred miles from the replenishment area. Here fleet attendant tankers would load from freighters, and the logistic support organized from here would include light repair ships, certain harbor facilities, and an airstrip for mail and personnel movement, and so on.[19]

The question that resurfaced then, as it had in 1944, was how all this would be fulfilled given that any sort of fleet train would have to be kept at a margin over minimum requirements in both personnel and material to ensure any chance of achieving a continuous efficient operation. Any such augmentation of the fleet train, in other words, would need to be directly proportional to any planned augmentation of the fleet. Meanwhile, it was suggested, a skeleton fleet train organization was essential to avoid losing lessons and experience because a full-service force in peacetime was clearly not feasible. As the Commander Fleet Train put it in June 1946, "The necessity to keep alive and develop the lessons learned from the Fleet Train and draw the conclusions that the establishment of a sound servicing force capable of rapid expansion in wartime, even at some sacrifice to the size of the Fleet, would undoubtedly enable more of the Fleet to be kept at sea and for a longer period."[20]

While the assumption was that the fleet train concept had, in Commodore Barraclough's words, "come to stay," its actual composition remained unsettled because no agreement could be reached on an appropriate overseas base policy.[21] This was partly due to the lack of any clear conclusion being reached on overall strategy that, even by 1947, was still being studied by the Inter-Service Future Planning Section of the Joint Planning Staff.[22] The question of whether to establish new shore or mobile bases had become quite a vexing issue for the Admiralty, not helped by the fact that as the logistics infrastructure invariably became more decentralized in peacetime, the finance was controlled ever more tightly at the center. One of the main advantages of forward bases in wartime, for example, was the "local" ability to repair damaged shipping, but this would become an expensive and redundant need in peacetime. While no definitive solution was ever reached during this whole period, the balance of thinking, at least in the Royal Navy, still seemed in favor of mobility, most particularly among those advocates who had been involved the first time around.[23]

For the U.S. Navy, despite many papers being produced in the early postwar years, no scientific study or definitive conclusions appear to have been agreed by the CNO planners or the Naval War College on which form of logistic support was the better—advanced bases or mobile support. The concept of mobile logistics support for naval forces was certainly more established throughout the U.S. Navy than in Britain's naval doctrine, and this really had to do with its roots in the American predilection for self-sufficiency.[24] This went back to the time when the engineer corps was amalgamated into the line in 1899, with the requirement that all line officers perform some engineering duty at sea as a prerequisite for promotion. This not only stimulated interest within command for logistics but also underlined the importance of self-maintenance as a factor in the materiel readiness of ships to carry out their missions. This eventually led to the policy of ships actually doing their own repair work, if necessary, assisted by tenders and repair ships from the Base Force (described in chapter 1), rather than calling on navy yards to do the work. It was this practice that not only ensured that self-maintenance characteristics were built into a ship's design construction and equipment but it also applied extra emphasis toward "improving the equipment and techniques for fueling and replenishing stores and ammunition with ships under way at sea."[25]

While this ethos did not change during World War II, what did change was the breadth and nature of methods developed by the U.S. Navy for retaining such self-sufficiency despite the exponential increase in technology, operational demands, and numbers of ships involved. With the benefit of some years of reflection, Admiral Furer privately expressed the view to Rear Admiral Eccles while he was still writing the history of the U.S. Navy Department, that "advanced shore bases were the answer during the early part of the war even though these were expensive, inelastic and often far from the front, but once the U.S. had command of the sea and say by mid 1943 then mobile floating support was more economical in manpower and costs and more effective in servicing the fleet."[26]

In Furer's subsequent published work, he went further by stating that if afloat facilities such as Service Squadron Ten had existed initially, then there was "no doubt" that much of the cost and headaches associated with building the advanced bases could have been avoided.[27] Rear Admiral Eccles meanwhile responded that any evaluations to date, including his own, were essentially intuitive because no one could agree the ground rules for basing the evaluation. On balance, however, he thought the answer was to have both but, if possible "every effort should be made to have all floating support self-propelled."[28] If Eccles had to express any single conclusion, it was

> Other things being equal, it is cheaper, more effective, and more efficient to support a fleet by floating mobile forces than by fixed overseas bases. However, "other things" are not always equal and therefore each situation, or at least a series of probable situations, should be carefully analyzed before reaching final conclusions. In view of the great variety of situations, it is unlikely that any large naval force can be effectively supported without some overseas bases. However, it seems wise to keep these as few and small as possible.[29]

Despite their many misgivings, both navies not unnaturally still regarded their recent total war experience as the "norm," to such a degree that most expectations—indeed plans—perpetuated the same total war dimension. What would strengthen this credo was the additional fear provoked by the prospect of nuclear confrontation, with its consequence upon fleet and base protection in general and fleet endurance in particular.

When war eventually did strike in 1950, the role of Japan providing host nation support for U.S. naval bases was critical but, once again, the economy to be achieved by using afloat support was largely ignored. This was borne out by a Bureau of Supplies and Accounts (BuSandA) study after the Korean War that showed that 85 percent of naval material that left the West Coast went to supporting the bases while only 15 percent went to forces afloat.[30]

Endurance

Although endurance is very much an amalgam of distance, speed, and time, the one particularly important factor found in any formula associated with sustainability is distance. Combatant endurance, transportation routes, and potential enemy targets all required an ability to cover distance globally. How long ships would have to remain at sea would depend on whether a task force was required to be on station for a up to, say, six months during a period of strained relations or, for example, three months in time of war. The former would challenge a navy to keep the fleet somewhere near the enemy territory but sufficiently far away to make discovery unlikely. In war, in addition to tactically more demanding operations, the fleet would need to retreat sufficiently out of range to enable a trouble-free replenishment operation. Both would require extending ship endurance beyond normal base replenishment cycles. The postwar theoretical assumption for how long ships might have to remain at sea was constantly tested as the expectations and limitations placed upon endurance became increasingly affected by the introduction of more complex platform and ordnance technology.

Understanding these limitations is important. Complex variables of wind, sea, employment, and machinery conditions can all affect the fuel performance of ships; at a given propeller speed under apparently stable operating conditions, fuel consumption could fluctuate considerably even within the same class. The intensity of wartime activity would also seriously exacerbate consumption behavior with speeds above 20 knots causing fuel consumption to rise exponentially. This can best be illustrated by using two examples of daily wartime fuel consumption rates, the first for an American *Essex*-class aircraft carrier where high-speed for launching aircraft was essential, and the second for a destroyer, its vital escort but with the weakest endurance.

The carrier typically consumed daily 915 barrels (bbl) at 14 knots, increasing by 684 bbl to 1,599 bbl at 20 knots. However, for every incremental 2 knots thereafter, the burn-off jumped each time by 343 bbl, 437 bbl, 561 bbl, and 780 bbl so that by 30 knots the daily consumption rate reached 4,767 bbl, a fivefold increase when compared to 14 knots. Because it would take fewer than three weeks of cruising at 19 knots to empty its tanks, the need for regular refueling to sustain flying operations and execute evasion tactics becomes compelling. For destroyers, the curve was even sharper despite their comparatively large (for a destroyer) cruising radius of typically between 5,500 and 6,000 miles, designed to address the logistic demands of War Plan Orange. For the interwar-built *Farragut* class, consumption between 14 and 30 knots increased nearly tenfold while the relatively modern *Fletcher* class and the latest *Gearing* class increased by over six and seven times, respectively.[31] Assuming designed cruising speeds of between 14.7 and 16.5 knots, their respective fuel tanks would be totally expended in as little as eight days.[32] The problem of regular replenishment becomes particularly compelling if sustained high-speed maneuvers, such as antisubmarine or aircraft evasion tactics, are required, which would cause a dramatic increase in consumption rates.

Inevitably, the question for the postwar planners and, indeed, ship designers was how much would this pattern change given the expectation that global carrier task force operations would continue, albeit less intensively, and the fleet train concept would therefore remain the kingpin for logistics planning. Preliminary postwar estimates for *Essex*-class carrier deployments assumed about a 7:3 ratio between being under way and in port, consuming some 15,648 bbl per month, not unlike heavy cruisers or 35,000-ton battleships. Clearly, these estimates were still influenced by contemporary values of the importance of carrier task forces, even when no specific enemy was envisaged. Not surprisingly, therefore, from 1945 onward the plans for both the displacement and fuel capacities of new American carriers and destroyers were increased substantially.[33]

The British, too, had to readjust to postwar expectations. The BPF's refueling plans during the Okinawa ICEBERG campaign had projected daily fuel consumption, assuming 18 knots cruise speed for TF37, as 380 tons for battleships, 300 tons for fleet carriers, 180 tons for escort carriers, 140 tons for cruisers, and

95 tons for destroyers.[34] By 1949 it was estimated that fleet carriers such as HMS *Eagle* would typically consume about 425 tons per day (tpd), which, given her storage capacity of 7,300 tons, meant that replenishment could be stretched to well beyond a week or two. But, like the Americans, storage capacity and consumption of aviation fuel was becoming more and more the limiting factor, exacerbated for the British by the relatively slow pumping rates due to the small hoses. According to Exercise "Trident," the optimum ratio of demand–consumption between boiler fuel and aviation fuel, used for establishing pumping rates/volumes to carriers, was 4:1. The U.S. Navy's Pacific War ratio, by comparison was 7:1, reflecting the relatively economic piston engines in 1945. The Korean War, conversely, witnessed the introduction of significant numbers of jet aircraft on American carriers that led to a soaring demand for aviation fuel. This not only forced replenishments to be conducted every four days, usually at night, but also resulted in the transfer ratio between bunker and aircraft fuel dropping dramatically to as low as 2:1, with avgas taking three times longer to transfer than bunker fuel due to the smaller size and number of available hoses. The plan for a new British freighting type tanker proposed in 1949, discussed later, might seemingly have just coped with this if the Royal Navy had found itself in similar circumstances because it could theoretically pump bunker fuel at 1,500 tph and aviation fuel at 600 tph, giving a ratio of 2.5:1. But the modernized *Wave* class was not so efficient. Although bunker fuel could be pumped adequately enough at 1,100 tph, aviation fuel struggled across at a very low 50 tph, producing a ratio of 22:1.[35]

While endurance and fuel capacity were always regarded by the U.S. Navy as critical parameters in destroyer design, these had always received less attention in British design. The problem of fuel endurance for British escorts remained particularly acute because of the unrealistic prewar endurance parameters forged from World War I experience that prescribed small hull sizes for relatively long-range tasking. Inevitably, any provision for more fuel storage would have to lead to compromise, and this usually meant "at the expense of other offensive qualities," therefore making it imperative that all tankers and escorts retain the capability for refueling under way.[36] But with the passage of experience, particularly operating in the Pacific, the emphasis about what really mattered in terms of endurance started to change. Fuel remained critically important in any calculation because fuel consumption for all classes of ships was increasing for any number of reasons, not least the demands for increased speed and power to support evermore-complex technology, including faster and heavier aircraft. What was also changing, though, was how refueling at sea was increasingly recognized as just another routine evolution. Extensive wartime experience had shown, for example, that built-in endurance capacity at sea could last thirty to ninety days "provided that re-supply of fuel and ammunition was assured every three to five days."[37] It was not, however, just a question of fuel but also having adequate levels of fresh water due to higher wartime complements levels. By 1950 the Admiralty now specifically ignored the question of fuel capacity by defining endurance as "the period during which war rates of expenditure, with full war complements, could be sustained without replenishment of victualling, medical and naval stores, including spare gear."[38]

The Director of Tactical and Staff Duties Division (DTSD) then noted that the Admiralty still considered the minimum acceptable endurance for aircraft carriers as ninety days; battleships and cruisers, seventy days; and destroyers or smaller, forty-five days.[39] But how best to determine the optimum configuration of precious space for competing requirements was difficult because of the continuing uncertainty as to what fleet carriers were expected to do in the future. Nor was he alone in feeling this uncertainty. The Director of Naval Operational Research (DNOR), for example, considered replenishment at sea should not exceed one day, thus "should not affect carrier design—only the planned ratio of logistics to operational tonnage, i.e., a longer fleet train would be required to complete the replenishment in one day."[40] However, he also believed that "a fleet carrier designed to operate for three months without a fleet train is bound to be a relatively inefficient weapon of war, since something will have to be sacrificed to achieve this extreme self-sufficiency."[41]

While the distance from forward or main bases to actual or potential operating areas would clearly vary, wartime experience still weighed heavily in setting endurance parameters. For instance, in 1945 typical supply routes were extremely extended. The Okinawa ICEBERG operation, often regarded as the benchmark for comparison because it involved both British and American naval task forces, was 4,800 miles from the U.S. Navy's primary base in Pearl Harbor, Hawaii, and 4,200 miles from the Royal Navy's main base in Sydney, Australia. Underway refueling routinely occurred well over 2,000 miles from fuel depots in Eniwetok. In the postwar period, much would naturally depend on what type of operation was envisaged since the requirement for logistic mobility would be less critical for, say, defending the Atlantic sea-lanes compared to a long-range carrier strike or amphibious operations in a hostile theater. One of the consequences for seeking such diversity was the difficulty in determining the nature and size of appropriate logistic support. With both navies becoming increasingly obliged to focus on the Mediterranean and North Atlantic/Arctic, which required less extended lines compared to the Pacific, this at least helped to define the problem better, although warship endurance was still vulnerable in the Northern latitudes where hostile conditions made replenishment at sea more hazardous. By 1951, partly in response to the belief that the Korean War was a Soviet-inspired diversion, Admiralty planners assumed that offensive carrier forces would operate in both the Atlantic and Mediterranean in support of land operations. While the U.K. contribution "has not yet been definitely stated," it was expected that the Royal Navy would play their part, as either a separate unit or forming part of an American one. The key underlying assumption, however, remained unchanged in that "even if the offensive carrier force operations were limited to intermittent strikes at targets in Northern Norway and Russia it would be necessary for them to be replenished at sea to avoid the long passage to and from the U.K. and the operational area."[42] Consequently, it was acknowledged that "mobile or floating logistic support is the means by which this end can be attained; therefore fuelling at sea must be regarded as an everyday operation."[43]

Again, note the emphasis placed on refueling as being a routine evolution; as will be discussed in chapter 7, this emphasis would become very much the leitmotif for all replenishment doctrine issued during and after the Korean War. What would eventually change was not so much the routine per se but unexpectedly the frequency, as carrier endurance became increasingly defined by its capacity to receive aviation fuel on an almost continuous basis.

Fleet Speed

The term "fueling at sea" has wide connotations because, strictly speaking, it covers all aspects for moving the oil from its main shore storage to the actual rendezvous at sea. The relative importance attached to tanker speed depends on the underlying task; transporting bulk supplies over long distances demands a lower speed threshold compared to operating alongside fast combat task forces. In addressing the value and risks associated with mobile logistic support, the primary consideration is the extent to which a tanker's ability to replenish warships under way is constrained by its lack of speed and power. From a ship design perspective, speed was becoming a crucial element. Until 1947, no real experience existed of replenishing at speeds above 15 knots.[44] Yet the growing fear among Allied commanders was the belief that the Russians had developed a very fast submarine, based on several German type XXI fast submarines captured in 1945, that would prove difficult to evade unless higher speeds could be achieved compared to those established during World War II.[45] Nor did the fear appear to recede over time, with the need to protect shipping "against attack by high speed submarines" being emphasized again in Britain's Navy estimates during the Korean War.[46] There was also a new factor that had not existed in World War II—the introduction of increasingly heavy naval aircraft, including those powered by jet engines, which now required higher launch speeds from the carriers. By 1948, for example, flank speed for U.S. Navy major warships was 32 knots, with auxiliaries and amphibious craft set at 20 knots.[47] Even though Royal Navy speeds were believed to be slightly lower, the average commercial tanker even by 1950 would still only be managing 13¾–14½ knots while the more modern RFA freighting tankers typically achieved about 15½ knots. The bulk of the British replenishment tanker fleet, that is, the modernized *Wave* class, still only averaged a modest 12½ knots.[48]

A further increasingly significant factor for determining the right propulsion or power plant for a replenishment ship, was the extra auxiliary power required to handle the new power winches, pumps, and oil tank heaters so replenishment could be undertaken under all conditions (in particular the Arctic). This extra demand for power alone equated to some 2 knots of speed, which when combined with the demand for higher hull speed already, exacerbated the gap in the size of power plant for wartime needs compared to the overriding need for fuel economy in peacetime.[49] Meanwhile there were an enormous number of slow freighters and several slow tankers that were clearly unsuited for fleet duties but might still be useful for station duties or freighting in need. Most of these were in the United States languishing in the reserve fleet but in poor condition, their retention justified on the grounds they were not yet obsolete because the limitations of naval architecture made high speed such an expensive quality in ships. It was therefore argued, these may be "good twenty years from now as they are now, and who will say what problems foreign sea powers will present twenty years from now?"[50] In the end, the advocates for retaining everything, whether fast or slow, eventually lost the battle but, as shall be seen in chapter 6, this had as much to do with budgets as whether ships were potentially obsolete.

What could not be ignored was that if the need for more speed continued to rest on accommodating both military and commercial/economic prerogatives, then auxiliary ship design had to overcome some increasingly difficult and contradictory challenges ahead.

Auxiliary Design

Well-informed judgment, usually based on experience, combined with advances in technology can significantly influence how ship design matches strategic requirements. But the parameter that determines most outcomes is usually financial. The effect of warship endurance limitation and minimum fleet speed requirements, discussed earlier, combined with the need for auxiliaries to issue their cargoes more efficiently under differing conditions invariably stimulated design during wartime. But much of this work was ad hoc and often expedient to cope with demand. The development of oiling-at-sea equipment, for example, always lagged behind fleet requirements due to the difficulty of removing, even temporarily, from service the tankers of which there were too few. Lack of available labor and materials exacerbated the difficulty in keeping tankers up to date. In peacetime, a different but more intractable challenge presented itself. To attract scarce financial resources away from warship building, auxiliary specification for fleet replenishment needed to be fast enough for wartime fleet requirements but still economical to build and operate, using economies of scale through standardization to produce an acceptable return on capital. These wartime and peacetime parameters were inherently in conflict with each other. Could time, effort, and scarce money be better spent on ship design in advance, which would reduce the delay between authorization and commissioning as and when the occasion demanded?

Royal Navy: Fraser Fleet Train Recommendations

The Royal Navy's proposed postwar operating parameters for new auxiliary ship design were extremely ambitious and derived principally from a study of fleet train experience produced a few months after the end of the war by Admiral Fraser, who had been commander in chief of the BPF.[51] Included were staff requirements for fleet issue ships and an "Ideal Tanker" equipped to replenish under way at 15 knots with the whole range of petroleum products while capable of simultaneously transferring limited quantities of ammunition and provisions.[52] Yet within six months, progress in developing these ideas had apparently ground to a halt. Those, for example, that related to air stores deficiencies and ASIS conversions were still being "referred to Fourth Sea Lord" while new tanker programs were merely "being borne in mind." Others, such as the standardization policy were "acknowledged by Director of Trade Division and Director of Plans but no action [proposed]." Specific suggestions for new tanker and VSIS designs remained simply "noted by Director of Naval Stores."[53]

What had happened? After all, these were progressive but wholly sensible designs for coping better with the next war, albeit assuming it would be the same as the last one. Not surprising, either, was the preference for having dedicated fast fleet naval tankers that would no longer have to be designed with economy in mind to get built.[54] The trouble was that for this to happen, given the long lead times involved, the tankers would still have to be built in peacetime, in direct competition with other naval-related shipbuilding programs, and the only new construction authorized by the Admiralty during these austere postwar times were warships—and very few at that. Virtually all completions until 1949–50 (including, as it happens, some small-harbor tankers discussed later) were critical replacements from earlier authorized programs.[55]

In fact, however, there had been some progress across many fronts on the fleet train recommendations, although it was admittedly extremely slow. This was partly to ensure an increasingly wider consultation or scrutiny was undertaken among the various departments within the Naval Staff, as well as other government bodies like the Ministry of Transport. In effect, though, it was a decision process reflecting a deliberate "wait and see" policy as new technologies appeared that might need to be accommodated into the final specifications. But this lack of pace was also due to the degree of postwar weariness, absent fresh emergencies, that pervaded the bureaucracies anyway, exacerbated possibly by the debilitating effect caused by the erosion of those personnel familiar with fleet train issues who had since been demobilized. Only after all these collective contributions have been garnered could the proposal then be developed into a formal requirements outline from which could then be developed the necessary detailed construction plans within the Department of Naval Construction.[56]

Yet even though the concept of having an agile fleet train still seemed to be the intention, the underlying question remained as to how it would be composed, given the existing war-built vessels had poor seagoing and issuing capability, and were invariably slow, wrongly sized, or underpowered.[57] The options ranged from retaining and coping as best as possible with the existing auxiliaries, perhaps with some selective modernization where funds allowed. Or ships could be mothballed to be modernized or augmented once identified for reactivation. Or—the boldest plan of all—they could all be scrapped and replaced by modern new ships incorporating all the necessary wartime lessons to ensure that Britain's new but smaller navy was ready for all contingencies worldwide, thanks to a modern versatile fleet train. As usual, the answer came down to money.

Civilian and Admiralty Competition for Hull Design

Unfortunately for the Admiralty planners, no funds were available for new fast fleet tankers, so the only alternative was to compete along with other government agencies for a share of merchant ship hulls that could become eligible for conversion in the event of war. This would at least allow planning to continue for new replenishment ships while the Admiralty ensured that pre-agreed arrangements were in place to undertake conversion work on its allocation immediately after war was declared.[58] But the challenge of developing a satisfactory replenishment ship design was not confined to fuel only. Many other ships essential to a fleet train, with such attributes as cargo refrigeration for provisions, distilling, heavy lift, and so on, were also in demand by other agencies, including the Ministry of Food (MOF) and Ministry of Transport (MOT).[59] Many of these would require special equipment fitted in time of war, and this made conversion work quite complicated. In fact, at one point the Admiralty was skeptical whether multiple conversion work, up to fleet issue standard, would ever be feasible in time for the result to be useful.[60] For instance, better solids and liquids cargo segregation was needed, and more steam capacity was required for heating the oil, pumping cargo, and working all deck machinery. Then there was the ability to handle Arctic conditions or provide enough accommodation space for wartime manning. On top of these considerations, any specification would still have to meet the various Admiralty specifications related to naval vessels in general.[61] As Rear Admiral Hughes-Hallet, Director of Administrative Planning during this period, subsequently emphasized, there was no real alternative but to make clear "to [the MOT and MOF] that the Navy's ability to support offensive operations against enemy-held territory will depend upon the provision of an adequate fleet train."[62]

So, unlike the previous altercation between the Admiralty and MOWT over the availability of auxiliaries for the BPF Fleet Train back in 1944—in which, it will be recalled, the Admiralty lost—this time there was to be no allowance for a repetition.

Admiralty Director of Stores

Unlike the U.S. Navy, which owned and operated all its naval auxiliary support as an integral part of its complement, the Admiralty relied upon having to balance both naval and civilian shipping assets, with all their attendant design and manpower issues, to support the fleet either in harbor or at sea. This was managed through the Director of Naval Stores, who was responsible to the Fourth Sea Lord for, among other things, the storage of fuel and transportation to Admiralty bases or direct to the fleet. He was, in the commercial sense, the effective owner and operator of a variety of such tankers ranging from harbor attendants to large ocean-going freighting tankers. When not needed, these were chartered out to avoid being laid up. One of his primary concerns therefore was that all vessels should operate economically—in other words, that he could freight oil in peacetime at a price per ton comparable to commercial companies.[63]

For this to work, the ships had to be economically and commercially efficient, which meant that their basic design was a compromise, particularly in terms of speed. In wartime, when the freighting tankers could be withdrawn from commercial operation and replaced by commercial hulls, these could then be used for naval replenishment, much as had prevailed during World War II. Hence the necessity for having an inbuilt allowance for reserves of additional power to fulfill these tasks. Apart from the otherwise essential requirement that the ship should be the smallest possible to carry the deadweight cargo required, there were two other major considerations that uniquely affected RFA civilian (as distinct from naval) design parameters. To comply with the rules and regulations of the MOT, Lloyds, and other classification bodies, it was necessary to allocate more hull space than their naval equivalent to the type of machinery and its layout, as well as a more generous allowance for crew accommodation. Unlike their American counterparts, and in many ways to their disadvantage, RFAs were never designed to accommodate—let alone be allocated—the size of crew necessary for multirig operations and simultaneous handling of miscellaneous stores, hoses, and so on.[64] Needless to say, deadweight cargo space would have had to be sacrificed accordingly.

The Director of Naval Stores was responsible for initiating new replenishment ship design, and it was through him that the Fraser recommendations for "Ideal Replenishment Ships" would circulate until ready for promulgation as part of a formal Outline of Requirements. This proposal, however, could not be developed in isolation. He had to consult first with many other staff divisions about specific aspects such as speed, endurance, or the extent to which the vessel would be used for replenishment at sea.[65] It was this process that took so long. A very fast 20-knot tanker, fully equipped for the fleet, with offensive and defensive/protective armament and driven by high-powered, lightweight naval machinery with high pumping capability would be a one-off and, therefore, expensive proposition. It was becoming more and more self-evident that only the contingencies of war could justify such and, even then, it would probably require a class order to spread the cost more effectively. In peacetime, such a ship would not only still have to compete with warships for the limited funds but it would also have to be measured against the performance of the existing freighting/replenishment tankers. Meanwhile, absent any advance on converting designs into plans for a dedicated replenishment ship, a compromise had to be reached, if possible, between the conflicting commercial and naval specifications. But nearly a decade after the Americans first discovered the same dilemma before World War II, it was still proving extremely difficult for the Admiralty to conjure up a workable solution. The conflicts between speed and economy seemed irresolvable.

Plant Design for Speed

The most immediate of these conflicts was to be found in the size and type of power plant to be adopted, which had two important ramifications. The first affected the speed of the auxiliary, the second its endurance.

Although the difference between 15 knots and 16 knots (by then regarded as the minimum safety level against submarines) may not appear huge, every extra knot had a direct bearing on the size of the propulsion plant, which in turn affected cargo capacity since a greater proportion of the ship's load carrying capacity—its deadweight tonnage—would have to be allocated for storing bunker fuel. This would be at the expense of cargo space, thus increasing the direct operating costs as a proportion of cargo carried. Add to this the increase in fuel consumption for the larger plant and operating profitability suffered accordingly.[66] The implication was that, unless the engines were designed for maximum efficiency at the most economical commercial speed, the additional fuel cost for commercial use became disproportionately large. Nor was there much that could be done to mitigate this. The additional boiler capacity, required for higher speeds in need, would only be justified in a commercial context if its extra capacity could be utilized for, say cleaning or underway maintenance, thereby reducing turnaround time. But that seemed about it.

Plant Design for Endurance

The question of establishing the right type and capacity in plant and machinery was also crucial to the choice of plant design because RFA tankers generally worked between refits for 10½ months of the year and were seldom in harbor for longer than thirty-six hours. In other words, they spent at least 75 percent of the year at sea.[67] It was essential, therefore, that the main and auxiliary machinery had to be of a simple and robust construction capable of continuous running with much less maintenance than warships required. As a result, the machinery was heavier and more bulky than for "normal" commercial tankers, with its inevitable effect on deadweight cargo capacity and ultimate operating profitability.

Fleet Issue Design

In hindsight, the Royal Navy's immediate postwar vision for a successful replenishment ship design was actually quite bold. The suggestion, based on all the lessons of the Pacific, was to produce a 10,000-ton fleet issue ship capable of 6,000–8,000 miles endurance at an operational speed of 17 knots, with good rudder and handling characteristics. The ship would have every conceivable modern facility including essential navigation equipment—that is, gyrocompass—and a full communications suite. Most importantly, there would be no loss of speed due to diverted power for the pumps, and the very latest burton and jackstay cargo-handling rigs would be installed (including an ability to lift boats, if necessary, and an ability to carry two medium landing craft).[68]

   Equal attention had also been given to endurance. Not only would it have three months of victualling stores (including refrigerated) on board for its own use, it would also have electric or oil-fired galleys, bakeries, and laundries plus ample water distillation capacity and an ability to be refueled at sea.[69] This was an impressive aspiration in line with modern warship design even though economics would rule out many of these options. Still, it remained important enough for the Admiralty to establish in 1946, through the Shipping Defence Advisory Committee, a study of what type of special features should be incorporated to make freighters and store ships "adaptable for war purposes" thereby enabling the various necessary fleet issuing ships to replenish ammunition as well as fleet stores and provisions. The study soon concluded that since the conversion only applied to a limited number of ships, it would be better not to have shipbuilders design a class of merchant ships in anticipation of meeting any potential but yet undefined fleet train specifications; rather, the Admiralty should be kept informed of design progress within the shipbuilding industry, and when the time came for needing a fleet train ship, it would then contact the ship owner direct.[70] Given that it would take about eight months to convert a merchant ship into a VSIS, clearly some planning was paramount, but this was proving to be quite problematic, absent any clear overseas base policy.[71] The existing fleet issue ships for victualling/naval stores and ammunition were all *Fort*-class conversions of 8,000–10,000 tons displacement, most of which remained on freighting duties to earn their keep until required for a fleet train. Although none was equipped to undertake large transfers while under way at sea, they were still very useful. Indeed, an indication of their value (whether as part of a mobile logistic support group or as a remotely located "service station," should U.K. bases and dockyards be attacked by conventional or nuclear weapons) can be gauged from the fact that each one was designed to support over a period of six months up to forty-two destroyers, frigates, and minesweepers; or four cruisers and twenty-one destroyers; or eight cruisers and eight light fleet carriers.[72]

Part of the thinking behind this new design had been that combining the attributes of ships that issue provisions (VSIS) with those issuing naval stores (NSIS) would reduce from three to two the number of auxiliary types needed for any replenishment operation. Thus, any warship would have to go alongside either tankers or only one of these general issuing ships instead of three or even four. Equally important, in peacetime one general issuing ship could take the place of all three specialized cargo ships, that is, NSIS for stores, VSIS for victualling, and ASIS for ammunition, which would save on manpower, training, and operating costs—an increasingly important consideration postwar. Doubts remained, however, as to whether this was really feasible; the problem was that the combined "shop" and "warehouse" (victualling and naval stores) would not be consumed at equal rates, so the ships would be required to reload one type before the other was depleted.[73] Others believed any such handicap was overridden by the benefits to be had in terms of cost control and maximizing efficiency by integrating them into one design. Not surprisingly, the strongest support came from those who advocated the need for a naval replenishment ship designed from the hull upward. Then it could provide provisions ammunition and fuels from one or at most two hulls, thus reducing reliance upon other parties with their inherently inadequate hulls, which would always require messy conversions anyway.

British Tanker Design

There were three broad categories of tankers operated by the RFA. Harbor tankers attended the fleet in harbor but were unsuitable for freighting oil in bulk. Intermediate tankers serviced the fleet in harbor but provided limited freighting and replenishment at sea. Large tankers were primarily used for freighting in peacetime but were often fitted out for underway replenishment in need, in which event their freighting duties would then be taken over by requisitioned commercial tankers.[74]

Despite the impression that the 1946 auxiliary plans had been allowed to languish, a new initiative during 1950 resurrected once again the idea of a fully flexible fleet train reflecting a more efficient use of these different types of tankers.[75] In fact these new initiatives called for an even more sophisticated variant but that, again, depended on a fully navalized design from the keel up (see appendix R). The new proposal was for a fast "replenishment tanker" that would operate as part of any fleet train by remaining in theater replenishing under way the whole carrier task force. As stocks ran low, it would then depart to rendezvous with and refill from shuttle tankers bringing oil to the refueling area from forward or intermediate bases. These shuttle tankers would in turn refill from freighting or bulk tankers that had transported the oil from its source. The proposed fast fleet tankers were even more advanced than the Admiralty 1946 design, capable of steaming at 22 knots, with a cargo of 15,000 tons and pumping oil at 2,400 tph and aviation fuel at 250 tph. With such high pumping capacity, she would then be able to service four ships simultaneously, including two destroyers astern, all at 20 knots.[76] The proposed shuttle tanker design, first produced in 1949 (although not expected to be ordered until 1952), was comparable to any American specification. Capable of carrying 15,000 tons at 18 knots, these would be able to deliver oil abeam or astern at 1,500 tph and aviation fuel at 250 tph to two ships simultaneously at a respectable 15 knots.[77] This then left the transportation of fuel from Admiralty stocks to the forward or intermediate base with bulk tankers that would typically be normal commercial tankers.

It was believed within the Admiralty that these proposals, combined with the aforementioned fast fleet issue ship for all types of solids requirements, would meet overall fleet sustainability needs at a stroke. Whether they were realistic remained questionable, although the basic concept itself was very much in line with that adopted by the U.S. Navy; in fact, the specifications for the very fast tanker were superior to anything on American drawing boards at the time. The U.S. Navy was actually quite impressed. As Captain Pare described it, the British specifications were "much superior to any we now have, or have under design. This ship is just about what we want in a replenishment vessel, and a homogenous group of such ships would represent the modern replenishment group as we see it. If these specifications are translated without much change into an actual ship the British will have once more indicated their superior skill in shipbuilding."[78]

While Captain Pare's motivation must have been to prod his own navy into building a one-stop replenishment ship, this still provided a rare example of

American recognition that the Royal Navy had something superior to contribute in the logistics sphere. In fact, the British were still only developing a "two-stop" ship arrangement, one type for fuels and the other for solids. In the end, of course, without the necessary funding, all these designs were to remain for several years just that—a design.

Programs for New Construction

Nevertheless, some practical progress was made by the Royal Navy, even if not in producing an actual new naval replenishment ship. At the end of World War II an emergency program had been undertaken to replace several worn out harbor and intermediate tankers, eight being completed during this period costing £3½ million each.[79] This outlay absorbed virtually all the available funds for brand new auxiliaries for the next few years. Indeed, the only modernization was to eight of the twenty *Wave*-class tankers, each of which cost £1 million and half of which had served with the BPF Fleet Train in 1945. Two freighters were also converted to ammunition supply ships, which at least was a step forward. By 1950 however, the RFA tanker fleet really was starting to look a little weary, consisting as it did of a considerable number of "overripe ships, many of which were built as early as 1919."[80] It would take another war before any of this would improve.

U.S. Navy Progress in Design

Unlike within the Admiralty, there was no conviction in the U.S. Navy after 1945 to build any new naval tankers as replacements, either for those lost or otherwise scheduled for scrapping. Although in May 1946 Fleet Admiral Nimitz recommended construction of a high-speed 25–30 knot oiler (Project 22) and a very fast armaments/provisions ship (Project 23), neither was taken up, ostensibly because of the overriding concern for demobilizing the existing abundance of auxiliaries as quickly as possible.[81] Even design improvements were slow to crystallize, as the lessons learned from the war took their time to percolate through the system.

That the U.S. Navy progressed so slowly would at first glance appear somewhat surprising. After all, the momentum gained from successful wartime experience should have encouraged new designs for special underway replenishment ships and transfer techniques. Instead, research and development had been virtually frozen and most of the wartime auxiliaries mothballed. Plans, on the other hand, were relatively cheap, so it was recognized that it still made sense at least to develop these to such a level that when the next war started—and it must be remembered this was still regarded as a real possibility not lightly dismissed at the time—then all that was required was to go ahead and build in the numbers desired. Encapsulating the problem well, Captain Pare acknowledged that "a mobile support organization, necessary in war, is not nearly so necessary in peacetime, and cannot expect to get the attention we think it deserves as an arm of the Fleet. . . . We only ask that plans be finished, and not for completed ships, because under present circumstances it would be an idle dream to request the building of such a ship."[82]

Consequently, there was little change from wartime practice in the first few years after the war because the few auxiliaries still deployed had simply not changed. Interestingly, though, the conclusions reached by the U.S. Navy for new designs were not too dissimilar from the British. For example, in terms of the optimum size for fleet issue ships, both concluded this should be 10,000 dwt.; a larger capacity might be advantageous economically, but it was conceded this would cause many problems with port facilities as well as cargo handling and storage.[83] Earlier in this chapter it was noted that the British struggled to reconcile the competing demands of speed over economy. For the Americans, this was less of an issue. Tankers used for underway replenishment were fully navalized anyway, and for the time considered to be fast enough. If commercial tankers needed to be converted to naval freighting duties, these could theoretically be drawn from the U.S. merchant marine fleet, 90 percent of which was relatively modern, having been built between 1939 and 1946. In fact, only a relatively small core of some 14 percent of the 683 tankers were more than twenty years old and incapable of more than 12 knots, whereas nearly 60 percent of the newer T-2 and T-3 class could at least achieve 14–14½ knots, thus qualifying them for conversion to naval auxiliaries in need.[84] If the U.S. Navy had a problem at all, it related to certain types of AKA cargo vessels that might need to be converted for fleet train purposes. The U.S. Maritime Commission, for instance, apparently took "a dim view" of the U.S. Navy's demand for a 20-knot freighter, settling instead for a limit nearer to the British, at around 18½ knots based on full load displacement—not that this seemed to have posed much of a hurdle for the U.S. Navy, which circumvented this constriction by "unloading them again to the point where an 18½ knot ship will make 20 knots."[85] There is no evidence that the Royal Navy took the same expedient approach, but then their speed threshold was lower anyway.

However, if speed was not the primary problem for the U.S. Navy, then other matters were brewing that could sooner or later affect plans for new auxiliary ships. The cause lay primarily in the condition of many of the so-called inactive fleet of 1,891 merchant vessels owned by the Maritime Commission laid up in reserve, all but 135 of which were dry cargo vessels.[86] Too many were either too slow or damaged and in a state of deterioration that they no longer warranted the cost of maintenance and preservation, let alone conversion. Although conversion in World War II of slow or medium speed cargo or cargo/passenger ships into naval transports was considered expedient and necessary, by 1949 this was regarded as "an unacceptable course of action for adoption in a future war because of the known increased effectiveness of modern submarines."[87] So ships below 14 knots no longer qualified for reactivation, leaving many destined for scrap or sale. What is notable is that any replacement program designed to avoid repeating the mistakes of the past was still not regarded as cost justified. Korea, admittedly, was still a year or two away, but very little new construction or even contracts were made during this period—no dry cargo ships, just fifty-four tankers and five passenger ships.

Anglo-American Exchange

Having looked at the slow progress by either navy for getting beyond the drawing board to the shipyard, the question arises as whether it would have been possible to cross-own auxiliaries, or at least exchange design research information so that, as and when funds became available, the chances of expediting the latest design into production would be enhanced. It would appear, however, that there was little prospect of any convergence in ship design, partly because American dimensions were considerably greater than the British dimensions, given that they needed higher levels of built-in self maintenance and endurance capacity. British docking facilities were also "more neglected, and therefore restricted [and] would have to receive a good deal of attention if it were found desirable to follow to any extent the American trend in size."[88] As for research exchange, this was completely one-sided in favor of the Americans. Considerable evidence shows the frustration and disappointment felt within the Admiralty that, despite all the—often secret—research information handed over to the Americans, not just during the war but in subsequent years, there had been a singular lack of reciprocity at anything like the same level.[89] Nor did the U.S. Navy deny this one-sidedness. At the U.S. Navy General Board Hearings, convened in 1948 to discuss shipbuilding and design requirements for the forthcoming decade, it was acknowledged that the British were "very open minded about exchange" that proved to be "much better for us than it is for them."[90] While the U.S. Navy was conversant on whatever the British were researching, including hull and equipment design, virtually all the return flow was unclassified information unless U.S. naval intelligence gave particular dispensation for the release of classified information. And this was only even considered if the British had specifically asked for it. The onus was therefore on the British to anticipate what classified work might have been undertaken by the U.S. Navy.

Although the U.S. Navy's Office of Naval Research sought to excuse their position as merely complying with JCS policy, the real reason appeared to be the fear that if American industrial research reached the British, there might be patent infringement, given the lack of patent harmonization between the two countries. It was felt this might disadvantage American industry, which the U.S. Navy wanted to protect, particularly because so much British research information was allegedly channeled through its Ministry of Supply, which "together with certain aspects of their military establishments," made it possible for civilians to acquire information that "might be leaked out into industry." The British might also see the implications of such American research before the Americans did and "thus stymie us over here." It also seemed to be the case that the Americans had in fact previously given classified information to the British that "turned out to have considerable risk attached to it from an intelligence and security point of view."[91] The implication was that this had been a mistake too far.

Conclusion

As the Americans had first discovered just prior to 1941, only the contingencies of actual war justified setting aside normal commercial constraints to build a fast, purpose-built replenishment tanker. But then at the time speed was the overriding priority. Whether this was still justified under peacetime conditions was simply not an available option. In fact, it would take another war to resurrect such an idea. Even then, no attempt was actually made by the Americans to integrate naval and commercial speed parameters into design until after the Korean War in 1954, when the JCS approved an immediate requirement for 175 T-2 equivalent oilers for the mobilization reserve, "constructed with a sustained speed of from 16–20 knots with the speed selected in this range [to] be governed by economic considerations."[92]

And it was not until Korea, when the magnitude of the problems encountered by the U.S. Navy in handling the huge volumes of ordnance and aircraft and furnace fuel necessary to sustain the carrier at sea, that the U.S. Navy felt it was necessary to seek a complete review in 1952 of how underway replenishment should be conducted. The combination of this review and, more critically, the release of the necessary funds, very quickly helped resurrect—literally—the plans for a new 36,000-ton displacement 20-knot fleet oiler specifically engineered for replenishing warships at sea. The first of the class was called USS *Neosho*, shown in plate 5.1. Launched in 1953, she incorporated for the first time such features as a full-length cargo deck to support both fuel and solid cargo stations employing the highline and burton methods.[93]

The *Neosho* was the first oiler to be designed from the keel up since USS *Kanawha* was laid down in 1913, and while it did not represent a revolutionary step forward—this would still have to come later—the result was notwithstanding the most important and comprehensive advance in mobile logistic ship design since 1945. Five new ammunition ships were also designed and built from the keel up, specifically to issue ammunition under way at higher speed using new methods of storage and improved handling machinery.[94] The primary triggers for getting beyond the planning stage? Simply the manifest failure of old designs to cope with the new demands, particularly for ammunition and aviation fuel while under way, combined with the sudden availability of funds during the Korean War.

As for the Royal Navy, while the pressure for faster replenishment continued, there was no prospect of new tankers coming on stream even by the Korean War, so reliance remained on further ad hoc modifications to replenishment gear on what remained of the underpowered inadequately designed commercial hulls that still formed the RFA fleet. While this was expedient, given the financial circumstances, at some point the law of diminishing returns would apply. A more radical approach in rig technology and hull design had to be found, but again the solution did not appear until after the Korean War. The genesis for a new design, however, had come much earlier. As will be demonstrated in chapter 7, the real breakthough for both tanker and rig design was derived from a series of important replenishment trials that the Royal Navy undertook using a captured German replenishment ship during the late 1940s. But if these trials provided a solution, it was the subsequent experience gained in the Korean War that provided the catalyst for obtaining the vital funds. As a result, four purpose-designed fast fleet replenishment ships, each projected to cost £2 million, were built after the Korean War. These were the 17,715 dwt *Tide* class, introduced in 1955, an example of which can be seen in plate 5.2. Capable of 17 knots, these new tankers were fully equipped to transfer oil and jet aircraft fuel as well as modest amounts of food, stores, ammunition, by jackstay or derricks even under arctic or tropical service.[95] Although smaller and slightly slower than USS *Neosho*, the new *Tide* class was really a huge stride forward for the RFA, even though much of the design had been on the drawing boards for so many years. Indeed, appendix R shows just how little had changed (at least superficially) between the original 1946 tanker design discussed earlier and this result, the *Tide*-class, launched eight years later.

When comparing this new breed of replenishment tanker, which each navy introduced at more or less the same time, it nevertheless really becomes quite remarkable how much further and faster replenishment design and technology had progressed in the Royal Navy since 1945 when, it will be recalled, American naval tanker design and performance was immeasurably ahead of any rival. Given the lack of new construction by either country before the Korean War, this says as much about the value of continuing research and development inherent in so much of British ship design as it does about the value of trials and the progress in doctrine. Yet the real revolution in ship design had still to come, because among the many lessons learned from Korea was the need to have fast combat support ships remaining on station, permanently assigned to the task force and able to dispense simultaneously fuel ammunition and provisions whenever required. This was truly one-stop shopping that demanded a wholly fresh approach to design from the keel up. This could be the only way forward.

6 | Strategic Mobilization
The Case for Reserve Fleets

WITH BOTH NAVIES at their peak strength by the end of World War II, the most immediate postwar challenge was to arrest the momentum and decelerate their complex machinery in an orderly and planned way. As the Vice Chief of Naval Operations (VCNO) of the U.S. Navy put it, "We could not choose the time and circumstances of our mobilization. But in demobilization the initiative is ours."[1] However, given the profound changes in the political, economic, and strategic landscape that affected both countries after 1945, their navies were presented with many unknowns to consider both from home and abroad. The immediate challenge was to determine the most appropriate type and size of forces required for conducting their peacetime responsibilities while remaining alert to the uncertainties ahead, not least those caused by the initially modest but growing tension between the West and the Soviet bloc that could ultimately lead to renewed military conflict.

This chapter looks at the force level effects upon both navies brought by rapid demobilization and their efforts to establish appropriate mobilization plans in the event of another war. It also seeks to establish how well the logistic dimension was addressed during this postwar period, particularly in the use of reserve fleets. Was this, for example, a useful way for preserving existing mobile logistic support capability? Using the Korean War as an example, did auxiliary fleet reserves for both navies prove to be relevant, and if so, was the original decision to create them therefore vindicated? At the broader level, was the whole concept of creating and managing reserve fleets strategically successful and cost effective?

Demobilization

For the U.S. Navy, an ambitious plan code-named Operation ZIPPER was proposed for demobilizing more than 3 million tons of naval ships.[2] Three levels of fleet readiness were initially identified: active, semiactive (i.e., still in commission and materially complete but not fully manned), and the inactive or mothballed 16th and 19th Reserve Fleets. Appendix S provides the provisional list of all three groups, produced in November 1945, separated into ship types with their proposed disposition.[3] This was the initial plan, but the reality proved far different. The abrupt cessation of hostilities, combined with increasing public demand for repatriation and demobilization, completely disrupted the planned schedules.[4] On the day of Japan's surrender, for example, a thousand ships were sailing west across the Pacific from the United States with huge stockpiles rapidly accumulating on naval bases. Virtually overnight, ships and war plans had to be reversed, creating immense logistical problems. Ships returned home laden with surplus equipment but were forced to lay at anchor for weeks in clogged ports waiting for space.[5]

Adding to the confusion was the recognition that any demobilization plan had to accommodate the possibility that an undetermined portion of such demobilized ships might need to be reactivated in emergency. What must be remembered is just how fast the U.S. Navy had grown in the last year of the war, with total tonnage increasing from 6.2 million tons in 1944 to more than 14 million tons in 1946.[6] As can be seen in appendix T, the cuts affected some types more than others, partly reflecting the way naval forces were expected to operate in peacetime and partly reflecting the inherent acute skilled manpower shortage, particularly for the larger ships. Battleships, escort carriers, and amphibious classes, for example, were reduced by nearly 90 percent, many scrapped and the balance placed in reserve. Fleet carriers were less affected because many were relatively new, but escort/ASW vessels were seriously eroded, particularly frigates until the Russian submarine threat became real enough to warrant their reactivation. The other severely mauled group was the naval auxiliaries, which by 1950 had been reduced by more than 80 percent.

For Britain, the pace of demobilization was no less brutal. As can be seen from appendix U, the total Royal Navy fleet had grown rapidly to more than 8,500 ships by August 1945. In less than two years, this would collapse by more than 75 percent to 1,848 vessels, of which nearly 60 percent were relegated to reserve status. The pressure for reducing overhead was, and indeed remained throughout the period, unrelenting.

Summary Strategic Overview

The U.S. Navy's postwar naval strategy, which shaped its postwar planning well into the mid-1950s, was very much founded on the potential for a possible global war breaking out against the Soviet Union, a perceived gap in ASW capability against the new Russian fast submarines, and an expectation that carriers would have to operate within range of enemy shore-based aircraft. Underpinning this was the recognition that European waters, including the Mediterranean and Middle East, now replaced the Pacific as the primary theater of naval operations.[7] Over the next two years detailed plans were drawn up to address how the U.S. Navy would respond to a number of future threats, despite the lack of any clear enemy on the immediate horizon. This meant in essence retaining the war-winning concept of carrier task forces, each supported by a fast replenishment group operating from the Western Atlantic up to the Barents Sea, down through the Mediterranean, leaving only a small carrier group for the whole Pacific. The U.S. Navy, with its military and political future increasingly predicated on the successful promotion in Washington of its proven superior carrier-based airpower, had therefore adopted its traditional offensive posture: to neutralize any maritime threat by "attacking at source" if necessary.[8]

Meanwhile, since the spring of 1948, American and British naval planners had been working on emergency war plans that would either deter or otherwise respond to and, if necessary, fight off a large-scale Soviet attack in Europe. Hence the introduction of NATO containment and the vital need for maintaining sea control to achieve convoy protection so Britain could be sustained and reinforced for the eventual counterstrike. For the Royal Navy, tasked with defending the sea-lanes but convinced its contribution could and should expand further and wider, the key to survival was to ensure its forces were adequately trained and prepared "with an appropriate backing of ancillary vessels" should war should break out.[9] Yet Britain's efforts to retain its great power status, with "sea power being an essential component, owing to its strategic mobility worldwide,"[10] required maintaining forces (including overseas garrisons) that by 1948, for example, were costing a disproportionately large percentage of GNP compared to other Western nations.[11] The Admiralty's early plans during this time, predicated as they were upon a repeat performance of the global battles recently fought and won, soon proved not merely ambitious but totally unrealistic, in both ships and manpower.[12] Demobilization and obsolescence had drastically reduced both, despite the continuing need for a balanced fleet capable of meeting worldwide commitments. Because financial constraints limited the number of ships in commission at any one time, the solution was to rotate active units through a reserve fleet, particularly the larger ships, which needed to be retained to avoid the prospect of long construction delays, should it become necessary once again to meet "the hazards of war."[13]

Within short order, however, Britain was forced to recognize that the security of her sea-lanes could no longer be guaranteed without American engagement from the beginning, so the central tenet of British policy assumed that savings could best be accomplished by canceling weapons upgrades (which might be obsolete by 1957 anyway) and concentrate on preserving and then modernizing the fleet. This in turn would be supplemented by completing hitherto virtually suspended construction programs, to ensure that new ships were brought on stream by the early 1950s in time for the peak critical risk in 1957—the so-called Nine-Year Plan.

The central dilemma for both navies during this period was how to deal with a range of different strategic and operational challenges that were constantly changing both in priority and in perspective. Some challenges were difficult to gauge, such as the risk of atomic attack due to the lack of any relevant precedent. Others were difficult to prepare for because of the uncertainty surrounding when or what type of forces might be appropriate. Meanwhile both navies needed to resume the myriad peacetime maritime (and, for the U.K., constabulary) obligations, including showing the flag to protect and promote Anglo-American commercial, political, and trading interests around the world. However, given the rapid redundancy of large wartime forces, the question for both navies was how best to harness economically the necessary combat and support forces to meet their existing maritime obligations and yet be ready and properly equipped to respond to future contingencies, including the possibility of global war. The North Korean invasion of South Korea in June 1950, as it so happened, came as a complete surprise both in its timing and in the nature of operations required from both Allied navies.

Logistic Mobilization Plans, 1946–1950

It is against this backdrop that mobilization plans were prepared. Early wartime experience had already shown how difficult it could be to mobilize effectively without being thoroughly prepared, so logistic planning and its influence on mobilization strategy assumed a much higher profile—particularly in the United States—through postwar organizational reform. The key was to introduce extensive phased mobilization programs that could draw upon properly maintained reserve fleets when required. In other words, a judicious split of affordable resources was required between active and reserve elements to meet all possible contingencies. To quote the U.S. Secretary of the Navy, James Forrestal, "If world conditions deteriorated so that the reserve vessels must be called to active duty, the Nation would have a navy as big as our wartime aggregation of power. Between the two extremes, a pre-war fleet and a wartime fleet, the nation should be able to vary its strength from time to time as world conditions require."[14] The challenge was to find the right balance despite the twin handicap of tight budgets and the effects of rapid and deep demobilization. Any belief that new technologies could solve all future needs problems had to be tempered by the several lessons drawn from recent experience that implied that nothing beats being simply well prepared. Or as Admiral Carney put it, "The magic of the future must be weighed against the proofs of the past."[15] Yet the time available for mobilization had historically not been decisive—important yes, but not decisive. In the future, time was expected to be not only a critical factor because of the suddenness of any outbreak of war, but with the recent advances in technology and weapons complexity, it would become increasingly difficult to plan the logistic implications of any sudden large-scale mobilization. As the Director of Procurement in Washington noted in 1947, "in both world wars, we had advance warning and a period of protection by our Allies in which to mobilize our strength. No enemy will make the same mistake the third time."[16]

Although mobilization planning should complement, not overshadow, force planning, its effectiveness or otherwise could still very much determine the outcome. This concern for having adequate time to prepare seemed to influence much of the military's thinking throughout the next decade, as the fear of Communist aggression breaking out on a global basis seemed to become self-perpetuating.[17] Actually, it was only by constantly reminding everyone of the country's vulnerability to being unprepared for future war that mobilization planning came to be taken seriously. The breakthough came when logistic and strategic planning was at last applied concurrently, that is, fully integrated and appropriately balanced.

U.S. Navy Mobilization Plans

The first stage of the planning process was for the CNO to distribute his interpretation of the naval component of the JCS's broad strategic plan, which set out the operational and logistical tasks, policy guidance, and an indication of the required forces together with applicable broad material requirements. This requirement would then cascade down to the Offices of the Navy Department, Commanders of Active and Reserve Fleets, and Naval Districts as well as the various bureaus, to enable them to produce sets of implementation plans covering both peace and war contingencies. These plans were expected to be addressed in two steps, first by establishing the requirements necessary to meet the various contingencies and second by determining capabilities, based on actual available resources.

The first of the postwar plans produced by the CNO under the Navy War Planning System that dealt specifically with logistics and mobilization was called the "Navy Basic Mobilization Plan" (NBM-1), promulgated on May 9, 1947. Its express purpose was to determine "the requirements for the expansion of the naval Establishment for total war" that "may occur at any time."[18] This replaced the mobilization section of the earlier all-encompassing "Preparation for Logistic Support Plan no. 1," originally produced in December 1945.[19] The balance of the logistical features contained in the aforementioned 1945 Logistic Support Plan were also overtaken by a new logistics plan titled "Navy Basic Logistic Plans, I-48, Part II (Mobilization)." Both plans were subsequently updated in 1950–51 to reflect revised requirements, but the essential underlying premise of NBM-1, namely that everything was predicated upon the outbreak of total war rather than a series of limited wars, remained essentially unchanged. What was new was the gradual adoption of a more sophisticated approach to phasing based on various levels of contingency.

It is important to remember, though, that these were requirement plans that did not reflect capabilities because the latter were always subject to budgets. This might explain why the plans appeared so ambitious. This first plan, for example, assumed that 98 percent of a reserve fleet of 1,982 vessels would be activated within nine months from mobilization.[20] This presumption, the Navy General Board learned, would "give us a chance to fight faster another time."[21] Whether the ships in question matched the task was not always apparent, nor was any logic provided as to how the split between warships, auxiliaries, and amphibious was derived.[22] What was also noticeable was that, of the fleet train component (some 268 ships, or 13 percent of the total), only 16 were designed specifically to replenish warships at sea.[23] Any expansion would therefore have to rely on new construction or conversions, with the vast majority only delivered two or more years into any war.[24] Yet the so-called defensive stage—that is, the necessary time to contain the enemy and prepare for and seize the offensive—was expected to last twelve months, leaving a further twelve months to reach maximum offensive effort.[25] Although it was true that during the peak of the wartime shipbuilding effort (following four years of expansion through 1945) it was possible for U.S. shipyards to build escort vessels in six months and submarines or destroyers in nine months, any future mass production on this scale would be difficult if not impossible to emulate as warships became increasingly complex and electronically more sophisticated.[26]

No capacity increase was expected within the first two years, and delivery in quantity was unlikely before the fourth year. In other words, as Admiral Wheelock put it at the hearings before the General Board of the Navy on the Reserve Fleet, "we shall have to fight for three years using, with but minor exception, ships already built."[27] It was a similar but less exacting predicament for merchant/auxiliaries, although acquisitions from the merchant marine would still be necessary.[28] Indeed, the other assumption to note from a mobility perspective was that in the light of their experience in World War II, the U.S. Navy intended (although it was not yet ratified) to progressively man with naval personnel all U.S. merchant vessels—potentially about three thousand—that would need to be acquired for the Naval Transportation Service.[29]

When, on September 22, 1950, some three months after the Korean War had unexpectedly broken out, the CNO promulgated "NBM-1A Navy Basic Mobilization Plan" to replace the 1947 version, a couple of significant steps forward were made. The new requirements plan provided for a more phased approach, commencing with minimum requirements for offensive operations ranging up to those necessary to prosecute total war. Second, it also tried to determine much better the scope of the logistical effort involved because "in planning for mobilization it must be kept constantly in mind by all planners that rapid mobilization is essential."[30] The general assumption as to where the preponderance of naval offensive effort would be required had now shifted from "Atlantic/Pacific and adjacent Arctic waters" (1947) to just the "Atlantic-Mediterranean" by 1950, recognition that Northeast Asia was still a sideshow despite the Korean War, with the real underlying threat remaining Euro-centric.[31]

U.S. Navy Logistic Plans

It is perhaps worth distinguishing at this stage the difference in meaning between "logistics planning" and "planning for logistic support." The first incorporated the various logistic considerations for helping commanders or the JCS estimate what was needed to formulate the broad strategic or operational plans. The latter applied to the more detailed analysis of the nature of logistic support required by combat forces for specific campaigns or operations.[32] To save time and ensure consistency in their compilation across the various joint plans, all naval logisticians relied on comprehensive lists of regularly updated "Planning Factors" that were documented in "Logistic Reference Data" covering a wide variety of variables including ship characteristics, ship and air component data, transportation formulas, turnaround times, and so on.[33] Naval logistics planning at this more practical level was channeled through the U.S. Navy's "Basic Logistic Plan Part II Mobilization" (NBL 2), of which a revised version was published in 1951.[34] This document formed the template for other logistic code plans, such as for Naval Transportation, which could then address in more detail the different contingencies both short and long range in scope, with any materiel consequences accounted for in the main logistic plan. The process of comparing material availability to requirements across all these plans then became an inevitably convoluted liaison between the various strategic, logistic, and implementation planners that became both vertical—that is, between the materiel bureaus and the JCS via the assistant secretary or munitions boards or the office of the Deputy CNO (Logistics)—or else horizontal—that is, between the various bureaus themselves.[35] Every opportunity was taken to remind those involved of the importance attached to achieving a sense of unity between the logistic and strategic planners, hence the deliberate intention for having logistic plans prepared concurrent to, rather than divorced from, strategic and tactical plans. Only by such integration was there any prospect of being able to state what was needed and who would provide it, how, when, and where.

It is quite striking, when looking at the various logistic plans as they evolved over time, that despite their size and the complexity of their production, they still managed to reflect changes in emphasis as events or experience dictated. A case in point was how the U.S. Navy's approach to mobility requirements changed as a result of early experiences in the Korean War. The summary of ships ready for deployment, as outlined in NBM-1A, dated 1950 reflected pre–Korean War assumptions. For instance, the effects of mobilization would only start crystallizing by month 12 with the larger capital ships arriving even later. What is more interesting to note, in terms of mobile replenishment, was that any expansion became relatively cautious with no further reliance on new construction. All sixty-seven oilers, for example, required to supplement the thirty-eight on the active list would be derived from conversions, with most only becoming available after fifteen months. Similarly with only three AKS's on the active list, the additional twenty-nine would all be conversions, and of the estimated thirty-nine AEs required, twenty-three would be conversions to support the eight active and eight mobilized from reserve.[36]

All these projections, however, had to be modified in the revised Basic Logistic Plan (NBL-2) produced by the Logistic Plans Division only a few months after publication of NBM-1A but, more significantly, also following several months of experience trying to provide mobile logistic support to the American carrier forces in Korea. Although the numbers of proposed AEs and AKSs were substantially increased, which was to be expected, these still relied entirely on conversions, but for fleet oilers the opposite was now the case. A complete new fleet was now proposed that would comprise ninety-five replenishment oilers spread over five years, sixteen delivered before Mobilization Day, M-Day, with peak output after three years.[37] What might have prompted such a radical change? First, this plan would have been the first produced when the U.S. Navy was no longer inhibited by lack of funds, and second, recent Korean experience had immediately reinforced the urgent need for building fast fleet oilers designed from the keel up to meet speed, cargo capacity, and transfer rates demanded by modern—that is, jet—air warfare. With the few oilers in reserve too slow and up for sale, only a new design would suffice. Not unlike the Admiralty, with their desire too for building a tailor-made naval replenishment tanker solution, the U.S. Navy's plans were still very prototype. Unlike the Admiralty's protracted experience, however, the American solution actually arrived comparatively quickly, for in November 1953 the new AO-143 *Neosho* class, designed specifically to meet modern fleet needs, was launched.[38] The significance of all this on ship design, strategy, and replenishment tactics was discussed in chapter 5—it is sufficient to point out here that compared to the inbuilt rigidity of the earlier logistics plans, there was now seemingly much more fluidity built into requirements and capabilities assessments for these new logistic plans.

Royal Navy Mobilization Plans

Unlike the American preference for a formalized planning process that was fairly rigid in construct and style to cope with the size and geographic spread of the U.S. Navy, the Admiralty adopted what appeared to be a much more central-ized but low-level, informal—even disaggregated—approach to the preparation of any logistic plans for mobilization. Debates over future fleet requirements and objectives were naturally circulated among the Board of Admiralty, but many of these papers were the outcome of various executive working party committees, a popular forum for examining important issues from all perspectives including that of planning.[39] Some working party reports were indeed transformed into cornerstone policy papers addressing the future number and disposition of com-missioned ships, as well as the size of a reserve fleet in the event of war.[40]

Potentially one of the most far-reaching of the early committee outcomes was the Harwood Committee, which produced its first report in 1949 looking at the shape and size of Britain's armed forces over the next few years within a set of predetermined financial constraints imposed by the Treasury. These constraints had the effect of layering priorities depending on the extent of "insurance" to be chosen in the event of future war breaking out, and while the committee did not outline any specific strategy for mobilization per se, it certainly attempted to de-termine the aggregation of resources in ships and facilities that could be finan-cially justified.[41] From the Admiralty's perspective, the report was devastating because it created such a geographic imbalance in both fleet and overseas bases. For them, it was not only inaccurate and debilitating but the Working Party's conclusions were "utterly unrealistic and militarily reprehensible."[42] To some degree, of course, the Admiralty was using the Far East as an example to justify retaining a significant part of the postwar fleet dependent upon retaining bases around the world—despite the absence of any clear threat abroad and despite the lack of any coherent national strategic and defense policy that reflected Britain's overall vested interests. Nevertheless, it fell upon the Director of Plans to produce a position paper on what might constitute a restricted fleet to meet this economic imposition, but when this was subsequently deemed to be still too ambitious, a further more circumspect policy document, called "Revised Restricted Fleet," was produced by the Admiralty in June 1949.[43] This educed into the policy for achieving a balanced fleet for war by 1957 with its size determined by whatever was "economically possible." However, although it would be fitted with modern armament and equipment, any new construction would still require mobilizing additional manpower resources because even current levels barely covered ex-isting warships even after the disposal of all those vessels considered either the least useful or in the poorest condition.[44]

It is interesting to note that these high-level policy papers make virtually no mention of what logistic support might be appropriate to service any fleet. One can only deduce that this was to be considered subordinate in every respect to first establishing the correct fighting fleet level. In other words, the logistic im-plications could be tailored afterward by the Naval Staff relying on interdepartmental consensus to reach a suitable recommendation. As with many aspects of establishing naval policy and implementation, such reviews would typically be collected or disseminated through the internal docket system; although this process undoubtedly encouraged a high degree of liaison and discussion between the various departments and divisions, it had its limitations. As far as can be established, the planning procedure was never converted into the adoption of a formal mobilization template that could be promulgated throughout the Naval Staff to provide a sense of continuity, consistency, or development. Meanwhile the logistic implications for fleet requirements were coordinated, as one might expect, from the Director of Plans (Q) to the various functional divisions and groups such as the reserve and active fleet commands, among others. Where separate plans were produced, for example, for personnel mobilization, these were then reconciled to other unit plans, such as those produced by, for example, the reserve fleet command.[45]

Because the Admiralty increasingly conceded their dependence on American support and even geographical control in any future conflict, the Director of Plans was actively encouraged to discuss with American JCS planners about what resources the Royal Navy could likely muster in the event of outbreak of war within the next eighteen-month period. But these were not plans in the formal sense, more the case of what steps needed to be taken "possibly short of actual mobilization."[46] There remained, however, the need to determine what long-term steps ought to be taken to reduce the period of unreadiness that was otherwise implicit in all the Admiralty's current plans.

Reserve Fleets

A number of reasons could account for the Admiralty's less rigid approach to mobilization planning. Not least was their natural predilection for regarding centralized administrative planning as merely part of the normal bureaucratic process rather than some exceptional exercise or hurdle that needed to be overcome. More important, though, was that throughout Britain's long history, the Royal Navy had always expanded in war and cut severely in peace, so the tradition of relying on reserves to cope with initial emergencies was nothing new. "In ordinary," as it was called, was the seventeenth-century English term whereby the cost of a ship's upkeep, while out of commission in the dockyard, came out of the "ordinary" naval budget in contrast to "extraordinary" taxes and levies that were raised to construct or keep ships at sea.[47] But the policy of having large numbers of line-of-battle ships in reserve to support a relatively small active fleet became untenable over time as the long average life of sail and timber gave way to the relatively faster obsolescence caused by technological advancement in weapons and materials.[48] The technical challenges for preserving warships—

particularly steel ones—so they could be quickly reactivated from reserve in the event of emergency was only really resolved after World War II, thanks partly to American technology that made a revolutionary impact upon mobilization throughout the subsequent decade.

But many mistakes had to be recognized by both navies to reach this point, more so perhaps for the Americans than the British. After World War I, the importance of keeping ships ready for future service was overlooked by the U.S. Navy, mainly because of the decision to scrap many ships to comply with the tonnage limitation treaties discussed in chapter 1. Those ships identified for inactive status were placed under an organization that unfortunately was so poorly managed with inadequate inspection facilities and personnel that the ships were improperly prepared, poorly preserved, inadequately serviced, or manned. As a result, by 1941 it took the U.S. Navy, for example, two or three times longer than planned, some seven months typically, to activate a destroyer, with an average of nine months to activate a submarine.[49] Given their subsequent short useful service lives because of their condition and inherent obsolescence (the fifty destroyers lend-leased to Britain, for example, were soon relegated or retired within a few years), some fresh thinking was required to avoid the next generation of ships being equally inadequately preserved.[50] Three years later on May 31, 1944, President Roosevelt wrote, "Both in 1917 and in 1941 we found that vessels in reserve commission were not in as good condition as we expected them to be. The Navy ought not to get in that condition again."[51] The mobilization experience of the Royal Navy had undertaken a different course during the last few decades, partly from necessity and partly due to circumstance. Professor Sumida notes, for example, that prior to 1914 "the rapid activation and concentration of Britain's navy in the event of war constituted the single most important logistical problem facing the Admiralty."[52] Interestingly, he then notes that, although the three years of intense planning had produced a successful outcome in terms of mobilization, when the time came to activate, the real logistical problems began to multiply as an expanded fleet with constantly increasing responsibilities had to be sustained throughout what became a very unplanned for and protracted war.[53] At least when peace finally returned in 1918, the Royal Navy had wisely taken steps to build the necessary infrastructure for not only for managing the seagoing but also preserving the static reserve fleets to meet any future emergency. Three divisions were established in Portsmouth, the Nore, and Devonport where ships could be adequately prepared (although by post–World War II standards still rather crudely) and occasionally tested to monitor any deterioration.[54] This at least had the benefit of identifying the problems—and there were many— before they became too serious or costly to correct. Overcoming the real practical problems associated with preserving ships was therefore an essential postwar task if the future contribution of any reserve fleet was not to be debilitated and their strategic value compromised. The design, composition, regulation, and organization of the reserve fleets established after 1945 were therefore very much the logical outcome of all the lessons learned from the unhappy experiences in mobilizing ships that both navies suffered at the outbreak of World War II. What was not so well anticipated was the need for better control in how ships would be qualified for reserve status. It soon became evident, particularly in the U.S. Navy, for example, that the reserve fleet concept was becoming as one observer put it, "somewhat starry-eyed in many of its implications."[55] Indeed, for a while it seemed anything military that could still float merited a reserve fleet tag.[56] Due to the growing threat from fast submarines, for example, even slow escorts were only protected from the scrap yard because, as Admiral Wheelock submitted "We have never found an occasion in any war when any hull that was in reasonably good condition, and had engines that run, wasn't an extremely valuable tool." To which it was noted that "all witnesses have pointed out pretty much the same thing . . . anything that floats, and has a gun on it, may be useful."[57] Not surprisingly, this penchant for trying to preserve everything in sight didn't survive once increasingly oppressive budgets encouraged measures to "get rid of ships we can't really see a need for."[58] However, it was not just the practical and often unforeseen difficulties of mothballing that absorbed time and money. There was also the massive infrastructure required to create and then support these fleets while the demobilization of navy personnel could be accelerated to satisfy other overriding political and military prerogatives.

The problem for the U.S. Navy was the huge scale of the task ahead. With some 2,100 ships looked after by only 18,000 enlisted men, the U.S. Reserve Fleet was severely constrained by having only 8 or 10 men per ship—hardly even a nucleus but all that could be found with the skills or allowed by the budgets.[59] There was also a growing concern about how to deal with the distribution and concentration risks, given the large numbers of ships involved. Criteria for choosing berthing sites were security, temperate climate, fresh water, and ready access to navy yards capable of berthing as many ships as possible in one area to reduce personnel and facility overhead. Some fifteen sites were chosen on both coasts; similar types and even classes were grouped together wherever possible.[60] For example, most escort carriers went to Boston and Tacoma, the prewar cruisers to Philadelphia, the battle cruisers to Bayonne, and the hundreds of destroyers and escorts were concentrated in California and Florida, along with the huge amphibious fleet.[61] Concentration by type, however, proved controversial. Apart from being vulnerable to enemy attack, many—particularly escorts—were distributed to berthing areas incapable of providing speedy reactivation, yet these were likely to be the first in line for required duty.[62]

The U.S. government also had to decide which ships to dispose from its wartime merchant fleet, with more than half of the four thousand vessels being slow

11-knot *Liberty* ships that had little commercial value, the rest being a mix of *Victory* ships, T-2 tankers, and troop carriers, which American and foreign shipping companies were eager to acquire. The 1946 Merchant Marine Sales Act enabled those that were considered surplus to be made available to the world market; this, for example, had contributed to Britain's prewar tonnage being completely replaced by 1948.[63] For the U.S. Navy there was also the additional windfall of thirty T-2 tankers that were commissioned as naval oilers to transport petroleum from the Middle East refineries to the Sixth and Seventh Fleets in the Mediterranean and Pacific, respectively.[64] Meanwhile, those government-owned ships not sold, transferred, or scrapped were placed into the newly formed National Defense Reserve Fleet (NDRF) stored in six major anchorages, two each in the Atlantic, Gulf and Pacific.[65] The Maritime Commission, "responsible for maintaining a Reserve Fleet in a laid-up status for the purpose of national defense in a future emergency," owned this inactive fleet of 1,891 ships (including 38 slow tankers), many damaged or requiring repair. The total, however, remained well below the 3,683 (43,240,000 dwt.) vessels originally planned for military requirements.[66] By 1948, the auxiliary reserve fleet had settled down to some 950 *Liberty* ships and 153 military auxiliaries, including tenders, hospital ships, ammunition ships, attack transports, and some 50 troopships. The *Victory* cargo and reefers and bulk cargo ships were spread between James River, Virginia, and Suisan Bay, California, but no tankers remained in the reserve fleet; the 17 still laid up were virtually all sub-14-knot tankers assigned for sale or scrap.[67]

In Britain, as appendix U shows, the Royal Navy's reserve fleet had already reached sizable proportions by mid-1945, but as the total fleet became radically reduced in subsequent years, that proportion of the total fleet allocated to reserve grew to more than 60 percent by the time Korea erupted. As new reserve fleet commands were established, these then expanded as the active fleets declined. Their task was "to maintain in mobilization readiness the large number of ships allocated to them, both organizationally and materially to ensure expeditious commissioning."[68] Because of the effects upon morale and Britain's standing with the Americans, it was important to ensure that not only the public in both countries but also the Russians understood exactly what was happening. Hence, the *New York Times* noted that the "British 'Ghost Fleet' is very much alive," and the *London News Chronicle* announced that the Royal Navy now had a powerful reserve fleet that "once given the labour, could be battle worthy within probably a little over a week," then quoted an officer who proclaimed, "We could de-pickle the ships while getting up steam."[69] The reality, however, was so very different.

As it was, all reserve ships were divided by the Admiralty into three categories: those required at short notice, those on extended notice, and those for sale (the so-called Z list). The first two formed the reserve fleet, organized initially into six divisions at Devonport, Portsmouth, Chatham, Sheerness, Harwich, and the Clyde. How they were allocated was governed by the type of berthing facilities most suited to the ship in question as well as manning availability. In fact, the reserve fleet's greatest enemy after damp was manning availability, a problem that never waned even during the Korean crisis.[70] For example, the 1947 planned manpower for the reserve fleet was 9,000 to look after 405 major warships compared to 5,600 in 1938 looking after 129 ships, both just less than 7 percent of total effective manpower.[71] By 1953, the reserve fleet, which had hitherto been confined to the royal dockyards, estuaries, and creeks, transferred for the first time about a third of its fleet to civilian maintenance firms at nine ports around the country, ostensibly to save on money, manpower, and services.[72] This transfer of responsibility contrasted with the U.S. Navy, which regarded civilianizing the process as "the blind leading the blind."[73]

For either navy, some practical problems with modern ships required remedies—some quite revolutionary—to ensure they remained fit enough to be of value upon reactivation. Not everyone in the active fleet, after all, was completely confident that any deficiency for meeting future wartime emergencies would necessarily be filled in a timely fashion from reserves. A case in point could be found in the Emergency Operating Plans of the U.S. Atlantic Fleet Logistic Service Force, which provided mobile support to all U.S. fleet units, including the Fast Striking Force and Eastern Atlantic and Mediterranean forces. Having noted in particular that there would be no further tankers available for logistic support, their planners went on to record that "the Reserve fleet reactivation program provides little if any assistance in Service Force ships except AE, AR, ARG, and ARS types. One additional fast AK would be available after 70 days and 2 tankers and 2 AEs, which would still be inadequate. A further 2 AEs would be available after 100 days and another two after 130 days. The whole operation is notably dependent upon reactivation to work."[74]

This was not exactly a ringing endorsement. Given the dependence that was being placed on these fleets that by now represented the majority of the total U.S. Navy, a series of hearings were conducted over two sessions in 1948 and 1949 before the General Board of the Navy in Washington charged with examining the composition, disposition, and costs of the U.S. Reserve Fleet.[75] It is from these reports that many of this chapter's observations are drawn.

Mothballing: Technical Aspects of Preserving Ships

With the introduction of many new revolutionary techniques in the preservation and mothballing of surplus vessels, both navies were able to calibrate their active force levels to suit existing or near-term future demands in a way that had not been possible to achieve in the past. The following therefore looks at how ships were prepared for mothballing and then deals with the troublesome problems associated with their repair and maintenance thereafter.

Preparation

Both navies categorized their ships into three groups according to condition and readiness. The best were maintained at fourteen days mobilization notice, the next were subject to thirty days, and the third were usually suffering from major defects requiring a refit and were maintained at extended notice or sold for scrap. As ships aged, they tended to migrate to the last group.[76]

Effectively, three preservation problems had to be overcome. Moisture, which caused corrosion and rust, had to be extracted before the ship was sealed. Second, the necessary removal of equipment, such as radar or electronics, was an expensive and time-consuming business with no guarantee that shore facilities would provide better protection. Third, the coating of machinery with rust-preventing compound was inadequate and had to be removed—a very tedious and long process—before machinery could be operated. The whole process for the U.S. Navy took four to six months, and for the Royal Navy a bit longer.[77]

After removing ammunition and perishable stores, and after checking that equipment and spare part levels were filled—an important consideration in case they were unavailable following reactivation—the ship was thoroughly cleaned before being sealed. Each compartment was made watertight, and all corrodible metal surfaces except machinery were treated with rust preventive compound to prevent oxidation. The real breakthrough, dehumidification, was developed by the U.S. Navy after tests showed shipboard materials would keep indefinitely without deterioration or corrosion provided that humidity was contained below 25–30 percent. Two types of dehumidification were used, dynamic and static. The former required a machine to circulate air in, for example, the living quarters. A ship was divided into zones each with a dehumidifying unit connected to the ship ventilation system, thereby enabling the ship to inhale dry air and expel the moist air, with desiccant inside the machine to absorb the moisture. The static method, deployed inside places like gun mounts or directors, involved a renewable drying agent containing silica gel or activated alumina which removed the moisture from the air.[78] All nonremovable items topside such as gun mounts were covered with an airtight casing either by a metal cover sealed to the deck or woven plastic by means of a spray gun, eventually both being replaced by cocoons connected by pipe to dehumidifying machines.

The biggest problem was the protection of weather surfaces. Apart from stripping and repainting with thick protective coating, aluminum paint was also applied to eliminate breathing caused by temperature changes. The ships' outer skin was protected by a poisonous hot-air plastic paint applied to the hull to kill barnacles, thereby quadrupling the time out of dry dock for active ships and protecting the hulls of inactive ships for more than fifteen years. In the 1950s, cathodic protection was also introduced in which a small electric current beneath the water around the hull negated the corrosive effects of salt water.

Repairs and Maintenance

Manpower shortages and limited resources invariably affected whether, when, and how reserve ships were prioritized for overhauls or refits. By 1949, for example, the Royal Navy concluded it was essential to bite the bullet so, after relegating a large number of ships particularly escorts to unmaintained status, it was decided that those remaining in the first two readiness categories by 1953 would be refitted at least once since their last commission. It was believed this would optimize the chances for a speedy reactivation.[79] Lack of money, however, or even available crews or expertise familiar with the ship often led to shortcuts being taken during deactivation, many of which were sufficiently serious to compromise the ship's seaworthiness or fighting capability upon recommissioning. This was not an isolated problem and often exacerbated the need for "cannibalizing" ships in the interest of still being able to run others.[80] Examples can be found in many postcommissioning reports of the effect poor preservation had upon morale and efficiency, but the root causes proved difficult to eradicate.[81]

Partly because of the sheer scale of the problem, the U.S. Navy had an even more difficult time ensuring ships were properly deactivated and adequately maintained thereafter. Theoretically, every year one-fifth of the American Reserve Fleet was to be overhauled to achieve a balanced uniformity, absent any indication for when ships might actually need to be activated. In 1945, most ships were relatively new, so the regular overhaul cycle had not peaked. After two years, with about a third of the fleet having been overhauled, it was decided that those in the poorest condition should thereafter be ignored to avoid wasting money in case the reserve fleet was cut. While overhauling reserve fleet units was not as cost-effective as overhauling the active fleet because the latter could be tested at sea, at least overhauls enhanced the likelihood that full operational status could be attained that much quicker.[82] Any such prospect, however, soon evaporated as U.S. naval budgets were tightened, causing maintenance and improvements to be deferred until the ship was actually picked for reactivation.[83] Nor was cannibalization considered to be the best solution, given the belief that what was short or worn in one ship was usually short or worn in all.[84] Because any piecemeal reductions among the reserve sites would not work either, because the fixed costs still remained, it was eventually concluded that any real cost improvements would only be forthcoming by closing down whole sites or yards, or dramatically cutting overhauls altogether.[85] With funding so tight (even for the active fleet), the call to withdraw scarce funds, increasingly regarded as merely supporting deteriorating assets, was growing ever stronger. But then, just as the pressure for more budget cuts reached its climax, North Korea invaded South Korea in June 1950, and from this moment, all such constraints were immediately cast aside. The rest of the chapter looks briefly at how mobilization occurred and then examines whether the reserve fleets provided the value expected from them in the opening phase of the Korean War.

Outcome in Korea

The Korean War was the first limited war since 1945 involving significant UN naval forces to which the Royal Navy, together with some of its Commonwealth allies, and the U.S. Navy were the dominant contributors and partners. The North Korean invasion was completely unexpected because concern in the West was focused entirely on the prospects of a global war against the Soviet bloc, with the center of gravity being Central and Southern Europe and the Atlantic. Both the British and American navies were obliged to adopt a two-theater strategy, which required retaining the majority of their fleets in the European arena, acting either as a deterrent or ready for mounting a response should war with the Soviet bloc break out. From the Royal Navy's perspective, Korean logistic support was rationed from existing resources, sufficient only to meet the various tasks as they unfolded, with no margin.[86] As the Admiralty's Director of Plans (Q) was to record, "it is essential if false conclusions are not to be drawn that the logistic aspect of the Korean naval operations must be viewed in correct context, the requirements of a two theater strategy. . . . Had there been no question of prejudicing European defence it would not have been too difficult to have filled all Korean wants."[87] A major difficulty in planning the appropriate type and level of support in Korea for both navies was the open-ended uncertainty about the duration of the war that dogged logisticians throughout. This handicap, combined with significant shortages in trained personnel (if not necessarily the ships after the initial hiatus), exacerbated the problem of striking an appropriate balance of combat and auxiliary forces. Both navies were compelled to mobilize reserves but the degree, timing, and emphasis between combat and support ships was quite different for each, partly reflecting the disposition of their active forces at the outbreak but mainly reflecting the difference in the size, type, and nature of logistics each found they required.

U.S. Navy Korean Mobilization

In June 1950, the U.S. Navy in the Pacific was only a shadow of its former self. Even the much-vaunted U.S. Fleet Train of the Pacific War had been virtually disbanded with only a destroyer tender, a refrigeration ship, an oiler on shuttle duty, a fleet tug, and an LST available to support the whole Western Pacific. Their only hospital ship and stores issue ship had been decommissioned. The rest of the ninety-one auxiliaries of the Pacific Fleet Service Force were mostly located in West Coast ports or at Pearl Harbor, Hawaii, covering East-Central and South Pacific—that is, everywhere but the Northwest Pacific.[88] Speed of concentration was therefore vital to compensate for both the lack of forces initially in theater or the availability of base facilities in the Pacific and Far East, most of which had been virtually deactivated. This meant that all the immediate support had to be projected in one huge thrust from the West Coast of the United States. Yet no logistic division existed on the staff of Commander Naval Forces Far East to organize this, nor were there any plans for conducting a war in the region.[89] According to the official U.S. Navy History of the Korean War, "there had been no prior planning for a minor war, or indeed anything short of full mobilization. In the sphere of fleet logistics, as elsewhere, the response to the North Korean invasion was to be an exercise in extemporization."[90] Although a service squadron was established within ten days to develop the requisite mobile logistics capability, it would take time to grow because virtually all the necessary oilers and ammunition ships had to be released from reserves, which would take several weeks to commission. The first underway replenishment to the carrier task force was eventually completed late July, and while availability of oilers and ammunition ships remained marginal for the rest of the year, the rate of replenishment expanded rapidly in both volume and regularity.[91] In fact, once the mobilization machine moved into gear, the build-up of combat and auxiliary forces was extraordinarily extensive; indeed, it was described by the official historian as "a concentration so rapid as to surprise friend and foe alike."[92] Altogether, some 381 ships were activated within the first nine months, although for some of the larger ships this took longer than expected, even taking up to a year or more—a far cry from the ten days naively promised at the end of World War II.[93] The recommissioned combat fleet included thirteen carriers, two battleships, two heavy cruisers, seventy-seven destroyer types, thirteen submarines, and numerous amphibious support vessels. But this nowhere near exhausted the available supply of ships still in reserve: eleven more battleships, sixty-six cruisers, plus hundreds of destroyers and escorts, escort carriers, and light carriers. Nonetheless, for a limited war this was a significant concentration.[94]

This massive build-up invariably placed a heavy demand on the Logistic Service Force, which had the difficult task of not only replenishing all operating forces at sea or in port but also providing salvage as well as various repair and maintenance facilities afloat. The four auxiliaries available at the outset, mentioned earlier, increased to seventeen within a month and to twenty-seven by mid-September, but this looked very marginal compared to the plans during the summer of 1950 for doubling the combat forces to nearly five hundred ships. Although these additions included four more oilers, there was still only one more refrigerated cargo ship and one ammunition supply ship available, forcing AKA fast cargo ships to be deployed in lieu. Within ten months, altogether some forty-seven fleet train logistic support ships had been mustered, including two destroyer tenders; six repair ships; six fleet replenishment oilers; six ammunition replenishment ships and two small ammunition cargo vessels; two general stores issue ships; four reefer ships, of which two could replenish under way; three fleet hospital ships; four fleet tugs; and various other sundry support ships.[95]

Once the war assumed a more routine pattern in terms of build-up and disposition, other issues started to impinge on maintaining adequate logistic mobility. It was no longer solely a question of force mobilization but increasingly about how to cope with the huge relentless increases in demand for fuel and ordnance expenditure, due to the introduction of modern jet aircraft with heavier payloads and their increasingly complex maintenance requirements. It was this additional challenge that started to define the limitations to sustainability that soon would force a rethink among planners about both the size and readiness capability of existing as well as future auxiliary forces. Nor did the consequences stop there; the Korean experience had had the most profound effect upon future replenishment ship design and on replenishment doctrine, which is discussed in the next chapter.

Royal Navy Korean Mobilization

In some ways, the Admiralty faced very different circumstances initially, at least so far as fleet disposition and mobilization were concerned. By June 1950, the active fleet and overall personnel levels were the lowest since World War II, reflecting the severe curtailment in naval estimates over the previous two years.[96] Despite significant reductions across the fleets generally, it was therefore fortuitous that when war broke out on June 25, 1950, a sizable force of twenty-two warships was already deployed in Far Eastern waters on various patrol duties or extending courtesy visits to Japan. Currently enjoying a summer training cruise in Japanese waters were a light fleet carrier, two cruisers with attendant destroyers, and frigates supported by a small fleet train comprising a stores ship, a large freighting tanker, and two smaller station tankers. In no time at all, this force joined the U.S. Seventh Fleet in Okinawa as part of Task Force 77. Given the many tasks to be undertaken with so few available ships, this addition "heartened" Admiral Turner Joy, the U.S. commander in Chief of U.S. Naval Forces, as he prepared an appropriate naval response to the invasion.[97] Soon additional reinforcements from Australia, Canada, and New Zealand were committed to assist in a blocking campaign with the west coast allocated to the British and Commonwealth navies including a carrier in the Yellow Sea, while the U.S. Navy blockaded the east coast, with their carrier group operating independently as a strike force from the Sea of Japan.

Within months, Britain's force level had stabilized and remained more or less the same for the remainder of the war. This was, however, not without some difficulty as the Royal Navy was soon stretched by its worldwide commitments, particularly given its aging fleet that required increasing maintenance support from home bases. Apart from carrying heavy responsibilities for the defense of Europe and Atlantic sea-lanes, deployments were also extended to Grenada, the Persian Gulf, Malaya, and China followed later by the Gulf of Akaba, Jamaica, and Egypt.[98] But it was really only Korea that presented the type of wartime logistic challenges last experienced in 1945, and it was Korea that would once again have to compete for scarce resources from London against other global imperatives.

The Admiralty had a number of options for augmenting the fleet. The most expedient was to mobilize warships from reserve. For example, by June 1950 total fleet resources had been dramatically cut by 85 percent to 1,381 vessels, of which 60 percent were by now in reserve; of the 495 major warships, 310 were in reserve.[99] In truth, however, these were deteriorating rapidly, particularly the larger capital ships for which there were no crews, as indeed was the case for many of the 150 escorts too.[100] However, the Korean War would change all this. 1951–52 was the first complete year of the rearmament program that provided additional carriers and destroyers, the largest the country could afford without transcending into a war economy. Following a moratorium on ship disposal, commercial work in royal dockyards was suspended to refit 100 mostly smaller warships, and the active fleet was soon increased by about a third. By July 1952, Britain's reserve fleet had contracted to its lowest postwar level of 232 major combatants, as ships were commissioned to replenish gaps in the active fleet.[101] Although the reserve policy had therefore been vindicated, the combination of stretched manpower and the complexities of mobilization nevertheless left their mark on operational efficiency. Indeed serious concerns were soon raised in the Admiralty about the wisdom of demobilizing often worn out ships to reserve, which had the potential to jeopardize the Royal Navy's ability to meeting future deployment requirements.

For the Royal Navy's fleet train, a different policy applied—in comparison to both warship mobilization and to the policy adopted by the U.S. Navy. It was accepted within the Admiralty that retaining in peacetime a permanent large Pacific-style fleet train for a future war was both uneconomical and an unnecessary drain on skilled manpower. What is quite striking to note, therefore, is the relatively small proportion of naval manned auxiliaries (in other words mainly depot/repair ships) that were retired from the active to the reserve fleet by August 1945. As can be seen in appendix U, only five out of sixty-seven were held back in reserve. This would change of course, as many vintage ships were eventually scrapped or converted back to civilian service while others were sold.

The postwar Empire Plan expected more than two-thirds of such auxiliaries to be held in reserve, and this in fact happened by 1948, but only after more than half of the wartime vessels had been scrapped altogether. Thereafter, the more modest balance of about thirty vessels stabilized at about fifty-fifty between active and reserve. Although the reserve portion increased during the Korean War, this reflected the lack of available crews even to cover emergencies nearer to home.[102] Other vessels, such as RFA freighting ships that could not be manned, stocked up, and brought forward at short notice for fleet duty, were employed to transport the Admiralty's own stores and fuel worldwide, with any surplus capacity chartered out to earn their keep.[103] Over time this practice proved the norm as it became increasingly unacceptable financially to leave auxiliaries in reserve when their reprieve could otherwise be assured in peacetime through their ability to earn their keep on Admiralty freighting duties (particularly the *Fort*-class freighters, some of which were to provide valuable service in Korea).[104]

Requisition of civilian ships for conversion, a traditionally important strategy for the Admiralty, was in fact confined to only two 10,000–ton tankers being privately built for Polish owners that in 1951 were outfitted for freighting.[105] The fleet train of twenty-two auxiliaries to support the Royal Navy and Commonwealth forces in Korea (see appendix V), represented nearly a third of the total number of fleet auxiliaries operated by the Admiralty.[106] Unlike the American Service Force though, it was drawn from both naval and civilian services with the vast majority still unmodernized. Hospital and headquarters ships were White Ensign; the rest, such as tankers, transports, stores issuing ships for armaments or provisions, or naval stores were operated by the RFA under the Blue Ensign.

While, unlike the U.S. Navy, the Royal Navy suffered less of an initial shock because it already had sizable forces in the region, the ongoing challenges for both in trying to augment their forces were not dissimilar as the naval contribution to the war effort exponentially increased in size and intensity. Manning and equipment shortages constantly hampered the speed at which American ships, principally the large capital ships, could be brought out of reserve and properly worked up prior to commission. For the Royal Navy, the problem was finding enough properly worked-up, fully manned destroyers to replace or augment existing forces, such that the Far East Fleet was sometimes forced to retain warships in theater much longer than planned. Appendix U shows clearly the extent to which this fallback was required. The reserve fleet as a proportion of the total fleet varied from 19 percent in August 1945, creeping up to 60 percent by June 1950, and then dropping fairly rapidly throughout Korea before recovering to the 50–54 percent level after Korea until 1959. The years 1952–53, however, witnessed major increases in spending and the first increase in personnel for over two years, with the highest active fleet level ever achieved in the same period.

When it came to augmenting auxiliary support, London's dilemma was more acute than Washington's because the number and variety of available ships, even those in reserve, were comparatively few. So pleas to the Admiralty from the British local commander, for example, to send out a depot ship to Sasebo, were dismissed as simply not possible "due to the essential duty allocated to the six available in the event of global war."[107] From the Admiralty's perspective, they had provided adequate resources to meet the local Korean circumstances, no less and no more.

Reserve Fleets: Value for Money?

So far the justification for having reserve fleets has been reviewed from the navies' perspective in terms of strategic deterrence. Yet an underlying problem for both throughout 1945 and 1950 was, to quote an American Admiral, that "it is hard to get money for the active fleet let alone the reserve fleet."[108] Because the alternative was to scrap, there are two key variables—replacement value and operating costs—that help to provide some indication of whether mothballing was cost-justified.

It has been estimated that the American mothballing program involved more than 2,263 naval ships totaling 5.6 million tons, with an original cost value of $13.6 billion against a replacement cost estimated at $23.2 billion.[109] Even by 1948—that is, relatively early on in the overall reserve cycle—the original cost of the reserve fleet of some 2,000 ships, according to the U.S. Navy's Bureau of Ships, was about the same as the active fleet—some $9 billion.[110] Added to this, mothballing and the provision of suitable berthing facilities had been estimated to have cost about 3 percent of their original value.[111] Dehumidification was the most significant preservation cost that was universally considered to be by far the most economical and satisfactory way of preserving ships in good condition at low cost.[112] Yet overall success ultimately depended on minimizing the operating/maintenance cost without degrading the quality of the initial or ongoing preservation.

The final cost variable was reactivation. Reactivating nearly four hundred badly needed ships for Korea had cost the U.S. Navy $120 million through April 1951—about 2.5 percent of their replacement cost.[113] Comparing this to the $2 billion just approved for new construction seemed to vindicate the mothballing strategy, but this line of reasoning becomes less compelling when it is recognized that the type of ships required for the future would need to be much more sophisticated and complex to perform the increasingly demanding roles expected of them. The Korean War was fought primarily with World War II technology and equipment, but the advent of jet propulsion and heavier ordnance requirements profoundly affected not just tactical replenishment doctrine (discussed in the next chapter) but carrier design and logistic support generally. This in turn demanded more sophisticated ships and technology, but it was simply uneconomic to modernize reserve fleet vessels that were aging and increasingly likely to be operationally deficient anyway.[114] The American JCS concluded, for example, that many of its huge reserve merchant fleet was war ravaged and, unless urgently repaired at a cost of up to $500,000 per tanker (which showed how poor their condition was), they would become "a doubtful asset."[115] In fact, although not vigorously pursued, the thought was even raised that it might be militarily more advantageous to dispose of most of the merchant fleet—particularly the slow, older vessels—to foreign governments for political value, rather than holding them idle for a potential emergency where their contribution was likely to be marginal at best. Such a thought also had the merit of freeing resources for building new faster ships to match the growing fears of Russian fast submarine technology. In the end, some U.S. ships remained in mothballs for decades untouched and, provided they could be properly preserved in good condition for twenty years (a rather confident broad assumption by the Navy General Board), then the program would justify being categorized as cost effective.[116] An annual maintenance cost of 0.5 percent per annum would, for example, project an outlay of 10 percent of original cost, which was considered at the time "a very appealing low rate of insurance in any kind of business."[117]

Although difficult to compare precisely, the Royal Navy suffered slightly higher annual maintenance costs, of between 0.6 percent and 1.2 percent of their original cost, although this was still marginal in the broad scheme of things. Table 6.1 shows examples of annual replacement cost for both warships and major auxiliaries, including tankers, as they applied in 1947. As an aside, it is interesting to note that the full cost of a new tanker was estimated at £500,000, whereas recall from chapter 5 that the first new naval tanker, when it was completed in 1953, cost more than £2 million.

It was therefore fair to conclude that the combination of high replacement cost but relatively modest maintenance expense (thanks to dehumidification) provided a low-cost insurance policy. But this comes with a health warning because as aging ships deteriorated and their weapons and propulsion systems become too complex to maintain in static preservation, the law of diminishing returns would inevitably start to apply.

For auxiliary support ships, the scale of the reserve problem for the Royal Navy compared to the U.S. Navy was minor. For the naval depot/repair ships, most of the wartime conversions were scrapped sold or converted back to civilian use. The more modern were kept but many relegated to reserve because there were insufficient crews to man them. The RFA freighters and tankers were either chartered out during this period or remained on active service, leaving only the smaller harbor vessels relegated to reserve. As such, determining the future com-

Table 6.1. Annual Replacement Costs for Warships and Major
Auxiliaries (1947)

Type	Cost of New Ships, £[a]	Av Life (yrs)	Annual Replacement Cost per Unit, £
Battleship	13,250,000	26	510,000
Fleet carrier	10,000,000	24	417,000
Cruiser	3,850,000	25	152,000
Destroyers	1,150,000	22	52,000
Frigates	163,000–510,000	22	14,100–23,200
Depot ships	2,000,000	30	66,700
Fleet oilers	500,000	30	16,700
Fleet repair	2,500,000	30	83,300

Note: a. Prices for contemporary modern designs

Source: TNA (Kew), ADM 167/124, "Annual Cost of New Construction to Keep in Being Post-war Fleet," Annex 2, appendix A.

position of logistic mobile support vessels rested on the knowledge that for the large purpose designed depot and repair ships, these were available in extreme circumstances, while the balance of the fleet train such as issue ships and tankers could either be returned from charter-parties or acquired from shipping companies or ship builders and then modified according the Admiralty's needs at the time.

Conclusion

Did the reserve fleets fulfill their expectations? The answer broadly is yes, but not necessarily by design. The original premise for creating the reserve fleets could be summarized as being partly

- Political, by providing an overt form of deterrence to potential enemies
- Economic, by being a relatively cheap insurance policy in the event of future emergencies
- Pragmatic, given the postwar manpower shortages created by demobilization[118]
- Opportunistic, in that many ships were relatively young with valuable potential
- Realistic, given virtually all warship building capacity was regeared toward commercial tonnage such that any incremental wartime demand

could never be satisfied within the first two years or so, except by re-activating reserves.

All of the above assumptions, however, were predicated on the ability to augment existing active forces quickly should global war suddenly break out. Yet the only occasion both reserve fleets were activated was for a limited war that was, admittedly, sudden but neither originally planned for nor in the end predictable. Because of the particular circumstances prevailing at the outset in 1950, the pressure for urgent relatively large-scale mobilization really fell upon the Americans, and to that extent having the reserve fleet had proved absolutely essential. For the British, reliance on utilizing the reserve fleet was relatively more gradual and continuous as ships moved in and out of reserve, depending on, among other things, the availability of manpower maintenance capacity.

But the use to which reserve fleets were eventually applied by the Royal Navy was not entirely consistent with the original intent behind their creation. To answer the question of their ultimate utility, therefore, requires having to project beyond the period under consideration for this book by looking in hindsight from a position in the late 1950s when the rationale conceived more than a decade earlier for having a reserve fleet policy became subject to severe scrutiny. With Western economic health remaining precarious or in recession virtually throughout this period, the substantial increases in military expenditure during Korea were soon curtailed after 1953. Britain, for example, recognized that her strategic problem was no longer a "one-off" build-up of forces to fight on some specific date but rather how to maintain in the long-term Cold War forces strong enough to deter an enemy yet cheap enough not to strain the economy.

This important philosophical change, originally set out in The Global Strategy paper of 1952, provided the strategic framework for British defense planning over the next five years and would lead to many difficult decisions, not least what to do with the reserve fleet. But the days for many of these capital ships were numbered anyway. The reality was that the broken-backed theory of war was weak because it required maintaining an aging and deteriorating reserve fleet rather than building a powerful modern active one.[119] The expectation by the mid 1950s of a hot war in the near future was receding and the need for retaining a "hot-war" navy therefore became questionable. The relentless pressure for more reductions in military spending continued under Sir Anthony Eden, who replaced Churchill as prime minister in May 1955. Lord Mountbatten, the new First Sea Lord, was convinced that infrastructural fat, including the reserve fleet, could be cut from the naval organization since immobilized reserves were not going to be of any use after a Soviet H-bomb attack anyway. Britain over the last decade, he argued, had retained too many ships, not too few. Bringing them up to modern standards or even maintaining them was beyond her financial and manpower means, so long as sufficient resources were prioritized to keep a modern fleet in commission. The eventual abolition of conscription and the consequent closing of some training establishments, together with the massive reduction in ready reserve manpower meant that, as Eric Grove succinctly put it "effectively the concept of mobilization for old-style wars was being abandoned.'[120]

After Korea, it had become increasingly clear that the policy must change from preparing for a future hot war to preventing one. And this essentially meant reducing the size and changing the character of reserve fleets from mobilization reserves to supplementary or replacement reserves. This conclusion had significant and potentially far-reaching implications for the Royal Navy's auxiliary fleet. It can be no coincidence that this important change of emphasis came to the fore at exactly the same time as revolutionary plans were also coming to fruition for transforming how fleets could be supported more dynamically and flexibly using fast combat support ships, one-stop replenishment, and helicopter-borne replenishment. All these were being developed and refined during the previous decade, but what had been missing, until now, were the necessary funds and justification to build and commission these very special auxiliaries that would actually help make this transformation happen.

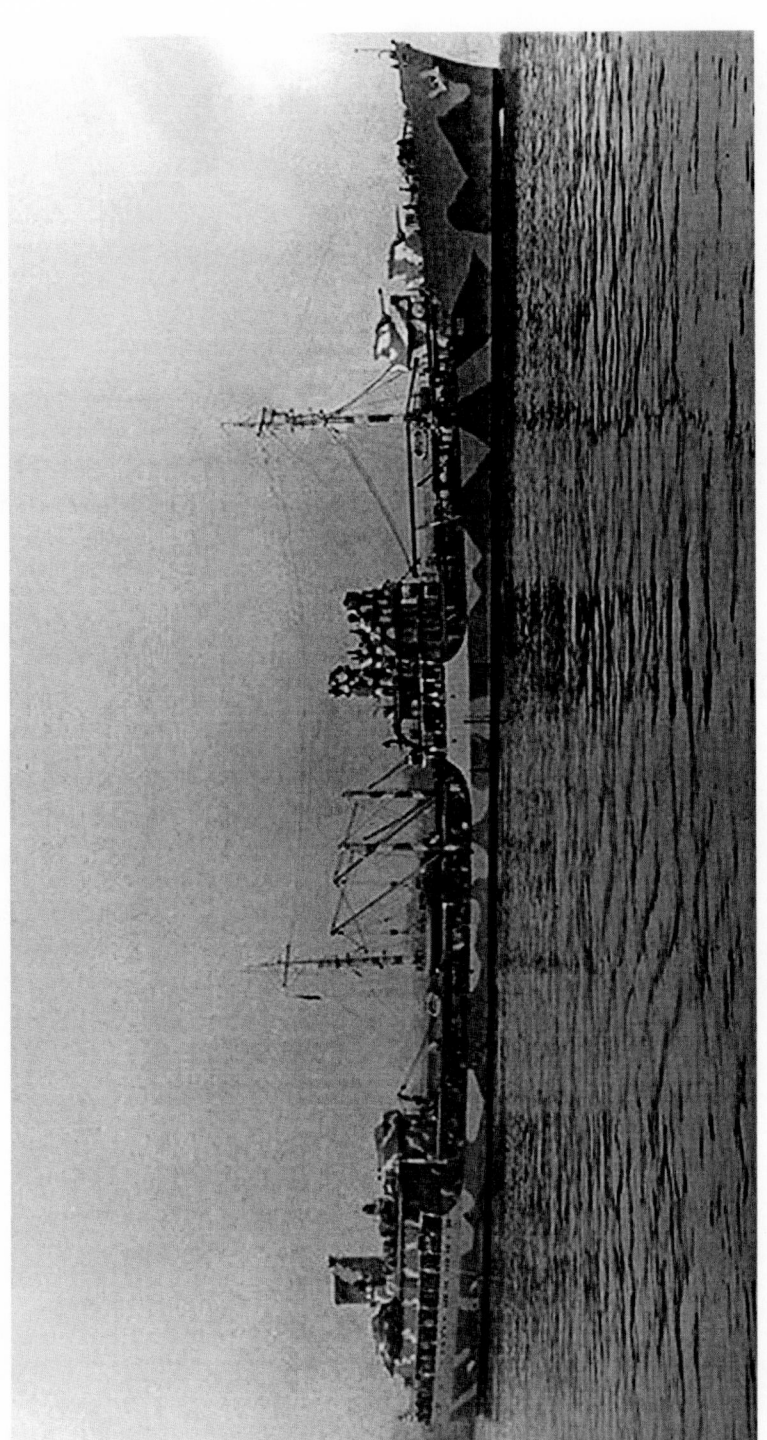

1.1. USS *Cimarron*, 1942. (National Archives, photograph 19-N-30121)

2.1. VSIS *Glenartny* transferring stores at sea to the New Zealand cruiser HMNZS *Achilles*, 1945. (Photo courtesy RNZN Museum Auckland)

3.1. Five USN ships consolidating abeam, Pacific 1945. (Courtesy Naval War College Historical Collection)

3.2. Battleship HMS *Duke of York* on her approach to HMS *Bulawayo*, whose fuel rig has been prepared for delivery. (TNA(Kew), ADM 1/21061)

3.3. HMS *Olna* refueling HMS *Implacable* with HMS *Newfoundland* on her starboard, on this occasion achieving a combined transfer rate of more than 1,000 tph. (Courtesy Naval Historical Branch)

3.4. Carrier HMS *Formidable* refueling astern from MFA *San Ambrosia*, with HMS *Euryalus* refueling abeam (1945). (Photograph courtesy of Imperial War Museum, London, ref. ABS 626)

3.5. Taken from a different angle, HMS *Victorious* refueling astern from MFA *San Ambrosia* with cruiser HMNZS *Gambia* abeam (1945). (Photo courtesy RNZN Museum Auckland)

3.6. HMS *Bulawayo* refueling HMS *Dunkirk* astern in rough channel weather.
(TNA(Kew), ADM 1/21061)

3.7. The cruiser HMNZS *Achilles* refueling the destroyer HMS *Ulysses* using her crane
fueling rig, 1945. (Photo courtesy RNZN Museum Auckland)

3.8. RFA *Dingledale* deploying the old 40-ft trough rig to refuel HMS *Ulysses* abeam while refueling astern the carrier HMS *Implacable*, 1945. (Courtesy Naval Historical Branch)

3.9. Large 70-ft derrick rig on HMS *Bulawayo*, 1947. (TNA (Kew), ADM 1/21061)

3.10. Saddle or hose trough on HMS *Bulawayo*, 1947. (TNA (Kew), ADM 1/21061)

3.11. HMS *Bulawayo* refueling the cruiser HMS *Cleopatra* by jackstay fueling rig. Distance between ships is about 240 feet. (NARA2, RG38, ATP-16 (1955)

3.12. HMS *Glory* and the Australian destroyer HMAS *Bataan* being refueled simultaneously from RFA *Wave Premier* during the Korean War, June 1951. Note the much wider gap between ships. (NARA2, RG38, ATP-16, 1955)

3.13. The ammunition ship USS *Rainier* replenishing the carrier USS *Antietam* and the battleship USS *Wisconsin* off Korea in 1952. (Naval Historical Foundation, Washington, D.C., photo 80-G-440189)

3.14. Transferring bombs from the AE *Mount Katmai* (AE 16) to the carrier USS *Philippine Sea* off Korea in 1950. At the beginning of the Korean War *Mount Katmai* was the only active AE in the Pacific Fleet, but it took some eighty days to collect and load her with ordnance and then transit to Korea. (National Archives, photo 80–G-439879)

3.15. Transfer of eggs by jackstay between the cruiser HMNZS *Achilles* and destroyer HMS *Wakeful*, 1945. (Photo courtesy RNZN Museum, Auckland)

3.16. Transferring an 18-inch aerial torpedo (about 1,800 lb) by one-ton jackstay storing rig from HMS *Bulawayo* to HMS *Dunkirk*, 1947. (TNA (Kew), ADM 1/21061)

3.17. Transferring personnel by stirrup/light jackstay between the Canadian destroyer HMCS *Athabaskan* and HMS *Unicorn*, 1951. (Photograph courtesy of Imperial War Museum, London, reference A31805)

3.18. Casevac transfer from the *Battle*-class destroyer HMS *Finisterre* to the light fleet carrier HMS *Glory*, 1946. (Courtesy Naval Historical Branch)

5.1. USS *Neosho* AO-143. (Courtesy AFS/Nobe Smith)

5.2. RFA *Tidesurge* refueling the cruiser HMS *Gambia* abeam. Note the single RAS deck with three port and two starboard fueling positions using new winch tensioned lattice rigs. Still no provision for helicopters at this stage, however. (Photograph courtesy of Imperial War Museum, London, reference FL 19999)

7.1. RFA *Olna* refueling a carrier during Exercise MAINBRACE, 1952. (TNA(Kew), ADM 1/24039)

7.2. HMS *Bulawayo* astern from HMS *Glory*. (Photograph courtesy of Imperial War Museum, London, reference FL 4221)

7.3. HMS *Dunkirk* refueling abeam of HMS *Bulawayo*. (TNA(Kew), ADM 1/21061)

7.4. Close-up of HMS *Dunkirk* refueling abeam from HMS *Bulawayo* using an experimental 7-inch hose. (TNA(Kew), ADM 1/21061)

7.5. HMS *Vanguard* refueling abeam from HMS *Bulawayo* using a large derrick rig, 1947. ((NARA2, RG38, ATP-16 (1955)

7.6. HMS *Bulawayo* rigging crews on deck during trials with the Home Fleet, 1947. (TNA(Kew), ADM 1/21061)

7.7. Ammunition transfer between the cruiser HMS *Superb* and HMS *Bulawayo*. (TNA(Kew), ADM 1/21061)

7.8. Ammunition skip box and netting. (RN 1947) (TNA(Kew), ADM 1/21061)

7.9. USS *Conecuh* fitted out for "one-stop replenishment" trials. (Courtesy AFS/ Nobe Smith)

7.10. War-gaming in Sims Hall, U.S. Naval War College. (Courtesy Naval War College Historical Collection)

7.11. RFA *Arndale* refueling a Canadian cruiser while an Australian destroyer is simultaneously transferring mail; photographed from an RN battleship, 1945. (Photograph courtesy of Imperial War Museum, London, reference AX 164A)

7.12. RN "C"-class destroyer refueling from USS *North Carolina*, 1945 (Courtesy Naval Historical Branch)

7.13. HMS *Ocean* and the Canadian destroyer HMCS *Nootka* refueling from RFA *Wave Sovereign* in the Yellow Sea, 1951. (Photograph courtesy of Imperial War Museum, London, reference KOR 28)

7.14. Fuel hose being extended from HMS *Bulawayo* to HMS *Duke of York*, 1947. (TNA(Kew), ADM 1/21061)

7.15. Australian destroyer HMAS *Warramunga* refueling from the American oiler USS *Manatee* off Korea in June 1951. (Naval Historical Foundation, Washington, D.C., photo NH 96261)

7 | Fleet Mobility
Tactical Development, 1945–1953

Despite the effects of demobilization and increasingly severe operational budgets, the challenge for the Royal Navy and the U.S. Navy was how to deploy tactically their most effective forces at the right level, mix, and capability to meet constabulary obligations and yet be ready for any potential high-intensity maritime threats. Over time, forces became increasingly shaped by the combination of the fast submarine, jet aircraft, and missiles, all of which introduced new technology and speed thresholds that would make much of the large wartime fleets obsolete. Meanwhile, any military response, whether global or national, oceanic or littoral in scope, needed to remain flexible and agile, which therefore meant that mobility and sustainability were going to be an increasingly integral part of any solution.

U.S. Navy Operational and Geographic Responsibility

In 1946, the U.S. Navy operated three main active fleets worldwide. The Fifth (later redesignated Third) Fleet covered Central and Eastern Pacific; the Seventh (Western Pacific) and the Eighth (later redesignated Second) fleets covered the Atlantic.[1] The CNO also retained administrative responsibility for certain other forces. For example, through the Deputy CNO (Logistics), the Reserve Fleets branch coordinated matters related to berthing and maintenance as well as activation and inactivation of vessels in the huge reserve fleets.[2] Additionally, under his wing were certain naval transports and merchant vessels chartered or allocated to the navy. All these came under the command of the appropriate Sea Frontier commanders (Western, Eastern, Gulf, and Caribbean); part of their job was to coordinate and administer the logistic and administrative activities of the various onshore Naval Districts as well as being tasked by the respective Pacific or Atlantic commanders in chief to supervise all logistic support required by their fleets from those shore activities located within their frontier.[3] An organizational chart for the Operating Forces is in appendix W.

The fleets themselves were divided into distinct commands: the Pacific Fleet (CinCPac), the Atlantic Fleet (CinCLant), and the U.S. Naval Forces in Europe (Eastern Atlantic and Mediterranean (ComNavEu/CinCNELM). For administrative purposes, each fleet was divided into forces, then divisions, squadrons, flotillas, groups, wings, and so on. Fleet units were also governed by a functional level of authority through Type and Task Force commanders responsible for, among other things, their readiness and operating ability. In some ways the similarities between the Pacific and Atlantic fleets ended there because these were two very independent, even competitive, autonomous organizations with different cultures and often different tactical doctrines tailored to suit their respective circumstances. Although not the case today, this dual autonomy seemed to have remained true for some while and is worth bearing in mind when comparing their respective progress.

Because the prospect of confronting enemy naval forces in the Pacific region post-1945 was considered very low, the subsequent level of demobilization was disproportionately huge for a Pacific Fleet that by 1945 had contained nearly 90 percent of the American active fleet worldwide. Indeed, most operational activity between 1945 and 1950 occurred in the Atlantic/Mediterranean region, where much of our attention will now be directed, including the various links between the American British and other NATO navies.

ComNavEu/CinCNELM

Headquartered in London, the C-in-C Naval Forces Europe was responsible from 1945 for the operation of all surface and air units transferred from the Atlantic Fleet into the Mediterranean theater or waters contiguous to Germany. The Northern European Force typically comprised a cruiser, several destroyers, and a repair ship operating out of Plymouth, England, covering the Northeast Atlantic and North Sea, with the aim of spending about a third of their time equally on logistics and upkeep, port visits, or training and special operations.[4] The Persian Gulf force initially comprised mainly naval transport tankers, but this became increasingly supplemented by other forces injected to conduct various special operations or cruises to ports in the Indian Ocean or Middle East. The Mediterranean force was the largest component, and because of the nature of their operations and distance from any home ports, it is perhaps instructive to look at how they were logistically supported during this period.

At the end of 1946, a peacetime force of cruisers, destroyers, and a carrier represented the first permanent American presence, called U.S. Naval Forces Mediterranean and designated TF125 of the Twelfth Fleet. Although these units were under the command of ComNavEu, they continued to operate logistically from their home ports on the East Coast of the United States, supported by ComServLant. On October 30, 1947, CinCNELM (Commander in Chief, U.S. Naval Forces, Eastern Atlantic and Mediterranean) was established to conduct naval operations in the Eastern Atlantic and Mediterranean but now extended to the Arabian Sea and Ceylon to cover the Persian Gulf. The practice of having the surface and naval air forces formally assigned on a four-month rotational basis from the U.S. Atlantic Fleet continued until June 1948, when the fleet was retitled Sixth Task Fleet augmented immediately by three ships permanently assigned to the region, a heavy cruiser (USS *Columbus* acting as flagship, home-ported at Plymouth England), the destroyer tender USS *Hamul*, and a gasoline tanker.[5] This deployment was particularly significant for two reasons. Not only was this a complete departure from the prewar practice of concentrating the U.S. Navy in the western Atlantic but, by stationing the fleet in friendly ports with their own logistic support, it signified that the priority of the Pacific, which had governed American naval logistic thinking for nearly a quarter of a century, had effectively ended.[6] This soon became evident by the number of Pacific Fleet ships passing through on their return to the United States; the ramifications of this shift would be far reaching, not least when North Korea invaded the South only two years later.[7]

In February 1950, six months after the Atlantic treaty came into force, the Sixth Task Fleet was redesignated as the Sixth Fleet, comprising a fast carrier strike force with a number of cruisers and a flotilla of destroyers supported by a large repair ship and other auxiliaries.[8] This was supplemented from time to time by a second carrier or submarines for training purposes. When the Korean War broke, however, further substantial reinforcements were quickly drafted in, and by late 1951, the Sixth Fleet had doubled in one year to nearly seventy ships. By 1953, ten cruisers and six carriers were deployed on four- to six-month tours during the course of that year. It was calculated that on average they spent their time 35 percent under way on U.S. fleet exercises, 15 percent under way on NATO and combined exercises, 35 percent in port on fleet visits, 10 percent in port for replenishment, and 5 percent in port on relief.[9]

As the task forces expanded, it became necessary to increase the number of replenishment oilers in the region and have on permanent station an ammunition supply ship to meet the CNO's requirement that "detailed operations must be planned with a view to mobility of effective forces."[10] The Royal Navy meanwhile provided docking facilities in Malta or Gibraltar for those serious repairs beyond the U.S. Navy's own afloat capability, as well as fuel, first agreed back in 1947.[11] As the forces increased, however, so the logistic infrastructure was expanded, and on April 27, 1951, the Commander Service Force Sixth Fleet was finally established.

U.S. Navy Command Structure

The U.S. Navy's method of organizing naval forces by task and type was unique and had a direct bearing on how and why British and American logistic organization structures were differently postured, including when British forces were operating under American task force commands in World War II and in Korea. It also helps to explain how logistics-related doctrine for fleet activities, described later in this chapter, evolved during this period.

The most typical terms used by the U.S. Navy for organizing ships or aircraft were "task force," "task group," "task unit," "type command," and "operational and administrative control." With the task type system, every ship's captain worked for two superiors. He was under the "administrative control" of a "Type commander" responsible for the ship's upkeep, supply, discipline, and training. But he was also under the "operational control" of a "Task commander" responsible for accomplishing some particular task within the Navy's mission, expressed as an "operational plan" or "order." Ships were therefore always under their Type commander but could be assigned, when needed, to a Task commander by a higher level superior. Task commanders were therefore concerned with purpose and Type commanders were concerned with support. This dual control was intended to provide maximum flexibility for adapting force levels commensurate with changing risks while continuity in ship administration, including logistics, was retained through the more permanent type command infrastructure. This separation of task and type evolved from experience but, rather paradoxically, the U.S. Navy had originally taken some inspiration for this from the British. That is, the eighteenth-century British, with their fleets acting essentially as task forces whose ships were assigned to fleets by the Admiralty but prepared by the Navy Board.[12]

Although the American task type concept was first properly developed at the Naval War College, it did not really become practice until the late 1930s. Task fleets were first created only when the Third and Fifth fleets alternated in the Pacific for a succession of operations within the overall strategic plan against Japan, using essentially the same ships but with different dedicated Flag staff for planning and operational command. Even then the concept remained so secret that at the time neither the Japanese nor even the American public was aware of this modus operandi.[13] Postwar, the idea of separating the strategic and administrative aspects of every ship remained unchanged. The U.S. Sixth and Seventh fleets permanently based in the Mediterranean and Far East, for example, each comprised ships temporarily assigned to them from the Atlantic and Pacific fleets, respectively, which effectively remained the administrative divisions of the U.S. Navy for all the Type commands covering the various classes of ship, including those auxiliaries organized for mobile support. Task assignment therefore related directly to the particular purpose for which they were designed, such as a fast carrier group or ASW, or reconnaissance through to expeditionary or logistic support. Additional task assignments also embraced detachments to the two major U.S. Navy training fleets, the First and Second fleets in the Pacific and Atlantic, respectively. This book examines these exercises and compares them with other joint naval exercises to see how these progressed during this period.

From the logistic perspective, while Type Commanders handled material and administrative matters, the logistic responsibility was concentrated under the three largest Type commands in the U.S. Navy—ComServForce, ComAirForce, and ComGenFMF (Commanding General, Aircraft, Fleet Marine Force), all of which were designated "Logistic Type Commanders."[14] For our purposes, the focus will primarily be on the ComServForce command, which delineated such responsibility between Commander Service Force Atlantic (ComServLant) and his Pacific counterpart (ComServPac). Their duties were quite embracing, covering everything from ship repair afloat or at advanced bases, planning procurement, and delivery to the fleet of provisions, fuel ammunition, and general stores for both ships and bases. Additionally, they were expected to study war requirements and the means for meeting them as well as rescue and salvage liaison with shore establishments.[15]

This organizational delineation was not without its share of confusion, waste, and duplication, particularly when ships were ordered from one theater to another even within the same fleet. But overall, this was regarded as an acceptable hazard, although evidence from later years suggests this confusion can still arise from time to time.[16]

Royal Navy Operational and Geographic Responsibility

With British naval forces comparatively more dispersed around the world after 1945, the Royal Navy once again resumed the many constabulary responsibilities associated with Britain's overseas commercial and political interests, using cruisers and frigates based at various locations both home and overseas to maintain "British prestige" (a frequently expressed objective, incidentally, throughout this whole period).[17]

By 1947 in addition to the Home Fleet, two other fleets patrolled the Mediterranean and Pacific, each centered on a pair of light fleet carriers that could provide the necessary mobility for responding to emergencies. The latter fleet, a severely pared down successor to the wartime BPF was then rebased to Singapore to become the new Far East Fleet. Over time some of the smaller stations were to close either for economic reasons, manpower, or garrison shortages or because the host country in question had gained its independence. Even the main fleets, however, were becoming increasingly emasculated, with the Mediterranean Fleet, for example (traditionally the largest of the Royal Navy's overseas naval forces), acting as more of a "swing force" or strategic reserve that also happened to provide good all-year round training.[18]

The essential difference between the U.S. Navy and Royal Navy command structures was that the British system was organized geographically by adopting the "Senior Officer present" approach, which empowered the commander in chief with immense autonomy and flexibility to manage the wide range of administrative and operational challenges. This difference affected at many levels the conduct of joint Anglo-American naval operations, particularly regarding command and operational responsibility in wartime. Where this became particularly sensitive was in establishing the right level of control for administering logistic support to their respective forces in theater. The Admiralty realized that, to avoid confusion in any future war, it would be prudent to adopt once again the American Task Force designation just as they had been obliged to do when the BPF was placed under American command as TF57 in 1945. In 1949, therefore, it was promulgated throughout the Royal Navy that the terms Task Force, Task Group, and Task Unit should be used in any wartime organization instead of the traditional Force, Group, and Sub-Group.[19] In fact, these new designations were almost immediately adopted, including the combined exercise conducted by two British fleets off Gibraltar some six weeks later.[20] This change of nomenclature notwithstanding, the traditional British regional command structure in theater remained unchanged even through the Korean War. Interestingly, one of the benefits of command devolution found within the British approach was admired by some Americans, illustrated by the following quotation taken from the American official historian of U.S. Naval Operations in Korea, who wrote

> The American tendency towards the de-personalized report (or, alternatively, the overwritten press release) leaves the historian to infer the atmosphere of any given period from a simple record of movements, orders and ammunition expenditures. The sense of urgency, the rising hopes, and dashed anticipations of war rarely appear. In this our British cousins appear to have the advantage of us, especially as regards the reports of commanders of task group level and above. In the Second World War no American reports from commanders of whatever service provide a satisfactory equivalent to those dispatches of British commanders published in the "London Gazette." Similarly in Korea, the Reports of Proceedings by the Flag Officer Second in Command Far East Station (Commander Task Group 95.1) are in many respects the most informative command reports of the war. This was noted by Admiral Dyer who, while commanding Task Force 95, forwarded FOSICFES "Report of Proceedings" for September 1950–November 1951 with the suggestion that U.S. Navy procedures might be modified to approximate the British. The historian can but reiterate this recommendation.[21]

Mention was made in chapter 2 of the planning and logistical support difficulties encountered in 1944–45 by having the logistics support function under vice admiral (Q) divorced, both physically and operationally, from the C-in-C within the BPF command structure. This dilemma seemed to remain a moot point for some years thereafter. When the British and American naval forces attempted to conduct joint planning for operations in the Mediterranean in 1948, for example, it was clear that the different command styles and structure adopted by both navies was causing problems, not least in the delineation of logistic support and responsibility. Not for the first nor last time, the Americans preferred to have the British logistic force subsumed under their Service Force command structure. When the C-in-C Mediterranean expressed exasperation at the lack of American empathy for "the advantages of our well-tried system," Lord Fraser, by now First Sea Lord, responded that "VA (Q) must be a separate Command, having full authority to make important decisions under an overall directive from Commander-in-Chief. I found this quite essential in the Pacific."[22]

The establishment of NATO in 1949 encouraged the gradual development by the member states of appropriate joint strategic/logistical plans, but any infrastructural support only came about beyond the period covered by this book. One guiding principle, among the many associated with international naval logistic planning, was that each member was responsible for its own logistic support, except where there existed bilateral agreements. While Allies were broadly intended to be mutually interdependent, it was nevertheless a fact that in most cases the United States was expected to underwrite the major portion of the logistical load.[23]

Cultural Appreciation

Any study of two navies operating together will invariably discover differences that might help explain why cultural misunderstandings occur, whether in style or substance. Sometimes these differences were ingrained and philosophically quite fundamental. Looking at, for example, the role of logistics in naval education, the Royal Navy's approach for instituting senior staff courses was consistent in keeping general line functions and knowledge separate from specialized functions such as engineering and aircraft management. Students were therefore discouraged from studying the detail that should be the concern only of those specialists trained precisely with that object in view. As one of the Royal Navy student officers at the NWC described it, "It is a waste of time to teach details until the principles are mastered." From the American perspective, it was acknowledged by the president of the NWC that "the American is in danger of losing the woods among the trees. The Englishman is always astonished when he discovers our penchant for details."[24] However, he then went on to argue, "the English system has its drawbacks, too. [He] is either a specialist or general line, and the demarcation between the two is sharp and clear. That is why we find English line officers on a destroyer shrugging off even general questions regarding fire control or radar by saying 'That is taken care of by one of our ratings.'"[25]

Lord Fraser, onetime C-in-C of the BPF and Adm. Sir Michael Le Fanu, who had been the BPF liaison officer with the U.S. Pacific Fleet (and who later also became First Sea Lord) both advocated closer ties with the U.S. Navy, even if this required emulating American practice—but within limits. While in their view everything should be done to encourage technological training among officers, for example, it was important to avoid what they perceived to be the trap, as the U.S. Navy had sometimes tended to do, of "enervating the command" by over-training deck officers at the expense of their "sea sense" or understanding tactics and weapons usage.[26] The question for debate within the NWC, therefore, was whether it was still possible to teach logistics by avoiding the detail and sticking to principles. Unfortunately experience had led American commanders to con-clude that subordinates could not be relied on for all matters of detail and needed to be checked occasionally but "to do this effectively he cannot afford too much impatience with details."[27]

Tactical Development in Replenishment at Sea Capability

In peacetime there exist few ways that navies can improve, in a practical sense, their replenishment capability at the tactical level. The choice is confined to fleet exercises for training, controlled trials for improving equipment and pro-cedure, and finally war-gaming, which can simulate a replenishment program from planning to breakaway but also provide context to the broader tactical or strategic picture that officers need to become more aware of. In all three, the Royal Navy and U.S. Navy adopted their own approach.

Postwar Fleet Exercise Experience

One of the many lessons learned from wartime experience was the worrying disparity between wartime and peacetime expectations of operational perfor-mance, particularly related to logistic support. Prewar cruises had become some-what perfunctory and devoid of any trial related testing, with the result that op-erational deficiencies were never discovered, other than those occurring under relatively benign circumstances.[28] While it was true that no wartime fleet opera-tion in the Pacific was ever curtailed or postponed on account of delays in de-livery of fuel, too much reliance nevertheless had been placed on extemporiza-tion and hard grind.[29] The Admiralty's postwar analysis of replenishment, for example, suggested that "it was a failure inasmuch as the time taken . . . was far greater than had been expected from peacetime fuelling at sea."[30]

The problem of upholding standards in peacetime replenishment was that fleet exercises could not effectively replicate the discipline or the fear that so con-centrates the mind in wartime. As Pare observed, "Our latest experience shows a tremendous drop in rates of transfer because of lack of personnel, lack of train-ing, and general lethargy due to lack of wartime incentive."[31]

Initially, both navies were constrained by the sudden loss of many skills and experience through demobilization; for a while, operational demands on fleet units ranging from minesweeping to repatriation took understandable priority over exercises. As force levels gradually stabilized, however, so each navy was able to reassess the composition, purpose, value and frequency of fleet exercises.[32] The dominant tactical exercise requirements tended to overwhelmingly emphasize either the air component or ASW. While replenishment practice was considered in general terms to be important, it was very rarely a key tactical component in any exercise. By the early 1950s, however, the pace and breadth of these exercises had intensified noticeably, including the value to be obtained from having the right level of logistic mobility. A number of reasons could be behind this. Firstly, the nature of naval threats, whether real in Korea or potential in the North Atlantic/Europe, had intensified and were seen to be requiring a more dynamic and dispersed response. Second, experience gained in the early stages of the Korean War had shown there was a desperate need for sea training at all levels and for better equipment. Third, funding for naval activity had been substantially augmented since 1950.

What follows is a brief look at how each navy conducted fleet exercises during this period and what relevance, if any, was attached to mobile logistic support.

ROYAL NAVY FLEET EXERCISES

Many of the lessons drawn from the BPF's Fleet Train experience in 1945, and the extent they were heeded, have been discussed earlier. Several initiatives floundered, usually due to financial constraints, but the one positive outcome was that inserted into the seamanship manual section on oiling and transferring stores at sea was the recommendation that "regular practice occur."[33] Exercises, however, were initially limited to modest operations usually concentrated on convoy and ASW tactics, minesweeping, and the like, which had little if any direct impact on ways to test or improve mobile logistic support doctrine.[34] Even then, the standard of analysis received by the Admiralty on such exercises was so poor that annual guidance had to be published to achieve more consistency and completeness.[35]

Over the postwar years, a pattern of Royal Navy fleet exercises evolved for the various fleets both home and overseas, called either Spring, Summer, or Autumn cruises, whose size and purpose varied according to the prevailing needs and resources of the time. Because of the immobilization of Home Fleet ships in 1947 "for manning difficulties" the first major Home Fleet tactical exercise to take place in eighteen months was Exercise SUNRISE in the West Indies in December 1948.[36] By American standards, it was small but nevertheless included a battleship, three carriers, several submarines, destroyers, and cruisers as well as land-based aircraft. Although the general level of competency was regarded as disappointing, as indeed was the weather, there were nevertheless some encouraging signs that at least some logistic lessons of the past had been remembered. Regarding replenishment at sea specifically, it was noted for example that "The frequent exchange of stores and correspondence at sea before this exercise was valuable and it is considered that now that this is standard procedure, every opportunity should be taken to practice it. The same is true for oiling, which would have to precede such a raid in wartime."[37]

One way of bringing more competitive realism into fleet exercises was to combine two fleets while each was conducting their own seasonal cruise. A case in point was having the Home and Mediterranean fleets conduct an air/surface/submarine search-and-destroy exercise, one against the other, using a number of large capital ships, including three carriers and two battleships as well as numerous destroyers and submarines, all deployed for two days off Gibraltar in March 1949. To the C-in-C Home Fleet it was a "source of strength to our Navy that we maintain two separate main fleets, one in the Mediterranean and one in the Atlantic," so the opportunity to exploit this was obviously valuable.[38] It was noteworthy, however, that notwithstanding the precondition that both "red" and "blue" fleets were purportedly low on fuel with one seeking an urgent return to base in North Africa, no further mention was ever made (let alone recognition given) to this important strategic dilemma. The aims, priorities, and subsequent analysis were instead heavily weighted toward the tactical advantages of achieving air superiority but little else. There was disappointingly no evidence that any consideration was given to the force multiplier benefits to be derived from having mobile logistic support. Perhaps the fact that the "area for the exercise was chosen [near land] because it was restricted, and therefore the opposing forces were bound to meet" could have had something to do with it.[39]

Other exercises were specifically designed to test procedures, men, and equipment under varying climatic conditions, and these were becoming increasingly relevant as the prospect of war intensified by the end of the decade. Arctic operations, for example, were seen as of growing importance for future deployments, yet they posed critical hazards for ships far from any base. Rigorous testing of replenishment gear and doctrine was considered essential, and the Home Fleet's two-week Arctic cruise, Exercise AUTUMN BEAR in November 1952, provided this opportunity. The RFA *Wave Premier*, having only recently participated in a major NATO exercise (MAINBRACE discussed later), acted as refueling tanker for this sizeable force that included a battleship, carrier, cruiser, five destroyers, three frigates, and two submarines.[40] The main lesson learned was that it was essential to have at least two replenishment tankers during such periods of short daylight and adverse weather conditions, otherwise the smaller ships were at risk of running out of fuel, only avoided on this occasion by prematurely returning to sheltered waters off Iceland to allow for simultaneous re-fueling abeam. Nevertheless, the C-in-C Home Fleet still considered the lessons learned overall made the cruise a success.[41]

U.S. NAVY FLEET EXERCISES

Compared to the Royal Navy, the U.S. Navy conducted surprisingly fewer full-blown fleet exercises in the early postwar period, primarily due to the "immobility of ships from a personnel viewpoint and higher operational commitments."[42] But from 1947 onward the intention was to provide for an annual fleet tactical exer-cise program for both the Atlantic and Pacific Fleets that would be multitasked to cover everything from amphibious assault to ASW, from bombardments to carrier-borne attack requiring extensive force deployment over large sea areas and lasting up to six weeks. In the Pacific these soon became disaggregated with shorter exercises specifically designed to address issues such as cold weather or ASW or (in keeping with recent history) amphibious training, often jointly with the Army or Marines.[43] Both fleets supplemented these exercises with midship-man training exercises, the most celebrated of which were the annual cruises for about three thousand naval reservists and midshipmen from the East Coast to Europe. These were substantial forces in their own right. In addition to several cruisers and destroyers, the 1947 cruise included two battleships and two fleet carriers, and although this was reduced in 1948 to one battleship and one carrier, a further battleship was added in 1951. Following the success of the first cruise to the United Kingdom and Scandinavia, the 1948 cruise was extended into the Mediterranean as TF84 to include North African ports for the first time.[44]

Typically, all participants were loaded to capacity prior to departure, al-though it was still envisaged that joint exercises should be undertaken with the Service Force of the U.S. Atlantic Fleet.[45] In the end, the number of refuelings was very few, mostly escorts being topped up by the larger ships. Although a stores ship was sent direct to Scotland, its value proved limited; it transpired that what was really needed for these cruises was a refrigeration ship available through-out.[46] This, however, was easier to request than effect. The lack of available aux-iliaries, even to cover operational needs, meant that short of reactivating more from the reserves, fleet exercises for auxiliaries had effectively to go on hold. In 1948, for example, the Atlantic Fleet had just one AE, USS *Great Sitkin*, continu-ously deployed to carry ammunition to and from the Atlantic bases, which had denied her participating in two fleet exercises, thereby "preventing the much needed vital training not only to the AE, but to ships that she replenishes dur-ing the fleet exercises."[47] In fact, the loading, transportation, and issue of ad-vanced types of weapons at sea remained completely untried in the Atlantic. Al-though CinCLant subsequently conceded that the AE should participate in the next exercise, the reactivation of a second AE from reserves was only possible "if

ComServLant's Emergency plans had to be implemented."[48] Unfortunately these were the very plans already being severely criticized for their total inadequacy to provide sufficient ships from reserve to support both a Fast Striking force as well as the Eastern Atlantic and Mediterranean forces, along with all the other overseas afloat support required by the Navy and Army.[49]

The fact of the matter was that achieving any improvements in peacetime logistic support had become a struggle. For example, based on previous wartime experience, the U.S. Navy had prescribed by 1947 that the standard replenishment rate should be ten days worth of supplies to a fleet in ten hours, which, according to Captain Pare would require a complete replenishment of a large carrier in three hours.[50] There is no evidence this was achieved at that time. Indeed, later doctrine became more circumspect in light of further peacetime experience, and expectations became increasingly cautious. Too often consideration of any replenishment problem overemphasized the quantitative aspects of any transfer at sea to the detriment of how long it was actually taking to achieve this. By 1948, underway replenishments were expected to take all day based on planning factors that reflected the inadequately designed or equipped merchant type hulls still operating in the Service Force. Moreover, changing replenishment rendezvous due to weather or enemy action could no longer be conducted at the existing 8–12 knot leisurely pace because this was considered totally inadequate under potential wartime conditions.[51]

By early 1950 the Sixth Fleet had been increased to about twenty ships with various task force exercises consuming about one-sixth of their time, usually conducted for about a week between port visits, with additional training undertaken during logistic and upkeep periods.[52] These exercises intensified significantly following the outbreak of the Korean War, both in frequency—often to two or more a month—as well as by type, that is, ASW, gunnery, convoy, or amphibious. Moreover, these exercises were increasingly conducted jointly with other navies, particularly the British.

One of the most fully documented of the large annual tactical exercises (but never published) was that conducted by the U.S. Atlantic Fleet Second Task Fleet from February 3 until March 18, 1947, involving nearly 150 ships including 3 fleet carriers, 2 light carriers, 1 battleship, 7 cruisers, 29 destroyers, 17 submarines, 32 amphibious assault, and some 34 other warships.[53] Reflecting the severe cutbacks in logistic support, all these warships were supported by a logistic support force comprising only 1 ammunition ship (AE), 5 oilers (AO), 1 supply ship fresh/frozen/dry (AF), 1 hospital ship (AH), 2 repair ship landing craft (ARL), 2 landing ship (LSD), and 1 attack cargo vessel (AKA) with escorts. Overall performance reports often made uncomfortable reading; one of the broader lessons was that without regular practice neither the commands nor the ships would ever operate together efficiently. In addition to the one huge annual exercise, it was therefore recommended that additional short fleet tactical exercises should be undertaken every three months for two weeks at a time to include a carrier task force and a submarine force supported by a logistic support force. In other words, leave the amphibious aspect to the annual exercise.[54]

As for the logistic challenges, these remained difficult to resolve, but as Vice Admiral Blandy emphasized from the outset, "In a future war it is probable that our ships will remain at sea for much longer periods than in the last war due to the greater vulnerability of ships at bases and anchorages on account of atomic bomb attack."[55]

But all the evidence suggested that the fleet auxiliaries were ill prepared or equipped for the task. In all, eleven representatives from various U.S. Navy departments were ensconced on logistic support ships to study all aspects of replenishment. Their reports were discouraging. For example, the report from a BuSandA observer on board AKA-92 USS *Wyandot* (which also carried a British observer from the Admiralty, whose report has yet to surface) criticized the performance of the supply ship and the combat ships that came alongside, including fleet and light carriers, battleships, and cruisers. It was his impression that these warships "attached little importance to the replenishment exercises as compared to the tactical exercises" (by which he would be alluding to gunnery and air sorties and the like) and he recommended that replenishment be elevated to a proper tactical exercise.[56] This is a revealing observation, and while the Task Force commander agreed with the sentiment, the cold reality for him was that insufficient personnel and stretched operational commitments made this initiative impractical.[57] Much of the blame for the perceived low morale was traced to lack of any training or organization, exacerbated by shortages of trained officers and absence of the right equipment to conduct transfers. His remedy was to institute a proper training program to increase the number of qualified personnel, particularly winch operators, an initiative, he wrote "that observers from the British Admiralty are also considering."[58] The problem might have been deeper than imagined because five years later, during the Korean War, Royal Navy observers witnessed similar lethargy from U.S. oilers, which was noted with considerable surprise at the time, given the most favorable impression already established for the U.S. Navy's extraordinary and unique ability to reammunition their carriers at sea in such large quantities.[59]

JOINT EXERCISES

Observer reports from either navy on logistic activities undertaken exclusively by the host force tended to be positive and instructive. When they acted jointly in the same exercise, however, some notably different perspectives arose on aspects ranging from purpose to procedure. This disparity could become a vexatious issue, and Exercise MAINBRACE on September 10–24, 1952, provides an interesting example. This was the first Supreme Allied Commander Atlantic (SACLANT) exercise involving, for the first time, a NATO striking fleet dominated by four American carriers and two British fleet carriers operating under difficult weather conditions for most of the time in the North Atlantic. Logistic support was provided by five American oilers and three RFA tankers. Table 7.1 shows the amount of fuel issued by each auxiliary and table 7.2 provides a summary of ships fueled.

The twenty-eight replenishments by the RFA to U.S. warships (which included a battleship, two light carriers, a cruiser, and numerous destroyers and auxiliaries) consumed approximately 37 percent of the total RFA fuel issue. Other nationalities consumed 3 percent, and British warships took the balance of 60 percent, about half of which went to the fleet carriers and battleship with the balance going to destroyers and cruisers.[60]

Two observations about these figures can be made at this juncture. First, in proportionate terms the American oilers issued significantly more avgas to carriers than the RFA, given the balance of carrier contribution by each navy for this exercise. Second, the British distributed a much higher proportion of fuel to non–Royal Navy warships compared to U.S. oiler distribution to their non–U.S. Navy customers. Behind these figures, however, are some interesting dynamics that reflect to some extent the broader challenges for navies trying to establish successful coalition cross-support. While these types of exercises cannot always be readily compared to wartime operations (even such relatively "benign" limited operations as Korea) they nevertheless provide the chance to compare progress and highlight lessons for consideration in future operations.

In analyzing the replenishment performance for this particular exercise, it was seen from the Admiralty's perspective that compared to the U.S. Navy the RFA transfer rates of fuel and avgas were disappointing. This was partly because American warships could receive fuel at much higher rates than everyone else (for reasons discussed in chapter 3). It was also the case that most of the American transfers occurred between U.S. Navy warships, all of which would be very familiar with their own UNREP doctrine. American oilers also had much more practical experience than the RFA in formation fueling for carrier task forces. Two of the British tankers, for example, were only recently taken off freighting duties and were still familiarizing themselves with the new 6-inch hose equipment recently taken on board. Their crews therefore lacked experience in replenishment even though their superb seamanship skill was recognized in all reports, particularly the American. But the main problems for the RFAs were their poor pumping rates, primarily because the *Wave* tankers were in urgent need of modernization; this would double their 700 tph pumping rate and provide the necessary new transfer rigs to do the job properly. Even so, they would still fall well below the 1,560 tph pumping rate of the RFA *Olna* (shown in plate 7.1 refueling a

Table 7.1. Summary of Fuel Issued during Exercise MAINBRACE (1952)

Ship	Oil Fuel (tons)	Avgas (tons)
USS *Chipola*	9,333	900
USS *Canisteo*	11,070	—
USS *Elokomin*	10,050	700
USS *Allagash*	4,000	700
USS *Salamonie*	7,432	285
RFA *Wave Prince*	3,477	—
RFA *Wave Premier*	7,209	4
RFA *Olna*	6,423	245

Source: TNA(Kew), ADM 1/24039: "Review of Replenishment at Sea: Compilation of Reports Received on Exercise MAINBRACE."

Table 7.2. Summary of Ships Fueled during Exercise MAINBRACE (1952)

Ship	U.S.	British	Norwegian	Dutch	French
USS *Chipola*	31	4	—	—	1
USS *Canisteo*	26	6	—	—	—
USS *Elokomin*	28	8	—	—	—
USS *Allagash*	11	—	—	—	1
USS *Salamonie*	24	7	—	1	—
RFA *Wave Prince*	10	13	1	—	—
RFA *Wave Premier*	10	18	—	1	—
RFA *Olna*	8	8	1	1	—

Source: TNA (Kew), ADM 1/24039: "Review of Replenishment at Sea: Compilation of Reports Received on Exercise MAINBRACE."

British carrier during Exercise MAINBRACE) and were even poorer compared to the designed 2,400 tph capacity for the new RFA tankers laid down that very year.[61]

Within the Admiralty a number of other criticisms surfaced about the disappointing performance of fleet replenishment, which had not been up to their staff requirements. Included were various explanations for the disparity between the British and American replenishment performance. Auxiliary ship design, for example, was highlighted as a cause when it was pointed out (not for the first time) that the U.S. Navy built and manned their oilers for fleet issue whereas the RFAs were designed as freighting tankers fitted out for replenishment at sea. While attempts to convert the RFA to naval specifications and manning had been proposed in the past, the main stumbling block—that it was uneconomic in terms of both ships and manpower—would thwart any progress. Corroboration for the need for further change can also be deduced from the American exercise report issued by ComServRonTWO (the American logistic support group for this exercise), which complained that the British oilers were civilian manned and were understood "to have had no previous experience with publications effective for MAINBRACE . . . or . . . the use of operation orders or operating as a part of a naval task force." It had therefore proved necessary "to restrict the formation and maneuvers of the entire group to those of a convoy type [of formation]." The American report went on to say that while the British oilers gave "an outstanding performance considering the above limitations . . . the mobility of the support group was considerably reduced."[62] Other concerns expressed in the American report centered on lack of speed of the British frigate screen, lack of understanding of American doctrine and rig structures, and the usual radio miscommunication issues.

In some senses, these reports were a useful reminder for the Admiralty that more work and significant change was still necessary if they were going to get the most out of future joint exercises. Not least, was "the need for a proper fleet train." In one respect, however, the RFA had excelled itself, for all three of their tankers were still able to refuel ships astern in particularly atrocious weather after the U.S. Navy oilers had been obliged to stop.[63] While this accomplishment says much about their seamanship, it also reflected the fact that whereas the U.S. Navy had relegated astern fueling to emergencies only, the Royal Navy was always more determined to practice astern fueling because this might prove to be the only available option when using commercial tankers in an emergency, such as in the initial stages of any war.

Unlike their joint experience during the Korean War, in which the general level of interoperability between both navies progressed well (partly because they had to), in peacetime such cooperation could occasionally become less harmonious. MAINBRACE again provides a case in point where there clearly existed a cultural difference of perspective on what was at stake. Take, for example, the collective view of the British liaison officers attached to the U.S. Navy, who believed that the Americans had adopted "a very haphazard approach to their task" with a lack of enthusiasm either to correct mistakes by their staff or show "any interest in the activities of any friendly forces, except for the logistic support force operating in the vicinity."[64] The strong impression in their report was that the American fast carrier task force felt so self-sufficient with their dedicated logistic support that it could afford to act independently from its ashore authority unilaterally; therefore no attempt was made to seek or share information from others, such as Coastal Command for submarine reconnaissance. It was thought that this attitude was perhaps forced on U.S. admirals at sea because "it is understood that they are not allowed even to make suggestions for the alterations of plans of their Senior Officers ashore."

As for achieving closer understanding, this seemed stillborn. As the report put it

> We had the greatest difficulty in getting them to understand British procedures and drills. We are certain this was not due to any reluctance to be taught by the British. Nor did it seem they did not understand our language. The lack of comprehension of other peoples' ideas seemed to be much more deep rooted. . . . Whatever may be the cause of this difficulty to understand and use other peoples detailed methods, it is considered to be a matter of great importance . . . otherwise . . . the efficient operating of a combined force under British or other NATO command is going to be difficult.[65]

Other observations seemed familiar to officers of the time, for example, that the U.S. Navy "had good equipment for providing information from all sources, but doesn't know how to use it." Not surprisingly at all, it was reported American aviators and their aircraft operations were "of a high standard" although everything was geared around Pacific doctrine with "no attempt made to alter these lessons in the light of the different Factors peculiar to operations in the North Sea" such as the weather, submarines, enemy raiders, and the need for radio security.

Overall, however, the major frustration was encapsulated in their feeling that "The U.S. Navy knows only one way of operating a Carrier Task Force, the Pacific way. This might work in Northern European waters in wartime with heavy submarine threat. It certainly didn't work in MAINBRACE but nothing short of a shooting war will force the Americans to change their methods."[66]

From the logistics perspective, there are perhaps three important inferences to be drawn from all this, all of them rather sobering. First, the commander's independence (thanks to his mobile logistic support) could induce a unilateral approach toward solving the strategic challenge at hand without investigating other available options, particularly if they were outside his control. Allowing room for initiative to theater commanders is something to be encouraged, but unilateral approaches based simply on precedent and the familiarity of one's forces do not necessarily all go hand in hand when undertaking joint operations. Second, operating the carrier task force "the Pacific way" would in all likelihood be more risky in the Atlantic, given the more modest logistic resources at his disposal, the climate, and a higher vulnerability to submarine or land-based air attack in more confined spaces. Third, the Royal Navy in particular urgently needed to find the necessary financial support to convert from plans the necessary improvements in the capabilities of their replenishment ships, equipment, and doctrine if the fleet was ever expected to operate in task forces for sustained periods at long distances away from base.

NATO

While it was envisaged soon after 1945 that, for peace to endure at sea, the "free" nations of Western Europe would need to pool their naval resources into some sort of international force, how this could be accomplished in peacetime would take time and commitment. It was not until 1949 that the first multinational naval exercise occurred under the direction of the Royal Navy. With its strong emphasis on convoy protection, Operation VERITY involved seventy British and thirty-nine Dutch, Belgian, and French warships. Although comparatively rudimentary in its aims, with its tactical emphasis on mine-sweeping and ASW, much progress nevertheless had been made in trying to operate together through extensive signaling and communications practice, to the extent that Admiral McGrigor was moved to note afterwards that "Now we can go forward in great confidence; before we only had great hopes."[67] The template was thus laid and all subsequent combined naval exercises, including those by NATO forces later (such as ACTIVITY in 1950 and PROGRESS in 1951), assumed the VERITY model. There were also numerous smaller bilateral exercises in various European waters, but the primary purpose for these, and the numerous multinational exercises under the NATO umbrella thereafter, emphasized antisubmarine and antimine tactics with no evidence that internaval mobile logistic support received any specific attention. Perhaps this was not surprising, however, since the only NATO navies operating for extended periods away from their bases beyond European coastlines would have been American, British, or Canadian. Within five years it was typical for the Royal Navy to undertake more than forty exercises a year, half of which involved NATO or other foreign navies covering "all aspects of sea warfare."[68]

Meanwhile, the first big exercise in the Mediterranean, held in 1951, was Anglo-American with carrier maneuvers involving the U.S. Sixth Fleet and Britain's Mediterranean Fleet together with units of the Home Fleet on its annual Spring Cruise.[69] For this and subsequent exercises, the main objective was always the defense of Malta, but again, no specific emphasis appears to have been given to the logistic dimension.

Postwar Replenishment at Sea Trials

Much of the real groundwork for improving the efficacy and capability in mobile logistic support originated from two unlikely resources that would become, for both navies, the indispensable cornerstone of their postwar replenishment trials. Both acquired a German replenishment ship of the same class, the *Nordmark* for the Royal Navy in 1945 and later the *Dithsmarschen* for the U.S. Navy. Each ship was built just prior to World War II displacing 22,500 tons fully loaded, designed specifically to provision German capital ships, raiders, and U-boats with fuel, ammunition, and stores either at sea or at anchor. Because time was not usually a critical issue, given the typical remoteness and secrecy of the replenishment rendezvous, German refueling was conducted alongside when stationary or, if conducted under way, only astern. Given the age of both vessels as well as their limited abeam capability, both the Royal Navy and U.S. Navy concluded initially that only with significant modification and expense could either be deployed as full-time replenishment tankers. Nevertheless, it was acknowledged there were some inherent real attractions to consider, not least their size, fast speed, replenishment gear including rubber hose, and multipurpose design. Indeed, what was particularly attractive was their capacity not only to hold 10,000 tons of bunker fuel and 300 tons of aircraft fuel but separate storage facilities were also available for ammunition, refrigeration rooms, and general stores. There was nothing similar anywhere. How each navy chose to exploit the opportunity now presented to them would in some senses reflect, in microcosm, their view of the broader logistic challenges confronting them during these difficult transitional years. Moreover, the circumstances provide a unique opportunity for comparing how they responded because, for once, the playing field was level.

ROYAL NAVY TRIALS

It soon became evident to the British that it would be uneconomic to convert *Nordmark* into an RFA auxiliary for the long term, so for a while she remained in reserve at short notice while other possibilities were explored. Given her excellent ship-handling characteristics, it was eventually decided she should become a platform to test new transfer techniques and equipment because the Admiralty was anxious to catch up with American knowledge. This vessel provided a suitable short cut. Furthermore, as both the U.S. Navy and Kriegsmarine auxiliaries had been naval manned, the Admiralty was keen to take the opportunity to experiment with a naval crew as well. In July 1947 she was accordingly refitted using many ideas derived from their BPF Fleet Train experience including new large cross-derrick posts for abeam refueling.[70] Soon her name was changed to HMS *Bulawayo*, shown in plate 7.2 coming astern of the British carrier HMS *Glory*.

Several trials, each spread over several weeks, were conducted between 1947 and 1949, with the main objectives being to simplify and standardize the equipment already in use before testing a radically different method for transferring liquids and then heavy stores with a rig that would cope better with ship motion and heavier seas.[71] The initial results even with the standard 70-ft derrick rig in 1947, as shown refueling HMS *Vanguard* in plate 7.5, were nevertheless extraordinary. HMS *Bulawayo* was comfortable replenishing at 20 knots (compared to the normal 12–14 knots preferred by U.S. Navy and RFA tankers) in strong winds force seven and rough seas. Fueling at night was feasible, and testing a new robust but light 7-inch hose proved to be "an unqualified success" (shown in plate 7.3 and plate 7.4). Even fueling astern with the new hose "was practicable in all but the most severe weather."[72] All this achievement was not just encouraging; for the Royal Navy it was groundbreaking.

During 1948 HMS *Bulawayo* had to spend several months freighting urgently needed oil from Trinidad to the United Kingdom, which delayed and subsequently curtailed her refit in preparation for the planned autumn trials using a new rig for transferring solids. The trials were therefore confined to the new jackstay fueling rig shown in diagram 3.4 and plate 3.12, which enabled a larger hose to be supported by four troughs slung on travelers that ran along a jackstay, a taut wire stretched between the two ships.[73] Despite encouraging results, the rig could not be fitted to other tankers because it required either more powerful steam winches or incorporating an efficient means of automatic compensation, such as the tensioning winch, which was still under development and unavailable to either navy for some years.[74]

Nevertheless, the advances achieved in replenishment performance were huge, so much so that the U.S. Navy observer on board was "genuinely impressed," noting particularly the close aboard work at high speed of the heavier ships that the U.S. Navy considered too risky to undertake as well as the high pumping rates that he noted were an advance on the highest American figures at the time.[75] In fact, the U.S. Navy proceeded to incorporate the data into their reference material for the underway replenishment "maneuvers" conducted at the NWC.[76] But HMS *Bulawayo* was, of course, no normal replenishment ship and it was stressed how she enjoyed a number of unique advantages compared to other fleet train ships. For example, "her fine lines slips through water easily, with good handling." Moreover, being naval manned, as shown in plate 7.6, serials were conducted on "traditional naval lines with precision skill and discipline."[77]

The 1949 trials series provided the chance to test new methods for transferring very heavy solids including ammunition, about which the British had less experience both in scale and frequency primarily due to the lack of any suitable store ships. Again, HMS *Bulawayo* was the ideal platform. In plate 7.7 the ammunition held in a skip box is transferred between the cruiser HMS *Superb* and HMS *Bulawayo*; plate 7.8 is a close-up photograph of the ammunition skip box and netting. An illustration of transferring a torpedo by jackstay can also be found in plate 3.16.

These trials were important for a number of reasons, not least by providing the Royal Navy with valuable practical experience about the new concept of jackstay rigs, for this new method would be an essential prerequisite for safely transferring either fuel or stores at the increasingly higher speeds demanded by operational commanders in virtually all types of sea and weather conditions. What these trials had also demonstrated to both navies was that, even in these very early stages, the British had quickly caught up with the Americans in refueling technology even if they were still significantly behind in transferring solids and ammunition. When representatives of the Admiralty's Director of Naval Construction, on a subsequent trip to the United States, met with the small team of U.S. Navy officers who had recently observed the trials, they recorded that from the U.S. perspective, not only had there been a complete exchange of information but "the two are now generally at about the same stage in the development of RAS arrangements and equipment."[78] This was no mean achievement, considering how wide the disparity had been in experience and technology less than three years earlier.

By 1950, with the trials series behind her, the proposal to refit HMS *Bulawayo* for more permanent replenishment duties was again rejected on financial and practical grounds, so she was placed into reserve. This was a huge disappointment to the Commonwealth naval forces in Korea who had been requesting she be redeployed as a peripatetic tanker, given her excellent reputation and capability.[79] But her legacy had now been established by providing the vital groundwork that would enable the next generation of naval replenishment ships to be the first designed from the keel up.

U.S. NAVY TRIALS

Nordmark's sister ship, *Dithmarschen*, which had also been taken over by the British in 1945, was allocated to the U.S. Navy in January 1946. She later sailed to Philadelphia and was renamed USS *Conecuh* in October 1946. Within three weeks, however, all conversion work was terminated due to lack of funds, and she was thereupon reduced to the inactive list for the next six years.[80] This change of heart reflected the initial conflicting bouts of enthusiasm and indifference regarding the value of further trials. Most of the impetus for progress came from Captain Pare, who persuaded admirals Nimitz and Mitscher to allocate scarce resources for exploring a design for a one-stop replenishment ship by using in trials the unique characteristics of the captured German supply ship. However, additional severe budget cuts killed the project and no further progress was made until after the groundbreaking Conference on Mobile Logistic Support was convened in April 1952 to study the lessons from the Korean War. Thereafter, life for USS *Conecuh* significantly changed and despite various delays, she was eventually commissioned on February 16, 1953, as the U.S. Navy's first 'one-stop' fleet replenishment ship (see plate 7.9). In September she joined the Service Force of U.S. Second Fleet for NATO's MARINER exercises in the North Atlantic where she conducted the first one-stop replenishment operation ever undertaken by the U.S. Navy. Her main legacy, though, was in providing a wealth of information from evaluations of one-stop versus multiple-source replenishment evolutions conducted with the U.S. Sixth Fleet in the Mediterranean on eighty-seven occasions the following year.[81] However, like her sister, by the mid 1950s she was so worn out that her upkeep was considered no longer viable, so USS *Conecuh* was subsequently decommissioned in 1955.[82]

A number of points should be made about these two different experiences using similar German ships. The most important is that each ship was deployed, albeit at different times and for different purposes, to help each navy resolve what it perceived at the time to be its most important weakness in providing mobile logistic support. For the British, it was the urgent need to catch-up with the Americans, and this was well vindicated, for HMS *Bulawayo's* contribution not only helped the Royal Navy toward parity but she provided the vital test bed for the next generation of fast replenishment ship designed exclusively for naval service. For the Americans, the purpose and timing were completely different. In 1946 the combination of scarce funds, lack of emergency, and the existence of a relatively well-equipped fleet of modern auxiliaries meant there was little incentive or institutional encouragement to experiment or even modify USS *Conecuh* just for the sake of it. Korea, however, changed everything. Now the U.S. Navy needed to learn fast about how to deliver almost daily both ordnance and fuel simultaneously to increasingly hungry warships, particularly carriers. The USS *Conecuh* was uniquely equipped to assist in resolving the specific challenges found with one-stop replenishment, and for this she fulfilled her role well.

War Games

Recall from chapter 5 that British and American officers attended logistics courses at the NWC that included an appreciation of the relevance of mobile logistic support in modern carrier warfare. One of the unique characteristics of these courses were the so-called war games, conducted using maneuver boards (as shown in plate 7.10) to simulate different strategic or tactical challenges requiring multidisciplinary solutions.

Using the replenishment-at-sea studies as an example, various competitive teams were required to plan, design, and implement fleet replenishment programs in exactly the same way that fleet exercises were conducted by the Commander Logistic Support Force at sea.[83] A full military appreciation would be provided, based on the number and type of combatant ships involved, geography of the area, projected fleet track, and estimated speed and signals traffic, including expected fleet activity and opposition. From all this information, complex schedules were then prepared for transferring ammunition and fuel, planes, and personnel replacement. Replenishment areas were then selected and—most importantly—the weather, wind, and sea conditions were factored in. Notably, all these exercises presumed very large-scale fleet train operations with all the data derived either from Pacific experience or recent fleet exercises (including data provided by Royal Navy students from very recent replenishment trials using HMS *Bulawayo*, discussed earlier).[84] Collective critical reviews were subsequently conducted after the exercises finished but, when all was said and done, even Pare would admit that "the plain tactical handling of the force with task forces maneuvering in the vicinity is a job for a *good officer*." This challenge gets exacerbated by the sheer variety of ships involved, all with differing characteristics, most with "no speed to speak of . . . slow unwieldy and not manned by the best trained officers, most of whom may be good seamen but have zero knowledge of tactics."[85]

To the extent that these war games enhanced naval officers' appreciation of the tactical dimension and strategic context for mobile logistic support, then such programs were regarded as very helpful but not necessarily essential. For the Royal Navy, the nearest equivalent, so far as can be discerned, was the Royal Naval Tactical School in Woolwich, which ran a number of courses for officers involving group discussions together with syndicates formed to resolve various tactical issues. Four such classes were conducted in 1952 to look at the tactical considerations involving the replenishment of a carrier task force with fuel and ammunition and aircraft following the theoretical outbreak of war between NATO and the USSR in 1953. The task force was to operate off the Lofoten Islands carrying out air strikes and bombardment against Soviet occupied Norway.[86] A comprehensive breakdown was provided to each student covering ship performances and requirements (both combat and auxiliary), replenishment capabilities, a detailed chronology of "events" together with several appendices of supporting logistic related information. Not only was this all remarkably similar to the type of replenishment material provided by the NWC for their war game syndicates but equally interesting were the underlying assumptions adopted for the exercise. The task force comprised two carriers, four cruisers, and a destroyer screen all supported by a fleet train of tankers, an ammunition issue ship, a rescue tug, and a replenishment carrier plus screen. Despite the lack of any existing ammunition issue ship that could replenish at sea in 1952, this apparently did not deter those setting up the exercise. It was clear the Royal Navy had every intention to operate an offensive carrier strategy in line with its aspirations to be a significant contributor to Anglo-American naval offensive capability. Such a challenge presumed that the "Pacific" model for task forces (including their own fleet train) was therefore alive and well.

Logistic Doctrine Development 1945–1955

A number of other practical educational initiatives were undertaken by both navies, partly out of concern that demobilization would lead to a significant loss of "corporate memory" and partly to ensure that after the lessons from World War II had been analyzed, these should be disseminated as widely as possible.

Each navy approached this task in slightly different ways. For the U.S. Navy, the accumulation over time of various academic, historical, and military research studies culminated in the promulgation throughout the fleets of a number of very formal detailed doctrine manuals, including standard fighting instructions that prescribed procedures and practices that embraced almost holistically every aspect or contingency in detail. The Royal Navy, conversely, adopted a more transactional "on time delivery when needed" type of approach, by publishing confidential "books" that included tactical directives, changes, or descriptions of lessons derived from recent tactical experience or exercises. As such, they were immediate and were often pragmatically applied, tending to leave more to the initiative and expertise of the on-scene commander.

The outcome from these two approaches is discussed in the following, including the extent to which any exchange or standardization was established between them as a way to achieve tactical logistic interoperability.

U.S. Navy Command/Strategic Doctrine

Following a considerable amount of preparation during the early postwar years, a new series of Naval Warfare Publications (NWP) was promulgated by the U.S. Navy during the Korean War designed to replace the early post–World War II USF series of publications. These would in effect act as source books for contemporary warfare doctrines of the U.S. Navy, although they were intended to perform two rather divergent functions—first as immediate reference on the bridge of a warship and second as guides for planning an operation or for command qualification.[87] This particular series commenced with NWP-10 *Naval Warfare*, which expressed a number of broad principles that provided the foundation upon which various doctrines and operating instructions were subsequently published. It was a widely embracing document that traced the development of sea power as an instrument of national policy followed by a description of the development and organization of the U.S. Navy. There then followed an analysis of the principles of offensive and defensive action closed by a summation of the probable future course of naval warfare in the light of technological development.

NWP-11 *Naval Operational Planning* was a guide for the commander and those staff confronted with operational planning problems. Additional sections were devoted to logistic and communications planning. At the Tactical/Task Force level, Naval Warfare Information Publications, or NWIP, also provided the detailed technical instructions not covered by the NWP, and these were issued with numbers that related directly to the respective NWP. A full list of relevant publications can be found in appendix X.

No formal doctrine manual for mobile logistic support along the lines adopted by the U.S. Navy existed within the Royal Navy. Instead, the Admiralty disseminated important ideas or changes through two so-called confidential books (CB) titled either as "The Fighting Instructions" or "Progress in Tactics." Logistics issues often featured in both. For example, CB04487 published by the Admiralty's Tactical Staff Duties Division in June 1947 under the name "The Fighting Instructions," provided insights on how the Admiralty at the strategic/ tactical level envisaged establishing and organizing various types of bases in order to achieve vital dispersion to protect fleet units from the atomic bomb.[88] A further section was also devoted to the role of a fleet train and the high level tactical procedures and ship disposition arrangements during replenishment at sea. It was not a detailed operational or procedural manual; this would be found in separate dedicated manuals, discussed later.

Another example of a tactical problem that merited dissemination was the trials results in replenishment at sea conducted by HMS *Bulawayo*, mentioned earlier, because of the growing fear that faster replenishment speeds were urgently needed to counter the vulnerability to submarine attack.[89] "Progress in Tactics" also included appraisals of the order book for various tactical fleet exercises undertaken from time to time, including replenishment at sea.[90] Finally, there were the Battle Summaries, again issued under BR references, which provided a succinct and balanced account of events covering a wide variety of wartime operations.[91]

Replenishment at Sea Doctrine

There was one very particular area of tactical doctrine that benefited immensely from the convergence of different operating procedures between the U.S. Navy and Royal Navy that would lead to increased interoperability and, by extension, strategic reach for both navies. This was to be found in Replenishment at Sea or UNREP.

American replenishment at sea was first fully codified in CominCH P-2 "Fueling at Sea Instructions," promulgated in November 1944 and very much based upon their early experiences in the Pacific war.[92] This document was replaced in August 1946 by USF-13 "Logistic Support Force Operating Instructions United States Fleets," which was "based on procedures used, and experience gained, in the operations conducted by Service Squadron Six in the Iwo Jima and Okinawa Campaigns." It was able to standardize for a commander the tactics and procedures within a Logistic Support Force and their liaison with associated commands.[93] "USF-83 Fueling and Replenishment at Sea" was published at the same time; it addressed in more detail operating procedures including interoperability, particularly with the Royal Navy.[94] British replenishment doctrine since 1945 had meanwhile been governed by the BPF's "War Orders" issued to its Fleet Train.[95] The first British publication dedicated to replenishment

at sea was apparently modeled after the American USF-13 but tailored from experience gained by the BPF; this was published in 1947 as BR1742/47 "Replenishment At Sea."[96] Both USF-83 and BR1742/47 formed the foundation for a lo-
calized version for UN naval forces in Korea that was revised in 1951, following
further Anglo-American replenishment experience, and subsequently promulgated throughout the Royal Navy's Far East Fleet in 1951.[97] Further operational
experience, combined with the results of the *Bulawayo* trials, was then codified
and promulgated in 1952 throughout the Royal Navy as BR1742 (52) "Replenishment at Sea."[98] Two subsequent addenda, BR1742/52B "Transfer of Liquids at
Sea," issued in 1952, and BR1742/52C "Transfer of Solids at Sea," were distributed along with BR1742 (52) to British, Canadian, and American warships in
1953, specifically intended to provide a common procedure for ships to replenish from each other.[99] The Admiralty's later "Manual of Seamanship Volume II"
BR67 (2) also provided useful guidelines on aspects of replenishment at sea
doctrine.

In 1953, the U.S. Navy issued "NWP-38 Replenishment at Sea," which reflected some of the procedural lessons gained from Korea.[100] Two years later
came ATP-16 "Replenishment at Sea," which in many respects was similar if not
identical to NWP-38 but, most importantly, now included procedures and rig
descriptions for operating with navies from NATO and France.[101] The American
ATP-16 and the British BR1742 thus became mutually compatible for joint operational requirements and, although modified from time to time since, ATP-16
provides to this day the standard operating procedures for underway replenishment between the U.S. Navy and all its NATO partners.[102]

Other Technical Publications

The first comprehensive glossary of logistic terms was produced in 1946 by the
U.S. Navy's BuSandA, which acknowledged that it was still incomplete so cor-
rections and additions "will be welcomed."[103] In 1950, the Bureau of Naval Personnel published the first compendium on naval logistics designed for all levels
of officers as a manual that encompassed subjects ranging from geopolitical/
economic issues of production to phases in logistic planning and the types of
organizational structures designed to implement them.[104] No similar literature
on logistics existed for the Royal Navy until a compendium of logistic planning
data was published in October 1952 titled "APM307 Logistic Planning Data" carrying a "secret" classification. It was the first of its kind specifically designed to
help British logistics planners prepare for Atlantic/Home Waters operations, as
the existing American logistics data was based almost entirely on Pacific criteria
that by then was regarded as "unsuitable."[105]

No literature was published during this period about British naval logistics policy, although there were the occasional articles in military journals that provided some insights whenever logistics was a consideration. Examples here would be I. McD. Black's excellent exposition on the state of fueling at sea from the perspective of a naval constructor.[106] Others could be found in the authoritative contributions from serving officers published by the Royal United Services Institute, which again have been extensively quoted elsewhere in this book.[107]

Nor was there any apparent rush in the Royal Navy to produce a historical record of logistic experience, despite postwar demands for such. The most comprehensive study was an account of the history of the Royal Navy's fleet train that was not released until 1953 and to this day remains in manuscript form only.[108] Its author, Capt. R. F. Leonard, RN, of the Admiralty's Plans Division (Q), wrote in the introduction what can best be described as either an illuminating reflection on the prevailing attitude toward logistic lessons from wartime experience or a heart-felt caveat having just produced a long and very comprehensive but complex history for the record. What he concluded was

> The term "Fleet Train" came to be loosely applied to any aggregate of Fleet auxiliaries, and surprise may be felt that Stations other than the Pacific are hardly mentioned in the History. There are several reasons behind these apparent omissions: The Pacific Campaigns of 1945 show the essentials of "Floating Support" without too many confusing side issues; the histories which are to be written of Bases and Combined Operations would, inevitably, duplicate much that might have been written here of "Fleet Train" work in the Mediterranean or Indian Ocean; and this history would be even longer and more tedious to read than it already is.[109]

Standardization

On a number of occasions during wartime both the Royal Navy and U.S. Navy had managed to standardize each other's operating procedures and signals where it was important for a joint approach, a notable example being the integration of the BPF alongside American units in 1945. Plate 7.11, for example, shows a multinational replenishment between British and Dominion warships using standard Royal Navy equipment and doctrine in 1945, whereas plate 7.12 shows the rarer occasion for its time, that of a British destroyer refueling from an American battleship. Yet the success in achieving at least some binational standardization during 1945 was somewhat diminished by the lack of standardization within the BPF's own fleet train.

British postwar efforts to achieve further standardization with the U.S. Navy, should there be another war, was therefore intensified through informal contacts in Washington, but the latter were generally less enthusiastic about reciprocating unless it happened to suit their needs such as in the development of astern fueling. In the immediate postwar years, the Commonwealth navies, conversely, still took their lead in operating methods, equipment, and training from the Royal Navy. In 1947 a formal agreement to progress further standardization between the United Kingdom, the United States, and Canada was signed, and in March 1949 the First Lord approved the formation of the Standardization Division within the Naval Staff to coordinate and advise on the naval aspects of various policy issues. One early result from all this was the all-important RN/USN/RCN standardization agreement, signed in May 1950; it was this agreement more than anything else that facilitated the extraordinary progress achieved in the key area of logistics interoperability—namely, replenishment at sea during and after the Korean War.

The other key area of standardization affecting logistics was the Burns-Templer U.K./U.S. agreement, also dated 1950, which introduced the use of formal Information Exchange Programs (IEPs). By satisfying the U.S. legal requirement that the U.S. Navy only divulge information via its Office of Naval Intelligence, these important programs enabled contact between naval staff wishing to exchange information on a variety of specified subjects. This was a considerable step forward for those advocating closer contacts between the two navies. The advent of NATO accelerated the need for further standardization, and so the NATO Military Standardisation Agency in London was created, headed by its own director but requiring support from the Naval Staff's Standardisation Division. By November 1951 the task of devising policy and setting up procedures had been complete, and the Standardisation Division was therefore dissolved and its work absorbed into the Admiralty's Training Staff Duties Division.[110]

Despite strong intentions following the closer links forged out of the Pacific partnership in 1945, other opportunities for both navies to achieve further standardization on a broader scale were actually quite limited. Harmonizing tactical differences like fueling signals, nomenclature, and fuel specifications helped, of course, as did the adoption of hose connectors to accommodate different hose sizes and so on. But harmonizing or merging logistics infrastructures was another issue, and this would only make sense if there were to be full interchange of air groups between naval carriers. The prospect for this was considered unlikely, although it was perfectly feasible for a single carrier or even task group from each navy to operate together. Even then it would still require each task group to have their own logistic support, so the inference was drawn that while it was not necessary to merge the infrastructures it was still the case that "standardization of techniques and tactics will be more important than standardization of equipment."[111]

Royal Navy/U.S. Navy Exchange

In 1945, reaction within the Royal Navy to the overwhelming American success in the Pacific had become somewhat ambivalent. To those who had physically operated alongside the Americans, their enthusiasm to perpetuate the close links after the war was very strong. In London, resentment festered in certain quarters at how Britain's naval superiority had finally been usurped. And it was logistics that proved to be the midwife for this transformation. As the Admiralty's Director of Plans noted, when reviewing American logistic success, "A major lesson of this war has been that naval operations can only be undertaken 'by courtesy of' adequate and efficient supply arrangements. It is possible to resent this fact but we cannot afford to ignore it."[112]

If exchanging ideas and experiences, even on quite sensitive issues, represented an indication of how close the two navies might have become since 1945, the truth was that the relationship between the two was neither static nor even predictable. On logistics matters, the relationship had deepened since operating together in 1945 such that by 1948 it was clearly one of growing mutual respect. A further case in point was the chance for U.S. Navy Service Force officers to visit HMS *Bulawayo* in Trinidad. It had also provided Captain Pare, U.S. Navy—regarded by the Royal Navy as "the naval adviser on replenishments" and a keen advocate for "one-stop replenishment"—with the opportunity to discuss British plans for new fleet issue ships. His initiative was "welcomed" by the Royal Navy that was only too willing, indeed flattered to share with Americans whatever they asked for—including a wealth of detailed operational information and trials information.[113] Although some found this too one-sided, the excellent cooperation on recent logistics planning and organization, together with the presence of an Admiralty observer during the recent U.S. Navy Second Fleet exercises (noted earlier in this chapter) had, in the Admiralty's eyes, proved "very valuable."[114]

But there were setbacks too: witness the abrupt cancellation of places for British officers on the logistics courses at the NWC with no official explanation. Although this was eventually put down to American political sensitivity over the sharing of atomic-related subjects in the course material, the nature and way this was handled left a sour taste in London. Notwithstanding the close working relationship developed in the Korean theater, the First Sea Lord was becoming increasingly concerned that relations with Washington risked further deterioration so long as the British government continued to seek cuts in the naval staff in Washington.[115] This concern was partly prompted by Admiral Pennant, heading the BJSM in Washington, who had felt for some time that the U.S. Navy was drifting away from the close association developed during and immediately after the war by their refusing to continue dealing on a bilateral basis in the belief that other NATO nations would demand the same. Although in some respects the U.S. Navy had increasingly warmed to new ideas from the British, this trend "has not reached the various fields of tactical doctrine." There was no willingness to accept British tactical books even when there was something new for both navies, and although they were eagerly read, "any tactical ideas which the U.S. Navy derives from them are usually heavily disguised before being incorporated in any of their own publications."[116]

As for intelligence, there was admittedly an increasing exchange of "raw" material, but this was diminished by the reluctance of the U.S. Navy's ONI to disseminate "processed" information. Although the Royal Navy still had some wartime friends in positions of influence, the reality was that Britain no longer gained anything by handing over ideas and information without strings. In Pennant's view, many Americans no longer regarded the Royal Navy as special but merely one of a crowd; therefore the British should be more "commercial" about negotiating quid pro quo. He concluded that "they certainly never expect to get something for nothing."[117]

Outcome: Korean Operational/Tactical Performance

The Korean War provided at the tactical level the opportunity to test and discover the strengths and limitations of Allied replenishment doctrine, interoperability, and transfer techniques under duress, all important considerations for achieving a more integrated and responsive logistic support capability, which expeditionary naval warfare increasingly demanded. This section is limited to progress in Anglo-American tactical doctrine for mobile logistic support; a more complete analysis of the broader operational and logistic dimension for Korean operations can be found in the author's contribution to a book recently published on British naval strategy east of Suez between 1900 and 2000.[118]

Nature of Korean Mobile Logistic Support Compared to Pacific War

Given that each navy had been obliged to deploy the same auxiliary ships and equipment they had used in the Pacific War five years earlier, the nature of mobile logistic support more or less followed past precedent. But there were some important differences. Although the core purpose of having mobile logistic support remained the same, that is, to replenish carrier task forces on station, this was about the only consistent aspect between both operations. Korean naval operations benefited from invaluable host nation support provided by nearby Japan, which, as can be seen in map 7.1, allowed for relatively modest transit time and distance to theater operations, with excellent repair and maintenance facilities available in need.

The smaller number of vessels on station at any one time also contributed to

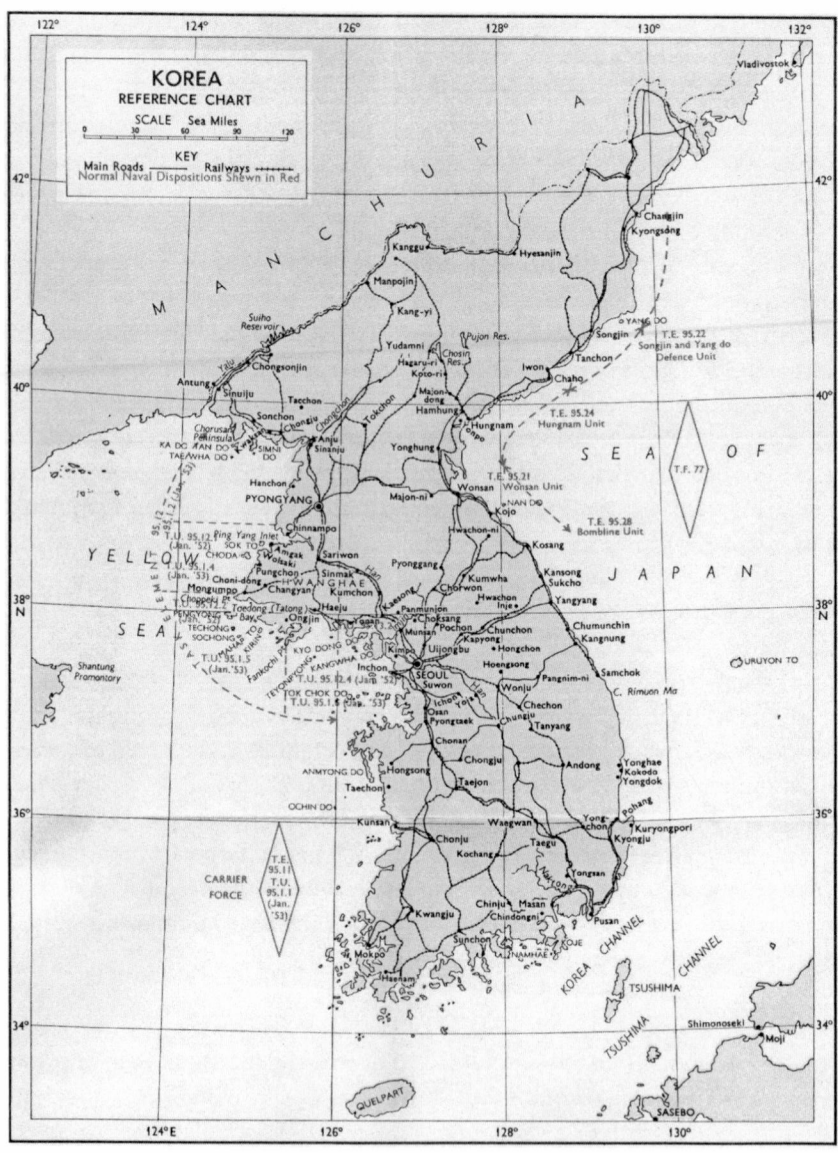

Map 7.1. Korean naval operations, 1950–1953. (NHB, "British Commonwealth Naval Operations, Korea 1950–1953,") Courtesy Naval Historical Branch

a more stable and containable set of challenges, although set against this were the unforeseen consequences of having to satisfy the much heavier ordnance and fuel requirements of the American carriers using jet aircraft, which "far exceeded anything accomplished or even contemplated during World War II."[119] As a result, whereas in the early stages of the Korean War American carriers, for example, typically operated for twenty-one days, with full replenishment undertaken every third day, this soon accelerated such that by the end of the war every replenishment for fuel and ordnance took up to nine hours and "nightly replenishment became the rule." As a consequence, U.S. oiler availability became so marginal that in-port fueling became dependent on using British or Japanese tankers.[120] Carrier replenishment had become the most far-reaching logistic headache uniquely affecting American forces during this time, and the magnitude of their problems encountered in replenishing Task Force 77 prompted the CNO to call a conference at San Francisco Naval Yard in 1952 to determine what corrective actions could be taken.[121] The outcomes were all essentially engineering based, culminating in new shipbuilding and new equipment projects, both of which were discussed earlier in chapters 3 and 5.

Korea: Royal Navy Performance

Although jet aircraft such as the Sea Vampire and Attacker could operate from British carriers, by 1951 they had neither the endurance nor sufficient radius of action (limited to high-level air defense) or weapons payload to operate effectively in Korea. In their absence and combined with the comparatively shorter transit times, it was possible for British on-station carrier cycles to be much shorter at ten days, with refueling at sea undertaken every fifth day. This left the balance either in transit or replenishing in port.[122] If the distances from base had been greater, or enemy counterattack more intense and the carrier air complement comprised jets not piston-engine aircraft, this would have presented severe logistic implications to the RFA that would have proved irreconcilable without considerable additional resources from the United Kingdom.

As it was, some fifty-five ships of the Commonwealth navies served in the Korean War for various periods: thirty-two from the Royal Navy (five light fleet carriers, six cruisers, seven destroyers, fourteen frigates), nine from the Royal Australian Navy (RAN) including a carrier, eight from the Royal Canadian Navy (RCN), and six from the Royal New Zealand Navy (RNZN). Plate 7.13, for example shows a British carrier and Canadian destroyer refueling from an RFA tanker. In addition, two naval HQ ships, a hospital ship, sixteen RFA auxiliaries, and two MFAs served in the fleet train.[123]

Of the seventy fleet auxiliaries operated by the Admiralty during this time, approximately one-third contributed to the Korean War effort carrying the fuel

and stores to the Far East and distributing them to the ships in the zone of operations. In the first two years, some 90,000 tons of fuel was transferred at sea.[124] This
was exactly half the amount transferred under way from twenty-one tankers to
the BPF's four-carrier task group in Operation ICEBERG during two four-week
periods in 1945.[125] While this cannot be a fair comparison in isolation because en-
vironmental conditions, fleet composition, and distances were all completely different, it places into context the Admiralty's decision that only two tankers were
to be kept available in the Korean operational zone, given the less extreme circumstances.

At least for the British, the early days proved less of a logistic problem than
expected, mainly for two reasons. First, experienced supply and engineering officers arrived early to plan and coordinate logistical arrangements—a lesson well
learned from 1944–45. Second and most fortuitously, arrangements had already
been made for supplying the Far East Fleet during its summer cruise in the Sea
of Japan, so the majority of provisions and naval stores were available from the
RFA *Fort Charlotte*, which provided enough breathing space until a routine could
be established for keeping Sasebo adequately stocked.[126]

In looking at the fuel transfer rates, generally speaking RFA and U.S. Navy
pumping rates were initially not that far apart at typically between 200–220 tph
per hose, with U.S. oilers preferring to use two hoses per evolution, a rig that for
some British destroyers was considered "uncomfortable and on occasions dangerous in a seaway."[127] No astern fueling was conducted from U.S. Navy oilers.
The record transfer rate from a British tanker was 612 tph, using three hoses to
a cruiser and destroyer (this, incidentally, was exactly the same rate that HMS
Bulawayo pumped to the battleship HMS *Duke of York* in trials, using just one new
7-inch hose in 1947, shown in plate 7.14).[128] Those frigates and destroyers capable
of only connecting one hose typically received oil at between 127–230 tph; the
highest recorded was 243 tph. By eventually using two hoses, destroyers averaged 300 tph, but this was still some way below 350 tph that American destroyers
typically received. Aviation gas to carriers, using two hoses, was pumped across
at 75 tph, still considerably slower than American transfer rates.[129] All these rates
were nevertheless broadly an improvement on 1945 due in part to technique, or
by using additional hoses for each evolution. Sometimes the improvements were
very significant; witness the observation about the 8th Destroyer Flotilla's replenishment performance to the effect that "They show clearly that great strides
have been made in fuelling at sea . . . during the past year. Since the start of the
Korean War the time lost in fuelling destroyers has been cut by half thereby making a notable increase in the effectiveness of the blockade and carrier screen. It
was a pity that this experience of the former British Pacific Fleet was not more
widely known."[130] This provides a useful example of why it was becoming important to fully codify and promulgate procedures and techniques into one re-

plenishment doctrine so that continuity of experience could be passed on to later commanders.

Perhaps the most important difference between the British and American logistic support operations in Korea was that the U.S. Navy carriers were entirely dependent on regular ammunition replenishment at sea whereas for the British no ammunition issuing ship was available with the speed and capability to transfer under way. While such an absence was not critical to the outcome, it meant that the type, rate, and intensity of aircraft sortie borne by the Royal Navy carrier had to match the rate of rearming every two weeks or so at Sasebo, where at least there were compensating benefits that helped to increase efficiency by having more dockside time. As for bombardment ammunition, both navies were eventually forced to invoke a more disciplined approach in the choice of targets to conserve ammunition, but demand generally outstripped supply, forcing British bombardment warships to occasionally rely for further ammunition from small American cargo carriers within theater.[131]

A challenge running throughout this whole period that affected replenishment performance for both navies was their continuing difficulty in acquiring, training, and retaining personnel for their auxiliaries. For the British, the civilian manning of the RFA auxiliaries including replenishment tankers had been broadly unchanged during war or peacetime. Often a voice within the Royal Navy called for a complete reorganization to address the vexing issues of discipline and inefficient management structures, so recruitment and career disillusionment remained a problem in the RFA throughout the 1950s.[132] Nevertheless, it is interesting to note that after nearly two years of replenishment operations in Korea, the Royal Navy concluded that in fact "far more damage has been sustained fuelling alongside in exposed anchorages [due to inadequate sponsons] than fuelling at sea," a testament to the professionalism of both the RFA and the Royal Navy in pursuing a properly conceived doctrine for underway operations.[133]

Command/Convergence

While the Anglo-American command relationship was complicated by the different expectations and practices for how command should function, the logistic arrangements between the two navies in fact worked extremely well. There was, however, the potential for disaster initially. In July 1951, a year of working together had highlighted a number of "difficulties and differences of approach between British and U.S. methods" relating to the methods for exercising command.[134] From the logistics perspective it had to be decided whether to have two separate organizations or "graft a limb into the American set-up."[135] Although initially the Americans had wanted to separate British operational and administrative command by attaching the British fleet train to their Service Force, this would have divided Adm. Scott Moncrieff's command and split his staff. Fortunately the strong operational links forged in recent years between both naval logistic groups was sufficient to the Americans that it was eventually agreed that Britain should retain control of her own logistic force.[136] In fact, the Korean War provided the best opportunity since 1945 for both navies to work very close together again at the tactical level, but this time helped because of the ease with which the Royal Navy and Commonwealth navies were able, once again, to adopt American signals books and practices.[137] Plate 7.15 shows the Australian destroyer HMAS *Warramunga* refueling from the oiler USS *Manatee* off Korea in June 1951.

Evidence for this working relationship can be seen by the extraordinary progress achieved in reaching new levels of standardization in replenishment doctrine between them. It happened because both realized the mutual benefit to be derived from achieving safe efficient and fast transfers at sea between each other's ships, given they were increasingly expected to operate together globally. Once again, though, it was a war that would provide the final impetus for such closer interoperability such that in 1952 the Admiralty was able to announce, for example, that

> Agreement has been reached between the U.S. Navy, Royal Navy and Royal Canadian Navy on the methods by which ships replenishment with furnace fuel oil, aviation spirit, diesel oil and water can be carried out at sea between ships of the different navies. Replenishment at sea is very largely a matter of seamanship. The expression in use in the Royal Navy "Different ships, different long splices" applies very much to the rigs used in the Royal Navy and U.S. Navy. The Principles are the same but there are differences in matters of detail. It has been decided there is little to be gained by standardising the rigs in use as long as ships can connect up their hoses, and effort has therefore been made to standardise at the point of connection only.[138]

In 1945 British warships would only occasionally refuel from American tankers or warships. The Korean War, however, witnessed ships of several navies able to replenish from either American or British tankers as a matter of routine, this latter point being the fundamental objective for any successful replenishment doctrine. This relatively simple expediency of having the right connectors on board had taken years in the making but provided the foundations for establishing coalition mobility as a key force multiplier in global expedition for the future.

8 | Conclusion

THIS BOOK HAS suggested that the Royal Navy and the U.S. Navy had neither the need nor motivation during the interwar period, or for that matter even in the early years of World War II, to foresee the full strategic and logistic ramifications of carrier-based air support for amphibious landings in the Western Pacific. This would explain why a robust form of mobile logistic support capable of sustaining such forces over extended periods was not prioritized until it was almost too late. The central premise underpinning this book, therefore, is that the logistic challenges confronting both navies in 1945 required such innovative solutions that their successful outcome was not only the most radical turning point in the history of mobile logistic support but their execution also formed the yardstick by which foreseeable future mobile logistic support (particularly for carrier-based warfare) was to be judged.

For the U.S. Navy, the combination of military might and a comparatively much clearer vision of what was required logistically, lead to their being much better planned, better prepared, and better equipped than the Royal Navy for prosecuting this new type of warfare in World War II. In a way, though, this should come as no real surprise given the size, motivation, and power of the U.S. Navy, underpinned as it was by the strongest economy in the world. Britain's naval and merchant fleets, conversely, had been severely debilitated by five relentless years sustaining and defending the United Kingdom as well as operating in many theaters including the Atlantic/Arctic, North Sea, and the Mediterranean. Perhaps what is surprising is that the Royal Navy, despite having started from so far behind in 1940, was able to accomplish, in terms of mobile logistic support, as much as it did in the Pacific given the limited resources available to it. Indeed the same analogy might equally apply after the war too, for despite Britain's comparatively much weaker economic and military status, the Royal Navy was still able to continue narrowing the logistic capability gap between the two navies in terms of refueling at sea, at least in technological terms if not in fleet size or numbers. It still had a considerable way to go before it could gain a comparable level in terms of rearming warships at sea, but at least some useful progress was achieved.

With both navies having reached their peak by 1945, a number of conclusions can now be drawn on the extent to which mobile logistic support had a role to play, which would influence how both pursued their respective strategies during the subsequent peace and how both were reengaged together during the Korean War.

1945: A New Benchmark

Replenishment at sea, in general terms, remained more or less in a state of arrested development until 1943–44 primarily because neither navy foresaw, particularly during the interwar period, any overriding need for stretching this specialized capability any further. The Royal Navy expected to continue relying on its network of bases for support, which only changed when the time came to prepare a fleet for the Pacific campaign, where the nearest friendly naval base in Australia was still a considerable distance away from the action. The U.S. Navy, conversely, always knew it could not rely wholly on fixed bases so was always more willing to experiment with new techniques to enable some degree of progress to be achieved in replenishment techniques. The real catalyst, however, was the increasing number of new aircraft carriers being commissioned that could soon be deployed in packs, as either battle or task groups or later to provide air-based support for amphibious operations. The size of the Pacific Ocean, the huge distances to cover, and the speed and unprecedented tempo of operations all dictated that the need for adequate task force sustainability was vital for success. This could only be achieved through operating fleet trains from temporary anchorages and bases safely located away from the constantly changing battle lines. As a result, the role and potency of carrier task forces was transformed, thereby producing the defining moment in the history of mobile logistic support as well as the benchmark for future logistic planning and execution.

Post-1945 Culture

The speed and depth of postwar demobilization affected both navies dramatically. Cuts were savage in both personnel and ships, operating budgets were severely pared, and investment in new ships and technology curtailed to the minimum. The consequent potential for losing "corporate memory" combined with the recognition that lessons must be heeded if mistakes were not to be repeated induced both navies to conduct research into their wartime experience relating to naval logistic support. Much of this analysis would eventually be codified into doctrine and other training manuals, but it was also recognized that there was a much broader cultural issue to address—understanding how logistics fitted within the broader scheme of things. Any understanding among naval officers of logistics in general was still relatively poor, despite its manifestly successful contribution to the Pacific war. Yet neither navy found it easy to overcome years of traditional prejudice about the status of "supply," which for many officers would now become synonymous with logistics. Only the U.S. Navy felt compelled to address this as an educational need by elevating logistics to the same priority as other strategic subjects in the various Naval War College curricula.

This difference in culture toward logistics generally was evident at several levels both in theater command and in how logistics was organized. For example, the U.S. Navy adopted a more formalized template approach to logistics planning that transcended from the joint military strategic level to the lower operational echelons. The Admiralty, however, relied on its traditional committee-driven approach to administrative planning that was neither colocated with operational staffs, nor given the autonomy or authority enjoyed by their American counterparts. This difference again partly reflected cultural differences in management style but also, in the earlier postwar years, was in some degree due to bureaucratic inertia absent any particular crisis.

Endurance and Ship Design

Postwar naval logistics had been very much shaped by the threat of the atomic bomb and the fast submarine; as these advanced, along with the introduction of other new technologies such as the jet aircraft, so logistic support needed to keep up. Korea had demonstrated to everyone that jet aircraft fuel was now increasingly determining carrier endurance, which required a radical new approach in terms of design for warships and auxiliaries. This was impossible to accomplish without suitable funding. Although progress in ship design was actually more robust than perhaps could have been expected, this prevailing financial vacuum denied both navies any opportunity to convert designs into practice. Moreover, auxiliary design for the Royal Navy remained hampered so long as it was constrained to producing dual-purpose auxiliary vessels to satisfy fleet speed and flexibility, on the one hand, yet still deliver peacetime economy for charter purposes, on the other. Compounding this dilemma was the continuing uncertainty over whether to rely on fixed bases or afloat facilities for logistic support in the next war. Since both navies were therefore forced to rely more or less on the same ship types, jury-rigged modifications, and procedures that had prevailed in World War II, their subsequent uncomfortable experience in Korea called for urgent attention to fund the design and construction of the very first tailor-made naval fast fleet replenishment tankers and, further down the line, fast combat replenishment ships for multiproduct delivery, both liquid and solid.

Mobilization Planning and Mobilization for Korea

The reasons for creating reserve fleets were various. They had provided an overt form of deterrence to potential enemies; they were a relatively cheap insurance policy in the event of future emergencies; and having them was a pragmatic solution given the postwar manpower shortages created by demobilization. The concept of mothballing helped to avoid the pitfalls of poor preservation experienced in the past and this proved a generally successful strategy, particularly for the U.S. Navy. Their investment, after all, had been vindicated by the substantial number of warships and auxiliaries reactivated for the Korean War. The Royal Navy's approach toward drawing down on reserves had been less dynamic mainly because of manning constraints, so most of the auxiliaries remained in reserve given that their need for reactivation was less critical to the overall operation.

Limited Progress in Tactical Development through Exercises

Both navies discovered that to some degree the benefits to be achieved through fleet exercises were not exploited as much as should have been hoped or expected. Clearly, exercises could not simulate war conditions, and the lack of such stress certainly had a dampening effect on standards and efficiency, particularly in practicing replenishment at sea. However, there was also an institutional reluctance to regard replenishment at sea as meriting the same attention for exercises as, say, gunnery or air tactics, and this was not helped by the real vacuum of lost knowledge and experience resulting from earlier manpower demobilization.

Korea the Catalyst for Change

The Korean War, however, brought mobile logistic support to the forefront of fleet dynamics in a number of other ways. The war itself was a limited but protracted and open-ended operation that bore little logistic resemblance to the postwar "Pacific" model based on Allied experience in 1945. The comparatively modest distances, virtual absence of enemy attack, and excellent host nation support from Japan, for example, all created a comparatively benign logistic environment. However, both navies were forced to adopt a two-theater strategy in case global war broke out simultaneously, and this led to two broad consequences. First, at the financial level, both the U.S. and Britain were obliged to release vital funds to enable both navies to restock with more ships and commissions to meet their objectives. This not only significantly bolstered what had otherwise become quite demoralized and comparatively neutered forces but Korea was also the catalyst for stimulating vital research and development in logistic capability.

Conversely, because the perception that naval operations in Korea were relatively less critical than the defense of Europe, the already scarce logistic resources available to both countries remained tightly rationed. Consequently, the RFA was stretched and often inadequately equipped, although—and this is worth emphasizing—never to the point where its effectiveness was critically impaired.

Even ammunition supply at sea, the Royal Navy's most significant shortcoming, was met by other means despite the well-recognized need for having such a fleet capability, as reflected in their replenishment doctrine. American mobile logistic support was certainly more robust generally, due to significant reactivation from reserves, but they were now faced with a unique new challenge in carrier support for which they were ill prepared. Korea had demonstrated that an increasingly important consideration for the future, in addition to distance speed and endurance, was the ability to provide continuous throughput of fuel and ammunition at levels previously unheard of. This had huge and far-reaching repercussions on future auxiliary and carrier design and carrier replenishment doctrine, which the U.S. Navy in particular was to address with considerable vigor and urgency.

Doctrine: Convergence at Last

The Korean War provided an important opportunity to test Alliance command, with all its tactical consequences, while under duress. A significant and oft-repeated lesson of World War II was that the commander must have control of his logistic support to ensure proper responsiveness, and conversely, the logistics support system must be in harmony with the deployment and operation of the fighting force.[1] Putting scale to one side, the comparatively modest Korean experience at the operational level appeared to corroborate this. While the Anglo-American command relationship was complicated by the different expectations and practices for how command should function, the logistic arrangements between the two navies in fact worked extremely well. Evidence for this working relationship can be seen by the extraordinary progress achieved in reaching new levels of standardization in replenishment doctrine between the two navies. Moreover, by 1953 replenishment doctrine had been so successfully fortified by the recent wartime experience that it was now robust enough to anticipate the changes just around the corner with the introduction of the new generation of auxiliaries. While it would take time before these changes could become regarded as routine, the template was nevertheless set and the foundations laid for the future.

Trials: The Key to Progress

Unlike the interwar period in the 1930s, where trials had become rather perfunctory and unchallenging, postwar efforts to improve both replenishment equipment and techniques (including the use of helicopters) took on a more determined approach, even if they were constrained by the limited funds that were available at the time. Perhaps the least recognized to date but undoubtedly the most important of these trials were those using captured German replenishment ships, which in many respects offered superior replenishment characteristics to Allied auxiliaries with the opportunity to experiment using naval crews. Although deployed at very different times, these trials provided a vital breakthrough at a very critical moment for each navy in their continuing efforts to satisfy the increasingly complex and difficult demands associated with replenishing fleets at sea. For the U.S. Navy it produced the prototype of the new generation one-stop, multiproduct replenishment ship, designed to overcome the many problems encountered during the Korean War in supporting fast carrier operations. For the Royal Navy, it enabled them to catch up in refueling techniques for the very first time with their American cousins in two important respects: first, in pumping output and speed under way, with the latter even exceeding American designs still on the drawing board, and second, as the test bed for many of the design features incorporated into the Royal Navy's first fast tanker, which was not only specifically tailored to meet the exacting standards for fleet replenishment at sea but was also comparable at long last to the latest American equivalent. Given where the Royal Navy had stood in 1945, this had all been a truly remarkable achievement.

Legacy

Through three hot wars entwined by a vacuum of uncertain and frugal peace, the concept of mobile logistics underwent enormous change that ultimately transformed forever how strategic maritime objectives could be pursued on a global scale. By 1945, each navy had sought and developed, albeit sometimes differently, the necessary mobility and independence from geographic limitations to achieve what they desperately required—maximum sustainable advantage. The legacy created by this revolutionary concept remained enduring and relevant for future naval strategies even though the geopolitical circumstances under which such logistics skills were originally acquired, as it turned out, were never going to be quite the same in future limited conflicts.

Take for example the Cold War: for several years after 1945 the U.S. Navy had always retained a very clear vision of carrier task forces acting as the primary weapons platforms for pursuing their dual defensive–offensive strategy. The Admiralty, although fully embracing the carrier as the new capital ship, was nevertheless uncertain where or how they should best be deployed while its contribution to the Allied naval effort was constricted to protecting trade routes in addition to her constabulary role policing Britain's Empire. This uncertainty invariably hampered plans to establish appropriate levels and composition for any mobile logistic support. It was only some two years after the Korean War, with the threat of thermonuclear weapons, that the Royal Navy's policy on mobility crystallized, when it was publicly announced that it was "well placed to meet this new threat with battle groups of carriers, guided missile ships and their escorts as part of its contribution to the Allied navies of the future."[2] This new concept would not only effectively replace the concentrated main fleets of past wars but would "provide a mobile offensive force which can be quickly deployed wherever it is required." This ability to disperse and concentrate at will, it was argued, would establish "an elusive and hard-hitting fighting force." For the first time in a long time, the Admiralty was now confident to express the conviction that "in war, two outstanding qualities of sea power become more evident; namely mobility and relative independence of land bases."[3] In other words, the Admiralty explicitly recognized that any such war strategy was entirely dependent on having an adequate mobile logistic infrastructure, and—so far as the Royal Navy was concerned—it now had one. In 1957 the term "afloat support" was mentioned for the first time in the Naval Estimates, together with a list of naval White Ensign auxiliaries including depot and repair ships.[4] A year later, this was even further expanded to include, again for the very first time, all the various types of fleet issue ships under the RFA that "fly the Blue Ensign, but are in a very real sense part of the Strength of the Fleet."[5] This confidence stemmed from the successful if belated efforts to build the right sort of vessels to enable this to happen, and this can only be attributed to their experience in the Korean War and earlier.

The fact that the gestation period took so long was not unusual. The process from when the challenge is first identified, a technological solution found, and plans then brought to fruition is usually a long one—described by Professor Till as sometimes the deliberate policy of "gradualistic incrementalism."[6] But there were two particularly important developments in mobile logistics that merit further comment because their contribution not only revolutionized the conduct of replenishing warships at sea but also enabled auxiliaries for the first time to become a force multiplier in their own right. The best early evidence for this can be found in the U.S. Navy's logistic experience in Vietnam. Despite the fact that in the initial years some 93 percent of the logistics support force comprised ships that were twenty years or more old, the fighting power of the U.S. Navy's Seventh Fleet still managed to reach new heights, made possible according to the official record, "by levels of achievements of the underway replenishment ships."[7] What had made all the difference was the introduction of vertical replenishment (VERTREP), using helicopters, together with the deployment of two fast one-stop replenishment ships, a concept originally promoted by none other than Captain Pare back in 1947. During one seven-month deployment by the AOE USS *Sacramento* in the Vietnam War, for example, well over a third of stores and ammunition was transferred night and day, just using VERTREP alone.[8] The point here is that these were built directly in response to the many problems experienced during the Korean War replenishing modern fast carriers carrying large complements of fuel and ordnance-hungry jet aircraft.

Not unlike 1945, the Falklands War in 1982 was another case of power projection for the British that used carrier-borne naval aircraft to determine the outcome of the campaign. Moreover, this too was logistically sea-based dependent, given the lack of friendly bases and the very similar distances involved. But here, in some senses, the analogy with the 1945 "Pacific" model must finish. While the Falklands logistic operation indeed assumed many of the characteristics developed from earlier generations of mobile logistic support, including replenishment at sea, in one important respect the Royal Navy's experience in 1982 fundamentally changed forever how logistic support vessels would be designed and deployed by the RFA in the future. No longer would auxiliaries be merely the supporting cast in theater operations. They would now be defensively armed and "navalized" to reflect their strategic value, importance, and, therefore, capacity to act independently or as an integral part of any fleet or task force structure. Admittedly, the argument for navalizing the RFA had been around for decades, but the debate in the 1940s–1950s centered on manning policies that (for the agents of change) were never satisfactorily resolved at the time. Yet, 1982 was different because the issue then and, for that matter ever since, has been the value of the auxiliary as a force multiplier in its own right. While such a degree of versatility is of paramount importance today, given the diminished size of the fleet overall to undertake the Royal Navy's global mission, the underlying attributes of mobility and sustainability at different tempos and force levels have nevertheless remained unchanged from the principles that forged the doctrine of 1945. What is new is the flexibility offered by the RFA, particularly given that available resources and operational requirements will rarely, if ever, be in harmony. Interestingly, in terms of underway replenishment, the Americans have effectively taken a slightly different tack since 1945 that nevertheless entirely complements the way the U.S. Navy has chosen to operate their powerful carrier task forces in the modern world. As part of the U.S. Navy's Military Sealift Command, the mission of its Naval Fleet Auxiliary Force is to act as the supply line to naval forces worldwide. Although such logistic support is no longer militarized in the way it used to be (for a variety of reasons but essentially economic) each carrier task force continues to have its own dedicated logistic support group fully integrated and protected by the combatant defense system. This vital but particularly difficult aspect of carrier replenishment, first developed on a grand scale by the U.S. Navy in 1945, remains to this day a capability that in terms of complexity and scale remains unsurpassed by any other navy.

It is important to remember, then, that the legacy from the past does not just resurrect itself in wartime. Mention was made earlier of the tremendous progress achieved by 1953 in harmonizing and converging replenishment procedures to provide vital interoperability between the U.S. Navy, the Royal Navy, and the Royal Canadian Navy. That very early doctrine provided the foundation for establishing NATO replenishment doctrine, which has more or less remained in the same form ever since. In some senses then, everything has changed yet nothing has changed. Nearly half a century later, for example, no naval doctrine would dare ignore the vital enabling role of logistics support, yet the underlying principles have only recently been intellectually harvested from history. In 1995, for example, Britain's Ministry of Defence published the first edition of "British Maritime Doctrine," which is described as a "synthesis of experience and theory" designed to provide a foundation for debating the fundamentals of doctrine in peace or war. Chapter 8, titled "Maritime Logistics and Support" was introduced with the following statement: "Logistics play an important part in determining a nation's capacity to sustain *war*. The control, distribution and availability of *materiel* will directly influence the *tempo*, shape and outcome of *any campaign*."[9]

In the second edition, four years later, logistics was promoted to chapter 5, where its relevance at both the grand strategic level and at the operational level was further articulated and underpinned by a summary of logistic principles.[10] What is so striking, however, is the extent to which these principles, portrayed with such clarity in these contemporary documents, reflect—occasionally almost word for word—those same logistic principles enunciated forty-five years earlier by Rear Admiral Eccles as part of his educational crusade to place logistics alongside strategy and tactics to form the three major branches of military science and command.[11] Today, according to the authors of BR 1806, "the sailor is so used to the level of organic logistic support that is provided routinely in a ship and its tactical formation that logistic considerations are intrinsic to maritime doctrine."[12] In truth, no strategy without logistics can ever deliver planned tactics, but then, as was succinctly noted in a recent article in the *Naval Review*, "Logistics is no longer a specialisation but a core competency."[13] Such an assertion might have been hard to find in the hallways or on the bridge during the postwar era, but arguably when it came to war, this was in fact a very fair representation of the underlying professionalism that did exist in both navies, given the tools available at the time. The proof was in the outcomes, even if this was rarely articulated as such.

This book has tried to demonstrate how and why Anglo- American naval strategy in the Pacific relied on mobile logistic support to provide the critical mobility and endurance that enabled the potency of carrier warfare to determine the outcome of the campaign on their terms. This revolution in power projection had been entirely dependent on the ability to harness all the necessary complex logistic support in the right place, at the right time, and all of the time.

But it was more than just about good organization. The period between

1945 and 1953 was in fact a landmark time when the ground rules for mobility were devised and tested, when the seeds of technological change were sown that would soon be cultivated by peacetime trials and further tactical wartime experience. This fundamentally changed forever the way navies would be able to fight in the global arena. Understanding whether and how this core capability could or should be preserved in peacetime is therefore fundamental, for everything that was discovered, experienced, recorded, or codified during this time also touched the future. As has been demonstrated time and again at critical points in naval history, the contribution of mobile logistics has always proved decisive as it has continued to mature and adapt to meet the challenges posed by both navies throughout the rest of the century. That is its unique and enduring legacy; that is why it mattered.

Appendix A.
U.S. Naval Train Squadron, 1926

Type	In Commission	AV Displacement	In Reserve
Destroyer tenders	6	12,900	3
Submarine tenders	7	7,640	0
Repair ships	2	11,300	1
Store ships	2	10,500	3
Aircraft tenders	1	11,000	0
Colliers	2	19,250	3
Oilers	10	13,500	10
Ammunition ships	1	10,600	1
Cargo ships	4	7,700	4
Transports	2	11,700	0
Hospital ships	2	10,000	1
Miscellaneous	7	7,700	0

Source: NMM, Dew 20, K. G. B. Dewar Papers

Appendix B.
BPF/Fleet Train: *Planned* and Actual Strengths, 1941–1946

Warship Type	December 1941[a]	December 1944[b]	April 1945	August 1945[c]	May 1946[d]
Fleet carrier	4	6	4	5	4
Light carrier	—	2	—	3	7
Escort carrier	—	6	6	9	18
Battleship	9	5	2	3	4
Cruiser	10	16	7[e]	8[f]	12
Destroyer	24	38	18[g]	34[h]	60
Fast minelayer	—	3	2	3	3
Escorts[i]	—	90	5	18	100[j]
Submarines	—	29	17	27	24
Sub depot[k]	—	2	2	3	3

Fleet Train Type	December 1941[l]	December 1944[m]	April 1945	August 1945[n]	1st Qtr 1946[o]
Fleet tankers	undecided	5	10	15	31
Small tankers	undecided	—	1	9	15
Repair	0	8	3	5	7
Depot	1	4	1	3	7
Maintenance	1	7	0	4	7
ASIS	20–30	13	12	15	16
VSIS	2	10	5	5	12
NSIS	1	6	1	2	5
Stores carriers	18	14	2	7	11
Air train	—	9	3	5	11
CVE–Ferry/CAP	—	—	6	9	15
Hospital	—	2	3	5	6
HQ/accommodation	—	6	4	4	10
Other	15	6	6	15	42
Escorts	—	—	22	28	119

Notes: a. Italics indicate planned strength. All other figures are actual. David Brown, *The Forgotten Bases*, table 1.

b. Ibid.; NHB, BSR 453, "History of the Fleet Train," Vol. 2 appendix B, "Representative Planning Estimates."

c. V-J Day includes units en route to the Pacific.

d. David Brown, *The Forgotten Bases*, table 1. These were the planned British objective during discussions at the OCTAGON conference in September 1944.

e. Includes 1 RNZN and 1 RCN.

f. Includes 2 RNZN.

g. Includes 4 RAN.

h. Includes 4 RAN.

i. Excludes escorts assigned to Fleet Train shown in Fleet Train table but includes unknown proportion referred to in footnote j.

j. Includes 36 RCN frigates. Unknown proportion to be assigned to Fleet Train escort numbers described further down.

k. Not allocated to Fleet Train. Excludes HMS *Bonaventure* and her XE submarines.

l. 1938 Supply Ship Committee plan.

m. S. W. Roskill, *History of the Second World War,* appendix P.

n. V-J Day: Includes units at sea, at Manus or advanced bases, en route for the Pacific.

o. TNA (Kew), ADM 199/1766, "Fleet Train Records 1944–1946," Vol. 2 , para. 2, "Composition and Buildup of TF 112," "Tables of Procurement."

Appendix C.
Admiralty Plans (Q) Division, 1944

PLANS (Q) DIVISION 1944

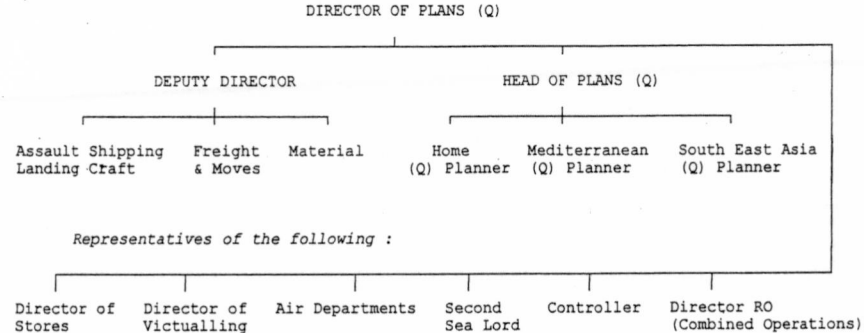

DIRECTOR OF PLANS (Q)

DEPUTY DIRECTOR   HEAD OF PLANS (Q)

Assault Shipping   Freight   Material   Home   Mediterranean   South East Asia
Landing Craft   & Moves   (Q) Planner   (Q) Planner   (Q) Planner

Representatives of the following :

Director of   Director of   Air Departments   Second   Controller   Director RO
Stores   Victualling   Sea Lord   (Combined Operations)

Source: NHB, "The Organisation of the Naval Staff," Cdr. N. L. Stewart.

Appendix D.
Pacific Ocean Distances (miles)

San Francisco to Pearl Harbor	2,091
San Francisco to Manila	6,000
San Francisco to Singapore	7,000
San Francisco to Colombo	8,500
Canal Zone to Pearl Harbor	4,692
Pearl Harbor to Sydney	4,000
London to Sydney	12,500
Sydney to Yokohama	4,970
Sydney to ICEBERG	4,200
Sydney to Leyte	3,500
Sydney to Manus	2,000
Manus to Leyte	1,524
Manus to TF 37 refuel area	2,500 (3-week roundtrip)
Leyte to TF 57 refuel area	800
Leyte to Tokyo	1,689
Pearl Harbor to Eniwetok	2,567
Eniwetok to ICEBERG	2,200
Eniwetok to TF 37 refuel area	1,700
Eniwetok to Ulithi	1,333
Ulithi to Okinawa	1,185
Ulithi to Leyte	870

Appendix E. Task Force 37, BPF, July 13–August 20, 1945

1 battleship; 4 fleet aircraft carriers; 6 cruisers; 18 destroyers

Fleet Train TG112.2	MANUS/ ENIWETOK	(Of Which LSG)	Refit	Total
Tankers	13	(12)	1	14
Harbor tankers	4	—	—	4
Water tankers	4	—	—	4
ASIS	8	(2)	2	10
VSIS	4	(2)	—	4
Tug	4	(1)	1	5
Hospital ship	4	(1)	—	4
Repair	2	—	1	3
Maintenance	3	(1)	—	3
Depot	1	—	—	1
Armament stores	3	—	—	3
Naval stores carrier	5	—	—	5
Boom defense	1	—	—	1
NSIS/Deperming	2	—	1	3
Air support	4	—	—	4
Accommodation/HQ	4	—	1	5
Collier	1	—	1	2
Salvage/Distiller	—	—	3	3
Floating dock	1	—	1	2
Total auxiliaries	68	(19)	12	80
Replenishment Carriers	5	(5)	—	5
CAP Carrier	1	(1)	—	1
Escorts	37	(23)	—	37
Total	111	(48)	12	123

Sources: NHB, BSR 453, TSD 4122/53, S.567B, "History of the Fleet Train," Volume 2, appendix A, annex 11; Ministry of Defence (Navy), *War with Japan*, appendix U.

Appendix F.
The BPF Fleet Train in the Pacific, December 1944–January 1946

Ship type	Dec. 1944 Estimate	Mar./May 1945 TF112	July/Aug. 1945 TF112	VJ-Day[a]	VJ-Day naval only	Expected 1/1/46	Actual 1/1/46
Naval and RFA Auxiliaries							
Fleet tankers	5	10	14	15	1	31	—
Small tankers	c	1	4	9	—	15	—
Heavy repair ships[b]	7	3	3	2	2	4	1
Hull repair[b]	1	0	0	1	1	1	1
Auxiliary repair[b]	0	0	0	2	2	2	2
Destroyer depot[b]	2	1	1	2	2	2	—
Escort maintenance[b]	3	0	1	2	2	3	—
Minesweeper maintenance[b]	1	0	1	1	1	1	—
Motor craft maintenance[b]	1	0	0	0	—	1	—
Armament maintenance[b]	2	0	0	0	—	1	—
Radio repair/maintenance[b]	c	0	1	1	1	1	—
Accommodation/HQ/Command[b]	6	4	5	4	3	10	2
Harbor craft carrier/depot[b]	0	0	0	0	—	3	—
Naval store carrier	8	2	5	5	—	9	—
Naval store issue (NSIS)	6	1	2	2	—	5	—
Victualling store issue (VSIS)	10	5	4	7	—	12	—
Armament store issue (ASIS)	13	12	10	15	—	16	—
Armament store carrier	6	0	3	2	—	2	—
Mine issue/depot	2	0	0	1	—	2	—

(Continued on the next page)

(*Appendix F continued*)

Ship type	Dec. 1944 Estimate	Mar./May 1945 TF112	July/Aug. 1945 TF112	VJ-Day[a]	VJ-Day naval only	Expected 1/1/46	Actual 1/1/46
Mine carrier	0	0	0	0	—	0	—
Hospital	2	3	4	5	—	6	3
Distilling	2	1	1	1	—	1	—
Netlayer[b]	c	1	0	1	1	2	—
Boom defense[b]	c	0	1	0	—	1	—
Deperming[b]	c	1	1	1	1	1	—
Salvage[b]	c	0	2	3	3	3	—
Water tanker/carrier	1	1	4	2	—	13	—
Collier	c	1	2	1	—	3	—
Tug	c	2	5	2	—	14	—
Floating dry dock	c	0	2	2	—	4	1
Amenity	1	0	0	0	—	1	—
Air stores issue	3	1	1	2	—	2	—
Aircraft maintenance[b]	3	0	1	1	1	2	—
Aircraft/engine repair[b]	3	2	2	2	2	7	—
Total Naval and RFA Auxiliaries	88	52	80	94	23	181	10
Naval Warships							
Ferry/replenishment carriers	c	5	5	9	9	15	—
CAP carrier	c	1	1	0	0	0	—

Escorts[c]	0	22	37	28	28	119	—
Total Naval Warships	28	37	43	37	37	134	—
Total Vessels	88	80	123	131	60	315	10
Officers and men[d]			26,200			53,800	

Notes: a. Includes units at sea, at Manus or advanced bases, or en route to the Pacific.

b. Includes naval auxiliaries prefixed by HMS.

c. No estimate given.

d. Total projected personnel of 53,800 derived as follows: 14,600 in 41 HM ships in Fleet Train (including one fleet tanker), 13,500 civilian crew in 140 auxiliaries, and 25,700 in 134 escorts and escort carriers.

Sources: 1) December 1944 figures taken from NHB, BSR 453, TSD 4122/53, S.567, "History of the Fleet Train," Vol. 2, appendix B, "Representative Planning Estimates"; and S. W. Roskill, *War at Sea*, appendix P.

2) March–May 1945 and July–August 1945 figures taken from NHB, BSR 453, TSD 4122/53, S.567,"History of the Fleet Train," Volume 2, appendix A, annex 1 "Fleet Train State"; Ministry of Defence (Navy), *War with Japan*, vol. VI, appendixes T and U.

3) VJ Day derived from Ministry of Defence (Navy), *War with Japan*, vol. VI, appendix ZC; and H. P. Willmott, *Grave of a Dozen Schemes*, appendix C.

4) TNA (Kew), ADM 199/1766, "Fleet Train Records 1944-1946 (Part 32)," "History of the Fleet Train, paragraph 2, "Composition and Buildup of Task Force 112."

5) Actual Fleet Train composition 1/1/1946 derived from NHB "History of the Fleet Train," Vol. III, "Post Hostilities," 177–79.

Appendix G

Replenishment Formation for USN Task Group, 1946

Replenishment Formation 13–F-1 Normal Service

Unit Formation for Replenishing One Combatant Task Group

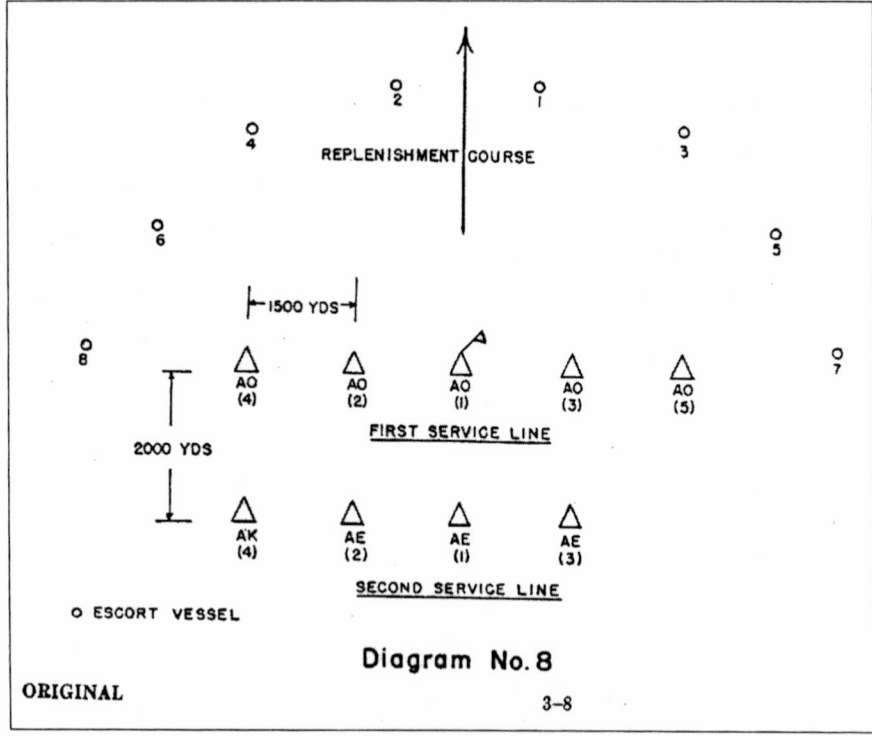

Source: USNHC, "USF-13 Logistic Support Force Operating Instructions," sec. 330, dia. no. 8. (Courtesy U.S. Naval Historical Center)

Appendix H.
Royal Navy Cruising Disposition during Replenishment, 1947

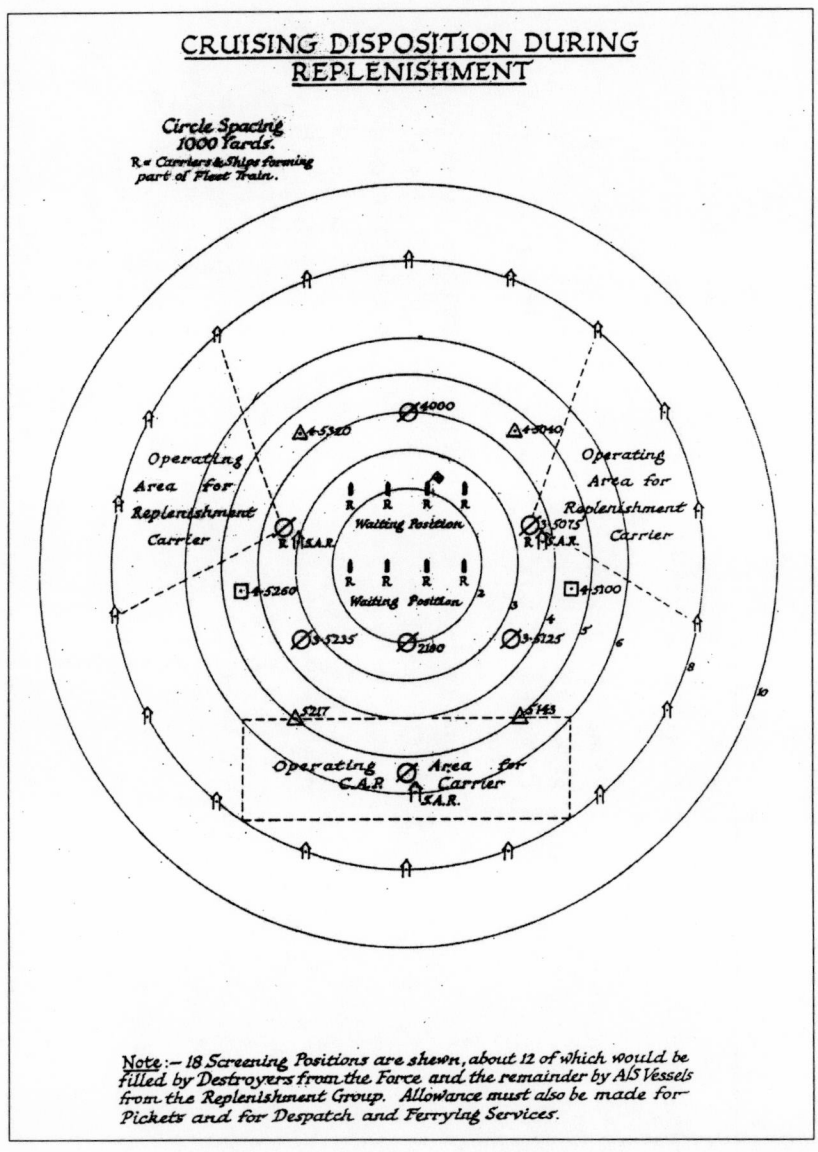

Source: NHB, "The Fighting Instructions," dia. no. 6. (Courtesy Naval Historical Branch)

Appendix I.
Replenishment at Sea Liquids Transfer Rig Comparisons

USN/RN	Rig Name	Introduced	Purpose	Working Distance in feet	Comment
USN	Riding abeam	1925	Primary method for capital and smaller ships	40–80	Larger vessel "tows" other alongside; fuel transferred by booms and lines
USN	Broadside	1941	Primary method for capital and smaller ships. Prewar known as riding abeam	40–80	Larger vessel "tows" other alongside; fuel transferred by booms and lines
USN	Astern		Secondary method for escorts/destroyers	300–500	Emergency refueling from capital ships or when broadside not possible
USN	Close-in fueling		Principal fuel rig during most of WW II, formerly known as alongside	60–80; 80–120 for larger	6-inch hose supported by boom whips and bight lines to destroyer or smaller
USN	Span wire (Elwood)	1944	Safe for bad seas	140–80; by 1953 60–100 for DD, 80–120 for larger max 180	Eliminates need for tow and spring lines and allows greater distance between ships than broadside method. Four 6-inch hoses extended by single spans between two ships.

Navy	Method	Year	Use	Distance (ft)	Notes
USN	Elokomin	1946	Combination of Elwood and close-in methods	160–200	Also known as oil-inhaul rig, as oiler supplies power to haul hose, etc.
USN	Tensioning span wire	1956	Destroyers in sea state 5 with gale winds	300	Developed 1953; fully operational by 1956
RN	Hose hawser	1924	Trials for oiling at sea, until abandoned in 1932	430	Towing hawser passes through floating hose to support it
RN	Astern: stirrup	1932	Standard for oiling at sea and in exposed anchorages	200	Hose suspended by stirrups from hawser first tried in 1906
RN	Trough: abeam	1937	For fueling destroyers from capital ships/Oilers	20–30	First use of Abeam transfer; evolved into wartime beam-derrick rig
RN	Astern: buoyant hose	1943	Initially only for British escort oilers	400–600	Passed either by float or gun line; distance governed by weather/seas
RN	Large derrick	1945	Standard for tankers fitted with 70-ft rigs. Appropriate for most sea and weather conditions	100–60; best 120	Originally called derrick two trough rig; in 1945–46 it also became known as the "ND" rig.

(Continued on the next page)

(Appendix I continued)

USN/RN	Rig Name	Introduced	Purpose	Working Distance in feet	Comment
RN	Jackstay	1949	Tanker to heavy ship when greater distance required than provided by Derrick method	150–250; best 200	Only fitted to HMS Bulawayo by 1952
RN	Crane and small derrick		Cruiser or above to another warship	80–110; best 95	Originally called derrick one trough rig
RN	Small Ship jackstay		For small ships	50–70; best 60	

Sources: NARA2, RG38; USNHC, USF-13; USNHC, NWP-38; TNA (Kew), ADM 116/6231: FEFM 29/51; TNA(Kew), ADM 116/5813; TNA(Kew), ADM 234/393, ADM 234/394, ADM 234/395.

Appendix J.
Replenishment at Sea Solids Transfer Rig Comparisons

USN/RN	Rig Name	Introduced	Purpose	Working Distance in feet	Comment
USN	Manila highline		Transfer personnel	60–80	Hand tended and safer to use; easy to set up and no boom necessary
USN	Wire highline		Standard transfer to destroyers; never personnel	60–80	If receiver ship has special fitting, load can be increased to 3,500 lb
USN	Housefall		Same as wire highline but less safe than highline in rough weather	60–80	Can be accomplished with one or two booms; U.S. DDs limited to 800 lb
USN	Double housefall		When multiple housefall transfers impossible	60–80	Two adjacent housefall rigs attached to single suspension point
USN	Modified housefall		Keeps loads higher above water than housefall	60–80	Additional trolley block on transfer whip with the advantage of total control of both whips and winches vested in supplier
USN	Burton	Feb. 1945	Preferred method for rearming carriers in calm seas	60–80 (1945+) 60–100 (1953)	One boom for transfer and one for hoisting loads from hold; beyond 3,500 lb, only appropriate under special circumstances

(Continued on the next page)

(*Appendix J continued*)

USN/RN	Rig Name	Introduced	Purpose	Working Distance in feet	Comment
RN	Heavy jackstay	1949	Heavy loads including ammunition	80–200; best 110	Wire; preferably good weather unless with auto-tensioning winch
RN	Light jackstay		Transferring men, provisions, and light stores	80–200; best 110	Rope; suitable for any weather
RN	Auto-tension winch	1951			Prototype RFA *Fort Duquesne* standardized on tankers mid 1950s

Sources: NARA2, RG38; USNHC, "USF-13"; USNHC, NWP-38; TNA (Kew), ADM 116/6231: FEFM 29/51; TNA (Kew), ADM 116/5813; TNA(Kew), ADM 234/393; TNA (Kew), ADM 234/394; TNA (Kew) ADM 234/395.

Appendix K.
USN Logistics Plans Division OP-12, 1944

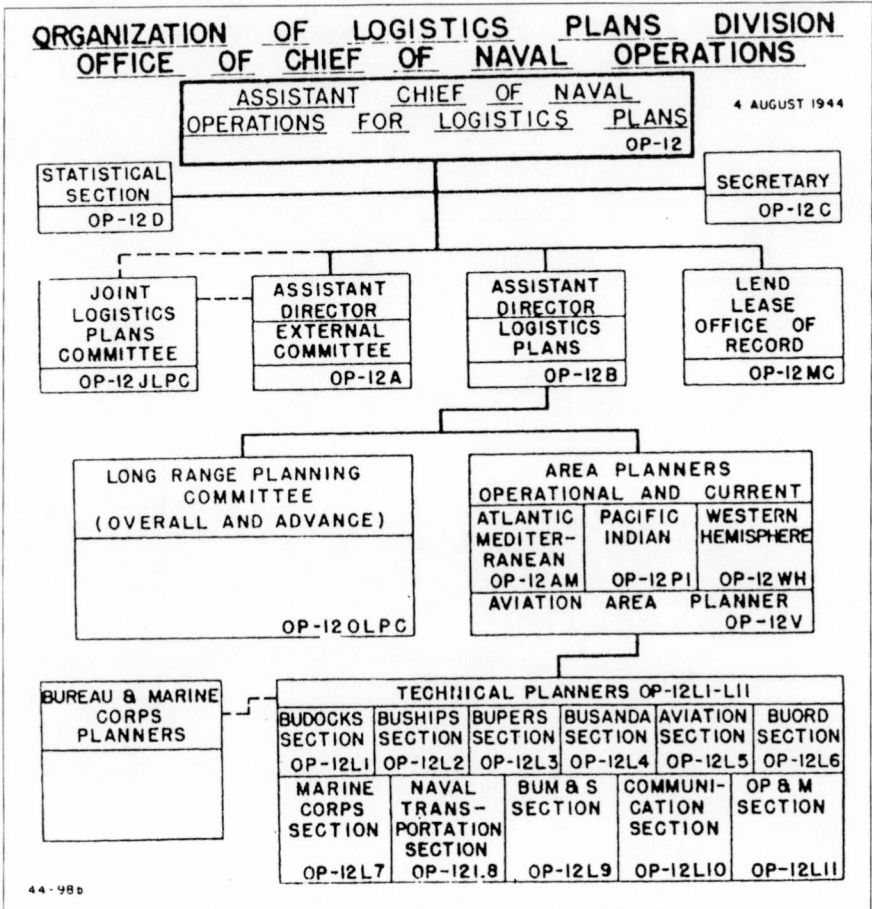

Source: NWC, RG14, Cdr. T. A. Brown, "Logistic Planning Agencies of CominCh and CNO."
(Courtesy Naval War College Historical Collection)

Appendix L.
USN CNO Organization, 1945

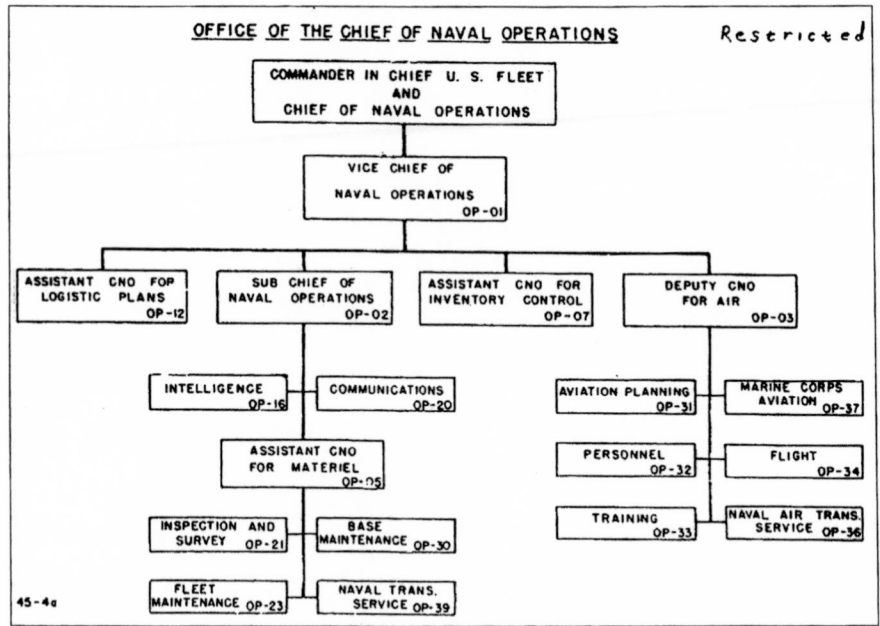

Source: NWC, RG14, Cdr. T. A. Brown, "Logistic Planning Agencies of CominCh and CNO."
(Courtesy Naval War College Historical Collection)

Appendix M.
USN CNO Logistic Agencies, 1942–1946

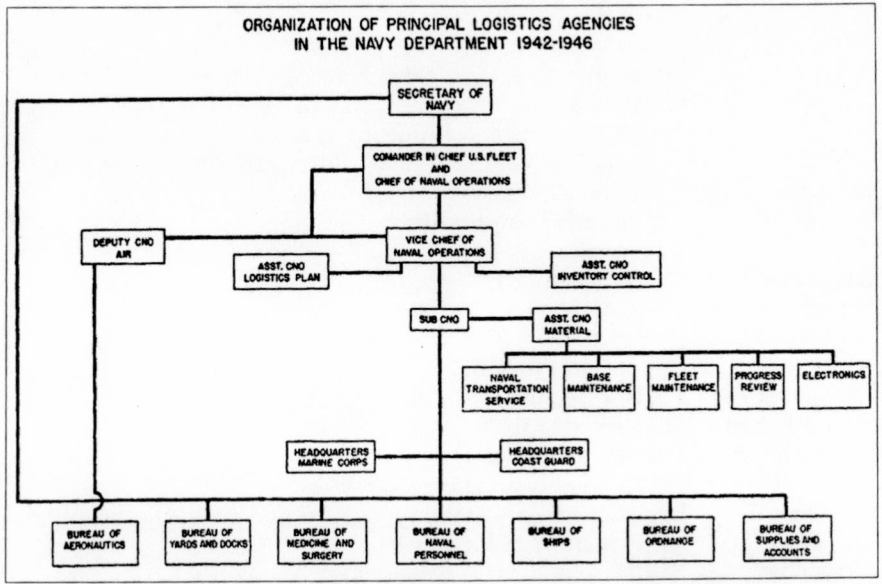

Source: NWC, RG14, Cdr. T. A. Brown, "Logistic Planning Agencies of CominCh and CNO." (Courtesy Naval War College Historical Collection)

Appendix N.
USNWC First-Year Logistics Course, 1947–1948

July 11	Shake-down; draw material
July 12	Opening Address
July 14	Orientation; the Atomic Bomb
July 15	Capabilities and employment of ships, aircraft, and their weapons; search exercises, screening and task force dispositions
July 31	Critique of screening and task force dispositions exercises
August 2	Operations Problem 1
August 16	Critique of Operations Problem 1
August 16	Intelligence
August 26	Communications
September 2	Board Maneuver Exercises
September 5	Logistics
September 9	Operations Problem 2
September 12	Logistics, cont'd
September 19	Strategic area study
September 23	Logistic principles and procedure
October 6	Atomic energy and nuclear physics
October 9	Logistics principles and procedure, and mobile fleet support
October 22	Operations Problem 3
November 3	Base development and operation
November 4	Operations of World War II
November 10	Critique of Operations Problem 3
November 13	Strategic area study
November 14	Base development and operation, cont'd
November 15	Operations of World War II, cont'd
November 25	Base development and operation, cont'd
November 27	Thanksgiving Holidays
December 1	Base development and operation, cont'd
December 8	Operations Problem 5
December 18	Naval History
December 19	Critique of Operations Problem 5
December 24	Christmas Holidays
January 5	Strategic area study
January 5	Fleet and base logistic support
January 14	Thesis critique
January 16	Fleet and base logistic support, cont'd
January 26	Logistics of amphibious warfare
February 9	Logistics Staff Study for Operations Problem 11
February 24	Naval History
February 25	Operations Problem 9
March 24	Critique of Operations Problem 9

March 26	Logistics in major operations
March 30	Strategic area study
April 1	Operations Problem 11
April 13	Naval History
April 21	Presentation by Marine Corps School
April 26	Operations Problem 11, cont'd
May 7	Thesis critique
May 11	Critique of Operations Problem 11
May 14	Turn in publications and material
May 15	Graduation

Note: During the above schedule, the logistics class attends the same lectures given by visiting speakers as those attended by the senior and junior classes

Source: NWC, RG27, Ralph E. Smith, "A History of Logistics at the Naval War College," Tab D. (Courtesy Naval War College Historical Collection)

Appendix O.
Naval Staff Admiralty, 1949

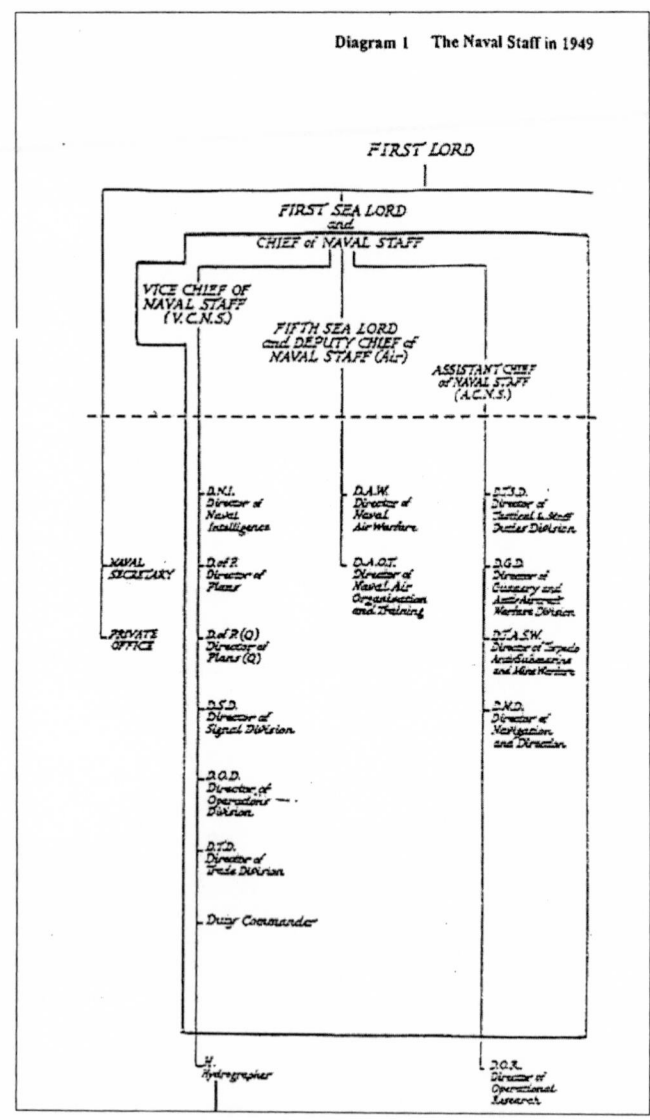

Diagram 1   The Naval Staff in 1949

Source: NHB, Cdr. David Hobbs, "A Brief Study of the Naval Staff 1945–1997." (Courtesy Naval Historical Branch)

Appendix P.
Naval Staff Admiralty, January 1952

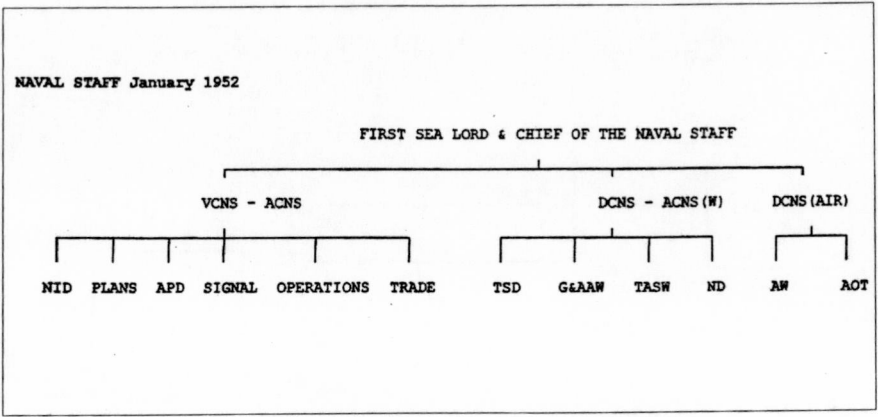

NAVAL STAFF January 1952

FIRST SEA LORD & CHIEF OF THE NAVAL STAFF

VCNS - ACNS   DCNS - ACNS(W)   DCNS(AIR)

NID PLANS APD SIGNAL OPERATIONS TRADE   TSD G&AAW TASW ND   AW   AOT

Source: NHB, Cdr. N. L. Stewart, "The Organisation of the Naval Staff."

Appendix Q.
Office of the Chief of Naval Operations, 1947

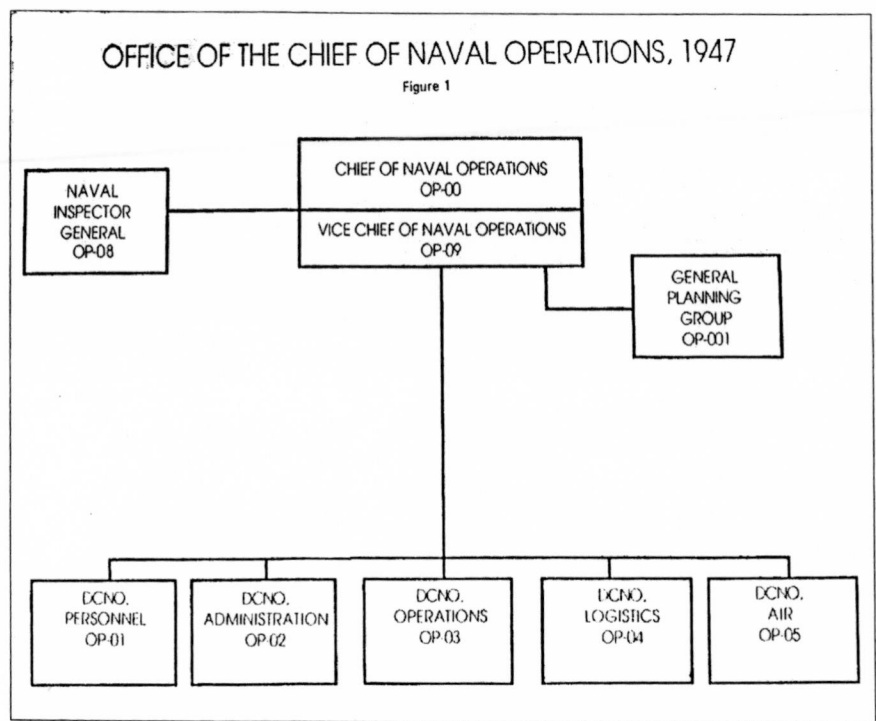

OFFICE OF THE CHIEF OF NAVAL OPERATIONS, 1947
Figure 1

Source: NWC(L), Thomas C. Hone, *Power and Change*.

Appendix R.
RFA Tanker Plan, 1946

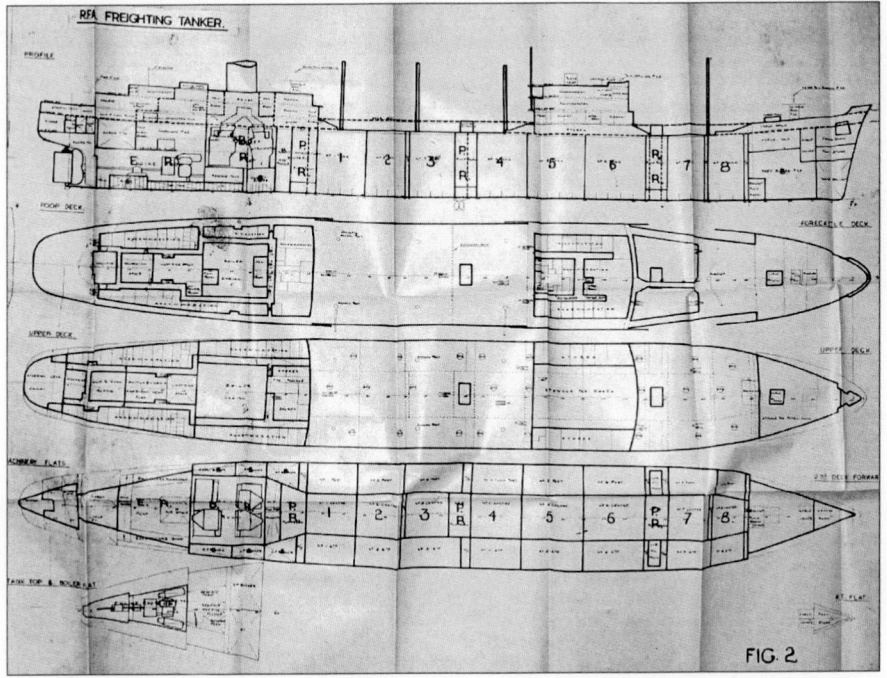

Source: NHB, J. B. Crawford, "The Problems Involved in Designing an RFA Tanker." (Courtesy Naval Historical Branch)

Appendix S.
Proposed USN Postwar Fleet Dispositions, November 1945

U.S. Pacific Fleet	First Fleet (Active)
18 CV and CVE/CVT	carrier divisions 1, 3, 5, 15, 17 (marines), 19 (transports)
2 BB	battleship division 1
24 CA/CL	cruiser divisions 1, 3, 11, 13, 15
78 DD	18 destroyer divisions
16 DE	3 escort divisions

U.S. Pacific Fleet	Third Fleet (Reserve)
2 CV	carrier division 7
3 BB	battleship division 3
8 CA/CL	cruiser divisions 5, 17
18 DD	4 destroyer divisions

U.S. Pacific Fleet	19th Fleet (Inactive)
45 CV/CVL/CVE	carrier divisions 9, 11, 13, 21, 23, 25, 27, 29
3 BB	battleship division 5
15 CA/CL	cruiser divisions 7, 19, 21
93 DD	22 destroyer divisions
96 DE	16 escort divisions

U.S. Atlantic Fleet	Second Fleet (Active)
8 CV/CVE	carrier divisions 2, 4, 14
3 BB	battleship division 2
8 CL	cruiser divisions 10, 12
54 DD	12 destroyer divisions
20 DE	3 escort divisions

U.S. Atlantic Fleet	Fourth Fleet (Reserve)
3 CV/CVL	carrier division 6
3 BB	battleship division 4
10 CA/CL	cruiser divisions 2, 14
22 DD	5 destroyer divisions
4 DE	1 escort division

U.S. Atlantic Fleet	16th Fleet (Inactive)
40 CV/CVL/CVE	carrier divisions 8, 10, 16, 18, 20, 22, 24, 25
5 BB	battleship division 6
3 CB	cruiser division 4
18 CA/CL	cruiser divisions 6, 8, 16, 18
94 DD	20 destroyer divisions
145 DE	25 escort divisions

Source: NARA2, RG38, "Organization of Major Combatant Types Less Submarines," Box 3.

Appendix T.
U.S. Navy Force levels, 1945–1955

Type	8/14/1945	1946	1947	1948	1949	1950	1951	1952	1953	1954	1955
Battleships	23	10	4	2	1	1	3	4	4	4	3
Carriers, Fleet	28	15	14	13	11	11	17	19	19	20	21
Carriers, Escort	71	10	8	7	7	4	9	10	0	7	3
Cruisers	72	36	32	32	18	13	15	19	19	18	17
Destroyers	377	145	138	134	143	137	206	243	247	247	249
Frigates	361	35	24	12	12	10	38	56	56	57	64
Submarines	232	85	80	74	79	72	83	104	108	108	108
Mine Warfare	586	112	55	54	52	56	91	114	121	117	112
Patrol	1,204	119	74	50	50	33	40	29	23	22	15
Amphibious	2,547	275	107	86	60	79	208	189	226	223	175
Auxiliary	1,267	406	306	273	257	218	269	309	287	288	62
Total Active	6,768	1,248	843	737	690	634	980	1,097	1,122	1,133	1,030
Reserve Fleet	2,000	2,100	1,935	1,362							
Officers	375,359	62,000	49,019	57,540							
Enlisted	3,611,022	600,000	475,000	494,460							
Appropriations $B	28.5	24.1	4.1	3.3	3.7	4.3	12.4	15.6	13.0	9.3	9.8

Sources: Active Fleet figures as at June 30 each year 1945–1955: USNHC, Washington, D.C.
Reserve Fleet figures: USN General Board Hearings, 1948/1949.
Appropriations and personnel: *Jane's Fighting Ships*, 1947–1955.

Appendix U.
RN Naval Estimates: Personnel, Active, and Reserve Fleet Statistics, 1945–1955

	1945[a]	1945[b]	1946	1947	1948	1949	Korean War 1950	1951	1952	1953	1954	1955
Naval Estimates, £ millions[c]				£275	£197	£153	£189	£193	£279	£332	£330	£353
Personnel, thousands[d]				493	192	168	154	143	144	153	151	139
Total Fleet												
Active Status	6,979	5,812	3,210	799	705	617	548	591	598	687	662	637
Reserve Status	1,607	2,720	1,089	1,049	886	913	833	826	811	674	729	721
Total	8,586	8,532	4,299	1,848	1,591	1,530	1,381	1,417	1,409	1,361	1,391	1,358
Major Combatants Only												
Active Service	977	760	567	278	219	219	185	226	244	219	233	232
Reserve Fleet	59	289	401	466	414	349	310	246	232	245	274	316
Total	1,036	1,049	968	744	633	568	495	472	476	464	507	548
Depot/Repair Ships Only												
Active Service	74	62	68	18	10	15	14	13	10	10	11	11
Reserve Fleet	3	5	13	17	20	15	13	9	12	13	13	12
Total	77	67	81	35	30	30	27	22	22	23	24	23

(Continued on the next page)

(Appendix U continued)

	1945[a]	1945[b]	1946	1947	1948	1949	1950	1951	1952	1953	1954	1955
								Korean War				
Naval Estimates[e]												
Active						119	144	122	126	169	164	148
Training						55	52	41	43	55	56	42
Reserve/refit[f]						304	296	294	274	296	329	372
Total						478	492	457	443	520	549	562

Source: The above ship statistics, other than those shown under Naval Estimates are derived from Admiralty Pink/Green/Red Lists on or about June 30 each year (Source NHB). Excludes RFA vessels.
The Naval Estimates ship status statistics, recorded for comparison, are derived from the Annual Naval Estimates. These include only major combatants, and their definitions vary slightly from the rest of this appendix.

Notes: a. V-E Day
b. V-J Day
c. Statements on the Naval Estimates for each year; figures net subtracting U.S. aid and other receipts.
d. TNA(Kew), ADM 1/25569: F.O.C.R.F. Report No. 22 14/1/54 ref 30/3.
e. Statements on the Naval Estimates for each year.
f. Includes refits of all ships whether in reserve or active fleets.

Appendix V.
Royal Navy Fleet Train Deployed during the Korean War

Name	Type (gross registered tons)	Comment
Tankers		
RFA *Birchol*	1,440 tons harbor tanker	Stationed in Hong Kong
RFA *Oakol*	1,440 tons harbor tanker	Stationed in Singapore
RFA *Brown Ranger*	3,417 tons Fleet attendant	Limited underway capability
RFA *Green Ranger*	3,313 tons Fleet attendant	Limited underway capability
RFA *Echodale*	8,219 tons	Freighting only
RFA *Wave Chief*	8,097 tons Fleet tanker	Fitted for RAS
RFA *Wave Conqueror*	8,141 tons Fleet tanker	
RFA *Wave Knight*	8,187 tons Fleet tanker	Intermediate modification
RFA *Wave Laird*	8,187 tons Fleet tanker	Intermediate modification
RFA *Wave Premier*	8,175 tons Fleet tanker	Intermediate modification
RFA *Wave Prince*	8,197 tons Fleet tanker	Fitted for RAS
RFA *Wave Regent*	8,184 tons Fleet tanker	Freighting only
RFA *Wave Sovereign*	8,182 tons Fleet tanker	Fitted for RAS
Naval Stores (NSIS) and Victualling Issue (VSIS) Ships		
RFA *Fort Charlotte*	7,201 tons NSIS/VSIS	Sasebo: Stores depot
Armament Supplies Issuing Ships (ASIS)		
MFA *Choysang*	1,500 tons	Temporary Sasebo & freighting from Hong Kong
RFA *Fort Rosalie*	7,335 tons	Sasebo Sept 1950–June 1952
RFA *Fort Sandusky*	7,300 tons	June 1952 onward
MFA *Fort Langley*	7,285 tons	Transferred to RFA in 1954
White Ensign Naval Manned Ships		
HMHS *Maine*	7,515 tons	Hospital
HMS *Tyne*		HQ Sasebo April–July 1953
HMS *Ladybird*		HQ ship Ex-SS *Wusueh*
HMS *Unicorn*		Repair/Maintenance Ferry carrier July 1950–July 1953

Sources: NHB, "British Commonwealth Naval Operations, Korea 1950–1953," appendix B1; E. S. Sigwart, *Royal Fleet Auxiliary*; TNA (Kew), ADM 1/27143, "History of the RFA Service 1919–1958."

Appendix W.
USN Organizational Chart
for the Operating Forces, 1947

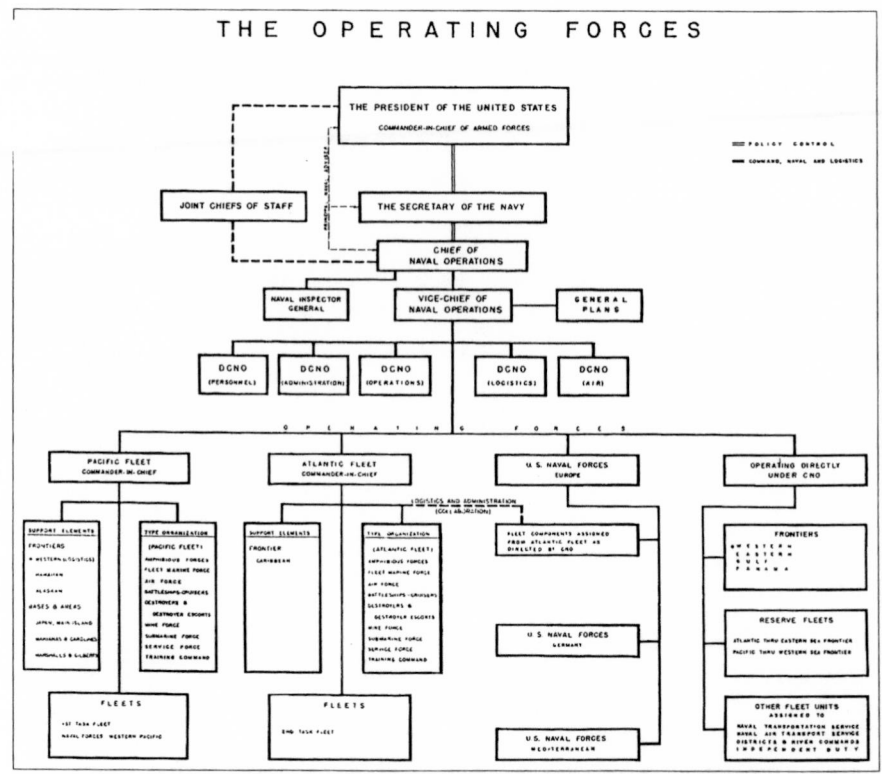

Source: NWC, RG4, "U.S. Navy 1947." (Courtesy Naval War College Historical Collection)

Appendix X.
Mobile Logistic Support: Related Doctrine Manuals

U.S. Navy

USF-1	Principles and Application of Naval Warfare
USF-2	General Tactical Instructions (1946)
USF-4	Carrier Task Force Tactical Instructions (1946)
USF-5	Surface Action and Tactics (1946)
USF-6	Amphibious Warfare Instructions
USF-7	Escort of Convoy Instructions
USF-8	ASW Instructions (1946)
USF-10A	Current Tactical Orders and Doctrine (1944)
USF-13	Logistic Support Force Operating Instructions U.S. Fleets (1946)
USF-15	CIC Operating Instructions
USF-70	Basic Rapid Communication Plan for the U.S. Fleets
USF-83	Fueling and Replenishment at Sea (1947)
OP-34P400	Fueling and Replenishment at Sea 1946: Alongside Refueling and Replenishment at Sea
CominCH P-2	Fueling At Sea Instructions, U.S. Fleet (1944)
NWP-4–01.4	Underway Replenishment (1996)
NWP-10	Naval Warfare
NWP-11	Naval Operational Planning part II Logistics
NWP-14	Underway Replenishment at Sea UNREP (c1970)
NWP-20	Striking Force Operations
NWP-25	Replenishment Formations
NWP-25A	Mobile Logistic Support Operations
NWP-38	Replenishment at Sea (1953)
ATP-16	Replenishment at Sea (1955)
ATP-16(D)	(Navy) Replenishment at Sea (2001)

Royal Navy

BR68	Manual of Seamanship, Volume II (1923)
BR68	Manual of Seamanship, Volume II (1932)
PFWO	Pacific Fleet War Orders, Part 3 (July 1945) Logistic Support Group
BR1742/47	Replenishment at Sea (1947)
BR67 (2)	Manual of Seamanship, Volume II (February 1951)
FEFM 29/51	Far East Fleet Memoranda: Replenishment at Sea-Fuelling (1952)
BR1742/52	Replenishment at Sea (1952)
BR1742/52B	Transfer of Liquids at Sea (1952)
BR1742/52C	Transfer of Solids at Sea (1953)
BR67 (2)	Manual of Seamanship, Volume 2 (Revised January 1967)
BR1806	British Maritime Doctrine (1995)
BR1806	British Maritime Doctrine (1999)

Notes

Archives or Museums cited with abbreviations

Citations to primary sources are given in the notes using the following abbreviations along with a document reference number or shortened title.

AL	Admiralty Library MoD, London
FAAM	Fleet Air Arm Museum, Yeovilton
IC(L)	Imperial College Library, London
IWM	Imperial War Museum, London
LHCMA	Liddell Hart Centre for Military Archives, King's College, London
TNA(Kew)	The National Archives (formerly Public Record Office), Kew
NARA2	National Archives and Records Administration 2, College Park, Maryland
NHB	Naval Historical Branch, Ministry of Defence
NL	Nimitz Library, Naval Academy, Annapolis, Maryland
NWC	Naval War College, Naval Historical Collection, Newport, Rhode Island
NWC(L)	Naval War College, Library, Rhode Island
NMM	National Maritime Museum, Caird Library, Greenwich
RNM	Royal Naval Museum, Portsmouth
RNZNM	Royal New Zealand Navy Museum, Auckland
USNHC	Naval Historical Center, Department of the Navy, Operational Archives, Washington Navy Yard

Other abbreviations that appear in the notes and bibliography include the following:

1SL	First Sea Lord, Admiralty
2SL	Second Sea Lord, Admiralty
4SL	Fourth Sea Lord, Admiralty
5SL	Fifth Sea Lord, Admiralty
ACNS	Assistant Chief of Naval Staff
AE	Fleet Replenishment Ammunition Stores ship (USN)
AF	Supply ship for fresh/frozen/dry provisions (USN)
AFIC	Armed Forces Industrial College USA
AFO	Admiralty Fleet Order
AK	General Stores/Cargo ship (USN)
AKA	Attack Cargo vessel (USN)

AKS	Fleet Replenishment Stores ship (USN)
AO	Oiler for all petroleum products (USN)
AOE	Fast Combat Support ship (1964 USN)
APD	Administrative Plans Division
ARL	Repair Ship Landing craft (USN)
A/S	Antisubmarine
ASIS	Armament Stores Issuing ship (RN)
ASW	Antisubmarine Warfare
BAD	British Admiralty Delegation, Washington, D.C.
BJSM	British Joint Staff Mission, Washington, D.C.
BNLUS	RN/USN Collaboration Committee, Naval Staff Admiralty
BPF	British Pacific Fleet (1945–46)
BSR	Battle Summary Report
BR	Book of Reference
BuSandA	Bureau of Supplies and Accounts (USN)
BuShips	Bureau of Ships (USN)
CAP	Combat Air Patrol
C-in-C	Commander in Chief
CinCLant	Commander in Chief, Atlantic (USN)
CinCNELM	Commander in Chief, U.S. Naval Forces, Eastern Atlantic and Mediterranean
CinCPac	Commander in Chief, Pacific (USN)
CinCPacFlt	Commander in Chief, US Pacific Fleet (USN)
CinCLantFlt	Commander in Chief Atlantic and US Atlantic Fleet (USN)
CNO	Chief of Naval Operations (USN)
CNS	Chief of Naval Staff, Admiralty
CominCH	Commander in Chief United States Fleet (USN)
ComNavEu	United States Commander Naval Forces Europe (USN)
ComServLant	Commander Service Force Atlantic (USN)
DCNAE	Deputy Chief of Naval Air Equipment, Admiralty
DCNS	Deputy Chief of Naval Staff, Admiralty
DNC	Director of Naval Construction, Admiralty
DND	Director of Navigation & Direction, Admiralty
DNE	Director of Naval Equipment, Admiralty
DOD	Director of Operations Division, Admiralty
D of P	Director of Plans Division, Admiralty
D of P(Q)	Director of Plans Division (Q), Admiralty
D of V	Director of Victualling Department, Admiralty
FO2FE	Flag Officer 2nd in Command Far East Station (RN)
FOCRF	Flag Officer Commanding Reserve Fleet
FT	Fleet Train
FO	Flag Officer
JPS	Joint Planning Staff
LST	Landing Ship, tank (USN)
M	Head of Military Branch, Admiralty
MoD	Ministry of Defence
MSC	Military Sealift Command (USN)
NID	Naval Intelligence Division (RN and USN)

NSWSES	Naval Ships Weapons Systems Engineering Station, Port Hueneme, California (USN)
ONI	Office of Naval Intelligence (USN)
OPNAV	Office of the Chief of Naval Operations (USN)
PRO	Public Record Office, Kew (now the National Archives, Kew)
SL	Sea Lord, Admiralty
TF	Task Force
TG	Task Group
TU	Task Unit
USNLO	United States Navy Liaison Officer
VCNS	Vice Chief of the Naval Staff

Introduction

1. Conventional forces only. The U.S. Pacific Navy comprised 4,067 warships and auxiliaries; the British Pacific Fleet (BPF) 247, including 125 acting as logistic support. Carter, *Beans, Bullets*, 9; TNA(Kew), ADM 199/1766, apx. A.

2. The fleet train used 8,745,000 barrels (bbl) of fuel oil (about ninety tankers' worth), 259,000 bbl of diesel and 21.48 million gallons of avgas (equivalent to 1.3 million tons of fuel oil, 34,000 tons of diesel, and 58,000 tons of avgas). Carter, *Beans, Bullets*, 361. See also NHB, BSR 453, apx. D, Logistic Support Group Statistics Parts III.

3. Wildenberg, *Gray Steel*, 203.

4. Ibid., 218.

5. Ballantine, *U.S. Naval Logistics*, 3.

6. Gray, *The Leverage of Sea Power*, xii.

7. Corbett, *Drake and the Tudor Navy*, 3.

8. Ballantine, *U.S. Naval Logistics*, 2–3; Eccles, *Logistics in the National Defense*, 59.

9. Ballantine, *U.S. Naval Logistics*, 7.

10. HMS *Vanguard* as flagship of the Home Fleet in 1952 was armed only with star shells, which were for her secondary armament. See Grove, *The Royal Navy since 1815*, 222.

11. Ballantine, *U.S. Naval Logistics*; Eccles, *Logistics in the National Defense*; Carter, *Beans, Bullets*; Dyer, *Naval Logistics*; Thorpe, *Pure Logistics*.

12. Carter, *Beans, Bullets*; Carter and Duvall, *Ships, Salvage and Sinews of War*.

13. Madsen, *Forgotten Fleet*.

14. Tupper Carey, "Fuelling at Sea"; Black, "Fuelling at Sea."

15. Sigwart, *Royal Fleet Auxiliary*; Adams and Smith, *The Royal Fleet Auxiliary*.

Chapter 1. Naval Logistics, 1900–1940

1. Baer, *U.S. Navy 1890–1990*, 83.

2. For example, see Sumida, "Forging the Trident," 229.

3. Gibson and Donovan, *The Abandoned Ocean*, 116.

4. Kennedy, *Rise and Fall of British Naval Mastery*, 316.

5. *Jane's Fighting Ships 1919*, 31–33.

6. Ferris, "Last Decade of British Maritime Supremacy," 133.

7. Ibid., 136.

8. Ballantine, *U.S. Naval Logistics*, 27–29.

9. Ibid., 29.

10. Neilson, "'Unbroken Thread,'" 64.

11. Ibid., 80.

12. Kennedy, *Rise and Fall*, 330.

13. Baer, *The U.S. Navy 1890–1990*, 103.

14. Ibid., 120.

15. The complete story of War Plan Orange is described in Miller, *War Plan Orange*.

16. Kennedy, "What Worth the Americans?" 98–99.

17. Ibid., 102.

18. Ferris, *The Last Decade*, 159.

19. Kennedy, *Rise and Fall*, 321.

20. Smith, *Conflict over Convoys*, 13–15.

21. Baugh, "Confusions and Constraints," 107, 111.

22. Kennedy, *Rise and Fall*, 347.

23. Baer, *The U.S. Navy 1890–1990*, 164.

24. NHB, Admiralty, Circular Letter No. 9, August 3, 1905.

25. Royal Navy records typically include only White Ensign naval auxiliaries, not RFAs, except in the Admiralty Pink Lists for the British Pacific Fleet (BPF) Fleet Train 1945.

26. TNA(Kew), ADM 1/27143: "The Early RFAs," Capt. J. R. Williams to D of S, October 29, 1953, unpublished draft article for *Naval Stores Journal*.

27. Adams, "Origins of the Royal Fleet Auxiliary Service."

28. TNA(Kew), ADM 1/ 27143: "Oil Fuel," Anon, Departmental Briefing Director of Naval Stores to Financial Secretary, 1919.

29. Ibid: "Royal Fleet Auxiliary Service: Historical Notes," D of S, June 1, 1945.

30. Ibid: Speech, 4SL, u.d. Ms. [given in 1951].

31. Ibid: "The Early RFAs," Capt. J. R. Williams to D of S, October 29, 1953.

32. Adams, "Origins of RFA," 36; TNA(Kew) ADM 53/94323: Ships' Logs "*Burma* June 30, 1911–October 8, 1911.."

33. NARA2, RG 38, "Oiling at Sea." I am grateful to Dr. Warwick Brown for this source of information.

34. "Liquid Fuel Bunkering At Sea," *Shipping Illustrated*, November 2, 1912, 118.

35. Sumida, "British Naval Operational Logistics," 468. This unique study is an excellent outline survey on the rarely published aspects of British naval logistics throughout World War I.

36. TNA(Kew), ADM 1/27143: "The Early RFAs," Capt. J. R. Williams to D of S.

37. Ibid: Internal memorandum, anon, "The Royal Fleet Auxiliary Service."

38. Ibid: "RFA Service: Historical Notes," D of S, June 1, 1945.

39. NMM, Dewar Papers, DEW 20, "Certain Suggestions."

40. NHB, Crawford, "Fuelling At Sea."

41. TNA(Kew), ADM 116/5813: Carter, "History of Fuelling at Sea," NS 1151/47, Vol. 14, para. 2–3.

42. NMM, Dewar Papers, DEW 20, "Certain Suggestions," para. 6, 7.

43. Ibid.

44. Ibid., para. 7.

45. Thomas Buell, Fleet Admiral King's biographer, noted that King before the war had considered Britain as one of America's greatest potential enemies. See Buell,

Master of Sea Power, xxxiii and 145. See also Coles, "Ernest King and the British Pacific Fleet," 125–29.

46. Gordon, "Admiralty and Imperial Overstretch," 76.

47. Quoted by the committee formed on November 5, 1936, and comprising the divisional directors of Plans, Stores, Victualling, Armament Supplies, and Military Branch. See NHB, BSR 493, vol. 1, chap. 1.

48. NMM, "Strategical Policy in the Far East."

49. TNA(Kew), ADM 1/27143: "Comparing 1935 and 1955 RFA fleets," Anon, Department of Supply [u.d. Mss.].

50. Sigwart, "Royal Fleet Auxiliary," 11.

51. TNA(Kew), ADM 1/ 27143: "Royal Fleet Auxiliary Service," D of S, NSO 3A, February 19, 1958, [u.d. Mss.], 4.

52. "Ultra-Fast Tankers for the United States Navy: British Naval Tanker Policy by Comparison," *The Petroleum Times*, January 15, 1938, 68.

53. Miller, "Refueling Warships at Sea."

54. NWC(L), "Underway Replenishment of Naval Ships," sec. 1, 6.

55. Miller, *War Plan Orange*, 90.

56. Wildenberg, *Gray Steel*, 4.

57. Gibson and Donovan, *Abandoned Ocean*, 115.

58. Ibid., 11–12.

59. NWC(L), "Underway Replenishment of Naval Ships," sec. 1, 8.

60. Ibid., 4.

61. Potter, *Nimitz*, 129.

62. Ballantine, *U.S. Naval Logistics*, 22.

63. Still, "Anglo-American Naval Logistic Co-operation in World War I."

64. NWC, RG15, Webber, "Capabilities of Logistic Support Forces," 7.

65. Carter, *Beans, Bullets*, 3. A useful description of the fueling techniques operating for this period, extracted from "NWP-14 Oiling At Sea" (1924), can be found in the NWC(L), "First Quarterly Report Oct–Dec 1982: WWI–WWII."

66. See Furer, *"Administration of the Navy Department in World War II,"* 697–98.

67. NMM, Dewar Papers, DEW 20, "Certain Suggestions."

68. Wildenberg, *Gray Steel*, 28–29, 39.

69. USNHC, "U.S. Navy Active Ship Force Levels 1917–1995."

70. NMM, Dewar Papers, DEW 20, "Certain Suggestions."

71. Carter, *Beans, Bullets*, 2.

72. Ibid., 3.

73. Wildenberg, *Gray Steel*, 41.

74. NARA2, RG19, Records of the Bureau of Construction and Repair. Carriers were consuming in Fleet exercises as much as 10 percent capacity in one day when operating aircraft in company with the Fleet requiring speeds up to 25 knots into the wind. The extended search in 1937 for Amelia Earhart also reinforced how carrier endurance proved completely inadequate without replenishment. See Wildenberg, *Gray Steel*, 129–30.

75. NWC, RG4, "The Industrial Reserve," *BuShips Journal*, November 1953.

76. These features included a variety of fittings such as gun mounts and oiling at sea gear. Twin screws and increased shaft horsepower would provide speeds in excess of commercial requirements.

77. Carter, *Beans, Bullets*, 4.

78. King, "U.S. Navy at War," 12.
79. Bokel and Clark, "Acquisition in World War II," 109.
80. Gibson and Donovan, *Abandoned Ocean*, 167.
81. Quoted in Friedman, *Postwar Naval Revolution*, appendix III.
82. Till, *Seapower*, 140.

Chapter 2. World War II

1. Pugh, *The Cost of Seapower*, 59.
2. See apx. B, col. 1, Planned Fleet Train, December 1941.
3. NHB, BSR 493, chap. 1, 3.
4. *Jane's Fighting Ships, 1939*, 92–93.
5. TNA(Kew), ADM 1/27143: "RFA Fleet in 1939," D of S, Internal Memorandum April 22, 1955.
6. Roskill, "*History of the Second World War*," apx. P, 426.
7. TNA(Kew), ADM 116/5813: "History of Fuelling at Sea," para. 5–10. See also NMM, DEW 20, "Present situation."
8. NMM, "The Chase and Sinking of the *Bismarck*." Criticism about the lack of fueling-at-sea capability was voiced by Vice Adm. K. G. B. Dewar, head of Historical Section in NMM, Dewar Papers, DEW 20, TSDD to VCNS. The *Bismarck* experience was also used as a case study by the U.S. Navy at the Naval War College. See NWC, RG15, Bell, "Mobile Logistic Support," 3.
9. TNA(Kew), ADM 199/1521: Minute, September 1, 1945, Director TSDD.
10. Roskill, *History of the Second World War*, 427.
11. NHB, BSR 493, chap. 2, 25.
12. TNA(Kew), ADM 1/13169: "U.S. and Admiralty Logistics Organizations Comparison, 1943."
13. At the time, the logistics admiral was Admiral Badger, USN, Director of Naval Logistic Plans; he was scheduled to visit the United Kingdom later in 1943 to see how logistics was being organized by the Admiralty.
14. TNA(Kew), ADM 1/13169: Minute, Capt. C. C. Hughes-Hallett, Deputy D of P(Q), July 12, 1943, M.07619/43.
15. Much of the description of Plans Division in the early years was gleaned from reading an early draft of an unpublished manuscript, "The Organisation of the Naval Staff within the Admiralty & Ministry of Defence 1927–2000," written by Cdr. N. L. Stewart, RN, domiciled with the NHB. I am grateful to both for the opportunity to review this.
16. The Fourth Sea Lord (4SL) organized the activities of the Victualling Department and the Naval Stores Department, both responsible for the provision, storage, and supply of all stores except armaments—this was governed separately by the Third Sea Lord (3SL) as controller.
17. Captain (later rear admiral) Hughes-Hallett was the first holder of the post.
18. TNA(Kew), ADM 1/13169: Minute, C. C. Hughes-Hallett, July 12, 1943.
19. Ibid.: Minute 2, 4SL, July 15, 1943 M.07619/43.
20. Ibid.: Minute 3, Controller, July 17, 1943.
21. Ibid.: Minute 4, 4SL, October 16, 1943.
22. Ibid.: ACS memorandum to 4SL, August 12, 1944.

23. Ballantine, *U.S. Naval Logistics*, 45, 60.

24. Furer, *Administration of the Navy Department*, 711.

25. NWC(L), Maddon, "Operational Logistics," 10.

26. For example, a force of forty thousand in Australia required nearly as much shipping as a force of one hundred thousand in the United Kingdom. See Gray, "Joint Logistics in the Pacific Theater," 329.

27. NWC(L), King, "Second Report," 108.

28. Ministry of Defence (Navy), *War with Japan Volume VI*, 69.

29. NWC(L), King, "Third Report," 197.

30. NWC(L), King, "Second Report," 155.

31. When the slow oiler USS *Neches*, for example, tried to refuel the carrier USS *Saratoga* and her escorts during the attempted relief of Wake Island, December 1941, the underway operation became protracted due to inadequate fueling rigs and bad weather. Time ran out to save the island, and the mission was abandoned.

32. USS *Kanawha* to USS *Saratoga*, June 12, 1939, See Dyer, *Naval Logistics*, 128. See also NWC(L), "First Quarterly Report," A-7.

33. USS *Brazos* to USS *Maryland*. See Dyer, "*Naval Logistics*," 128.

34. Wildenberg, *Gray Steel*, 180–83.

35. NARA2, RG143, "Fueling at Sea Instructions U.S. Fleet," v.

36. See Edward Baxter, "Rappahannock Saves Day,"

37. Buell, *Master of Sea Power*, 467.

38. USNHC, "U.S. Naval Administration in World War II," 288.

39. Postwar this became renamed "Logistic Support Force"—sometimes also referred to as the "Underway Replenishment Group" (URG). The concept and the supporting doctrine (USF-13) are discussed in more detail in the next chapter.

40. Maddon, "Operational Logistics," 9.

41. USNHC, "Logistics Support Group Historical Report Service Squadron 6 Task Group 16.6."

42. Ibid.

43. NARA2, RG143, "Logistic Reference Data."

44. USNHC, "NWP-38 Replenishment at Sea," 319; Carter, *Beans, Bullets*, 355–56; NWC, RG15, Webber, "Capabilities of Logistic Support Forces," 13.

45. Petroleum products transferred during Operation ICEBERG were 10,133,000 bbl fuel oil, 323,000 bbl diesel oil, and 25,573,000 gal of avgas. See USNHC, "Logistics Support Group Historical Report Service Squadron Six Task Group 16.6," A12/A3A-4.

46. NWC(L), King, "Third Report," 176.

47. NHB, BSR 493, 12, 36.

48. Willmott, *Grave of a Dozen Schemes*, 75.

49. TNA(Kew), ADM 199/1766: "Reports of Rear Admiral Fleet Train," Vol. 1, 47–48.

50. Ibid., 15. See also Smith, *Task Force 57*, 110–11.

51. Vian, *Action This Day*, 155, 161.

52. McCormick did concede, however, that the British eventually accomplished their role without "constituting an appreciable drain on our resources." See McCormick, "Logistics and Strategy."

53. Ibid.

54. NHB, BSR 493, 85–90; MoD(N), *War with Japan*, 16–17; TNA(Kew), ADM 199/1766, 59–60.

55. TNA(Kew), CAB 119/155: "War Cabinet JPS (44), January 3, 1945, annex 1, 226. See also TNA(Kew), CAB 119/160. MOWT estimates dated April 25, 1944.

56. TNA(KEW), PREM 3.164.5: directive April 9, 1944, 68.

57. Ibid., 140. See also NHB, BSR 493, 46.

58. NHB, BSR 493, 57; see also appendix F of this volume for a summary of requirements by December 1944.

59. TNA(Kew), ADM 1/27143: "Expansion of the RFA Service," D of S, N.S.019226/ 44, August 30, 1944.

60. TNA(Kew), ADM 199/1766: "Report of Liaison Officer," July 12, 1945, Vol. II, appx. T.

61. Roskill, *War At Sea*, 362.

62. Winton, *The Forgotten Fleet*, 269.

63. MoD(N), *War With Japan*, 16; Smith, *Task Force 57*, 59.

64. Stevens, *Royal Australian Navy in WW II*, 107; TNA(Kew), ADM 199/118: Report, Vice Admiral (Q), "Supply and Creation of the Australian Base," November 19, 1945, apx. 1. See also NHB, BSR 493, 83.

65. NHB, BSR 493, 79. See also "Valor," "The Fleet Train," *Naval Review*, 1946, 32.

66. Smith, *Task Force 57*, 111.

67. Humble, *Fraser of North Cape*, 267.

68. MoD(N), *War with Japan*, 15; NHB, BSR 493, 36.

69. Willmott, *Grave of a Dozen Schemes*, 75.

70. NHB, BSR 493, 55, 114.

71. TNA(Kew), ADM 116/5535: Letter, C-in-C BPF to Secretary, Admiralty covering Vol. II, October 24, 1945.

72. Willmott, *Grave of a Dozen Schemes*, 75.

73. MoD(N),*War with Japan*, 16; Winton, *The Forgotten Fleet*, 278–79.

74. NHB, BSR 493, 76, 81, 84.

75. MoD(N), *War with Japan*, 13.

76. TNA(Kew), ADM 199/1769: "Report of Engineering Officer," apx. I, "Report of Proceedings Fleet Train," Vol. 1.

77. Ibid., See also TNA(Kew), ADM 199/1766: "Report of U.S. Naval Liaison Officer," July 12, 1945, apx. T, Vol. II; TNA(Kew), ADM 199/118: "Report of Vice Admiral (Admin) VA(Q) Re Supply and Creation of Australian Base," Section 14 Personnel, apx. I.

78. Willmott, *Grave of a Dozen Schemes*, 139.

79. NHB, BSR 493: "Logistic Experience of the Fleet Train: BPF War Orders Part III" War Order No. 3000 issued to Fleet Auxiliaries by RAFT, FT 2610/438,July 1, 1945.

80. "Valor," "The Fleet Train," *Naval Review* vol. 34, 1946, 34.

81. TNA(Kew), ADM 116/5535: Letter, C-in-C BPF, to Secretary Admiralty, October 24, 1945.

82. NHB, BSR 493: "Logistic Support Group Statistics," apx. D, part 1 and 2.

83. See appendix F of this volume for a complete list of ship types during the various stages of the campaign.

84. TNA(Kew), ADM 199/1766: "Report of Proceedings Fleet Train," Vol. 1, "Inception—31/5/1945," section 11, "Operation Iceberg"; Vol. II, "1/6/1945–20/8/

1945,." See also NHB, BSR 493: "Logistic Support Group Statistics," apx. D, part 1 and 2.

85. MoD(N), *War with Japan*, 203.

86. NHB, BSR 493: "The Fleet Train in Operation," part 2, 110.

87. TNA(Kew), ADM 199/1478: D of P (Q), Review May 23, 1946.

88. HMS *Artifex*, HMS *Resource*, and HMS *Tyne*; MoD(N), *War with Japan*, 206.

89. TNA(Kew), ADM 199/1748: "Aircraft Damage Reports," "Aircraft Wastage in BPF March–August 1945," Flag Officer Naval Air Pacific to Secretary, Admiralty, October 24, 1945.

90. NHB, BSR 493: "Logistic Support Group Statistics," apx. D, parts I and II. Massive aircraft losses, including noncombat, were difficult to replace because these loss levels were beyond all expectations. MoD(N), *War with Japan*, 204.

91. NHB, BSR 453, 132–33, 137, 22.

92. NHB, BSR 493: "Logistical Support Group statistics," apx. D, part IV. See also TNA(Kew), ADM 199/1478: D of P(Q), Review May 23, 1946.

93. TNA(Kew), ADM 116/5813, para. 78.

94. NMM, Fraser Papers, MS 83/158; NMM, Fraser Papers, MS 86/096.

95. Crews were drawn from eleven nationalities each with different charter parties, articles, and so on. See TNA(Kew), ADM 199/1766: "Report by RAFT," Vol. II, para. 2, "Composition and Build-up of TF112"; and apx. B, "Personnel," August 20, 1945.

96. NHB, BSR 477, 179.

97. TNA(Kew), ADM 116/5813: "Fuelling at Sea," para. 10.

98. TNA(Kew), ADM 1/19248: Commodore BPF Fleet Train Memorandum April 26, 1946, "Admiralty Comments Concerning Recommendations," Enclosure No. 4, "Logistic Support of a Fleet Engaged in Ocean Warfare," 1946.

Chapter 3. Underway Replenishment at Sea (UNREP/RAS)

1. Tupper Carey, "Fuelling at Sea," 382. This article illustrates contemporary naval thinking about aircraft carriers remaining "the core of any striking force" with the concomitant need for mobile fleet train support very much reflecting recent Pacific war experience.

2. TNA(Kew), ADM 234/393, 4.

3. Ibid., 1.

4. USNHC, "NWP-38 Replenishment at Sea," sec. 100.

5. NARA2, RG 38, ATP-16, para. 110.

6. A fuller description can be found in AL, Admiralty, BR68 "Manual of Seamanship," Vol. II, 1932, 65.

7. Adams, "Origins of RFA," 36.

8. TNA(Kew), ADM 116/5813: Carter, "History of Fuelling at Sea," para. 8a.

9. Wildenberg, *Gray Steel*, 31–38.

10. Ibid., 30. The USS *Cuyama* successfully fueled eight destroyers in pairs (for the first time simultaneously) in calm weather at slow speed.

11. Ibid., 43.

12. TNA(Kew), ADM 116/5813: Carter, "History of Fuelling at Sea," para. 9 and 10.

13. Leutze, *Bargaining for Supremacy*, 30–33.

14. NMM, DEW 20, NID Admiralty to Dewar.

15. NHB, Crawford, "Fuelling at Sea," para. 12–13, 34; and TNA(Kew), ADM 116/5813: Carter, "History of Fuelling At Sea," apx. 1, item 8.

16. NMM, DEW 20, A. W. Brock TSD to Dewar. See also TNA(Kew), ADM 116/5813: Carter, "History of Fuelling at Sea," para. 10.

17. TNA(Kew), ADM 116/5813: Carter, "History of Fuelling at Sea," para. 3–4, 12(e).

18. Black, "Fuelling at Sea," 137.

19. TNA(Kew), ADM 116/5813: Carter, "History of Fuelling at Sea," para. 20.

20. NMM, DEW 20, A. W. Brock TSD to Dewar. See also TNA(Kew), ADM 116/5813: Carter, "History of Fuelling at Sea," para. 19–26.

21. TNA(Kew), ADM 116/5813: Carter, "History of Fuelling at Sea," para. 26.

22. Black, "Fuelling at Sea," 137.

23. NARA2, RG38, Naval Stores Department, Admiralty, "List no 16."

24. For example, the arrangements on American battleships were allegedly far superior to British ones, with six connections available on each side for oiling at sea. A tanker or battleship could oil two destroyers on each side at 12 knots. TNA(Kew), ADM 229/32, 329.

25. TNA(Kew), ADM 1/20418: Adm. Sir John C. Tovey, C-in-C Home Fleet to Secretary of Admiralty, Memorandum March 3, 1943, "Oiling at Sea—Buoyant Hose Method."

26. TNA(Kew), ADM 116/5813: Carter, "History of Fuelling at Sea," para. 48. Of the twenty-four tankers, only four were capable of 15 knots, the rest 11 knots. The tanker embodying all the improvements developed during the war, RFA *Wave Sovereign*, did not arrive in the Pacific until 1946.

27. Ibid., para. 21 and apx. 1, item 11.

28. Carter, *Beans, Bullets*, 110, 362.

29. MoD(Navy), *War with Japan*, 204.

30. NHB, BSR 493 and BSR 477: BPWO Part III (July 1945) "Logistic Support Group," para. 3010–13, "Cruising Dispositions."

31. USNHC, "USF-13 Logistic Support Force Operating Instructions," para. 110.

32. USNHC, "NWP-38 Replenishment at Sea," 319.

33. NWC, RG15, Webber, "Capabilities of Logistics Support Force," 13.

34. USNHC, "USF-13 Logistic Support Force Operating Instructions," para. 120–29.

35. NWC, RG15, Pare, "Mobile Fleet Support," 1947.

36. Ibid. For the British view, see NHB, "The Fighting Instructions," para. 759.

37. USNHC, "USF-13 Logistic Support Force Operating Instructions," "Replenishment Formations" sec. 2-4, 2-5, 3-8.

38. NHB, "The Fighting Instructions," para. 752–60, 769–73, and dia. 6.

39. Miller, "UNREP History of Aircraft Carriers," 320.

40. NARA2, RG38, ATP-16: USN "Maneuvering during Alongside Replenishment," (1955) para. 131.

41. NWC, RG27, Pare, U.S. Atlantic Fleet Service Force 2.

42. NHB, "The Fighting Instructions," para. 762–63.

43. TNA(Kew), ADM 234/393, 1.

44. USNHC, "USF-13 Logistic Support Force Operating Instructions," para. 211.

45. NARA2, RG143 "Fueling at Sea Instructions, U.S. Fleet," CominCH P-2 (1944), Annex A, "Elwood Method," para. 112.

46. As recommended in TNA(Kew), ADM 234/393. *Wave*-class tankers' optimum speed during Korean operations was 12 knots, which enabled them to pump to near capacity, and *Ranger*-class tankers' optimum speed was 10 knots. See TNA(KEW), ADM 116/6231: "Replenishment at Sea-Fuelling," para. 2(e), Far East Fleet Memoranda 1st February 1952, FEFM 29/51 (rev.).

47. TNA(Kew), ADM 234/393, 2.

48. USNHC, "NWP-38 Replenishment at Sea," para. 401. It is certain the British were relying on HMS *Bulawayo* trials to justify this claim. See chapter 7 for details.

49. Based upon conversations held with various RFA and MSC captains.

50. TNA(Kew), ADM 234/393, 7.

51. NARA2, RG143 "Fueling at Sea Instructions, U.S. Fleet," CominCH P-2 (1944), para. 106.

52. TNA(Kew), ADM 234/393, 7; TNA(Kew), ADM 234/394, 9.

53. AL, Defence Council, BR67 (2) "Admiralty Manual of Seamanship," Vol. II, 386.

54. Black, "Fuelling at Sea," 144.

55. These conclusions were based on interaction trials conducted in 1947 by the battleship HMS *King George V* with RFA *Olna* (which had recently been transferred to the RFA from the Royal Navy). See TNA(Kew), ADM 226/64.

56. TNA(Kew), ADM 234/393, 2. Such lines were discarded during World War II.

57. TNA(Kew), ADM 1/23443, point 6. DND minute 304/52 noted that while automatic pilots were a bone of contention with RFA masters, they were a valuable aid with any delay to hand steering no longer than four to five seconds. For a contrary view, see TNA(Kew), ADM 1/24041: Commander Norrington, "Master RFA *Wave Premier* Report to D of S, November 29, 1952, regarding Arctic Cruise of TG 47.1/2, November 17, 1952."

58. TNA(Kew), ADM 234/393, apx. 4, 34.

59. Ibid., 6.

60. Ibid., 1.

61. TNA(Kew), ADM 116/5813, para. 49.

62. TNA(Kew), ADM 1/24041: Commander Norrington, Memorandum, November 29, 1952.

63. TNA(Kew), ADM 234/393, sec. X, 20–21; AL, Admiralty, BR67 (2/51), 468–69.

64. AL, Admiralty, BR67 (2/51), 472–73.

65. TNA(Kew), ADM 234/393, apx. 2, 27.

66. Black, "Fuelling at Sea," 138.

67. NARA2, RG143, "Fueling At Sea Instructions, U.S. Fleet, "CominCH P-2 (1944), sec. 2.

68. TNA(Kew), ADM 1/24039: "Reports from the Masters of RFA's *Olna, Wave Prince* and *Wave Premier* covering September 10–24, 1952."

69. TNA(Kew), ADM 234/393, 1.

70. Hughes-Hallett, "Naval Logistics in a Future War," 238.

71. TNA(Kew), ADM 234/393, 1. See also the TNA(Kew), ADM 239/144, 3. DTSD considered all cruisers and larger must be capable of supplying oil fuel to smaller ships by both abeam and astern methods. See TNA(Kew), ADM 1/20418.

72. TNA(Kew), ADM 1/23443: "Oiling at Sea Astern Method," point 9. A destroyer abeam in bad weather inside of 200 ft suffered from water disturbance created by the tanker. Speed control became difficult because of pitching and the propellers coming out of the water. This, he argued, would not occur in the astern method. However, evidence of its decline in use is found in TNA(Kew) ADM 116/6231: FEFM 29/51 (rev.) 1952, para. 4(g)(i).

73. TNA(Kew), ADM ADM 234/394, point 11 (amended). See also NHB, Crawford, "Replenishment at Sea" para. 27.

74. See, for example, NARA2, RG143, "Fueling at Sea Instructions, U.S. Fleet," paragraph 102.

75. P. S. Newell, DNE, memorandum, November 7, 1951, 1218/51, to C-in-C Far East Station, suggests it will take twelve months to issue the new flexible hose as requested in their "First Report" under cover letter FO2FE/21176/1; TNA(Kew), ADM 116/6230: Vol. XXI, part IV "Administration, Maintenance and Logistics," sec. 3, "Logistics," para. 21.

76. TNA(Kew), ADM 239/144, "Progress in Tactics," para. 20.

77. TNA(Kew), ADM 234/393, 27.

78. TNA(Kew), ADM 239/439.

79. NWC(L), Miller, "UNREP History of Aircraft Carriers," 317.

80. Black, *"Fuelling at Sea,"* 138.

81. AL, Admiralty, BR67 (2/51), 454.

82. TNA(Kew), ADM 234/393, 15. See also Rippon, *Evolution of Engineering*, 385; TNA(Kew), ADM 116/5813, para. 47.

83. AL, Admiralty, BR67 (2/51), 468.

84. TNA(Kew), ADM 234/393, 16; TNA(Kew), ADM 234/394, Introduction, point 11; TNA(Kew), ADM 234/395, 2. It is ironic to think that the last occasion a form of hose tensioning was tried was nearly half a century earlier, when it was soon discarded as being too cumbersome for its time. A prototype supplied by Clarke Chapman was fitted to the RFA *Fort Duquesne* in 1951, and although successful it took several years to become the standard for both liquids and solids transfers. See Rippon, *Evolution of Engineering*, 383.

85. TNA(Kew), ADM 1/23434.

86. NARA2, RG143, "Fueling at Sea Instructions, U.S. Fleet": Annex A, "Elwood Method of Fueling At Sea."

87. USNHC, NWP-38, para. 423.

88. TNA(Kew), ADM 1/21061: Minute, D of V, April 27, 1948.

89. TNA(Kew), ADM 239/144.

90. USNHC, NWP-38, para. 600b. Ships were usually loaded to about 75 percent capacity. See NARA2, RG143, "Logistics Reference Data," 8–11.

91. TNA(Kew), ADM 234/393: apx. 3, 32 fig. VIII.24.

92. NWC(L), Miller, "UNREP History of Aircraft Carriers," 317–18.

93. NARA2, RG15, Denebrink, "Logistic Support to the Naval Forces."

94. Hughes-Hallett, "Naval Logistics in a Future War," 238.

95. TNA(Kew), ADM 234/394: BR1742B, Introduction.

96. This was according to the Admiralty's director of Victualling. See Hughes-Hallett, "Naval Logistics in a Future War," 243.

97. NHB, "The Fighting Instructions," para. 767.

98. NWC(L), "Underway Replenishment of Naval Ships," 331.

99. TNA(Kew), ADM 199/1766: "Victualling Stores," apx. H, "History of the Fleet Train," Vol. II. American statistics tend to be on an all-in "evolution" basis, that is, including time for connecting and disconnecting, whereas British records tend to be either pumping time (for fuel) or "first-to-last net basis" (for solids) with connect times occasionally shown separately, if at all.

100. NARA2, RG313, "Task Organization for TF 89."

101. NARA2, RG143, "Report U.S. Atlantic Fleet," 17.

102. NWC, RG15, Austin, "Mobile Logistics," 4.

103. TNA(Kew), ADM 116/6231: FO2FE "Third Report," part III, para. 14. The report noted that American ships "transfer phenomenal quantities of ammunition to the carrier task force at sea. Recently USS *Chara* transferred 203 tons to a carrier in one load."

104. NARA2, RG15, Denebrink, "Logistic Support Korean Operations," 15, 21.

105. TNA(Kew), ADM 116/6230: FO2FE/21176/1, part IV "Administration, Maintenance and Logistics," sec. 3, "Logistics," para. 8.

106. TNA(Kew), ADM 116/6231: Minute, D of V, April 27, 1948.

107. TNA(Kew), ADM 234/393, 9–10.

108. NARA2, RG38, ATP-16, 1–4; and USNHC, NWP-38.

109. TNA(Kew), ADM 234/393, 1.

110. TNA(Kew), ADM 116/6231: FEFM 29/51 (Rev.), para. 4(b).

111. TNA(Kew), ADM 234/393, 1.

112. TNA(Kew), ADM 116/6231: FEFM 29/51 (Rev.), para. 4(d) and 6(a).

113. NWC, RG15, Austin, "Mobile Logistics," 6.

114. TNA(Kew), ADM 1/21061: Minute, DND, February 6, 1948, Report No. 13AR, December 12, 1947.

115. TNA(Kew), ADM 1/26858: Minute, U. H. R. James, D of P (Q), August 28, 1948, "Report of Rear Admiral Schofield's RN/USN Standardisation Review, BAD 1687/47, May 31, 1948.

116. TNA(Kew), ADM 1/21061: Minute, D of P(Q), June 2, 1948, DND 29/48; and Minute, DCNAE, May 14, 1948.

117. TNA(Kew), ADM 1/21061: Minute, D of S, DND 29/48, March 22, 1948.

118. Rippon, *Evolution of Engineering*, 385.

119. Case, USS *Sacramento* (AOE1)."

120. NWC(L), "Underway Replenishment of Naval Ships," 36.

Chapter 4. Postwar Logistics

1. NWC(L), King, "Second Report to the Secretary of the Navy," 146.

2. Ballantine, *U.S. Naval Logistics*, 3. See also Eccles, *Logistics in the National Defense*, 44; and Dyer, *Naval Logistics*, 14.

3. NWC(L), King, "Third Report to the Secretary of the Navy," 198.

4. Fleet Admiral Ernest J. King, USN, to a staff officer in 1942, taken from "Logistics Quotes," Navy Supply Corps Newsletter, May 1, 2003 (U.S. Department of the Navy, Naval Supply Systems Command). King's observation was also noted with some dismay by Capt. John E Jackson, SC USN Military Chair of Logistics, NWC, in his introduction to the NWC Logistics Leadership Series republication of George C. Thorpe, *Pure Logistics*, ix.

5. Buell, *Master of Sea Power*, 566.

6. NWC, Ms. Coll., Furer to Eccles.

7. NWC, Ms. Coll., Carney to Eccles. Admiral Carney became VCNO (Logistics) Washington, D.C. The term "kiss of death" was a popular attribution that resonates through a number of different documents, for example, Ballantine, *US Naval Logistics*, 295.

8. Hughes-Hallett, "Naval Logistics in a Future War," 234.

9. Buell, *Master of Sea Power*, 406.

10. King, "U.S. Navy at War 1941–1945," 34.

11. Hayes, "Logistics of Necessity," 689.

12. Thorpe, *Pure Logistics*, 5.

13. Eccles, *Logistics in the National Defense*, 22.

14. Ibid., 44–50.

15. NWC, "Logistics Presentations Naval Command Course," sec. II, 3; sec. I, 1.

16. TNA(Kew), ADM 199/1457.

17. TNA(Kew), ADM 116/5535: Minute, D of P, August 12, 1945.

18. Ibid.: Minute, D of P, November 22, 1945.

19. Eccles, *Logistics in the National Defense*, 224.

20. TNA(Kew), ADM 199/118: Minute, D of P (Q) October 19, 1946, "C-in-C BPF Dispatches Summary of Staff Division's & Department's Remarks."

21. This was acutely observed by Rear Admiral Eccles during his visit to Europe in 1956. See memorandum prepared under the sponsorship of the George Washington University Logistics Research Project, NWC, Ms. Coll. ,Eccles, "Report No. 7," 81.

22. Eccles, *Logistics in the National Defense*, 59.

23. USNHC, "U.S. Naval Administration in World War II": "Narrative at Joint and Fleet Command Level," part VI, Logistics, 187.

24. Ballantine, *U.S. Naval Logistics*, 289.

25. NWC, Ms. Coll., Adm. J. Furer, USN, to Rear Admiral Eccles.

26. Ballantine, *U.S. Naval Logistics*, 290.

27. Stevens, *The Royal Australian Navy*, 106.

28. NMM, MS 83/158, "Task Force 57."

29. TNA(Kew), ADM 199/118: "Summary of Staff Divisions for Plans, Dockyards and Naval Stores." See also, TNA(Kew), ADM 199/2376: C-in-C, March 15, 1946, part III, "Recommendations from Experience Gained," sec. 1 and 2.

30. TNA(Kew), ADM 199/118: "Supply and Creation of the Australian Base," "Recommendations," apx. 1, Report by Vice Admiral (Q) BPF, November 19, 1945.

31. Ibid.

32. Furer, *Administration of the Naval Department*, 735.

33. These issues are well developed in a paper given by Col. Vincent J. Esposito at the Industrial College of the Armed Forces; NWC, Ms. Coll., Esposito.

34. NWC, RG14, Brown, "Logistic Planning Agencies of CominCH and CNO."

35. NWC, Ms. Coll., Eccles, "Pacific Logistics," 6.

36. Furer, *Administration of the Naval Department*, 696.

37. Hughes-Hallett, "Naval Logistics in a Future War," 233.

38. Ibid., 241.

39. NWC, Ms. Coll., Eccles, "Mobile Support versus Overseas Base Support," 1.

40. Eccles, *Logistics in the National Defense*, 103, 146.

41. Ibid., 133.

42. Furer, *Administration of the Naval Department*, 734.

43. Eccles, *Logistics in the National Defense*, 133.

44. Ballantine, *U.S. Naval Logistics*, 177.

45. NWC, Ms. Coll., Eccles, "Pacific Logistics," 15.

46. USNHC, "Logistics Support Group Historical Report Service Squadron 6."

47. NWC, Ms. Coll., Eccles, "Pacific Logistics," 10.

48. NHB, BSR 493, "History of the Fleet Train," 55 and 114.

49. TNA(Kew), ADM 199/1457: "C-in-C BPF and Eastern Fleet War Diaries 1943–1946," sec. 2, "Analysis: Logistic Lessons." See also TNA(Kew), ADM 116/5535: C-in-C BPF cover letter for History of the Fleet Train, Volume II, October 24, 1945.

50. TNA(Kew), ADM 199/1457: Part III, "Recommendations for Fleet Conducting Ocean Warfare," sec. II, "Staff Requirements for Ships," (b), C-in-C BPF, March 15, 1946.

51. Verbatim from the biographical sketch contained in the "Register of the Papers of Henry E. Eccles," 2nd ed., 1988, produced by the Naval Historical Collection at the Naval War College, Newport, Rhode Island. Additional material in the paragraph has also been drawn from this document.

52. NWC,(L), Vice Admiral Beary, Foreword to "Operational Naval Logistics."

53. NWC, Ms. Coll., Eccles to Moore, March 4, 1952, MS 52, Series II, Folder 28.

54. Ibid. A view shared by Commodore B. Horace, RN, a logistics graduate (1950) who was taught by Eccles, in a letter to the author February 24, 2003.

55. Furer, *Administration of the Naval Department*, 691.

56. Vogelsang, *Logistics: Its Bearing on the Art of War.*

57. Eccles, "Logistics—What is it?"

58. NWC, RG27, Smith, "A History of Logistics," 4.

59. NWC,(L), "Operational Naval Logistics," 2.

60. Ibid.

61. NWC, RG4, "Report of Committee to Study Post-war Logistic Training," "Post-war Logistic Training," CNO to Rear Admiral Jennings, letter Op-04–MC Serial 55–04, November 23, 1945. Its findings were approved by the Secretary of the Navy on June 25, 1946. See NWC, RG27, Smith, "A History of Logistics at the NWC."

62. NWC, RG4, "Report of Committee to Study Post-war Logistic Training," para. 11.

63. Ibid., para. 12.

64. Ibid., "Conclusions," para.18; "Recommendations," para.22.

65. NWC, RG27, Smith, "A History of Logistics at the NWC," 6–8.

66. NWC, Ms. Coll., Eccles to Admiral Cooley, July 7, 1950; NWC, RG27, Smith, "A History of Logistics at the NWC," Tab K.

67. NWC, RG27, Smith, "A History of Logistics at the NWC," "Logistics Course—Establishment of," Department of Strategy and Logistics to Chief of Naval Personnel NWC, serial 3p24,Enclosure A, para. 10, January 6, 1947, Tab B, 5.

68. NWC, RG27, Smith, "A History of Logistics at the NWC."

69. NWC, RG27, Pare letter to Eccles, March 28, 1947.

70. Till, *Seapower*, 46.

71. NWC, Ms. Coll., Eccles to Admiral Cooley, July 7, 1950; NWC, RG27, Smith, "A History of Logistics at the NWC," Tab K,5.

72. NWC, RG4, "Logistics Department Organization and Instructions."

73. NWC, RG27, Smith, "A History of Logistics at the NWC," 15.

74. Ibid., Tab E and K, "Report on Logistics Course" para. 12, president of NWC to CNO(Op-40), July 16, 1948.

75. NWC, RG3, "Royal Navy Graduates of the U.S. NWC 1947–1951." See also NWC, RG27, Smith, "A History of Logistics at the NWC," 18 and Tab M.

76. NWC, Ms. Coll., Eccles to Whitaker.

77. NWC, RG27, Smith "A History of Logistics at the NWC," 18, Internal Memorandum 4–51 NWC, December 28, 1950. See also NWC, RG3, "1950 Logistics Class," Box 28.

78. NWC, RG27, Smith, "A History of Logistics at the NWC," 19–21 and Tab O.

79. Ibid., 35.

80. Ibid., 36.

81. Ibid., 37.

82. Ibid., Tab K, Eccles memorandum to Cooley, July 7, 1950.

83. Ibid., Tab R, Algire, "Thoughts on Logistic Research." Commander Algire was the deputy head of the logistics department and one of the representatives at the George Washington Logistic Research Conference.

84. NWC, Ms. Coll., Eccles to Ballantine, letter October 5, 1949, MS 52, Series II, Box 4.

85. NWC, RG27, Smith, "A History of Logistics at the NWC," Tabs P and Q.

86. See the bibliography, Imperial College Library [IC(L)] for selected articles.

87. NWC, Ms. Coll., Eccles to Dyer, August 1, 1958, MS 52, Series II, Box 15. George Dyer was cautioned by Eccles not to fall into the same trap. Dyer published "Naval Logistics" two years later, in 1960. See also NWC, Ms.Coll., Eccles, "Notes on the Requirements for Logistics Books."

88. NWC, Ms. Coll., Eccles, "Notes on the Requirements for Logistics Books."

89. NWC, Ms. Coll., Eccles, "Detailed Recommendations for the Consolidation of the S&T and S&L Courses," Enclosure (2), section 2(c).

90. NWC, RG4, "Operational Problem 6L-50," "Foreword." See also, NWC, RG4, "Maneuver Rules."

91. For good examples, see NWC, RG4, "Replenishment at Sea Exercise September 16 1948"; "Replenishment at Sea Study: Statement and Special Situation October 1952," and "Replenishment at Sea: An Illustrative Problem, April 28 1949."

92. NWC, RG27, Smith, "A History of Logistics at the NWC," Tab H.

93. NWC, RG27, "A History of Logistics at the Naval War College," Tab E, "Report on Logistics Course," President of NWC to CNO (Op-40), July 16, 1948. See, for example, NWC, RG4, "Operational Problem 6L-50."

94. Hattendorf, "A Special Relationship," 200–201.

95. NWC, RG 27, "British Naval Officer Students at NWC."

96. NWC, RG3, "Royal Navy Graduates of the NWC 1947–1951."

97. Cdr. H. Barnard, RN (Ret.), letter to author, February 24, 2003.

98. Penn, *HMS Thunderer*, 117.

99. TNA(Kew), ADM 1/25047: NM 455/1953.

100. Vice Adm. Sir Louis Le Bailly letter to author, December 26, 1999.

101. NWC, Ms. Coll., Acworth to Eccles, letter August 16, 1949.

102. NMM, MS 83/158, Fisher (RAFT) letter to C-in-C Fraser.

103. TNA(Kew), ADM 116/5670: "Minutes of meeting with Naval Staff on further-

ance of RN/USN Collaboration held on July 25, 1947," Item 10. For list of Royal Navy officer names, see NWC, RG3, "Royal Navy Graduates of the NWC 1947–1951."

104. NWC, RG3, "Royal Naval Staff College England 1949": Vice Adm. D. B. Beary, President NWC, responses March 21, 1949, July 7, 1949, and September 16, 1949, to Capt. J. W. Eaton, director, Royal Naval Staff College Greenwich letters of February 11, 1949, April 23, 1949, and July 27, 1949, Box 27.

105. NWC, Ms. Coll., Acworth to Eccles, letter August 11, 1949.

106. NWC, Ms. Coll., Eccles to Acworth, letter August 15, 1949.

107. NWC, RG3, "Instruction in British Military Schools"; NWC, RG3, "Royal Naval Staff College England 1949": Vice Adm.D. B. Beary, President NWC to CNO, memorandum January 3, 1950, CinCNELM serial 4680, Box 40, NC-10.

108. NWC, RG3, "Report on U.K. Field Trip March 10–19, 1972." See also NWC, RG3, "Students at Foreign War Colleges 1972–1973."

109. NWC, RG3, "Imperial Defence College."

110. TNA(Kew), ADM 116/5670.

111. TNA(Kew), ADM 1/24626: Rt. Hon. J. P. L. Thomas, M.P., to Anthony Eden, May 30, 1952.

112. TNA(Kew), ADM 1/24626: Sir Oliver Franks to William Strang, Foreign Office, letter June 13, 1952.

113. TNA(Kew), ADM 1/23841: Adm. Douglas Pennant, British Joint Services Mission (Navy Staff) Washington, to Adm. Sir Rhoderick McGrigor, First Sea Lord and Chief of Naval Staff, letter May 26, 1952, ref BNS 700/52.

114. NWC, RG27, "British Naval Officer Students at NWC."

115. In September 1945, the navigation branch became a technical division of the Naval Staff under DCNS.

116. NHB, "The Organisation of the Naval Staff," 110–14.

117. NHB, "A Brief Study of the Naval Staff," 2–3.

118. NHB, "The Organisation of the Naval Staff," 118.

119. Ibid., 118, 122.

120. See TNA(Kew), ADM 1/13169: Adm. D. W. Dorling to 1SL, memorandum July 7, 1943, and subsequent minutes and memoranda.

121. TNA(Kew), ADM 1/13169, "U.S. 'Logistics' Organisation," ACS to D of P(Q), memorandum January 25, 1946.

122. NWC, RG 15, Hughes-Hallett, "Naval Logistics in a Future War," 241.

123. Ryan, Paul B., *First Line of Defense,* 9.

124. NARA2, RG143, "Naval Logistics Organization," 4.

125. The departments of the Army, Navy, and Air Force were not changed from executive departments of Cabinet level to military departments within the [U.S.] Department of Defense until 1953.

126. Ballantine, *U.S. Naval Logistics,* 295

Chapter 5. Fleet Sustainability and Its Effect on Auxiliary Ship Design

1. Quoted from "Naval Necessities" (1904) in Adm. Louis Le Bailly, *Old Loves Return,* 61.

2. TNA(Kew), ADM 219/329.

3. NARA2, RG313, "General Appreciation of the Shipping Position."

4. See, for example, NHB, "Navy Estimates 1948–1949": "Naval New Construction and Repair Work for the Navy," 6.

5. This was primarily due to the lack of shipyard workers. See NARA2, RG 313, "Exercise 'Trident' April 1949—Part 1," chap. 1, Tab. 1: "British Flag Tonnage (U.K. Colonial and Dominion)," 19. See also, TNA(Kew), ADM 239/489; and TNA(Kew), ADM 205/69: "Maritime Policy as it affects Exercise 'Trident,'" Fraser, First Sea Lord, September 14, 1948.

6. NARA2, RG313, "Exercise 'Trident' April 1949—Part 1 chap. 1."

7. For example, Britain's annual shipbuilding capacity in 1945 was 3 million tons; this was expected to halve by 1957. See NARA2, RG313, "General Appreciation of the Shipping Position," item 9.

8. NARA2, RG313, "Exercise 'Trident' April 1949—Part 1 chap. 1, tab. 11, "World Merchant Shipping Tonnage," 20.

9. NARA2, RG218, "Merchant Shipping Requirements and Availability," 5.

10. Friedman, *Postwar Naval Revolution*, apx. III: "World Wide Docking Facilities," DNC Department Admiralty, DNC Papers NMM, "Exercise Trident: Wartime Lessons Learned and Future Ideas 1948," sec. 6.

11. TNA(Kew), ADM 116/5535: Minute, DOD, Admiralty, November 16, 1945.

12. TNA(Kew), CAB 131/2.

13. Tupper Carey, "Fuelling at Sea," 382.

14. TNA(Kew), ADM 167/124: "Composition of Post-War Navy," Paper B435, September 12, 1945.

15. Tupper Carey, "Fuelling at Sea," 384.

16. MoD(N), *War with Japan*, 203; Sigwart, "Royal Fleet Auxiliary," 12.

17. An example of this British concern is found in AL, Admiralty, BR67 (2), "Admiralty Manual of Seamanship, Vol. II," 1951, 383.

18. TNA(Kew), ADM 1/19248: "Objects of the Fleet Train," "Logistic Support of a Fleet Engaged in Ocean Warfare Fleet," Enclosure No. 4.

19. Ibid., apx. A and B.

20. TNA(Kew), ADM 1/19248: "Commander Fleet Train Report on Replenishment at Sea," April 26, 1946. See also TNA(Kew), ADM 199/1766: "U.S. Naval Liaison Officer Report," Vol. 2, apx. T.

21. TNA(Kew), ADM 1/19248: "Admiralty Comments concerning Recommendations," "Logistic Support of a Fleet Engaged in Ocean Warfare," Commodore BPF Fleet Train Memorandum, April 26, 1946.

22. TNA(Kew), ADM 116/5824: "re: Appreciation Report dated April 8, 1947," R. D. Watson, D of P memorandum to 5SL, PD/OL022/47, February 5, 1951.

23. The arguments are well presented by Rear Adm. C. C. Hughes-Hallett, who was the first holder of the new post called the Directorate of Administrative Planning. See Hughes-Hallett, "Naval Logistics in a Future War."

24. For example, see Spruance " Victory in the Pacific," in particular his response regarding the future need for mobile support squadrons.

25. Furer, *Administration of the Naval Department*, 709–10.

26. NWC, Ms. Coll., Furer to Eccles, letter August 31, 1953.

27. Furer, *Administration of the Naval Department*, 713.

28. NWC, Ms. Coll., Eccles, "Pacific Logistics," 17.

29. NWC, Ms. Coll., Eccles, "Mobile Support versus Overseas Base Support."

30. NWC, Ms. Coll. Eccles, "Notes on the Logistic History of the Korean War."

31. *Farragut*, *Gearing*, and *Fletcher* class figures vary. Derived from NARA2, RG143, "War Service Fuel Consumption of U.S. Naval Surface Vessels," FTP218 Tab. 411A, 412A, and 414A, Navpers 91085.

32. These were 13, 8, and 11 days, respectively. See also USNHC, "NWIP 11–22 Fuel Consumption and Endurance Data."

33. Ibid.

34. NMM, MS 83/158, "TF37 projected daily fuel consumption."

35. See NARA2, RG313, "Exercise 'Trident' April 1949"—Part 1: Chapter 3, Part II, Annex 1, "Ship and Aviation Fuel Ratio," 105.

36. Tupper Carey, "Fuelling at Sea," 384. The issue of conflicting priorities of endurance and war-fighting effectiveness was also examined by Black, "Fuelling at Sea," 134.

37. Eccles, *Logistics in the National Defense*, 143.

38. TNA(Kew), ADM 1/19983: Minute, DTSD, June 5, 1950.

39. TNA(Kew), ADM 219/304, para. 23. See also TNA(Kew), ADM 1/24432. Conventional USN postwar thinking was that most combatants were self-sufficient for sixty to ninety days while refrigerated provisions were expected to be exhausted within two to three weeks. See NWC, RG15, Webber, "Capabilities of Logistics Support Force." The proposed unrefueled range of the Royal Navy's 7,200-ton Type 45 Destroyers currently being built, will be about 7,000 miles cruising at 18 knots. See Scott, "Cost and Capability."

40. TNA(Kew), ADM 219/304.

41. Ibid.

42. TNA(Kew), ADM 116/5824: "Appreciation Report"; D of P to 5SL, April 8, 1947, PD/OL022/47.

43. Tupper Carey, "Fuelling at Sea," 382.

44. This was achieved during trials with HMS *Bulawayo*, described in chapter 7.

45. See Llewellyn-Jones, *The Royal Navy and Anti-submarine Warfare, 1917–49* for an incisive appreciation of how this new technology affected postwar ASW doctrine.

46. NHB, "Navy Estimates 1950–51," 3.

47. NL, "Shipbuilding Program FY 1951–1960," 779, 781.

48. NHB, "The Problems Involved in Designing an RFA Tanker," 3.

49. Ibid., 5.

50. NL, "Composition and Costs of Reserve Fleet," Serial 4/49, 392.

51. TNA(Kew), ADM 199/1457: "Analysis: Logistic Lessons," "C-in-C BPF and Eastern Fleet War Diaries 1943–1946," sec. II.

52. Ibid., "Staff Requirements for Ships," (b), March 15, 1946, part III, sec. II.

53. TNA(Kew), ADM 199/118: "Status Report, September 1946." Approval had initially been sought from the Admiralty Board in 1945 for two fast tankers that, when not deployed with the fleet, would be available to undertake admiralty freighting between depots but not under commercial charter. No further progress was made at the time. See TNA (Kew), ADM 167/124: "Paper B403 New Construction Programme 1945," item 31.

54. Black, "Fuelling at Sea," 139.

55. NHB, "Navy Estimates 1950–51": "New Construction and Repair," 6.

56. Known as Section 40.

57. TNA(Kew), ADM 1/19248: Minute, (u.d.), DNC and apx. H.

58. TNA(Kew), ADM 1/19983: Minute, D of S, May 22, 1950.

59. This was called the Ministry of War Transport (MOWT) during World War II.

60. TNA(Kew), ADM 1/19248: "Admiralty Comments concerning Recommendations by Commodore BPF Fleet Train Memorandum," April 26, 1946.

61. Black, "Fuelling at Sea," 141–43.

62. Hughes-Hallett, "Naval Logistics in a Future War," 238.

63. NHB, "The Problems Involved in Designing an RFA Tanker," 2.

64. The complement of British tankers was generally only 20 percent to 40 percent of U.S. Navy oilers; TNA(Kew), ADM 1/23431. See also, TNA(Kew), ADM 199/1756: RAFT, "Re Oiling at Sea 1945–46," sec. 2, "Report on U.S. methods re USS *Platte*."

65. NHB, "The Problems Involved in Designing an RFA Tanker,"2–3.

66. Wildenberg, *Gray Steel*, 59, 65, 66.

67. NHB, "The Problems Involved in Designing an RFA Tanker," 9, 11.

68. TNA(Kew), ADM 1/19248: Memorandum "Repair and Maintenance Facilities Afloat," sec. H, apx. B, "Logistics Support Group or Service Squadron," RAFT April 26, 1946.

69. TNA(Kew), ADM 1/19248: "Objects of the Fleet Train," "Logistic Support of a Fleet Engaged in Ocean Warfare," apx. H, encl. no. 4.

70. TNA(Kew), MT 40/127.

71. TNA(Kew), ADM 1/19248: D of P (Q) docket, July 5, 1946.

72. TNA(Kew), ADM 1/26329: "Review of Naval Policy SMBA 4346 Working Party 3 Fleet Train."

73. TNA(Kew), ADM 1/19248: "Objects of the Fleet Train."

74. NHB, "The Problems Involved in Designing an RFA Tanker," 2.

75. Tupper Carey, "Fuelling at Sea," 384–85.

76. These plans eventually evolved into the new *Tide*-class tankers built in 1955.

77. TNA(Kew), ADM 116/5727: "8th New Construction Programme 1949–1950," PD 06/48, 3.

78. NWC, RG15, Pare, "Mobile Fleet Support," 1948.

79. TNA (Kew), ADM 1/27143: "RFA Additions Conversions since the War," Memorandum for File, April 22, 1955.

80. NHB, "The Problems Involved in Designing an RFA Tanker," 1.

81. Wildenberg, *Gray Steel*, 207.

82. NWC, RG15, Pare, "Mobile Fleet Support," 1947, 19–20.

83. NL, "Shipbuilding Program FY 1951–1960," 800.

84. Ibid., 733. In fact, thirty were transferred, see chapter 6.

85. Ibid., 802.

86. The rest were thirty-eight slow tankers (mentioned earlier) and ninety-seven passenger/transports. See NARA2, RG218: "Merchant Shipping Requirements and Availability," 5.

87. Ibid., 4, 6.

88. TNA(Kew), ADM 1/26858: "Ship Designs BAD 1687/47," ACNS, June 15, 1948, item 34.

89. See, for example, TNA(Kew), ADM 1/24626.

90. NL, "Shipbuilding Program FY 1951–1960: Ship Design," 514–15.

91. Ibid.

92. NARA2, RG218, "Review of Loss Factors and Mobilization Requirements."

93. Wildenberg, *Gray Steel*, 223.

94. Field, *History of UN Naval Operations*, 404.

95. TNA(Kew), ADM 239/439.

Chapter 6. Strategic Mobilization

1. NARA2, RG38, "Statement to Appropriations Committee," July 3, 1945, Box 4, 2.

2. *New York Times*, June 2, 1946.

3. NARA2, RG38, "Organization of Major Combatant Types less Submarines," Box 3.

4. Madsen, *Forgotten Fleet*, 12.

5. Eichelberger, "The Navy's Post-war Headache."

6. NARA2, RG38, "Statement of VCNO before the Committee on Appropriations," September 1945, "Summary BuShips maintenance, repair and fuel and transportation costs."

7. Palmer, *Origins of the Maritime Strategy*, 39.

8. Grove, *Vanguard to Trident*, 54–56.

9. CAB 131/1; see also, TNA(Kew), ADM 167/124: "Composition of the Post-war Navy," Paper B435, September 12, 1945.

10. TNA(Kew), ADM 167/124: "The Post-war Navy and the Policy Governing its Composition," Paper B424, July 17, 1945," 208.

11. According to Dr. Norman Friedman, Britain's defense budget in 1948 was $3.6 billion, or 10.3 percent of total GNP (35 billion), whereas the U.S. defense budget was $9.7 billion, or 3.8 percent of total GNP of $257.6 billion. See Friedman, *Postwar Naval Revolution*, 14.

12. TNA(Kew), ADM 167/124: "Composition of Post-war Navy," Paper B435, September 12, 1945, "Annex II Composition of Empire Navy in Peace."

13. TNA(Kew), ADM 167/124: "Post-war Navy and the Policy Governing its Composition," Paper B424, July 17, 1945, sec. III and sec. 25, 27, 28, 209, 214, September 12, 1945.

14. Cope, "Fighting Ships on the Leash," 165.

15. Adm. Robert B. Carney, deputy CNO (Logistics) [1946–1950], quoted in NARA2, RG143, "Navy Logistics and Logistic Planning," Box 7.

16. NWC, RG15, Lutes, *Logistics in World War II*, 244.

17. A typical example of an American perspective on war planning can be found in IC(L), Ruehlow, "The Interdependency of Logistic and Strategic Planning," a term paper for the Industrial College of the Armed Forces in 1954.

18. NARA2, RG38, "NBM-1 Navy Basic Mobilization Plan," June 1947, para. 1101/2 and 1105/6, Box 39.

19. NARA2, RG38, "NBM-1": Letter of Promulgation, CNO, May 9, 1947.

20. NARA2, RG38, "NBM-1," para. 2108.

21. NL, "Composition and Costs of Reserve Fleet," Serial 316: "USN General Board Hearings," March 31, 1948, 183 and 200.

22. 126 capital ships, 710 other warships, 689 amphibious and landing craft, 268 fleet train, and 189 yard and district craft.

23. Three type examples are chosen to reflect typical mobile logistic support replenishment ships: thirteen AE (ammunition), one AK (stores issue), and two AO (oiler).

24. Within thirty months from mobilization, the "New Build" target was sixteen AO, two AE, and six AK; "Conversions" were fifty fleet AO, twenty-eight AE, and twenty-eight AKS. See NARA2, RG38, "NBM-1," para. 2221 and 2231.

25. NARA2, RG38, "NBM-1," para. 1109.

26. NL, "Composition and Costs of Reserve Fleet," Serial 316: Rear Admiral Wheelock, BuShips, "USN General Board Hearings," March 31, 1948, 200.

27. NL, "Composition and Costs of Reserve Fleet," Serial 4/49: Rear Admiral Wheelock, BuShips, "USN General Board Hearings," May 27, 1949, 391.

28. NARA2, RG 38, NBL-NTS-2, para. 4023, Box 31.

29. NARA2, RG38, "NBM-1," para. 2501–2.

30. NARA2, RG 38, "NBM-1A Navy Basic Mobilization Plan," Box 39, para. 1108.

31. NARA2, RG38, "NBM-1," para. 1201d; NARA2, RG 38, "NBM-1A," para. 1202a.

32. Dyer, *Naval Logistics*, 88.

33. NARA2, RG143, "Logistic Reference Data." The British equivalent, "APM 307 Logistic Planning Data," was first published in 1952.

34. NARA2, RG38, "NBL-2 Basic Logistic Plan Part II Mobilization," Box 31.

35. NARA2, RG143, "Navy Logistics and Logistics Planning," Box 7.

36. NARA2, RG38, "NBM-1A," apx.

37. "NBL-2": "New Construction and Conversion Program, 1951, Mobilization Fleet Replenishment," part III–II, 14.

38. Wildenberg, *Gray Steel*, 221.

39. An example of a powerful working party would be the Way Ahead Board Committee, which recommended, among other things, the wind-down of the Reserve Fleet. See TNA(Kew), ADM 1/27460.

40. TNA(Kew), ADM 167/124: "Composition of the Post-war Navy," Paper B435, September 12, 1945; and TNA(Kew), ADM 167/124: "Post-War Navy and Policy Governing its Composition," Paper B424, July 17, 1945.

41. Grove, *Vanguard to Trident*, 47–51.

42. Murfett, *In Jeopardy*, 92.

43. TNA(Kew), ADM 205/83, and TNA(Kew), ADM 205/84.

44. TNA(Kew), ADM 116/5864: Memorandum, "Disposal of Ships," VCNO to 1SL, May 16, 1950.

45. See, for example, TNA(Kew), ADM 239/409, or TNA(Kew), ADM 1/24432.

46. TNA(Kew), ADM 116/5724: Memorandum, "Defence Policy: Improvement in Date of Readiness Forces," DCNS, April 10, 1948.

47. Rodger, *Safeguard of the Sea*, 232.

48. Pugh, *Cost of Seapower*, 335–38.

49. NWC, RG15, Sigel, "Mobilizing the Reserve Fleets."

50. Cope, "Fighting Ships on the Leash"; Madsen, *Forgotten Fleet*, 7.

51. Quoted in NWC, RG15, Sigel, "Mobilizing the Reserve Fleets," 4.

52. Sumida, "British Naval Operational Logistics 1914–1918," 449.

53. Ibid., 450.

54. "Spindrift," 147–48.

55. Quoted in NWC, RG15, Sigel, "Mobilizing the Reserve Fleets," 6.

56. According to BuShips, the cost of retaining ships in inactive status was $10.92

million for 709 combatants, 1,182 auxiliaries, and 1,663 craft (total 3,554, which was higher than the 2,255 identified in Demobilization Basic Post-war Plan No 2. See NARA2, RG38, "Statement of VCNO to Appropriations Committee of House of Representatives," July 3, 1945, "Cost of Ships Shown in Demobilization Plan 2 BuShips' March 10, 1945," and "Comparison of Number of Vessels in Proposed Navy Basic Post-War Plan No.1," April 6, 1945, serial 028503.

57. NL, "Composition and Costs of Reserve Fleet," Serial 316," 179.

58. NL, "Composition and Costs of Reserve Fleet," Serial 4/49, 354.

59. NL, "Composition and Costs of Reserve Fleet," Serial 316, 166.

60. Boston; New London, Connecticut; Bayonne, New Jersey; Philadelphia; Hampton Roads/Norfolk; Charleston, South Carolina; St John's River, Florida; Orange, Texas; Bremerton and Tongue Point, Oregon; and Mare Island, San Diego, Hunters Point, and Long Beach, California. NARA2, RG38, "Statement of VCNO before the Committee on Appropriations" September 1945, 9.

61. Madsen, *Forgotten Fleet*, 13–14.

62. NL, "Composition and Costs of Reserve Fleet," Serial 316, 148.

63. Gibson and Donovan, *The Abandoned Ocean*, 170.

64. Wildenberg, *Gray Steel*, 217.

65. Gibson and Donovan, *The Abandoned Ocean*, 170; Bryan and Sparks, "The National Defense Reserve Fleet," 39.

66. NARA2, RG38, "NBL-NTS-2 Mobilization Logistic Plan I-48 (Transportation), Box 31, para. 4011 and 4031.

67. Ibid., paragraph 4011 and 4031–33, and part IV, sec. 4, apx. II, note 1.

68. In all Admiralty fleet orders regarding the Reserve Fleet, the first line always carried the mantra "The object of the Reserve Fleet is to provide for the maintenance of ships (or craft) laid up." TNA(Kew), ADM 1/23666: AFO 4080 (48),3636 (49), 3556 (50), 2786 (51), and 2834 (53), "Reserve Fleet–Administration of Ships in, or reducing to, Reserve-Preparation of Ships Prior to Acceptance into Reserve."

69. *New York Times*, September 4, 1948, quoted in "British 'Ghost Fleet' Is Very Much Alive," USNI *Proceedings* no. 549 (November 1948): 1447.

70. Waymouth, "The Reserve Fleet Today," 150.

71. TNA(Kew), CAB 131/1, DO (46)97.

72. Hartlepools, Cardiff, Penarth, Barrow, Great Harbour, Greenock, Lisahally, Llanelly, and Northumberland Dock. TNA(Kew), ADM 1/25569: Report, FOCRF Report No 22, 30/3, January 14, 1954.

73. NL, "Composition and Costs of Reserve Fleet," Serial 4/49, 383; NL, "Composition and Costs of Reserve Fleet," Serial 316, 167 and 171.

74. NARA2, RG313, "Emergency Operation Plan Op Plan 2-47," Box 93.

75. Originally constituted in 1917 but wound up in 1950, the General Board comprised a group of senior officers tasked with advising the Secretary of the Navy on major issues. The reason for initiating the four sessions spread over two years was that whenever the secretary flew back to his New Hampshire home from Washington, D.C., he became agitated by the sight of huge concentrations of reserve ships vulnerable to potential attack. The author is particularly grateful to Dr. Norman Friedman for bringing the existence of these hearings to his attention.

76. TNA(Kew), ADM 1/24477: Minutes of meeting, "Administration and Organisation of the Reserve Fleet," DCNS, May 26, 1953. Using the carrier HMS *Indomi-*

table as an example, it would be very difficult to move her main machinery within six months, if unused; in twelve months, it would require wholesale renewals, making her "a paper unit only."

77. TNA(Kew), ADM 1/23577; Cope, "Fighting Ships on the Leash," 162–64; and Madsen, *Forgotten Fleet*, 75.

78. Cole, "Fighting Ships on the Leash," 164.

79. NHB, "Navy Estimates 1952–53," Statement of the First Lord of the Admiralty, Cmd.8476, "Modernisations and Conversions," 7.

80. Waymouth, "The Reserve Fleet," 150.

81. TNA(Kew), ADM 1/23577. See, for example, the numerous reports written by commanding officers of various destroyers in 3rd Destroyer Flotilla to the Flag Officer Destroyers Mediterranean August–December 1949.

82. NL, "Composition and Costs of Reserve Fleet," Serial 4/49, 357–58, 389–90.

83. NBM-1A, paragraphs 2201–15.

84. NL, "Composition and Costs of Reserve Fleet," Serial 316, 163.

85. NL, "Composition and Costs of Reserve Fleet," Serial 4/49, 396 and 404.

86. TNA(Kew), ADM 116/6231: Minute, D of P, Mo2227/51, re Folder C-in-C FES 916/FES/1190/31/1," August 13, 1951, "Report of Experience in Korean Operations January to June 1951."

87. TNA(Kew), ADM 116/6230: Minute, D of P, "Logistics," part iv, sec. 111, apx. X, "Supply at Sea," October 18, 1951.

88. Field, *History of UN Naval Operations*, 78.

89. NWC, Ms. Coll., "Notes on The Logistic History of the Korean War."

90. Field, *History of UN Naval Operations*, 78.

91. The underway replenishment took place July 23, 1950, to TF77.

92. Field, *History of UN Naval Operations*, 364.

93. Cole, "Fighting Ships on the Leash," 165.

94. Isenberg, *Shield of the Republic*, 223. See also Sir O. Franks memorandum from the British Embassy, Washington, D.C., to the Foreign Office London, attaching report by Capt. John Holmes RN: TNA(Kew), FO371/90987: "Section 1, Jan–June 1950 . . . Section 2, June–December 1950."

95. NWC, RG15, Denebrink, "Logistic Support Korean Operations," 3.

96. NHB, "Navy Estimates 1948–49," Cmd. 7337; NHB, "Navy Estimates 1949–50," Cmd. 7632.

97. Cagle and Manson, *Sea War in Korea*, 32, 35.

98. NHB, "The Royal Navy—Incidents since 1945."

99. NHB, Admiralty Pink Lists June 20, 1950; Reserve figures derived from Operational/Supplementary/Extended categories, "Z" lists, reserve refits, and ships being placed into reserve. Active Fleet includes training ships, active refits, or "non-operational" but excludes foreign-manned or loans to other countries. RFA ships not recorded.

100. As reported in *The Christian Science Monitor*, January 8, 1951, and the *New York Herald Tribune*, September 22, 1948.

101. NHB, Admiralty Pink Lists June 20, 1951; July 1, 1952.

102. NHB, Admiralty Pink Lists June 24, 1946; June 23, 1947; June 30, 1948; June 30, 1949; June 20, 1950; June 26, 1951. Also see TNA(Kew), ADM 1/27143.

103. TNA(Kew), ADM 1/27143.

104. TNA(Kew), ADM 1/27631, Memorandum, D of V, November 1960.

105. *Surf Pioneer* and *Surf Patrol*.

106. NHB, "British Commonwealth Naval Operations, Korea 1950–1953," 299, and apx. J.

107. TNA(Kew), ADM 116/6231: Minute, D of P, Folder C-in-C FES 916/FES/1190/31/1, M02227/51, August 13, 1951. See also TNA(Kew), ADM 116/6230: Minute, D of P(Q), December 5, 1951, "First Report July–December 1950."

108. NL, "Composition and Costs of Reserve Fleet," Serial 316, Admiral Curts (CNO), March 30, 1948, 159.

109. NWC, RG15, Sigel, "Mobilizing the Reserve Fleets."

110. According to BuShips. NL, "Composition and Costs of Reserve Fleet," Serial 316," March 30, 1948, 148, 200.

111. Isenberg, *Shield of the Republic*, 223.

112. NARA2, RG 38, "Statement of VCNO before Committee on Appropriations," September 1945, 8.

113. Isenberg, *Shield of the Republic*, 223–24.

114. Thirty years later, for example, it would cost $500 million to refurbish just one carrier, the USS *Oriskany*. Even taking into account inflation and other mitigating circumstances, the benefit of applying replacement values to reserve ships was no longer so transparent. A similar conclusion was reached with America's ageing auxiliary fleet too, most of which had to be scrapped after 1956.

115. NARA2, RG218, "Merchant Shipping Requirements for National Defense": Memorandum, Fleet Adm. William D. Leahy USN, Chief of Staff to C-in-C of the Armed Forces, to Secretary of Defense, November 21, 1947, "Joint Chiefs of Staff Central Decimal File 1948–56."

116. Escort carriers completed in 1946 were immediately mothballed in Tacoma but never left the reserve fleet until stricken in 1970–71, Madsen, *Forgotten Fleet*, 158.

117. NL, "Composition and Costs of Reserve Fleet," Serial 316, March 31, 1948, 148, 200. See also NARA2, RG38, "Statement of VCNO before Appropriations Committee of the House of Representatives," July 3, 1945, 2–3.

118. As reported in *Christian Science Monitor*, July 15, 1949, the manpower saved on one battleship, for example, could keep three flotillas of antisubmarine ships at sea.

119. Grove, *Vanguard to Trident*, 82–85, 95–96.

120. Ibid., 209

Chapter 7. Fleet Mobility

1. NARA2, RG38, "Organization of Major Combatant Types less Submarines."

2. "Historical Note," "Records of the Reserve Fleet 1947–1960," USNHC, March 1, 2005, http://www.history.navy.mil/branches/nhcorg10.htm.

3. NARA2, RG143, "Naval Logistics Organization," 79, 86–89.

4. USNHC, "Reports of Operations and Condition of Command July 1, 1949, to July 30, 1950."

5. USNHC, "Reports of Operations and Condition of Command July 1, 1948, to July 30, 1949."

6. Baer, *The U.S. Navy 1890–1990*, 284.

7. LHCMA, MF868: sec. 2, "Special Cruises and Operations."

8. USNHC, "Reports of Operations and Condition of Command July 1, 1949, to July 30, 1950."

9. USNHC, "Reports of Operations and Condition of Command June 14, 1952, to July 1, 1953."

10. NARA2, RG313, "Fleet Employment Last Half Fiscal Year 1949 and Fiscal Year 1950," CNO to CinCLant, CinCPac, CinCNELM, Serial 028p33, March 18, 1949, Box 525.

11. USNHC, "Quarterly Summary of U.S. Naval Forces Eastern Atlantic and Mediterranean July 1 to October 1, 1947," October 28, 1947, sect. 5, "Problems of Fuel Supply for the Mediterranean Fleet"; USNHC, "Quarterly Summary of U.S. Naval Forces Eastern Atlantic and Mediterranean October 1, 1947–March 31, 1948," May 12, 1948, sec. VI, "Supply of POL Stocks."

12. Hayes, "The Navy's Task Force," *Ordnance*, 2.

13. Ibid., 2–3.

14. NARA2, RG143, "Naval Logistics Organization," 79.

15. Ibid., 82.

16. NWC, Ms. Coll., "Informal Notes on Logistics Problems."

17. *Manchester Guardian*, October 20, 1947, quoted in "Professional Notes: Great Britain," USNI *Proceedings*, no. 539 (January 1948): 108.

18. Friedman, *Postwar Naval Revolution*, 41.

19. TNA(Kew), ADM 239/565: "Tactical Organisation of the Fleet," M/TSD 155/48, January 29, 1949, 93.

20. TNA(Kew), ADM 239/565: "Report on Combined Fleet Exercise 1949."

21. Field, *History of UN Naval Operations*, 463.

22. TNA(Kew), ADM 205/69: Memorandum, C-in-C Mediterranean Sir Arthur Power to Admiral of the Fleet Lord Fraser, SP/A9/1213E, December 21, 1948; memorandum 1SL to C-in-C Mediterranean Sir Arthur Power, 917/1SL25/48, January 5, 1949.

23. Dyer, *Naval Logistics*, 251.

24. NWC, Ms. Coll., Memorandum, Brown to Acworth.

25. Ibid.

26. Le Bailly, Vice Adm. Sir Louis, *From Fisher to the Falklands*, 95.

27. NWC, Ms. Coll., Letter, Acworth to Brown and Eccles; NWC, Ms. Coll., Memorandum, Brown to Acworth.

28. Quoted in Friedman, *Postwar Naval Revolution*, apx. III: "The Necessity for Extended Sea Trials or Special Cruises in Peacetime under War Conditions in Heavy Weather, Arctic and Tropical Conditions," DNC Department Admiralty, DNC Papers NMM, "Exercise Trident: Wartime Lessons Learned and Future Ideas 1948," sec. 2.

29. MoD(N), *War with Japan*, 205; Humble, *Fraser of North Cape*, 271; Smith *Task Force 57*, 116–17; Gray, *Operation Pacific*, 248–51; TNA(Kew), ADM 116/5535, 136.

30. ADM 199/1766, sec. 11, 7.

31. NWC, RG27, Pare to Eccles, March 28, 1947.

32. TNA(Kew), ADM 1/26858, 77.

33. TNA(Kew), ADM 199/118: "September 1946 status report."

34. See, for example, TNA(Kew), ADM 239/565: "Convoy Defence Exercise (LJX 123)," conducted in June 1948.

35. Ibid.: "Fleet Exercise Analysis," June 1948, 54; and TNA(Kew), ADM 239/143.

36. TNA(Kew), ADM 239/565: "Report on Exercise SUNRISE: Tactical Problems 12 & 15," para. 152, CB 03016/49, 62. However, the *London Times* reported on Sep-

tember 26, 1947, the cancellation was due to "the urgent need for economy in the consumption of fuel oil."

37. TNA(Kew), ADM 239/565, para.62. See also TNA(Kew), ADM 219/335.

38. TNA(Kew), ADM 239/565: "Report on Combined Fleet Exercise 1949," para. 195–204, 227.

39. Ibid., para. 230.

40. TNA(Kew), ADM 1/24041.

41. TNA(Kew), ADM 1/24041: Memorandum, Adm. Sir George Creasey, C-in-C Home Fleet to the Secretary Admiralty, December 11, 1952, HF 1425/2013/2.

42. NARA2, RG313, "Report of Atlantic Fleet Tactical Exercises February–March 1947," Memorandum, Blandy to CNO, April 25, 1947.

43. NARA2, RG313, "Fleet Employment Last Half Fiscal Year 1949, and Fiscal Year 1950," Memorandum, CNO to CinCLant, CinCPac, CinCNELM, Serial 028p33, March 18, 1949, Box 525.

44. LHCMA, MF868, "Special Cruises and Operations," sec. 2.

45. USNHC, "Quarterly Summary of U.S. Naval Forces Eastern Atlantic and Mediterranean, July 1 to October 1, 1947, sec. 8, "Midshipmen's Practice Cruise," October 28, 1947.

46. NARA2, RG313, "Report on Midshipman Practice Cruise."

47. NARA2, RG313, "Additional Type AE Vessel—Request for."

48. NARA2, RG313, "Report of Atlantic Fleet Tactical Exercises February–March 1947," Commander in Chief U.S. Atlantic Fleet, Memorandum, Blandy to ComServLant, April 17, 1948.

49. NARA2, RG313, "Emergency Operation Plan," Baker to CinCLantFlt, January 9, 1948.

50. NWC, RG15, Pare, "Mobile Fleet Support," 1948.

51. NWC, Ms. Coll., "Some Considerations of Re-supply at Sea Operations."

52. USNHC, "Reports of Operations and Condition of Command July 1, 1948 to July 30, 1949," "Sixth Task Fleet," sec. 3, NRS 610.

53. NARA2, RG313, "Report of Atlantic Fleet Tactical Exercises February–March 1947."

54. Ibid., "Comments and Recommendations" (2) "Areas and Schedules," encl. B.

55. NARA2, RG313, "Report of Atlantic Fleet Tactical Exercises February–March 1947," Memorandum, Blandy to CNO April 25, 1947.

56. NARA2, RG143, "Report U.S. Atlantic Fleet 2nd Task Fleet Replenishment at Sea Exercises," 1.

57. NARA2, RG313, "Report of Atlantic Fleet Tactical Exercises February–March 1947," Memorandum, Blandy to CNO, April 25, 1947, item 5(b) (1).

58. NARA2, RG143, "Report U.S. Atlantic Fleet 2nd Task Fleet Replenishment at Sea Exercises," 12–14.

59. TNA(Kew), ADM 1/23434: Memorandum, FO2FE to Admiralty, "Oiling At Sea," February 21, 1952.

60. TNA(Kew), ADM 1/24039: "Replenishment at Sea Report," Master of RFA *Olna*, September 10–24, 1952.

61. TNA(Kew), ADM 1/24039: Memorandum, "Principle Lessons of Exercise MAINBRACE—Fleet Replenishment Tankers," Director TSD, December 11, 1952, TSD 4333/52.

62. TNA(Kew), ADM 1/24039: Comments by ComServRonTWO, "Review of Replenishment at Sea: Compilation of Reports Received on Exercise MAINBRACE."

63. TNA(Kew), ADM 1/24039: S. 217 "Fuelling Reports," Masters of RFA *Olna*, RFA *Wave Prince*, and RFA *Wave Premier*.

64. TNA(Kew), ADM 1/23452: Lieutenant Commander Bullar of HMS *Mercury* and Lieutenant Commander Seely of HMS *Dryad*, Report to C-in-C Home Fleet, October 6, 1952, 1. See also TNA(Kew), ADM 1/24039 and TNA(Kew), ADM 1/24041.

65. TNA(Kew), ADM 1/23452, Annex A , "General" and (b).

66. Ibid., Summary Features (i), 1.

67. Hall, "Naval Exercises of 1951," 107–8.

68. NHB, "Explanatory Statement on the Navy Estimates 1957–1958," "Training and Combined Exercises."

69. Hall, "Naval Exercises of 1951," 111; see also, TNA(Kew), ADM 1/20719.

70. An interesting account of the history of the *Nordmark*/HMS *Bulawayo* can be found in Jones, *Under Three Flags*.

71. TNA(Kew), ADM 226/53: Memorandum, January 13, 1948, Superintendent, Admiralty Experimental Works Haslar, "Report No. 3/48" to DNC Bath and others. An assessment of the trials from the viewpoint of the Director of Naval Constructor's Department can be found in NHB, Crawford, "Replenishment at Sea."

72. TNA(Kew), ADM 1/21061: Report No. 13AR, December 12, 1947, Capt. K. A. Short to Flag Officer Commanding 2nd Cruiser Squadron.

73. See also AL, Admiralty, BR67 (2) "Admiralty Manual of Seamanship, Volume II," 1951, 468.

74. TNA(Kew), ADM 226/53; TNA(Kew), ADM 234/393; TNA(Kew), ADM 234/394; and TNA(Kew), ADM 234/395.

75. TNA(Kew), ADM 1/21061: "Conduct of Trials: Report No 13AR, December 12, 1947."

76. NWC, RG4, "Logistic Planning Factors: Replenishment at Sea."

77. TNA(Kew), ADM 1/21061.

78. TNA(Kew), ADM 281/123: "Miscellaneous 3 Replenishment At Sea," sec. IX.

79. TNA(Kew), ADM 116/6230: "Supply at Sea," part iv, sec. 111, "Logistics."

80. Dictionary of American Naval Fighting Ships, http://www.hazegray.org/danfs/auxil/aor110.htm, accessed August 15, 2005.

81. Wildenberg, *Gray Steel*, 212.

82. NWC(L), "Underway Replenishment of Naval Ships," 11–13.

83. NWC, RG27, Pare to Eccles, March 28, 1947. Captain Pare, who by 1947 was commander of Service Squadron 2 of the U.S. Atlantic Fleet during the Fleet Exercises mentioned earlier in the chapter, was invited by the NWC to help design these programs to ensure their authenticity.

84. NWC, RG4, "Logistic Planning Factors," sec. 1B, Box 231.

85. NWC, RG27, Pare to Eccles, March 28, 1947.

86. TNA(Kew), ADM 1/24039: "Syndicate Problem-Replenishment," Royal Naval Tactical School, Woolwich, u.d. [1952].

87. USNHC, "Presentation and Scope in the Naval Warfare Publications."

88. NHB, "The Fighting Instructions," CB04487: TSD Division Admiralty, chap. VII, "Bases," and chap IX, "Cruising," sec. V, "The Fleet Train and Replenishment At Sea."

89. TNA(Kew), ADM 239/144: "Logistics," TSD Division Admiralty, CB03016/48, chap. 2.

90. TNA(Kew), ADM 239/384: Short title FXOB Section B.4 "Exercise Orders for Replenishment at Sea." See also TNA(Kew), ADM 239/145: CB03016/51.

91. For example, NMM, "Naval Strategy in the Pacific February 1943 to August 1945."

92. This replaced appendix 4 of USNHC, "USF-10A Current Tactical Orders and Doctrine 1944."

93. USNHC, "USF-13 Logistic Support Force Operating Instructions."

94. NARA2, RG143, "USF-83 Fueling and Replenishment at Sea."

95. NHB, BSR 493: Pacific Fleet War Orders—Part III, "Fleet Train," rev. July 1, 1945, promulgated by RAFT FT 2610/438.

96. No copy of this document has been found by the author despite an extensive search.

97. TNA(Kew), ADM 116/6231: "Replenishment at Sea-Fuelling," Far East Fleet Memoranda, February 1, 1952, FEFM 29/51 (rev.).

98. TNA(Kew), ADM 234/393: BR1742 (52).

99. See TNA(Kew), ADM 234/394 and TNA(Kew), ADM 234/395. See also TNA(Kew), ADM 116/6231: "Fourth Report," "Report of Experience in Korean Operations, July 1, 1952–April 30, 1953," FO2FE, para. 11.

100. USNHC, "NWP-38 Replenishment at Sea."

101. NARA2, RG38, ATP-16 "Replenishment at Sea."

102. See "Sundry Unclassified Naval Documents," in ATP-16D (Navy), "Replenishment at Sea" (December 2001). The modern equivalent of NWP-38, which remains applicable only to U.S. Navy replenishment operations, is NWP4–01.4, the full title of which can be found in NWC(L) "NWP4–01.4 Underway Replenishment."

103. NARA2, RG143, "Glossary of Logistics."

104. USNHC, "Naval Logistics Manual," Dupre, Box 420.

105. TNA(Kew), ADM 1/24432: "APM307 Logistic Planning Data."

106. Black, "Fuelling at Sea," 133–51.

107. Lombe, "The Royal Navy in the Pacific," 335; Trimingham, "The Composition and Design of our Post-War Fleet," 73 ; Hughes-Hallett, "Naval Logistics in a Future War," 232–45; Tupper Carey, "Fuelling at Sea," 382–86.

108. NHB, BSR 493, "History of the Fleet Train," Vol. 1; NHB, BSR 453, "History of the Fleet Train," Vol. 2; NHB, BSR 477, "History of the Fleet Train," Vol. 3. Although some of this is similar to documents forming Fleet Train histories under TNA(Kew), ADM 199/1766 and TNA(Kew), ADM 199/1769, much of the story, particularly the prewar introduction and some of the appendices, remain unpublished.

109. NHB, BSR 493/453/477, "Introduction."

110. NHB, "The Organisation of the Naval Staff," 115–16.

111. TNA(Kew), ADM 1/26858, item 46.

112. TNA(Kew), ADM 199/1521: Minute, D of P, September 16, 1946, "Service Squadron Ten Logistics Data Okinawa."

113. TNA(Kew), ADM 116/5670: "Minutes of meetings with Naval Staff on furtherance of RN/USN Collaboration held on July 25, 1947, item 6, and on March 22, 1948."

114. TNA(Kew), ADM 116/5670: Minute, Capt. Hall Thompson D of P (Q), "Min-

utes of meeting with Naval Staff on furtherance of RN/USN Collaboration held on April 25, 1947." A number of these meetings were chaired by Capt. S. W. Roskill, N.I.D. (BNLUS).

115. TNA(Kew), ADM 1/23841: Memorandum, Adm. Sir Rhoderick McGrigor, GCB, DSO., First Sea Lord and Chief of Naval Staff, June 4, 1952.

116. TNA(Kew), ADM ADM 1/23841: Letter, Adm. Douglas Pennant, BJSM (Navy Staff), Washington, DC, to McGrigor, May 26, 1952, 700/52. His public position can be gleaned from a speech given at the NWC in 1951. See NWC, RG15, Pennant, "Britain's Place in Global Strategy," May 31, 1951.

117. TNA(Kew), ADM 1/23841: Pennant to McGrigor May 26,1952.

118. Nash, "The Royal Navy in Korea."

119. Field, *A History of UN Naval Operations*, 454.

120. Ibid., 378, 380.

121. See NWC(L), "Underway Replenishment of Naval Ships," 9–10.

122. TNA(Kew), ADM 116/6230: "Administrative Lessons," "Second Report," part IV.

123. NHB, Naval Staff History, BR 1736(54), Korean Operations, 298. See apx. V in this volume.

124. Ibid., 299.

125. NHB, BSR 493: apx. D, "Logistic Support Group Statistics Parts I and II."

126. TNA(Kew), ADM 116/5794: "Korean War Report of Proceedings," July 14–16, 1950, para. 25.

127. TNA(Kew), ADM 1/23434, sec. 5, Capt. (D) HMS *Cossack* November 20, 1951.

128. Ibid.; see also TNA(Kew), ADM 1/21061.

129. TNA(Kew), ADM 116/6231: FEFM 29/51, part 4(B) iv, sec. vi.

130. TNA(Kew), ADM 1/23434: Memorandum, FO2FE to Admiralty, February 21, 1952, "Oiling at Sea."

131. NHB, Naval Staff History, BR 1736(54), Korean Operations, 73.

132. "Replenisher," "What Is Wrong with the RFA?" *Naval Review* Vol. 45 (1957): 308 and 312.

133. TNA(Kew), ADM 116/6231: FEFM 29/51, "Fuelling at Sea" (rev.) 1952, para. 9.

134. TNA(Kew), ADM 116/6230: Memorandum, Rear Admiral Scott-Moncrieff, July 27, 1951, "Second Report: Report of Experience in Korean Operations."

135. Ibid., "Second Report," part II, "Command," para. 67.

136. Ibid., para. 38.

137. TNA(Kew), ADM 116/5794: Report, "Activities at Sasebo Base," sec. 13, Rear Admiral Andrewes, Report No. 11, July 5, 1950.

138. TNA(Kew), ADM 234/394, "Introduction."

Chapter 8. Conclusion

1. Eccles, *Logistics in the National Defense*, 225.

2. NHB, "Explanatory Statement on the Navy Estimates 1956–57," sec. 3, "The Role of the Royal Navy in the Age of Thermo Nuclear Weapons."

3. Ibid.

4. Ibid., sec. 23, "Role of the Royal Navy."

5. Ibid., sec. 28, "Royal Fleet Auxiliaries."

6. Till, *"Seapower,"* 142.

7. Hooper, *Mobility Support and Endurance*, 58.

8. Ibid., 56.

9. Naval Staff Directorate, *British Maritime Doctrine*, 1st Ed., BR1806, 145.

10. Naval Staff Directorate, *British Maritime Doctrine*, 2nd Ed., BR1806, 78–85.

11. See Eccles, *Logistics in the National Defense*, for example, pages 17, 59, 64, 103, 108, 122, 251–58.

12. Naval Staff Directorate, *British Maritime Doctrine*, 2nd Ed., BR1806, 78.

13. Marsh, "Supply Charge at Sea."

Glossary of Replenishment Terms

abeam: Fueling or storing replenishment between ships close aboard.

alongside (of ships): Cruising side by side (or, in sheltered waters, also stationary and touching).

approach time: Time from Romeo (see entry) close-up signal until first line over.

astern fueling: Replenishment to (or from) a ship close astern (or ahead).

avgas: Aviation gasoline for piston aircraft.

bbl: Barrel of fuel oil (approximately 6.7 bbl = 1 long ton)

bight line: Used to support the bight of the hose.

cable: 200 yards.

consolidation: Transfer operations conducted at sea to empty partially loaded auxiliaries before they return to base for reload.

fathom: Distance of six feet.

FFO: Furnace fuel oil (RN).

gunline: Line passed by means of any type of line-throwing gun (RN).

HEAF: Jet aircraft fuel, renamed JP-5 Avcat.

hose line: Line secured by a hose, by which it is passed to receiving ship.

inhaul: Line used to haul a traveling block to the supplying ship.

jackstay: Fueling = a span wire; rearming = highline.

jackstay line: Highline messenger (U.S.); line secured to a jackstay, passed to a receiving ship (U.K.).

jet mix: Mixture of JP-5 and avgas.

JP-5/AVCAT/kerosene: jet aircraft fuel (formerly HEAF).

Logistic Support Force: A USN Task Force (or Group) of fleet auxiliaries screened and supported by combatant ships operating in or near the combat zone equipped to provide logistic replenishment under way to combat Task Forces.

Logistic Support Group: RN term for fleet of auxiliaries and screen operating at or near the combat zone providing replenishment at sea to BPF TF37/57 in 1945.

messenger: Light line used to carry a larger line across.

NSFO: Navy special fuel oil (USN).

outhaul: Line used to haul a traveler block out of the supplying ship.

POL: Petroleum, oil, and lubricants (USN).

replenishment time: From commencement of approach until replenishment operation completed, all gear secured, and battle stations ready for carrying out mission.

Romeo signal: Flag flown by both supplier and receiver at half-mast to indicate readiness to proceed, and then at full-mast when approach has begun for receiver vessel to come alongside.

rope manila: Size by circumference in inches (USN if 1½" or less by thread).

rope wire size: Nominal diameter in inches (USN); circumference in inches (RN).

tactical diameter: The perpendicular distance between the path of a ship on the original course, and the path of a ship when steadied on an apposite course, after having turned through 180 degrees with a constant rudder angle.

towline: Distance line for astern fueling (RN)

tpd: Tons per day.

tph: Tons per hour.

Transfer Rigs

burton method (USN): The receiving and delivering ships each operate a winch and wire to transfer the loads. The receiving ship's suspension point (burton point), wire, and winch act as an extended movable yard of the yard-and-stay rig. The delivering ship's boom, wire, and winch take the part of the stay.

close-in method (USN): Standard method used in fueling between ships. The hose is supported by boom whips and bight lines, which lead from saddles on the hose to booms or other high: projections on one or both ships

double housefall (USN): Two adjacent housefall rigs, employing two housefall blocks shackled together and suspended from a single suspension point on the receiving ship. One housefall rig delivers a loaded net while the other returns an empty one.

double trough: RN term meaning two hoses carried on one rig.

Elwood method (USN): Name changed to span-wire method.

heavy jackstay method (RN): The jackstay line, on the end of which are the jackstay and outhaul, is clipped to the messenger and passed over the water. When secured the jackstay and inhaul are tended by winches on the supply ship. The loads are slung from a block called "the traveler" which is hauled along the jackstay.

highline method (USN): Transfer of light and medium cargo in which a highline between the two ships supports a trolley with cargo hook attached. The load is secured to the cargo hook and moved between ships by means of an inhaul and outhaul line. Tension is maintained on the highline by the supplier ship Standard method for use with destroyers and smaller ships. Normally the highline is wire, but for light loads a manila line is substituted, which is tended by hand or gypsy head.

housefall method (USN): Transferring cargo under way in which the delivering ship operates and tends all transfer winches and whips, thus taking entire control of the load during transit.

light jackstay method (RN): Rope jackstay line normally tended by the supply ship by hand, not winch; used typically for transferring personnel.

modified housefall(USN): Method by which the housefall and highline methods are combined. A trolley block is added to the standard housefall rig that rides on the transfer whip, which then doubles as a highline and outhaul line, thereby keeping the load higher during transfer.

span-wire method (USN): The hose is extended by stretching a single span-wire between the two ships. The hose hangs from trolley blocks that ride along the wire.

Bibliography

Primary Sources

AL—Admiralty Library Ministry Of Defence

Admiralty, BR67 (2) "Admiralty Manual of Seamanship," Vol. II (London: HMSO, 1951).

Admiralty, BR67 (2/51), "Admiralty Manual of Seamanship, Vol. II" (London: HMSO, 1952).

Admiralty, BR68, "Manual of Seamanship, Vol. II" (London: HMSO, 1923).

Admiralty, BR68, "Manual of Seamanship, Vol. II" (London: HMSO, 1932).

Admiralty, BR68, "Manual of Seamanship, Vol. II" (London: HMSO, 1937).

Admiralty, BR103, "Conversion Tables for Admiralty Fuel Oils" (Ottawa: King's Printer, April 1942).

Defence Council, BR67 (2), "Admiralty Manual of Seamanship," Vol. II (London: HMSO, 1967).

IC(L)—Imperial College Library, London

Campbell, Robert D., Frank D. Dorey, Richard E. Murphy. "Concept of a Logistics System," *Naval Research Logistics Quarterly* (Dept. of Navy Office of Naval Research) vol. 4 (June 1957): 101–16.

Carney, Adm. Robert B. (Ret.). "Some General Observations and Experiences in Logistics," *Naval Research Logistics Quarterly* (Dept. of Navy Office of Naval Research), vol. 3 (March & June 1955): 1–9.

Eccles, H. "Logistics: Conditio Sine Qua Non for NATO Defense," *Naval Research Logistics Quarterly* (Dept. of Navy Office of Naval Research), vol. 8 (March 1961): 111–16.

Hayes, Rear Adm. John D. "Logistics the Word," *Naval Research Logistics Quarterly* (Dept. of Navy Office of Naval Research), vol. 1 (September 1954): 200–202.

Henn, LCDR Carl L., Jr. "Multinational Logistics in the Nuclear Age," *Naval Research Logistics Quarterly* (Dept. of Navy Office of Naval Research), vol. 4 (June 1957): 117–29.

Morgenstern, O. "Note on the Formulation of the Theory of Logistics," *Naval Research Logistics Quarterly* (Dept. of Navy Office of Naval Research), vol. 2 (September 1955): 129–36.

Ruehlow, Capt. S. E. "The Interdependency of Logistics and Strategic Planning," *Naval Research Logistics Quarterly* (Dept. of Navy Office of Naval Research), vol. 1 (December 1954): 237–57.

Sachaklian, Col. Harry A. "Risk and Hazard in Logistics Planning," *Naval Research*

Logistics Quarterly (Dept. of Navy Office of Naval Research), vol. 2 (December 1955): 217–24.

St. John, Lt. Col. Lawrence R. "Trends in Logistics," *Naval Research Logistics Quarterly* (Dept. of Navy Office of Naval Research), vol. 1(Sept 1954): 182–89.

Wilson, Capt. A. H., USN. "Improvise or Plan?" *Naval Research Logistics Quarterly* (Dept. of Navy Office of Naval Research), vol. 4 (December 1957): 263–67.

LHCMA—Liddell Hart Centre For Military Archives, King's College, London

MF868, ComNavEu Administrative History 1945–1949. "Semi-Annual Summary of US Naval Forces Eastern Atlantic and Mediterranean, April 1, 1948–September 30, 1948."

MF868, "Special Cruises and Operations," Section 2. "Semi-Annual Summary of US Naval Forces Eastern Atlantic and Mediterranean, April 1, 1948–September 30, 1948."

TNA (Kew)—The National Archives Kew (formerly Public Record Office)

ADM 1. ADMIRALTY AND SECRETARIAT PAPERS

ADM 1/13169, "U.S. and Admiralty Logistics Organizations Comparison, 1943."

ADM 1/19248, "Fleet Train Skeleton Organisation for the Future based off BPF Experience."

ADM 1/19983, "Fleet Train Requirements: Consideration 1946–1951."

ADM 1/20418, "Refuelling HM Ships at Sea Including Aircraft Carriers, Buoyant Hose Method: Reports."

ADM 1/20719, "Home Fleet Exercises: Spring Cruise" (1947).

ADM 1/21061, "Replenishment at Sea Trials Autumn 1947 by HMS *Bulawayo* with Home Fleet."

ADM 1/23431, "Additional Personnel required when employed on Replenishment at Sea" (1952).

ADM 1/23434, "Oiling at Sea: Reports by HMS *Cossack* and Other Ships" (1951–1952).

ADM 1/23443, "Royal Fleet Auxiliary Oiler *Wave Chief*: Report by Master of Experience gained in Korean waters 1951–1953."

ADM 1/23452, "Exercise MAINBRACE: Report on Experience gained in USS *Midway* by RN Liaison Officers" (1952).

ADM 1/23577, Memorandum, FOCRF, "Commissioning Ships from the Reserve," submission 696 RF 277/14/24, July 15, 1953.

ADM 1/23666, "Preparation of Ships for Reserve" (1952).

ADM 1/23841, "Review of Relations between Royal Navy and United States Navy."

ADM 1/24039, "Exercise MAINBRACE—(Fuelling at Sea): Orders and Reports" (1952–1953).

ADM 1/24041, "RFA Wave Premier: Exercise AUTUMN BEAR: Report of Fuelling At Sea."

ADM 1/24432, Drafting of APM 307 "Logistic Planning Data," October 1952.

ADM 1/24477, "Reserve Fleet: Administration and Organisation."

ADM 1/24626, "American Attitude to Co-operation between the USN and RN."

ADM 1/25047, "RN Engineering College: HMS *Thunderer* Schemes of Complement and Formulation of Courses 1945–1954."

ADM 1/25569, "Activities of Reserve Fleet," 1953: Report.
ADM 1/26329, "Composition of Fleet Train: Review of Number of Ships Needed to Support an Active Fleet" (1955).
ADM 1/26858, "RN/USN Standardization: Review by Rear Admiral Schofield."
ADM 1/27143, "History of the RFA Service 1919-1958."
ADM 1/27460, "Abolition of Reserve Fleet Command."
ADM 1/27631, "Concept of Afloat Support," Memorandum, D of V, November 1960.

ADM 53. Admiralty and Ministry of Defence: Ships' Logs

ADM 53/94323, "*Burma* June 30, 1911–October 8, 1911."

ADM 116. Admiralty and Secretariat Cases

ADM 116/5535, "History of the Fleet Train, British Pacific Fleet: Reports of Proceedings Covering Period May 1945 to January 1946."
ADM 116/5670, "Reports on Liaison between RN Scientific Service HQs and U.S. Services London."
ADM 116/5724, "Post War Cuts in the Armed Forces Manpower and Finances: Admiralty Objections."
ADM 116/5727, "New naval construction programmes—consideration by Joint War Production Staff and the Ministerial Committee on Production before submission to Defence Committee: New construction programmes for 1949/1950 and 1950/1951 with supplementary programme for 1950/1951 submitted and passed by Joint War Production Staff and by Defence Committee 1947–1951."
ADM 116/5794, "Korean War: Naval Reports of Proceedings Nos. 1–29 in period June 25, 1950–January 17, 1951, with covering remarks by C-in-C Far East Station, and general summary of activities at Sasebo (fleet base)."
ADM 116/5813, "History of Naval Store Department 1939–1945: Role of Yards and Depots Overseas (including North America) and History of Fuelling at Sea during Second World War."
ADM 116/5824, "Requirement in Replenishment of Carriers and Aircraft Transports in Peace & War."
ADM 116/6230, "Special Report of Experience in Korean Operations—Flag Officer, Second in Command, Far East Station July 1950–June 1951."
ADM 116/6231, "Special Report of Experience in Korean Operations—Flag Officer, Second in Command, Far East Station 1950–1953 and collection of Departmental comments Jan–July 1951."

ADM 167. Board of Admiralty: Minutes and Memoranda 1869–1976

ADM 167/124, 1945 Board Minutes and Memoranda.

ADM 199. War History Cases and Papers

ADM 199/118, "BPF Operations versus Japan Narrative of Events 1944–1947."
ADM 199/1457, "Report of Experience of the BPF, January to August 1945," "C-in-C B.P.F. and Eastern Fleet War Diaries 1943–1946."
ADM 199/1478, "BPF Operations vs. Japan Narrative of Events 1945."
ADM 199/1521, "Okinawa campaign (Operation Iceberg): Reports."
ADM 199/1748, "Fleet Train: Electrical maintenance, Aircraft Damage reports, Ships."
ADM 199/1756: "Fleet Train: Oiling at Sea 1944–1945."

ADM 199/1766 "Fleet Train Records 1944–1946" (Part 32), "History of the Fleet Train."
ADM 199/1769, "Fleet Train: History of the Fleet Train," "Procedure for Fleet Train with BPF, Memoranda and Office Notes."
ADM 199/2376, "BPF Report of Experience, January–August 1945."

ADM 205. FIRST SEA LORD PAPERS

ADM 205/69, "First Sea Lord's Diaries 1939–1945:1948 Part 1."
ADM 205/83, "Future Size and Shape of Royal Navy" (1949).
ADM 205/84, "Revision of Restricted Fleet" (1949).

ADM 219. DIRECTORATE OF NAVAL OPERATIONAL STUDIES: REPORTS

ADM 219/304, "Fleet Carriers-Maximum Period away from Base or Fleet Train": Report No. 19/46.
ADM 219/329, "A Study of Factors Governing the Size of Merchant Ships in Wartime": Interim Report No. 18/47.
ADM 219/335, "Comments by Observers on Home Fleet Exercises-Exercise SUNRISE," Report No. 6/48.

ADM 226. ADMIRALTY EXPERIMENT WORKS: REPORTS 1874–1987

ADM 226/53, "Interaction between Ships: Replenishment at Sea: Series 1 Trials."
ADM 226/64, "Fuelling at Sea: Interaction between Ships; Second Report," No.14/47, March 31, 1947.

ADM 229. DEPARTMENT OF THE DIRECTOR OF NAVAL CONSTRUCTION: DIRECTORS PAPERS

ADM 229/32, "Notes on Captain Laing's Visit to Assistant Controller (Warship Production)," December 3, 1943.

ADM 234. NAVY REFERENCE BOOKS: BR [BOOKS OF REFERENCE] SERIES

ADM 234/393, "BR1742(52) Replenishment at Sea," Department of Navigation and Direction, DND 46/50, 1952.
ADM 234/394, "BR1742/52B Addendum to transfer of Liquids."
ADM 234/395, "BR1742/52C Addendum to transfer of Solids."

ADM 239. NAVY REFERENCE BOOKS: CB [CONFIDENTIAL BOOKS] SERIES

ADM 239/143, "Progress in Tactics: 1947," CB03016/47, 1947.
ADM 239/144, "Progress in Tactics: 1948," CB03016/48, 1948.
ADM 239/145, "Progress in Tactics: 1951," CB03016/51, 1951.
ADM 239/384, "Fleet Exercise Order Book CB04495."
ADM 239/409, "Instructions for Mobilising Personnel," CB03162, 1948.
ADM 239/439, "Particulars of RFAs," CB04587, 1955.
ADM 239/489, "Exercise 'Trident,' Volume I," CB004520, 1949.
ADM 239/565, "Progress in Tactics: 1949," CB03016/49, 1949.

ADM 281. ADMIRALTY: NAVAL CONSTRUCTION DEPARTMENT, LATER SHIP DEPARTMENT, NAVAL CONSTRUCTION DIVISION: REPORTS 1914–1979

ADM 281/123, "Visit of DNC's Representatives to USA 31/10/47–28/11/47."

CAB 119. JOINT PLANNING STAFF FILES

CAB 119/155, "Provision of Munitions and Manpower for War against Japan, 1943–1945."

CAB 119/160, "Far Eastern Shipping Implications 1944–45."

CAB 131. CABINET OFFICE: DEFENCE COMMITTEE (POST-WAR) RECORDS

CAB 131/1, "Cabinet Defence Committee Paper D.O. (46) 5th meeting."

CAB 131/2, "Military Merchant Shipping Requirements," Cabinet Defence Committee Meeting, March 7, 1946: Annex 1, D.O. (46) series, Serial 36.

FO371. FOREIGN OFFICE GENERAL CORRESPONDENCE

FO371/90987, "Naval Attaché's Annual Report on the U.S. Navy for 1950."

MT. MINISTRY OF TRANSPORT

MT 40. Sea Transport: Correspondence and Papers

MT 40/127, "Shipping Defence Advisory Committee Minutes and Reports: Sub Committee No. 3 Motor Transports and Store Ships Sea Transport: Correspondence & Papers," 1945–51.

PREM. PRIME MINISTER'S OFFICE: OPERATIONAL PAPERS

PREM 3.164.5, "British Fleet Train," December 1943–July 1945."

NARA2—NATIONAL ARCHIVES AND RECORDS ADMINISTRATION, College Park, Maryland

RG19. RECORDS OF THE BUREAU OF SHIPS

Records of the Bureau of Construction and Repair 1794–1941, vol. 5, "Fueling at Sea, Large Vessels," Leahy, C-in-C, Memorandum to CinCUS, October 20, 1938, Gen. Corr. File S-55(9).

RG38. RECORDS OF THE OFFICE OF THE CHIEF OF NAVAL OPERATIONS:

-Registered Publications Section 1901–1960

U.S. Navy and Related Operational, Tactical and Instructional Publications, 1918–1970

Sub Chief of Naval Operations History 1942–1946: Formerly Classified Records Relating to Logistic History and Operations, 1942–1946

Registered Publications Section, Foreign Navy and Related Foreign Military Publications, 1913–1960.

ATP-16 "Replenishment at Sea: Corrected Version," Department of the Navy, Office of CNO, Washington, June 1955, "USN Operational Publications 1918–1970."

Naval Stores Department, Admiralty, "List no 16: Escort Tankers (Excluding RFA's) Showing Their Oiling Equipment," January 6, 1945, NS 011124/45/B.10521, "10th Fleet Convoy and Subject Files, British Admiralty Delegation Washington." Records of CIC US Fleet 1942–1945.

"NBM-1 Navy Basic Mobilization Plan," June 1947, CNO Navy Department, "CNO Registered Publications, 1901–1960."

"NBM-1A Navy Basic Mobilization Plan," September 1950, CNO Navy Department, "CNO Registered Publications 1901–1960."

"NBL-2 Basic Logistic Plan Part II Mobilization," January 24, 1951, CNO Division of Logistic Plans, "CNO Registered Publications 1901–1960."

"NBL-NTS-2 Mobilization Logistic Plan I-48 (Transportation)," March 1948, CNO Navy Department, "CNO Registered Publications 1901–1960."

"Oiling at Sea," Office of Naval Intelligence (ONI) No. 67, No. 12217, June 28, 1913, "Records of the Office of the CNO," E-10c, Box 838.

"Organization of Major Combatant Types Less Submarines," CNO Serial 0100PO3, November 19, 1945, "Sub Chief of Naval Operations History 1942–1946."

"Statement of Vice Chief of Naval Operations before the Committee on Appropriations on the Review of the Appropriations for the Fiscal Year 1946," Admiral Horne, VCNO, September 1945, "Sub Chief of Naval Operations History 1942–1946," Box 4.

"Statement of Vice Chief of Naval Operations before the Appropriations Committee of the House of Representatives," Admiral Horne, VCNO, July 3, 1945, "Surplus Property Statements," "Sub Chief of Naval Operations History 1942–1946," Box 4.

"Statement of Vice Chief of Naval Operations before the Appropriations Committee of the House of Representatives," "Cost of Ships Shown in Demobilization Plan 2 for Retention in the Inactive Status in the Reserve Fleet" BuShips memorandum, October 3, 1945.

"Statement of Vice Chief of Naval Operations before the Appropriations Committee of the House of Representatives," "Comparison of Number of Vessels in Proposed Navy Basic Post-War Plan No.1 with those in Navy Basic Demobilization Plan No.2, Revision No.1" memorandum dated April 6, 1945, from Captain Moore Department of the CNO to Admiral Horne Serial 028503.

"Summary BuShips maintenance, repair and fuel and transportation costs" addendum for 1946 Navy Budget produced by Admiral Horne VCNO: Navy Department, Office of Budgets and Reports 31 January 1945," Box 8.

"10th Fleet Convoy and Subject Files, British Admiralty Delegation Washington," Records of CIC US Fleet 1942–1945.

RG143. Records of the Bureau of Supplies and Accounts (BuSandA)

Papers, Speeches, Lectures, and Miscellaneous Publications and Documents, 1932–1960

"Glossary of Logistics," BuSandA, Department of the U.S. Navy, in "Navy Material Logistics Handbook: Reference Data," "Naval Logistics Organization," "Civil Logistics" (Washington, DC: December 2, 1947).

"Navy Logistics and Logistics Planning," Rear Adm. E. D. Foster, SC, USN Chief BuSandA: Speech to Air University, February 14, 1949.

Fuels Management Publications and Documents, 1934–1961

"Fueling at Sea Instructions, U.S. Fleet," Commander in Chief, U.S. Fleet, CominCH P-2, November 1, 1944.

"USF-83 Fueling and Replenishment at Sea," Navy Department, CNO, (1946).

Supply Management Publications and Documents 1943–1964

"Logistic Reference Data," 4th edition, BuSandA Navy Supply Corps School Logistics Research Department, December 1, 1948, NavSandA Publication No. 94, Navpers 91085.

"Naval Logistics Organization," BuSandA, (Navy Department, Washington, D.C.: NavSandA Publication 95, September 1, 1947, amended December 1, 1948).

"Report U.S. Atlantic Fleet 2nd Task Fleet Replenishment at Sea Exercises," R. A Moody, BuSandA, u.d.

"War Service Fuel Consumption of U.S. Naval Surface Vessels," "Logistics Reference Data," Navpers 91085 (July 1, 1946, modified 1947 and 1948), BuSandA Navy Supply Corps School.

RG218. JOINT CHIEFS OF STAFF CENTRAL DECIMAL FILE, 1948–56

"Merchant Shipping Requirements and Availability for National Defense," Report by the Joint Military Transportation Committee to the JCS, January 4, 1949, JCS1454 Series.

"Review of Loss Factors and Mobilization Requirements for Tankers in the light of Projected Sustained Sea Speed Loaded in Excess of 16 knots"; Report by CNO to JCS (Decision 1741/106 August 2, 1954).

RG313. RECORDS OF THE NAVAL OPERATING FORCES ("FLAG FILES")

Commander in Chief Atlantic (CinCLant) Secret Administrative Files, 1941–1949

"Additional Type AE Vessel—Request for," Rear Adm. W. D. Baker, ComServLant to CinCLantFlt, March 30, 1948, Serial 005, Box 93.

"Emergency Operation Plan," Rear Adm. W. D. Baker, ComServLant to CinCLantFlt, January 9, 1948, FF13/9/A16–3, Box 93.

"Emergency Operation Plan Op Plan 2–47," ComServLant, FF13–9/A16–3, August 1, 1947.

"General Appreciation of the Shipping Position, with Particular reference to the Comparison between 1941 and 1957," Ministry of Transport, March 1949, Exercise "Trident."

"Report of Atlantic Fleet Tactical Exercises February–March 1947," Commander in Chief U.S. Atlantic Fleet, Memorandum, Vice Adm. W. H. P Blandy, CinCLantFlt to ComServLant, April 17, 1948, Serial 0031, Box 93.

"Report of Atlantic Fleet Tactical Exercises February–March 1947," Commander in Chief U.S. Atlantic Fleet, Memorandum, Vice Adm. W. H. P Blandy, C-in-C U.S. Atlantic Fleet to CNO, April 25, 1947, A4–3/P11/(0284), Box 88.

Commander Naval Forces Eastern Atlantic and Mediterranean

"Report on Midshipman Practice Cruise," Commander, TF 81 to C-in-C US Atlantic Fleet, serial 680, Box 8449.

Records of Naval Operating Forces (CinCLant) General Admin Files, 1950

"Exercise 'Trident' April 1949—Part 1."

"Fleet Employment Last Half Fiscal Year 1949 and Fiscal Year 1950."

"Task Organization for TF89, U.S. Atlantic Fleet Service Force, November 2, 1950."

NHB—Naval Historical Branch, Ministry Of Defence

Admiralty, Circular Letter No. 9, August 3, 1905, Ewen MacGregor to all Commanders-in-Chief, Captains and C/O's of HM Ships and Vessels, T.3487/1905, Republished in "Force 4: The Newsletter of the RFA" (August 1980).

Admiralty Pink Lists: June 24, 1946; June 23, 1947; June 30, 1948; June 30, 1949; June 20, 1950; June 26, 1951; July 1, 1952.

BSR 493, TSD 4122/53, S.567B, "History of the Fleet Train," Vol. 1: "Inception-31st May 1945," Capt. R. F. Leonard, R.N., Plans Division (Q).

BSR 453, TSD 4122/53, S.567B, "History of the Fleet Train," Vol. 2: "June–August 1945," Capt. R. F. Leonard, R.N., Plans Division (Q).

BSR 477, TSD 4122/53, S.567B, "History of the Fleet Train," Vol. 3: "Post Hostilities," Capt. R. F. Leonard, R.N., Plans Division (Q).

"British Commonwealth Naval Operations, Korea 1950–1953," Naval Staff History, BR 1736(54) (London: NHB, 1967).

"A Brief Study of the Naval Staff and Its Replacement by Central Staff 1945–1977," Cdr. David Hobbs, MBE, unpublished memorandum S.10682 (London: NHB, December 1997).

Crawford, J. B. "Fuelling At Sea." DNC Department, Internal Lecture and Discussion Paper, May 1946.

——. "Replenishment At Sea," DNC Department, Internal Lecture and Discussion Paper, March 1949, DNC reference 51.

"Explanatory Statement on the Navy Estimates 1956–57," First Lord of the Admiralty, (London: HMSO 1956).

"Explanatory Statement on the Navy Estimates 1957–58," First Lord of the Admiralty, (London: HMSO 1957).

"The Fighting Instructions," CB04487, June 1947.

"The Forgotten Bases," David Brown, May 16, 1995, in Conference Paper, "Royal Australian Navy in World War II," Sydney, May 25–26, 1995.

"Navy Estimates 1948–49," Statement of the First Lord of the Admiralty, Cmd. 7337 (London: HMSO, 1948).

"Navy Estimates 1949–50," Statement of the First Lord of the Admiralty, Cmd. 7632 (London: HMSO, 1949).

"Navy Estimates 1950–51," Statement of the First Lord of the Admiralty, Cmd. 7897 (London: HMSO, 1950).

"Navy Estimates 1952–53," Statement of the First Lord of the Admiralty, Cmd. 8476 (London: HMSO, 1952).

"The Organisation of the Naval Staff within the Admiralty & Ministry of Defence 1927–2000," unpub. Mss., Cdr. N. L. Stewart.

"The Problems Involved in Designing an RFA Tanker," J. B. Crawford, DNC Department, Internal Lecture and Discussion Paper, March 17, 1950.

"The Royal Navy—Incidents since 1945: Notes of H.M. Ships Involved," MoD (Navy), Naval Staff Duties Division (Data and Doctrine), (MoD WP5U13.40), London: 1963.

NMM—*National Maritime Museum, Caird Library, Greenwich*

K. G. B. DEWAR PAPERS, DEW 20 "MISCELLANEOUS HISTORICAL SECTION PAPERS"

A. W. Brock TSD to Adm. K. G. B. Dewar, Mss. note May 21, 1941, "Oiling at Sea 1930–1941." Ref. Pre War Decision: Admiralty letter NS 02393/38/22570, December 20, 1938,."

A. W. Brock TSD to Adm. K. G. B. Dewar, Mss. note May 21, 1941, "Oiling at Sea 1930–1941." Ref. "Present situation in regard to oiling cruisers and heavier ships at sea,"

"Certain Suggestions Resulting from a Comparison between the Mobility of the British and American Fleets," Admiral K. G. B. Dewar, Deputy Director NID Admiralty, [u.d., but written in 1926].

"Strategical Policy in the Far East," Historical Section TSDD, Memorandum October 1939, D. Bonner Smith.

NID Admiralty to Vice Admiral K. G. B. Dewar (u.d.), Observation dockets HDC April 4, 1941, to DCNS, "Fuelling at Sea," TSD 467/41, March 28, 1941.

"Present situation in regard to oiling cruisers and heavier ships at sea," "Oiling at Sea 1930–1941," Admiralty letter NS 02393/38/22570, 20/12/38.

TSDD to VCNS, "Fuelling at Sea," March 28, 1941 (TSD 467/41).

LORD BRUCE FRASER PAPERS

MS 83/158, Fact Sheet BPF/ops/1009/1, "War Data," note 4, "Strength of Empire Forces," Folder 22.

MS 83/158, "TF37 projected daily fuel consumption," Memorandum from Assistant Staff Officer (Ops) BPF to C-in-C BPF, July 13, 1945, "Operational Correspondence Flag Officers 1944–1948," Folder 23, 2/15.

MS 83/158, "Task Force 57," Rear Admiral Fisher to C-in-C Fraser, letters April 21, 1945 and May 5, 1945, File 23.

MS 83/158, Rear Admiral Fisher (RAFT) letter to C-in-C Fraser, April 21, 1945, "C-in-C Operational Correspondence Flag Officers 1944–1948," File 23, Folder 7/5.

MS 86/096, Fact Sheet, Capt. V. Merry, Flag Lieutenant to Admiral Fraser BPF.

OTHER PUBLICATIONS

"The Chase and Sinking of the Bismarck," Naval Staff History Battle Summary No. 5, BR1736 (3/50), (London: HMSO, 1950).

"Naval Strategy in the Pacific February 1943 to August 1945," Naval Staff History Battle Summary No. 34, Admiralty TSD Division, BR1736 (28), (London: HMSO, 1946).

NWC—Naval War College: Naval Historical Collection, Rhode Island

RG3. CENTRAL FILES, 1903–1997"

"Imperial Defence College: Selection of Students for," R. L. Conolly, president NWC to CNO, March 20, 1953, serial 1004–53, Box 136.

"Instruction in British Military Schools," G. R. Henderson, Deputy C-in-C CinCNELM to CNO, December 16, 1949, Serial 4680, Box "Education P-11-1," Box 23.

"1950 Logistics Class," Box 28.

"Report on U.K. Field Trip March 10–19, 1972," Director of Naval Warfare, April 18, 1972, Box 214/5050.

"Royal Naval Staff College England 1949," Exchange of correspondence between president of NWC and director of Royal Naval Staff College Greenwich, Box 27.

"Royal Navy Graduates of the NWC 1947–1951," Box 136, internal memorandum October 21, 1953.

"Students at Foreign War Colleges 1972–1973," Rear Adm. C. A. Hill Jr., USN, to Rear Adm. W. D. S. Scott, commander British Navy Staff Washington, letter June 11, 1973, Box 220/5400.

RG4. PUBLICATIONS, 1915–1977

"The Industrial Reserve," *BuShips Journal*, November 1953.

"Logistics Department Organization and Instructions," Approved by Rear Adm. Allan E. Smith, Chief of Staff NWC, July 10, 1947, Box 221.

"Logistic Planning Factors: Replenishment at Sea," Department of Logistics 1949, Committee No. 6, Box 231, part 1 chap. vi, para. 1(b).
"Maneuver Rules," Academic Section, Department of Logistics, June 1947, Box 162.
"Operational Problem 6L-50: A Study of Mobile Fleet Support," Logistics Class March 20–24, 1950, Capt. H. Felt, Acting Chief of Staff, Box 171.
"Replenishment at Sea: An Illustrative Problem," Department of Logistics, April 28, 1949, Box 172.
"Replenishment at Sea Exercise," September 16, 1948, Box 162.
"Replenishment at Sea Study: Statement and Special Situation October 1952," Box 195.
"Report of Committee to Study Post-war Logistic Training," "Jennings Report," CNO, December 21, 1945, Box 221.
"U.S. Navy 1947," Chart E, Box 149, folder 2656D.

RG14. FACULTY AND STAFF PRESENTATIONS, 1886–1970

Brown, Cdr. T. A. "Logistic Planning Agencies of CominCH and CNO," Staff Presentation to ANSCOL, August 24, 1945.
McCormick, Lynde. "Logistics and Strategy," September 28, 1955.

RG15. GUEST LECTURES, 1894–1992

Austin, Rear Adm. Bernard, USN, "Mobile Logistics," 1952.
Bell, Capt. H. B., USN Commander Service Squadron Two, U.S. Atlantic Fleet, "Mobile Logistic Support," February 20, 1951.
Denebrink, Rear Adm. F. C. USN, "Logistic Support to the Naval Forces in the Korean Campaign," April 30, 1951.
Hughes-Hallett, Vice Adm. Cecil C., RN, "Role of the Royal Navy in a Future War with Emphasis on Control of North European Waters," March 11, 1954.
Lutes, Lt. Gen. Leroy, "Logistics in Grand Strategy," February 13, 1950.
Pare, Capt. E. E. USN, "Mobile Fleet Support," September 16, 1947.
———, "Mobile Fleet Support," August 16, 1948.
Pennant, Sir Cyril Douglas, "Britain's Place in Global Strategy," May 31, 1951.
Sigel, Capt. C. H., USN, "Mobilizing the Reserve Fleets," March 10, 1950.
Webber, Cdr. R. P. SC, USN, "Capabilities of Logistics Support Forces," September 16, 1947.

RG27. SUNDRY PAPERS, GENERAL SUBJECTS, 1884–2000

"British Naval Officer Students at NWC: Proposal to Reconsider," Capt. G. A. Moore, Academic Plans Section to Heads of Departments, memorandum, October 15, 1953, Command and Staff History (NCC Foreign Officers) folder.
Pare, Capt. E. E., U.S. Atlantic Fleet Service Force 2, Service Squadron 2 to Capt. Henry Eccles, Head of Logistics Department NWC, letter March 28, 1947.
Smith, Ralph E. "A History of Logistics at the Naval War College produced by the Department of Strategy and Logistics," 1951.

RG29. STUDENTS, STAFF, AND FACULTY, 1884–2000

Register of Faculty Officers and Graduates Naval War College, 1946–1959

Manuscript Collections

Manuscript Collection 52: Rear Adm. Henry Eccles Papers

Acworth, Cdr. H. W., RN, to Capt. H. E. Eccles USN, letter August 11, 1949, MS 52, Series IV Box 74, Folder 9.

Acworth, Cdr. H. W., RN, to Capt. H. E. Eccles, USN, letter August 16, 1949; MS 52, Series IV, Box 74, Folder 9.

Acworth, Cdr. H. W., RN, Letter to Admiral Brown, Chief of Staff NWC and Captain Eccles, Head of Logistics Department NWC, August 27, 1948.

Brown, Rear Adm., USN, Memorandum to Cdr. H. W. Acworth, RN, September 7, 1948, MS52/4/74/9.

Carney, Adm. Robert B., CinCSOUTH, to Henry Eccles, letter December 7, 1952, Box 18, Series II.

Eccles, Capt. H. E., to Dr. D. Ballantine, letter October 5, 1949, MS 52 Eccles Papers, Series II, Box 4.

Eccles, Rear Adm. Henry E., to Vice Adm. George Dyer, letter, August 1, 1958, MS 52, Series II, Box 15.

Eccles memorandum to Admiral Cooley, Chief of Staff, NWC, July 7, 1950.

Eccles to Cdr. H. W. Acworth, RN, letter August 15, 1949, MS 52/4/74/9.

Eccles to Rear Adm. Charles J. Moore, March 4, 1952, MS 52, Series II, Folder 28.

Eccles to Capt. Frank Whitaker, USN, NY Naval Shipyard, letter December 2, 1947, MS 52, Series II, Box 4, Folder 13.

Furer, Adm. J., USN, to Rear Admiral Eccles, letter August 31, 1953, MS 52, Series II, Box 18, Folder 5.

Furer, Adm. J., USN, to Rear Admiral Eccles, letter September 16, 1953, Box 18, Series II.

"Logistics Presentations Naval Command Course for Senior Foreign Officers," January 6, 1958, MS/3/31/12.

"Some Considerations of Re-supply at Sea Operations," Cdr. D. H. Hoard, SC USN, October 29, 1948, MS 52 Series II, Box 4.

Papers Authored by H. Eccles

"Detailed Recommendations for the Consolidation of the S&T and S&L Courses," Enclosure (2), September 9, 1955, MS 52/4/81/15, "Naval War College Mission and Curriculum, 1951–1973."

"Informal Notes on Logistics Problems," February 1, 1953.

"Mobile Support versus Overseas Base Support," November 1959, Logistic Research Project 047 001, George Washington University, MS 52/3/46/3.

"Notes on the Logistic History of the Korean War," March 25, 1959, MS 52/3/46/3.

"Notes on the Requirements for Logistics Books," u.d. [in 1956], MS 52/3/54/1.

"Operational Naval Logistics" (Navpers 10869 Bureau of Naval Personnel), April 1950.

"Pacific Logistics," Presentation to Joint Operations Review Board, March 30, 1945, MS 52/3/30/17.

"Report No. 7: Notes on European Logistics—England," George Washington University Logistics Research Project, N7 onr 41904, "European Logistics Report: Lessons," Box 45, 1956.

Other Authors

Beary, Vice Adm. D. B., USN, President NWC, Foreword to "Operational Naval Logistics" by Capt. Henry E Eccles, Department of Logistics, NWC (Navpers 10869, Bureau of Naval Personnel) April 1950.

Esposito, Col. Vincent J. "The Interrelationship of Strategy and Logistics," Industrial College of the Armed Forces, November 15, 1955, MS 52/3/33/5.

NWC(L)—Naval War College Library, Rhode Island

"First Quarterly Report Oct–Dec 1982: WWI–WWII," Naval Ships Weapons Systems Engineering Station (NSWSES), Port Hueneme.

Hone, Thomas C. "Power and Change: The Administrative History of the Office of the Chief of Naval Operations 1946–1986" (Washington D.C.: Naval Historical Center Department of the Navy, 1989).

King, Fleet Admiral Ernest J., USN. "U.S. Navy at War 1941–1945: Official Reports to the Secretary of the Navy," "First Report 1941–1944," (Washington: US Navy Department, 1946).

———, "Second Report to the Secretary of the Navy Covering Combat Operations, March 1, 1944 to March 1, 1945," issued March 27, 1945 (Washington, D.C.: U.S. Navy Department, 1946).

———, "Third Report to the Secretary of the Navy Covering Combat Operations, March 1, 1945 to October 1, 1945," issued December 8, 1945 (Washington, D.C.: U.S. Navy Department, 1946).

Maddon, Cdr. David M., SC USN. "Operational Logistics in the Pacific in WWII: Are the Lessons Learned Still Valid?" Unclassified Paper, May 11, 1988.

Miller, Marvin, "UNREP History of Aircraft Carriers," Underway Replenishment Department, USN, Port Hueneme, California, 1992.

NWP4–01.4, "Underway Replenishment" (Formerly NWP-14 (Rev E)), Naval Warfare Publication, Department of the Navy, CNO, Washington, August 1996.

"Underway Replenishment of Naval Ships," "UNREP: System Development of the UNREP Fleet." Naval Surface Warfare Center, Underway Replenishment Department, U.S. Navy, (Port Hueneme, CA, and Washington DC: US Government Printing Office, 1992).

NL—Nimitz Library, U.S. Naval Academy, Annapolis, Maryland

"Composition and Costs of Reserve Fleet," Serial 316, "Proceedings and Hearings before the General Board of the Navy," Washington, D.C., March 30 and 31, 1948.

"Composition and Costs of Reserve Fleet," Serial 4/49, "Proceedings and Hearings before the General Board of the Navy," Washington, D.C., May 26 and 27, 1949.

"Shipbuilding Program FY 1951–1960: Ship Design," (Serial 323), Proceedings and Hearings before the General Board of the Navy, Vol. III, Washington, D.C., November 2 and 24, 1948.

USNHC—Naval Historical Center, Department of the Navy, Operational Archives, Washington Navy Yard

"Logistics Support Group Historical Report Service Squadron Six Task Group 16.6," Cdr. D. Beary, Commander Service Squadron Six, Service Force Pacific Fleet, A12/A3A-4, October 3, 1945, "Command File World War II."

"Naval Logistics Manual: For Use by the Naval Establishment as a Basic Manual in Naval Logistics," M. M. Dupre, USN, (Washington DC: Navpers 10861, 1950),

CNO Series Naval Warfare Publications NWP-109–NWP-54; Command File Post January 1, 1946.

NWIP 11–22 "Fuel Consumption and Endurance Data" (1953), "Naval Operational Planning"—Part II, "Logistics" Dept. of Navy Office of CNO 1953, CNO Series Naval Warfare Publications NWP-10–NWP-54; Command File Post January 1, 1946.

"NWP-38 Replenishment at Sea," Office of CNO, January 1953, Command File Post January 1, 1946, CNO Series, "Naval Warfare Publications NWP-10–NWP-54," Microfiche Record Number F-3640.

"Presentation and Scope in the Naval Warfare Publications," Navy Department, CNO, April 1952, Command File Post January 1, 1946, NWP 10–NWP 54, Box 401.

"Quarterly Summary of U.S. Naval Forces Eastern Atlantic and Mediterranean July 1 to October 1, 1947," October 28, 1947, ComNavEu Administrative History 1945–1949 Command File Post January 1, 1946.

"Quarterly Summary of U.S. Naval Forces Eastern Atlantic and Mediterranean October 1, 1947–March 31, 1948," May 12, 1948, ComNavEu Administrative History 1945–1949 Command File Post January 1, 1946.

"Reports of Operations and Condition of Command July 1, 1948, to July 30, 1949," "ComNavEu CinCNELM Reports 1948–1955," Command File Post January 1, 1946, NRS 610.

"Reports of Operations and Condition of Command July 1, 1949, to July 30, 1950," "ComNavEu CinCNELM Reports 1948–1955," Command File Post January 1, 1946, NRS 610.

"Reports of Operations and Condition of Command June 14, 1952, to July 1, 1953," ComNavEu CinCNELM Reports 1948–1955, Command File Post January 1, 1946, NRS 610.

"USF-10A Current Tactical Orders & Doctrine," Commander in Chief U.S. Fleet," CominCH P-2, 1944, WWII Command File, Box 271.

"USF-13 Logistic Support Force Operating Instructions, United States Fleets," Navy Department, CNO, August 8, 1946; Command File Post January 1, 1946, "CNO Series Naval Warfare Publications NWP 10–NWP 54."

"U.S. Navy Active Ship Force Levels 1917–1995," Operational Archives. Washington, DC: Naval Historical Center, Department of the Navy.

"U.S. Naval Administration in World War II," Vol. 1, "Narrative at Joint and Fleet Command level," Commander in Chief U.S. Pacific Fleet and Pacific Ocean Areas, Office of the Chief of Naval Operations, Department of the Navy, (Washington, D.C.: Naval History Division), Microfiche Record Number 149A.

Sundry Unclassified Naval Documents

ATP-16D (Navy), "Replenishment at Sea." Washington, D.C.: Department of the Navy, Office of the Chief of Naval Operations, December 2001.

EXTAC 1003 (Rev. A) USN, "Replenishment at Sea" manual, Washington, D.C.: Department of the Navy, Office of the Chief of Naval Operations, 2000.

CORRESPONDENCE, INTERNET

Barnard, Cdr. H., RN (Ret.), Logistics Graduate (1950), letter to author, February 24, 2003.

Baxter, Edward. "Rappahannock Saves Day for Mine Countermeasures Ships," SEALOGFE Public Affairs, SEALIFT January 2008. http://www.msc.navy.mil/sealift/2008/January/rappahannock.htm, accessed December 1, 2008.

"Historical Note," "Records of the Reserve Fleet 1947–1960": http://www.history.navy.mil/branches/nhcorg10.htm, USNHC, March 1, 2005.

Le Bailly, Vice Adm. Sir Louis, letter to author, December 26, 1999.

Secondary Sources

Adams, Thomas A. "The Origins of the Royal Fleet Auxiliary Service," *Gunline*, no. 12 (July 1991).

Adams, Thomas A., and James R. Smith. *The Royal Fleet Auxiliary: A Century of Service.* London: Chatham Publishing, 2005.

Baer, George W. *The U.S. Navy 1890–1990: One Hundred Years of Sea Power.* Stanford, CA: Stanford University Press, 1993

Ballantine, Duncan S. *U.S. Naval Logistics in the Second World War.* Princeton, NJ: Princeton University Press, 1949.

Baugh, Daniel A. "Confusions and Constraints: The Navy and British Defence Planning, 1919–1939," in *Naval Power in the Twentieth Century*, ed. N. A. M. Rodger, 101–19. Annapolis, MD: Naval Institute Press, 1996.

Black, I. McD. "Fuelling at Sea," Royal Corps of Naval Constructors, *North East Coast Institution of Engineers and Shipbuilders*, vol. 68, (1951–52): 133–51.

Bokel, John E., and Rolf Clark. "Acquisition in World War II," in *Big "L" American Logistics in WWII: Industrial College of the Armed Forces Study*, ed. Alan Gropman, 97–143. Washington DC: National Defense University, 1997.

Brown, David, ed. *Forgotten Fleets: British Pacific Fleet and Eastern Fleet.* Liverpool: Brodie Publishing, 1995.

Bryan, Robert A., and Charles Sparks. "The National Defense Reserve Fleet: An Essential Element of National Defense," *Naval Engineers Journal*, April 1977: 39–44.

Buell, Thomas B. *Master of Sea Power: A Biography of Fleet Admiral Ernest J. King.* Annapolis, MD: Naval Institute Press, 1980.

Cagle, Malcolm W., and Frank A Manson. *The Sea War in Korea.* Annapolis, MD: Naval Institute Press, 1957.

Carter, W. R. *Beans, Bullets And Black Oil.* Washington, DC: Department of the Navy, U.S. Government Printing Office, 1953.

Carter, W. R., and E. E. Duvall. *Ships, Salvage and Sinews of War: The Story of Fleet Logistics Afloat in the Atlantic during World War II.* Washington, DC: Department of the Navy, U.S. Government Printing Office, 1953.

Case, William. "USS *Sacramento* (AOE1)," U.S. Naval Institute *Proceedings* 93, no. 12 (December 1967): 88–102.

Coles, Michael. "Ernest King and the British Pacific Fleet: The Conference at Quebec, 1944("Octagon")," *Journal of Military History*, 65 (January 2001): 105–129.

Cope, Harley. "Fighting Ships on the Leash," U.S. Naval Institute *Proceedings*, February 1947: 161–65.

Corbett, Julian S. *Drake and the Tudor Navy.* London: Longmans Green, 1898.

Dyer, George C. *Naval Logistics.* Annapolis, MD: Naval Institute Press, 1960.

Eccles, Henry E. *Logistics in the National Defense.* Harrisburg: Stackpole, 1959; reprint NWC Press, Newport, RI, 1997.

———. *Military Concepts and Philosophy*. New Brunswick, NJ: Rutgers University Press, 1965.

———. *Military Power in a Free Society*. Newport, RI: Naval War College, 1979.

———. "Logistics—What is it?" *Logistics Spectrum*, (Summer 1982).

Eichelberger, C. A. "The Navy's Post-War Headache," U.S. Naval Institute *Proceedings*, August 1946: 1047–53.

Ferris, John. "The Last Decade of British Maritime Supremacy, 1919–1929," in *Far Flung Lines: Essays on Imperial Defence*, eds. Greg Kennedy and Keith Neilson, 124–70. London: Frank Cass, 1997.

Field, James. *A History of UN Naval Operations: Korea*. Washington, DC: GPO, USNHC, 1982.

Friedman, N. *The Postwar Naval Revolution*. London: Conway, 1986.

Furer, J. A. *Administration of the Navy Department in World War II*. Washington, DC: Navy Department, 1959.

Gibson, Andrew, and Arthur Donovan. *The Abandoned Ocean: A History of United States Maritime Policy*. Columbia: University of South Carolina Press, 2000.

Gordon, A. "The Admiralty and Imperial Overstretch 1902–1941," in *Seapower Theory and Practice*, ed. Geoffrey Till, 63–83. Ilford, UK: Frank Cass, 1994.

Gray, Anthony W., Jr. "Joint Logistics in the Pacific Theater" in *Big "L" American Logistics in WWII: Industrial College of the Armed Forces Study*, ed. Alan Gropman, 293–337. Washington, DC: National Defense University, 1997.

Gray, Colin S. *The Leverage of Sea Power*. New York: The Free Press, 1992.

Gray, E. *Operation Pacific: The Royal Navy's War against Japan 1941–1945*. London: Leo Cooper, 1990.

Grove, E. J. *The Royal Navy since 1815*. Basingstoke, U.K.: Palgrave MacMillan, 2005.

———. *Vanguard to Trident: British Naval Policy since World War II*. London: The Bodley Head, 1987.

Hall, Nowell. "Naval Exercises of 1951," in *Brassey's Annual 1952*, ed. H. G. Thursfield, 107–15. London: William Clowes & Sons, 1952.

Hattendorf, J. "A Special Relationship: The Royal Navy and the US Naval War College," *Mariners Mirror* 72, no. 2(May 1986): 200–201.

Hayes, John D. "The Navy's Task Force," *Ordnance: The Journal of the American Ordnance Association*, (Nov.–Dec. 1957): 1–4.

———. "Logistics of Necessity," *Ordnance: The Journal of the American Ordnance Association*, (Jan.–Feb. 1954).

Haynes, J. B., and David A. Schrady. "Logistics Quotes," *Navy Supply Corps Newsletter*, May 1, 2003 (U.S. Department of the Navy, Naval Supply Systems Command).

Hobbs, David. *Moving Bases: Royal Navy Maintenance Carriers and Monabs*. Liskeard, U.K.: Maritime Books, 2007.

Hooper, E. B. *Mobility Support and Endurance: A Story of Naval Operational Logistics in the Vietnam War 1965–1968*. Washington, DC: Naval History Division Department of the Navy, 1972.

Hughes-Hallett, C. C. "Naval Logistics in a Future War," CBE lecture given December 14, 1949, *Journal of the Royal United Services Institute*, vol. XCV (1950), 232–45.

Humble, Richard. *Fraser of North Cape*. London: Routledge & Kagan Paul, 1983.

Isenberg, Michael T. *Shield of the Republic: The United States Navy in an Era of Cold War and Violent Peace, 1945–1962*. New York: St. Martin's Press, 1993.

Jane's Fighting Ships, 1919. London: Sampson Low, Marston 1919.

Jane's Fighting Ships, 1939. London: Sampson Low, Marston, 1939.

Jones, Geoffrey. *Under Three Flags*. London: William Kimber, 1973.

Kennedy, G. "What Worth the Americans? The British Strategic Foreign Policy-making Elite's View of American Maritime Power in the Far East, 1933–1941," in *British Naval Strategy East of Suez, 1900–2000: Influences and Actions*, ed. Greg Kennedy, 90–117. London: Frank Cass, 2005.

Kennedy, Paul. *The Rise and Fall of British Naval Mastery*. London: Fontana Press, 1991.

Le Bailly, Vice Adm.Louis. *From Fisher to the Falklands*.London: Marine Management (Holdings) for the Institute of Marine Engineers, 1991.

——. *Old Loves Return*. Edinburgh, U.K.: Pentland Press, 1994.

Leutze, James R. *Bargaining for Supremacy: Anglo-American Naval Collaboration, 1937–1941*. Chapel Hill: University of North Carolina Press, 1977.

Llewellyn-Jones, M. *The Royal Navy and Anti-submarine Warfare, 1917–49*. London and New York: Routledge, 2005.

Lombe, Evans. "The Royal Navy in the Pacific," *Journal of the Royal United Services Institute* XCII, no. 567 (August 1947): 333–47.

Madsen, D. *Forgotten Fleet: The Mothball Navy*. Annapolis, MD: Naval Institute Press, 1999.

Marsh, D. J. "Supply Charge at Sea: The Evolution from Pusser to Logistician," *Naval Review* 88, no. 3 (July 2000): 235–41.

Miller, Edward S. *War Plan Orange*. Annapolis, MD: Naval Institute Press, 1991.

Miller, S. "Refueling Warships at Sea," *Trans. Society of Naval Architects and Marine Engineers New York*, vol. 22, 1914.

Ministry of Defence (Navy), *War with Japan*, vol. VI. London: HMSO, 1995.

Murfett, Malcolm H. *In Jeopardy: The Royal Navy and British Far Eastern Defence Policy, 1945–1951*. Kuala Lumpur, Malaysia: Oxford University Press, 1995.

Nash, P. V. "The Royal Navy in Korea: Replenishment and Sustainability," in *British Naval Strategy East of Suez, 1900–2000: Influences and Actions*, ed. Greg Kennedy, 154–77. London: Frank Cass, 2005.

Naval Staff Directorate. *British Maritime Doctrine* 1st Ed., BR1806. London: HMSO, 1995.

——. *British Maritime Doctrine*, 2nd Ed., BR1806. London: HMSO, 1999.

Neilson, Keith "'Unbroken Thread': Japan, Maritime Power and British Imperial Defence 1920–32" in *British Naval Strategy East of Suez, 1900–2000: Influences and Actions*, ed. Greg Kennedy, 62–89. London: Frank Cass, 2005.

Palmer, Michael A. *Origins of the Maritime Strategy: The Development of American Naval Strategy, 1945–55*. Annapolis, MD: Naval Institute Press, 1990.

Penn, Geoffrey. *HMS Thunderer: The Story of the Royal Naval Engineering College Keyham and Manadon*. Emsworth, U.K.: Kenneth Mason, 1984.

Potter, E.B. *Nimitz*. Annapolis, MD: Naval Institute Press, 1976.

Pugh, Philip. *The Cost of Seapower*. London: Conway Maritime Press, 1986.

"Replenisher," "What Is Wrong with the RFA?" *Naval Review* Vol. 45 (1957): 306–13.

Rippon, P. M. *The Evolution of Engineering in the Royal Navy*, vol. 2, 1939–1992. London: Marine Management (Holdings) Ltd., for the Institute of Marine Engineers,1994).

Rodger, N. A. M. *Safeguard of the Sea: A Naval History of Britain*, vol. 1, 660–1649. London: Harper Collins, 1997.

Roskill, S. W. *History of the Second World War: The War at Sea 1939–1945*, volume III, part II, June 1, 1944–August 14, 1945. London: HMSO, 1961.

Ryan, Paul B. *First Line of Defense: The U.S. Navy since 1945*. Stanford, CA: Hoover Institution Press, Stanford University, 1981.

Scott, Richard. "Cost and Capability: The Balancing Act for Type 45," *Warship World* 7, no. 1 (September 2000): 2–3.

Sigwart, E. S. *Royal Fleet Auxiliary*. London: Adlard Coles, 1969.

———. "Royal Fleet Auxiliary," *Navy International*, February 1975: 10–12.

Smith, K. *Conflict over Convoys: Anglo-American Logistics Diplomacy in the Second World War*. Cambridge, U.K.: Cambridge University Press, 1996.

Smith, Peter C. *Task Force 57: The British Pacific Fleet, 1944–45*. London: Crecy Books, 1969.

"Spindrift," "The Reserve Fleet: Post War Organisation 1919," in *Brasseys Annual 1952*, ed. H. G. Thursfield, 147–48. London: William Clowes, 1952.

Spruance, Raymond A. "The Victory in the Pacific," speech October 30, 1946, *Journal of the Royal United Services Institute* XCI (November 1946): 540–58.

Stevens, David, ed. *The Royal Australian Navy in World War II*. St. Leonards, NSW: Allen & Unwin, 1996.

Still, William N. "Anglo-American Naval Logistic Co-operation in World War I," *The American Neptune* 55, no.3 (1995): 213–22.

Sumida, Jon Tetsuro. "British Naval Operational Logistics, 1914–1918," *Journal of Military History* 57 (July 1993): 447–80.

———. "Forging the Trident: British Naval Industrial Logistics, 1914–1918," in *Feeding Mars: Logistics in Western Warfare from the Middle Ages to the Present*, ed. John A Lynn, 217–49. Boulder, San Francisco, and Oxford: Westview Press, 1993.

Thorpe, George C. *Pure Logistics: The Science of War Preparation*, Stanley L. Falk ed. Newport: Naval War College Press, 1997. First published 1917.

Till, Geoffrey. *Seapower: A Guide for the Twenty-First Century*. London: Frank Cass, 2004.

Trimingham, D. "The Composition and Design of our Post-War Fleet," *Journal of the Royal United Services Institute* XCI (February 1946): 73–76.

Tupper Carey, P. C. S. "Fuelling at Sea," *Journal of the Royal United Services Institute* XCI (1946): 382–86.

"Valor," "The Fleet Train," *Naval Review* vol. 34, 1946, 31–36.

Vian, Philip. *Action This Day: A War Memoir*. London: Frederick Muller, 1960.

Vogelsang, C. T. *Logistics: Its Bearing on the Art of War*. Newport, RI: Naval War College, 1911.

Waymouth, G. R. "The Reserve Fleet Today," in *Brasseys Annual 1952*, ed. H. G. Thursfield, 149–56. London: William Clowes, 1952.

Wildenberg, Thomas. *Gray Steel and Black Oil: Fast Tankers and Replenishment at Sea in the U.S. Navy, 1912–1992*. Annapolis, MD: Naval Institute Press, 1996.

Willmott, H. P. *Grave of a Dozen Schemes: British Naval Planning and the War against Japan, 1943–1945*. Shrewsbury, U.K.: AirLife Publishing Ltd., 1996.

Winton, John. *The Forgotten Fleet*. London: Michael Joseph, 1969.

Index

Page numbers in *italics* refer to illustrations. The letter *t* following a page number denotes a table, the letter *n* a note. The word *bis* indicates the item appears twice and *ter* three times on the page cited.

After retiring from Barclays Bank International in 1994, **Peter V. Nash** studied naval history for his master's degree at King's College, University of London. In 2006 he was awarded his doctorate degree, also from King's College. He has spent several years researching archives in the United States and the United Kingdom on naval logistics, including a period as the Edward S. Miller Research Fellow in Naval History at the U.S. Naval War College in Rhode Island.

He has written "The Royal Navy in Korea: Replenishment and Sustainability" in *British Naval Strategy East of Suez, 1900–2000: Influences and Actions,* edited by Greg Kennedy (2005).

Peter Nash, who lives in London, is Honorary Treasurer of the Society for Nautical Research, a councillor of the Navy Records Society, a vice president of the Marine Society and Sea Cadets, and a fellow of the Royal Society for the encouragement of Arts, Manufactures and Commerce.

NEW PERSPECTIVES ON MARITIME HISTORY AND NAUTICAL ARCHAEOLOGY
EDITED BY JAMES C. BRADFORD AND GENE ALLEN SMITH

Maritime Heritage of the Cayman Islands, by Roger C. Smith (1999; first paperback edition, 2000)

The Three German Navies: Dissolution, Transition, and New Beginnings, 1945–1960, by Douglas C. Peifer (2002)

The Rescue of the Gale Runner: *Death, Heroism, and the U.S. Coast Guard*, by Dennis L. Noble (2002); first paperback edition, 2008

Brown Water Warfare: The U.S. Navy in Riverine Warfare and the Emergence of a Tactical Doctrine, 1775–1970, by R. Blake Dunnavent (2003)

Sea Power in the Medieval Mediterranean: The Catalan-Aragonese Fleet in the War of the Sicilian Vespers by Lawrence V. Mott (2003)

An Admiral for America: Sir Peter Warren, Vice-Admiral of the Red, 1703–1752, by Julian Gwyn (2004)

Maritime History as World History, edited by Daniel Finamore (2004)

Counterpoint to Trafalgar: The Anglo-Russian Invasion of Naples, 1805–1806, by William Henry Flayhart III (first paperback edition, 2004)

Life and Death on the Greenland Patrol, 1942, by Thaddeus D. Novak, edited by P. J. Capelotti (2005)

X Marks the Spot: The Archaeology of Piracy, edited by Russell K. Skowronek and Charles R. Ewen (2006, first paperback edition 2007)

Industrializing American Shipbuilding: The Transformation of Ship Design and Construction, 1820–1920, by William H. Thiesen (2006)

Admiral Lord Keith and the Naval War against Napoleon, by Kevin D. McCranie (2006)

Commodore John Rodgers: Paragon of the Early American Navy, by John H. Schroeder (2006)

Borderland Smuggling: Patriots, Loyalists, and Illicit Trade in the Northeast, 1783–1820, by Joshua M. Smith (2006)

Brutality on Trial: "Hellfire" Pedersen, "Fighting" Hansen, and the Seamen's Act of 1915, by E. Kay Gibson (2006)

Uriah Levy: Reformer of the Antebellum Navy, by Ira Dye (2006)

Crisis at Sea: The United States Navy in European Waters in World War I, by William N. Still Jr. (2006)

Chinese Junks on the Pacific: Views from a Different Deck, by Hans K. Van Tilburg (2007)

Eight Thousand Years of Maltese Maritime History: Trade, Piracy, and Naval Warfare in the Central Mediterranean, by Ayşe Devrim Atauz (2007)

Merchant Mariners at War: An Oral History of World War II, by George J. Billy and Christine M. Billy (2008)

The Steamboat Montana *and the Opening of the West: History, Excavation, and Architecture*, by Annalies Corbin and Bradley A. Rodgers (2008)

Attack Transport: USS Charles Carroll *in World War II*, by Kenneth H. Goldman (2008)

Diplomats in Blue: U.S. Naval Officers in China, 1922–1933, by William Reynolds Braisted (2009)

Sir Samuel Hood and the Battle of the Chesapeake, by Colin Pengelly (2009)

Reg for new acct

Training / My Role / View Rec Training

Available Rec Training

DTS basic